Questions & Answers
ON THE
SHORTER CATECHISM

BY
JOHN BROWN
OF HADDINGTON

REFORMATION HERITAGE BOOKS
GRAND RAPIDS, MICHIGAN

2006

Published by
Reformation Heritage Books
2965 Leonard St., NE
Grand Rapids, MI 49525
616-977-0599 / Fax 616-285-3246
e-mail: orders@heritagebooks.org
website: www.heritagebooks.org

Originally titled *An Essay towards an Easy, Plain, Practical, and Extensive Explication of the Assembly's Shorter Catechism.* This facsimile is taken from the edition published in New York by Robert Carter in 1846.

10 digit ISBN 1-60178-004-4
13 digit ISBN 978-1-60178-004-1

For additional Reformed literature, both new and used, request a free book list from Reformation Heritage Books at the above address.

CONTENTS

Biographical Introduction

Eighteenth-century Scotland produced many noted ministers, scholars, and educators, but none greater or so greatly loved as John Brown of Haddington. He was a devout Christian, an able preacher, and a prolific theological writer. He was also a shining soldier of the cross who did not falter in the face of opposition. In the course of his life he saw his beloved church torn by painful conflicts, especially in the great breach that divided the Seceders, but he never lost faith that Jesus Christ is King of His church. As a faithful steward, Brown felt his highest calling was to shepherd Christ's flock and defend the truths of the Reformed faith.

Brown's life and career are all the more remarkable considering he began in obscurity and poverty, with no advantages of wealth, position, title, or education. Yet God favored him with unusual gifts and an enormous capacity for hard work, and providentially opened the way for him. Best of all, God favored him with a profound experience of the truth of the gospel as "the power of God unto salvation." That experience left its indelible stamp on every aspect of John Brown's many-sided ministry.

Early Life and Education
John Brown, named after his father, was born in 1722 in the village of Carpow, near Abernethy in the county of Perth, Scotland. His mother was Catherine Millie. His parents were poor (his father was a weaver) and could not afford an education for their son, though his father did teach him how to read. His parents also taught him the basics of true Christianity and conducted family worship every morning and evening.

The year of his birth, 1722, is remembered in Scottish church history as the year in which the General Assembly of the Church of Scotland reaffirmed its 1720 condemnation of the book, *The Marrow of Modern Divinity,* and rebuked twelve ministers who had defended the book's theology. Included among the twelve was the minister of the parish church of Abernethy, Rev. Alexander Moncrieff. Moncrieff and his colleagues were permitted to return to their charges, but the Marrow Controversy set in motion forces that would later divide the Scottish church. Born under the shadow of this controversy, Brown's faith and work were deeply impacted by all that resulted from it.

When Brown was eight years old, he pushed through a large Sabbath crowd outside the church at Abernethy and discovered that the Lord's Supper was going to be administered. Since non-communicants were excluded from such services, he was forced to leave but not before he heard a minister who spoke highly of Christ. Brown later wrote, "This in a sweet and delightful manner captivated my young affections, and has since made me think that children should never be kept out of the church on such occasions."

Brown's formal training was meager, but he did study Latin. He also enjoyed memorizing catechisms. "I had a particular delight in learning by heart the Catechisms published by Vincent, Flavel, and the Westminster Assembly, and was much profited by them," he wrote later. His mother noted his eagerness to learn and envisioned him one day standing among Scotland's preachers.

In 1733, Ebenezer Erskine (1680-1754), James Fisher (1697-1775), Alexander Moncrieff (1695-1761), and William Wilson (1690-1741) seceded from the Church of Scotland. Banding together as the Associate Presbytery, they fathered a new organization which came to be known as the Secession Church. As a member of Moncrieff's flock in Abernethy, Brown joined the Secession Church early on and stayed in it until his death.

When Brown was eleven years old, his father died and shortly after his mother, leaving him an orphan at the age of thirteen. He stayed with various families but was separated from his two brothers and sister. "I was left a poor orphan, and had nothing to depend on but the providence of God," he wrote, "and I must say that the Lord hath been 'the father of the fatherless, and the orphan's stay.'"

In his thirteenth and fourteenth years, Brown was irresistibly attracted to the gospel. He read the major religious books of the period, such as Joseph Alleine's *An Alarm to the Unconverted*, William Guthrie's *The Trial of a Saving Interest in Christ*, William Gouge's *Christian Directions Shewing How to Walk with God All the Day Long*, and the letters of Samuel Rutherford. Though Brown profited by what he read, and was often convicted by it for several days, he resisted resting on free grace alone. "Such was the bias of my heart, under its convictions, that I was willing to do any thing rather than flee to Christ, and trust to his free grace alone for my salvation," he wrote.

Shortly after his mother died, Brown himself became very ill and nearly died. Everyone but his sister thought he would not recover. While praying for her brother, the sister was struck with the promise, "With long life will I satisfy him, and show him my salvation," which set her mind at ease. Her brother became well again.

A Teenage Shepherd Converted

John Ogilvie, an elderly man with little education, employed the teenage Brown to tend his sheep. Ogilvie asked Brown to read to him, and Brown did so on numerous occasions. They soon became friends and met often to read the Word of God, pray, and sing psalms. Brown treasured those times.

After a severe fever in 1741, Brown became greatly concerned about his soul's eternal welfare. While his sheep were resting in the fold, he went to hear a sermon two miles away, running to and from the church. He heard three sermons in this manner, the last of which was preached on John 6:64, "There are some of you that believe not." That sermon pierced his conscience. He was convinced that he was the greatest unbeliever in the world.

His anxiety was greatly eased the next morning when he heard a sermon on Isaiah 53:4, "Surely he hath borne our griefs, and carried our sorrows." "I was made, as a poor lost sinner, as the chief of sinners, to essay appropriating the Lord Jesus as having done all for *me*, and as wholly made over to *me* in the gospel, as the free gift of God; and as my all-sufficient Saviour, answerable to all my folly, ignorance, guilt, filth, slavery, and misery," he later wrote.

Through this sermon and another on Isaiah 45:24, "Surely in the Lord have I righteousness and strength," he was drawn to the Lord Jesus Christ. He was given a clearer view of the freeness of God's grace and the exercise of taking hold of the promises of God.

False Accusations

By age nineteen, through diligent self-study, Brown had acquired some fluency in Latin, Greek, and Hebrew. He had learned the Greek alphabet by poring over notes in his copy of the Latin poems of Ovid, which contained Hellenic words, and by analyzing the Greek forms in the English Bible. Some of the Seceding students were suspicious of Brown's amazing feat and accused him of having learned Greek from the devil! Rumors about Brown and alleged dealings with the devil circulated for years. Brown agonized about them, though the Lord provided comfort. Brown especially found comfort in Psalm 42:8, "The Lord will command his loving-kindness in the day-time, and in the night his song shall be with me, and my prayer to the God of my life." In later years, he remarked that affliction is one of God's kindest blessings to the believer.

While still under suspicion, Brown went to a bookshop in St. Andrews and asked for a Greek New Testament. As the story goes, a professor in the university was struck with Brown, whose shabby clothes announced his deep poverty, asking for such a book. The professor declared that if Brown could read it, the professor would purchase the volume for him. Thus Brown obtained the New Testament at no cost.[1]

Peddler, Soldier, and Teacher

For several years, Brown was a peddler, shouldering a pack and traveling into neighboring counties to sell odds and ends at cottage doors. He did not have great success in this line. The books in people's homes and lengthy discussions would often divert him from selling merchandise.

During this time, Brown traveled great distances to attend Communion services. He once traveled over twenty-five miles to attend a Communion season at Ebenezer Erskine's church. It was customary at that time for the Lord's Supper to be administered only once or twice a year in a congregation, and many people would come from afar to take part in the several days of services devoted to the sacrament.

In 1745, Charles Edward Stuart, a staunch Roman Catholic, made an unsuccessful attempt to recover the British throne in Scotland. The Seceders were loyal to the Protestant faith, of course, and to the reigning House of Hanover. They took up arms to defend their church and country. John Brown fought alongside other Seceders in defense of Edinburgh Castle.

Afterwards Brown returned to peddling but soon was dissatisfied with his work. From his earliest days, he had felt called to proclaim God's truth from the pulpit, but lacked a university education. The next logical step for him was to assume the role of teacher, which he did in 1748.

John Brown first taught at Gairney Bridge, near Kinross, then at Spittal, a village in the parish of Penicuik. One of his students during this time was Archibald Hall (1736-1778), who later became the well-respected minister of Wall Street, London.

During this period Brown learned much about divinity and literature. He committed large portions of Scripture to memory. He acquired a working knowledge of Arabic, Syrian, Persian, Ethiopian, and major European languages, including French, Spanish, Italian, Dutch, and German.

He studied long into the night, regularly sleeping no more than four hours. Much later he confessed the error of such unhealthy habits.

The Breach in the Associate Synod

In April 1747, a division called "The Breach" took place in the Secession Church over the legitimacy of the Burgess oath. Citizens of Edinburgh, Glasgow, and Perth were required to take the oath in 1744. Taking this "loyalty oath" was a prerequisite to engaging in trade, belonging to one of the artisans' guilds, or voting in elections. Included in the oath was this clause: "Here I protest before God, and your Lordships, that I profess, and allow with my heart, the true religion presently professed within this realm, and authorized by the laws thereof . . . renouncing the Roman religion called papistry."

Those who condemned the oath believed that it was an endorsement of the Church of Scotland, with all its prevailing errors and corruptions. They were known as Antiburghers. Those who supported the oath were called Burghers, holding that the oath merely required one to profess to be a Protestant, over against Roman Catholicism. Brown and the Erskines sided with the Burghers. Twenty-three church leaders of the Antiburgher party, under the leadership of Alexander Moncrieff and Adam Gib (1714-88), declared that they were the rightful continuation of the Secession. They formed the General Associate Synod.

The secession of the General Associate Synod forced the Associate Synod to form a new seminary to train pastors for the ministry. The Associate Synod appointed Ebenezer Erskine to begin training students for the ministry at Stirling. Erskine accepted the appointment, though reluctantly, since he was already sixty-seven years old. The Synod therefore chose James Fisher of Glasgow as an alternate. Fisher is remembered for his *Exposition of the Shorter Catechism*, published in two parts beginning in 1753.

The first student to present himself at Stirling was John Brown. A university education was an entrance requirement, but Brown had already distinguished himself as a scholar through self-education. Some members of the Presbytery questioned his credentials, but Ralph Erskine (1685-1752), Ebenezer's younger brother, came to Brown's defense, saying, "I think the lad has a sweet savor of Christ about him."

Brown was approved for theological studies and started training for the Associate ministry under Ebenezer Erskine. The basic theology text used at the time was Francis Turretin's (1623-1687) *Institutes of Elenctic Theology*. Erskine's method was to read from Turretin and comment on its major doctrines. He excelled in teaching homiletics.

After two years, James Fisher took over the professorship. Brown moved to Glasgow to sit under Fisher's teaching. Fisher was often compared to an eagle, due to the keenness of his mental vision and the swiftness with which he swooped down upon fallacies and heresies. Brown learned much from Fisher and so refined his preaching skills that on November 14, 1750, at the age of twenty-eight, he received his license to preach from the Presbytery of Edinburgh.

Pastor in Haddington

A short time after his ordination, Brown received calls to be the minister of the Associate congregation of Haddington, the county town of East Lothian, and of Stow, Mid-Lothian. He accepted the call to Haddington, the smaller of the two congregations.

Brown served the small church in Haddington for thirty-six years, from 1751 until his death. He preached three times every Lord's Day, and visited and catechized his flock during the week. With all his learning, he tried to preach as if he had never read any book but the Bible. He often quoted Archbishop Ussher's saying, "It will take all our learning to make things plain."

During the course of his pastorate, Brown suffered many trials in his personal life, including the loss of a wife and several children. He was married eighteen years to

Janet Thomson, a God-fearing daughter of a Musselburgh merchant. They had eight children, of which only two survived. After his first wife died, Brown married Violet Croumbie, of Stenton, East Lothian, who outlived him by thirty-five years.

Brown often agonized that he was a trial to his congregation. He begged God to help him lead this flock, but if his ministry was not for God's glory, to remove him by death. He strongly disapproved of ministers who frequently switched pastorates.

On the other hand, he found great pleasure in studies that prepared him for the coming Sabbath. Personal spiritual experience also enriched his sermons. As he said, "Any little knowledge which I have had of my uncommonly wicked heart, and of the Lord's dealing with my own soul, hath helped me much in my sermons; and I have observed, that I have been apt to deliver that which I had experienced, in a more feeling and earnest manner, than other matters." Brown's main focus in preaching was the beauty and glory of Christ against the backdrop of man's wretched depravity. He wrote, "Now after near forty years preaching of Christ, and his great and sweet salvation, I think that I would rather beg my bread, all the labouring days of the week, for an opportunity of publishing the gospel on the Sabbath to an assembly of sinful men, than, without such a privilege, to enjoy the richest possessions on earth."

Brown loved to study the great theologians. He was particularly fond of the old divines—Francis Turretin, Benedict Pictet, Petrus VanMaastricht, John Owen—and contemporary writers such as Thomas Boston, James Hervey, and Ebenezer and Ralph Erskine.

Brown was a lifetime scholar. As Thomas Brown noted, "He was never more in his element than when in his study, and here he spent the greater part of his time." He would often rise at four or five o'clock in the morning fervently praying for his dear flock before discharging the day's duties, though he often lamented his deficiency in prayer.

Brown delighted in prayer, often setting aside entire mornings for it. His tender love for God would often spring up spontaneously, such as his response to an extra loud peal of thunder. "That's the love-whisper of my God," he would say.

Brown also organized group prayer meetings. For some years, he held prayer meetings with seven or eight children in his parsonage. He also led a prayer meeting for adults from both the Church of Scotland and the Seceder congregations. In later years, he wrote guidelines for how prayer meetings should be conducted.

In 1758, Brown published his first book, *An Help for the Ignorant: Being an Essay Towards an Easy, Plain, Practical and Extensive Explication of the Assembly's Shorter Catechism, composed for the Young Ones of his own Congregation.* The book offers 4,400 questions based on the Shorter Catechism. Brown prefaces his book with an introduction to children, urging them to serve the Lord, flee the world, and trust in Christ alone for salvation. This volume, reprinted here, is a photolithographed reprint of the sixth Edinburgh edition done by Robert Carter in New York in 1846. We have retitled it as *Questions and Answers on the Shorter Catechism.*

Questions and Answers on the Shorter Catechism is one of the most remarkable and unique doctrinal books we have ever perused. Each question of Westminster's Shorter Catechism prompts numerous questions from the author, who provides remarkably succinct answers, each of which is supported by Scripture. We know of no catechetical work that packs so much Reformed doctrinal truth in such a short compass. Brown is a master at providing pungent, scripturally based, sound, and experiential answers that can be understood readily by both older teenagers and adults. We have often turned to this practical work in preparing for teaching catechism class, and have found it more helpful than any other not only in its answers, but also in its questions! If you'd like a succinct handbook that asks thousands of good questions and provides wise and pastoral answers, buy and read this book. Read it slowly— a few pages an evening will suffice, and then meditate and pray about it.

For the most part, the book was well received. Some Antiburghers, however, charged Brown with heresy because he wrote that, though Christ's righteousness is of infinite value in itself, it is imputed to believers only in proportion to their need. The Antiburghers maintained that the righteousness of Christ is imputed to believers in its full infinite value so that God's people are infinitely righteous in Christ.

The debate appeared more speculative than edifying. Nonetheless, Brown responded the following year with his *A Brief Dissertation concerning the Righteousness of Christ* (1759), in which he wrote, "Let them do to or wish me what they will, may their portion be redemption through the blood of Jesus.... [Let them] call me what they please, may the Lord call them 'the holy ones, the redeemed of the Lord.'"

That response was typical of Brown. He seldom spoke a negative word about anyone. He also treated rumor as rumor, saying that when it was spoken of those in public office, it usually was not true.

Brown once wrote to Rev. Archibald Bruce, a respected professor of divinity with the Antiburghers: "Our conduct on both sides of the Secession I have often thought to be like that of two travelers, both walking on the same road, not far from one another, but in consequence of a thick mist so suddenly come on they cannot see one another, and each supposes the other to be off the road. After some time the darkness is removed, and they are quite surprised to find that they are both on the road, and had been all along so near one another."

That proved true of the Burghers and the Antiburghers. In 1820, thirty-three years after Brown died, the two denominations were reconciled as the United Secession Church. In 1847, a union was forged between the United Secession Church and the Relief Church, founded in 1761. The new body was known as the United Presbyterian Church.

Brown's ministry was blessed by God. People in his congregation grew in grace under the Word and sacrament, as did others who heard him preach wherever he traveled. Many regarded him as their spiritual father.

Professor of Divinity

After the death of John Swanston of Kinross in 1767, Brown was appointed Professor of Divinity by the Associate Church Synod. For twenty years he filled that position with distinction. He taught theological students in the Associate Church for nine weeks each year, packing in 160 hours of instruction, examination, and student presentations.

Brown taught about thirty students a year in languages, theology, church history, and homiletics. Some of those lectures are included in his publications, such as *A General History of the Christian Church* (2 vols.; 1771), and most importantly, his systematic theology, *A Compendious View of Natural and Revealed Religion* (1782). This book, republished several times in the nineteenth century, is a work of great merit. Other lesser known works that grew out of his theological teaching are *Letters on Gospel Preaching* and *Ten Letters on the Exemplary Behaviour of Ministers,* printed in Brown's *Select Remains* (1789).

In his teaching, Brown continually stressed the necessity of heart-religion. He taught students as a father teaches his children, loving them and admonishing them for their good. After hearing a practice sermon, he said to one student, "I hope never to hear such a sermon again while I live." To another, he wrote, "I hope the Lord has let some of the wind out of you that I thought was in you when first I knew you. Beg of Him to fill its room with Himself and His grace." Such severity, however, was tempered with kindness. His concern for students earned their affection and respect. Many of his lectures stirred their souls. His annual closing address particularly searched their consciences. Here is an example:

> What state you are in, what are the reigning principles in your breasts, what are the motives by which you are influenced, and what are the ends you have in

view—whether you are, indeed, what you profess, and what your outward appearance would indicate—all is known to God. To commend a Saviour for whom one has no love; to preach a gospel which one does not believe; to point out the way to heaven and never to have taken one step in that way; to enforce a saving acquaintance with religion, and to be an entire stranger to it one's self—how sad, how preposterous!

One biographer wrote of Brown, "Many of his sayings at those times, it is believed, will never be forgotten by those who heard him. The many able, useful, and acceptable ministers, both in Great Britain and Ireland, whom he trained up for the sacred office, evince the ample success with which the Lord crowned his labours." Some of the students Brown trained were George Lawson (1749-1820), John Dick (1764-1833), and his eldest son, John Brown (1754-1832), later minister of Whitburn.

During his years as professor, Brown was also busy in the work of his denomination. For the last twenty years of his life he served as clerk of the Synod. He missed only two of forty-one synodical meetings in those years. He also served on many denominational committees.

Sickness and Death

In early 1787, Brown suffered from indigestion, which became more acute as months passed. His health could no longer sustain the ruthless workload he had carried most of his life. But he was determined to keep working. "How can a dying man spend his last breath better than in preaching Christ?" he asked.

February 25, 1787, was his last Sabbath in the pulpit. In the morning, he preached from Luke 2:26, "It was revealed unto him by the Holy Ghost, that he should not see death, before he had seen the Lord's Christ." In the evening, his text was Acts 13:26, "To you is the word of this salvation sent." He told his congregation these were his last sermons and commended them to the grace of God.

While his health continued to decline, the man who had always been reluctant to speak of his own religious

experience seemed to become as a little child. The doors of
his affections sprung open. He said loving things to his
children, urging them to persevere in the faith. Forty-five
pages of deathbed expressions conclude his *Memoir* edited
by his son William. Here is a sampling of what Brown said:

- If Christ be magnified in my life, that is the great
  matter I wish for.
- O! to be with God! to see him as he is in Christ! to
  know him even as we are known! It is worth not
  merely *doing* for, but *dying* for, to see a gracious
  God.
- I have served several masters; but none so kind as
  Christ. I have dealt with many honest men; but no
  creditor like Christ. Had I ten thousand hearts,
  they should all be given to Christ; and had I ten
  thousand bodies, they should all be employed in
  labouring for his honour.
- Oh! commend Jesus. I have been looking at him for
  these many years, and never yet could find a fault
  in him. Many a comely person I have seen, but
  none so comely as Christ.
- Oh! what must Christ be in himself, when he
  sweetens heaven, sweetens Scriptures, sweetens
  ordinances, sweetens earth, and sweetens even
  trials!
- Once I got a ravishing sight of the necessity of his
  loving me, *the sinner*. He said, "Other sheep I have;
  them also I *must* bring."

Brown had a powerful sense of his own sinfulness. He
degraded his weakness as thoroughly as he exalted Christ.
Here are some samples of that self-knowledge:

- My life is and has been a kind of almost perpetual
  strife between God and my soul. He strives to overcome my enmity and wickedness with his mercies,
  and I strive to overcome his mercy with my enmity
  and wickedness. Astonishingly kind on his side,
  but worse than diabolically wicked on mine! After
  all, I wish and hope that he, not I, may obtain the
  victory at last.

- I know the outrageous wickedness of my heart; such wickedness as would have provoked any but a God of infinite love to have cast me into hell.
- I have no more dependence on my labours than on my sins.
- It has been my comfort these twenty years, that not only *sensible* sinners, but the most stupid, are made welcome to believe in Christ.
- Since Christ came to save sinners, even the chief, why, thought I, should I except myself?

In a letter to his congregation, Brown wrote movingly of these two themes of a hellworthy sinner and a precious Christ:

I see such weakness, such deficiency, such unfaithfulness, such imprudence, such unfervency and unconcern, such selfishness, in all that I have done as a minister or a Christian, as richly deserves the deepest damnation of hell. I have no hope of eternal happiness but in Jesus' blood, which cleanseth from all sin—in "redemption through his blood, the forgiveness of my sins, according to the riches of his grace."

Ordinarily Brown went to the congregation in Stow during June to take part in their Communion season. A friend who realized that the ailing Brown wasn't planning to go to Stow asked, "You are not journeying thither this year?" Brown answered, "No, I wish to be traveling to God, as my exceeding joy." On June 19, 1787, he uttered his last words, "My Christ," and died. He was sixty-five years old.

After Brown died, this "Solemn Dedication to the Lord," dated June 23, 1784, was found among his papers:

LORD! I am now entering on the 34th year of my ministry; an amazing instance of sovereign mercy and patience to a cumberer of the ground! How strange that thou shouldest have, for more than sixty years, continued striving to exercise mercy and loving-kindness upon a wretch that hath all along spoken and done all the evil that I could; nor ever would yield, but when the almighty influence of free grace put it out of my power to oppose it. Lord! how often have I vowed, but never grown better; confessed but never amended! Often thou hast challenged and corrected me, and yet I have gone on frowardly in the way of my heart. As an evil man, and seducer, I have grown worse and worse.

But where should a sinner flee but to the Saviour? Lord! all refuge faileth me, no man can help my soul. Nothing will do for me, but an uncommon stretch of thy almighty grace. To thee, O Jesus! I give up myself, as a foolish, guilty, polluted and enslaved sinner; and I hereby solemnly take thee as mine, as made of God to me wisdom, righteousness, sanctification, and redemption. I give up myself, as a poor, ignorant, careless and wicked creature, who hath been ever learning, and yet never able to come to the knowledge of the truth. To thee, O Lord! that thou mayest bestow gifts on the rebellious, and exalt thy grace, in showing kindness to the unworthy.
O Saviour! come down, and do something for me, before I die. I give up myself and family, wife, children, and servant, to thee, encouraged by thy promises, Gen. xvii. 7; Jer. xxxi. 1; Isa. xliv. 3, lix. 21. I commit my poor, weak, withered congregation, deprived by death of its pillars, that thou mayest strengthen, refresh and govern it. I commit all my students unto thee, that thou, O Lord! mayest train them up for the ministry. May never one of them be so unfit as I have been! Lord! I desire to take hold of thy new covenant, well ordered in all things, and sure. This is all my salvation, and all my desire.

A Prolific Writer

Brown published thirty books. He was best known for his *Self-Interpreting Bible* (2 vols., 1778) and, to a lesser extent, *A Dictionary of the Holy Bible* (2 vols., 1769). "Brown's Bible" contains history, chronology, geography, summaries, explanatory notes, and reflections—in short, it is a miniature library that covers everything a typical reader desires. It was reprinted twenty-seven times in

Britain and America, often increasing in size through editors' additions. The latest and best edition (4 vols., 1914) contains more than 2,200 pages; the numerous aids include a system of marginal cross-references. This library in itself became nearly as common in eighteenth-century Scottish households as Bunyan's *Pilgrim's Progress* and Thomas Boston's *Fourfold State*. It incorporated material from the *Dictionary*, which explained English vocabulary and grammar, making it useful for home schooling, and it also applied the Scriptures practically and personally. The complete work is exemplary in its directness and accuracy.

Robert Mackenzie's book, *John Brown of Haddington*, devotes an entire chapter to commending *The Self-Interpreting Bible*. MacKenzie writes:

> No work carried the reputation of the author so far afield as his *Self-Interpreting Bible....* Its success from the first was extraordinary.... It will be evident that an extraordinary amount of valuable material was thus placed at the command of the ordinary reader. It was the information that a student of the Scriptures hungered for, who had not access to the learned works dealing with such subjects.... Brown states that his avowed aim in his publication is not to depreciate the valuable commentaries of these writers (referring to some of the most famous Reformed commentators of the past), but "to exhibit their principal substance with all possible advantage"...and in referring particularly to the New Testament, he adds that "there the explication is peculiarly extensive, and attempts to exhibit the substance of many learned and expensive commentaries."

Charles Simeon of Cambridge (1759-1836) used Brown's book in his morning devotions. He wrote to Brown, "Your *Self-Interpreting Bible* seems to stand in lieu of all other commentaries; and I am daily receiving so much edification and instruction from it, that I would wish it in the hands of all serious ministers."

Brown also wrote a trilogy of books over a fifteen-year period on the figures, types, and prophecies of Scripture titled: *Sacred Tropology; or A Brief View of the Figures and Explication of the Metaphors contained in Scripture* (1768), *An Evangelical and Practical View of the Types and Figures of the Old Testament Dispensation* (1781), and *The Harmony of Scripture Prophecies, and history of their fulfillment* (1784). He wrote the books, he said, because "in the first, we observe the surprising eloquence of Heaven, and discern, in almost every form of nature, a guide to and an illustration of inspired truth. By the second, we perceive the whole substance of the Gospel of Christ, truly exhibited in ancient shadows, persons, and things: in laws apparently carnal and trifling. In the third, we observe how astonishingly inspired predictions, properly arranged, and compared with the history of nations and churches, do illustrate each other; and modern events, as with the evidence of miracles, confirm our faith in the oracles of God."

He also loved writing biographies and church history. For ministers, he wrote, *The Christian, the Student, and Pastor, exemplified in the lives of nine eminent Ministers* (1781). *Practical Piety Exemplified* (1783) presents the lives of thirteen eminent Christians, illustrating various cases of conscience. *Casuistical Hints, or Cases of Conscience* (1784) was originally written for personal use, but later Brown offered it as "an appended illustration of *Practical Piety Exemplified,* or an appendix to my system on the head of sanctification." It handles temptations, indwelling sin, heresy, and division in the church. His last published work was *The Most Remarkable Passages in the Life and Spiritual experiences of Elizabeth Wast, a Young Woman, sometime Matron of the Trades Hospital, Edinburgh* (1785). As for church history, in addition to his two-volume overview, he wrote *An Historical Account of the Rise and Progress of the Secession* (1766) and *A Compendious History of the British Churches in Scotland, England, Ireland, and America* (2 vols.; 1784).

At times, Brown wrote polemically to defend or attack a position. He attacked the papacy in *The Oracles of Christ and the Abominations of Antichrist Compared; or, A Brief View of the Errors, Impieties, and Inhumanities of Popery*

(1779) and *The Absurdity and Perfidy of All Authoritative Toleration of Gross Heresy, Blasphemy, Idolatry, and Popery in Britain* (1780). He defended the Burgher position in *The Re-exhibition of the Testimony vindicated, in opposition to the unfair account given of it by the Rev. Adam Gib* (1780). (Gib was a prominent anti-Burgher minister, who had written *An Account of the Burgher Re-exhibition of the Secession Testimony.*)

Brown also published the following sermons: *Religious Steadfastness recommended* (1769), *The Fearful Shame and Contempt of those professed Christians who neglect to raise up spiritual Children to Christ* (1780), and *The Necessity and Advantage of Earnest Prayer for the Lord's Special Direction in the Choice of Pastors* (1783).

In 1765, Brown published his journal, titled *The Christian Journal; or, Common Incidents Spiritual Instructions.* The journal is divided into five parts: spring, summer, harvest, winter, and the day of rest. Lessons from nature and the Sabbath are applied to spiritual life. He also wrote a bit of fiction. *Letters on the Constitution, Government, and Discipline of the Christian Church* (1767) contains nineteen letters addressed to a fictitious person named Amelius, who lacks understanding of the constitution of the church and how members are accepted into the church. Brown offers the scriptural groundwork for promoting a strong view of the organized church and its Solemn League and Covenant.

The Psalms of David in Metre (1775), recently reprinted, include Brown's notes on the Psalms. *A Brief Concordance to the Holy Scriptures* (1783) was useful in its time. *Devout Breathings,* which emphasized experiential faith, was printed sixteen times by 1784. *The Awakening Call: Four Solemn Addresses, to Sinners, to Children, to Young Men and Women, and to Aged Persons,* sometimes bound with *Devout Breathings,* was also widely circulated.

One of Brown's best books, *A Compendious View of Natural and Revealed Religion,* was printed in 1782 at the request of his theological students. It was reprinted by Reformation Heritage Books and Christian Focus in 2002 as *The Systematic Theology of John Brown of Haddington*.[2] The work, which includes seven "books" and twenty-four chapters, offers biblical focus, exegetical insights, a covenantal theme, experiential depth, and compelling applications. Brown's style is methodological and includes numerous scriptural proofs, divisions, and sub-points to aid students. Brown's reflections at the end of nearly every chapter are a unique feature of his systematic theology. In these warm reflections he teaches us how to apply doctrine to our souls to examine whether God's grace and holiness truly shine in us. Brown's systematic theology, said to be "one of the most profound, and at the same time perspicuous, views which have been given of the theology of the Westminster Confession," is an indispensable tool for the student, pastor, and professor of theology. It was used as a textbook in several colleges and seminaries, including the Countess of Huntingdon's college at Trevecca.

Brown was also concerned to bring doctrinal piety to children. His *The Young Christian; or, The Pleasantness of Early Piety* (1782) encourages the fear of God in youth. His catechism books for children that were first published under one cover as *Two Short Catechisms, mutually connected* (1764) came to be known as "Little Brown" and "Big Brown." "Little Brown" contains 202 questions, many of which are short, personal, and designed for young children, whereas "Big Brown," written for older children, contains 743 questions based on the Shorter Catechism.

Brown's last words spoken in this world, "my Christ," summarize all his doctrinal books, for his one great aim was to cultivate love for Christ in the soul of the believer. The Christ-centeredness of his *Questions and Answers on the Shorter Catechism* is aptly reflected in Brown's last letter to the Countess:

> There is none like Christ, none like Christ, none like Christ.... There is no learning nor knowledge like the knowledge of Christ; no life like Christ living in the heart by faith; no work like the service, the spiritual service of Christ; no reward like the free-grace wages of Christ; no riches nor wealth like "the unsearchable

riches of Christ"; no rest, no comfort, like the rest, the consolation of Christ; no pleasure like the pleasure of fellowship with Christ. Little as I know of Christ, I would not exchange the learning of one hour's fellowship with Christ for all the liberal learning in ten thousand universities, during ten thousand ages, even though angels were to be my teachers.

By the time of his death, Brown's name was a household word among Presbyterians in Scotland and throughout the English-speaking world. His books, pamphlets, tracts, and catechisms were read by increasing numbers of people. Even after his death, additional works continued to be published. *Select Remains* (1789), which includes some of Brown's voluminous correspondence, a number of tracts, and his dying advice, was edited by his oldest son, John. *Posthumous Works* (1797) and *Apology for the more Frequent Administration of the Lord's Supper* (1804) were also published. In *Apology*, Brown argued for more frequent observation of the Lord's Supper, countering those who taught that infrequency safeguarded solemnity with, "Why not pray seldom, preach seldom, read God's Word seldom, that they may become more solemn too?"

A Spiritual Dynasty

Brown had many children, some of whom became prominent Christian leaders. His son John (1754-1832) was minister of Whitburn for fifty-five years and was a prolific devotional writer; Ebenezer (d. 1836) was a prominent preacher at Inverkeithing, Fife, for fifty-six years; Samuel (1779-1839) helped start circulating libraries; and William (1783-1863) was a historian of missions and an excellent biographer of his father. Grandson John Brown (1784-1858) served as pastor at Broughton Place United Presbyterian Church, Edinburgh, and was Professor of Exegetical Theology in the United Secession and United Presbyterian College, Edinburgh. Great-grandson Robert Johnston (d. 1918) was a professor in the United Presbyterian College, Edinburgh, and United Free Church College, Aberdeen. Another great-grandson, John (Rab)

Brown (1810-82), became a medical doctor and writer. And great-great-grandsons John (1818-92) and David Cairns (1862-1946) became outstanding Presbyterian teachers and writers. Brown's descendants so respected him that some traveled to Scotland from the United States in 1987 for events marking the bicentennial of Brown's death.

– Joel Beeke and Randall Pederson

---

[1] That story has never been verified. Robert Mackenzie, biographer of John Brown in the early twentieth century, considered it true. Brown's grandson, however, questioned its authenticity in his edition of his grandfather's *Memoirs*.

[2] Most of this introduction is taken from the 2002 introduction of this reprint.

An Address to the Young Readers of This Catechism

My dear young people, for whom my heart's desire and prayer to God is that you be saved, let me beseech you, while you read this, and especially while you read your Bible or hear its precious truths preached to you, to "hearken and hear for time and eternity to come." Now in the perfect season of youth, "get wisdom as the principal thing," and with all your "getting, get understanding" of the infinitely important concerns of your salvation.

Do you not know your own selves? For the Lord's sake, seriously consider what souls you have—immortal souls, worth inconceivably more than ten thousand worlds; souls that are capable of enjoying an infinite God as their everlasting All in All; souls which must and shall, before long, enter into an eternal state of either inconceivable misery or happiness. Alas, my young friends! Must souls formed by God Himself—endowed with an understanding and will, formed to live forever for the everlasting and immediate service and enjoyment of God, solemnly devoted to Him by His mercy in baptism and other covenant relationships; souls on which parents and pastors have bestowed so many prayers, instructions, and exhortations, and God Himself hath bestowed such instructions, warnings, loving allurements, and strivings of His Spirit—must they be lost forever? Must they be condemned forever by you who possess them in order to obtain some trifling, earthly, destructive gratification?

Consider before God what state you are in while you remain careless and unconverted. Being without Christ and "strangers to the covenant of promise," you are completely guilty before God, "alienated from the life of God," and are His enemies. You are cursed and condemned by God because you have not believed in His only begotten

Son. Having no holiness, you have no hope and are "without God in the world." Being children of the devil, your heart is filled with all unrighteousness, pride, deceit, malice, and hatred of God; it is full of ignorance and unbelief. It is "deceitful above all things, and desperately wicked." Its "carnal mind is enmity against God," and "is not subject to his law, neither indeed can be." It is infected with every defiling, fatal plague; every sinful lust reigns there, and it is inhabited by Satan, ready to tempt you to everything wicked. Out of it, as permitted by God in your past, have "proceeded evil thoughts, murders, adulteries, fornications, thefts, false witness, idolatries, blasphemies." You have lived "after the course of this world, according to the prince of the power of the air," who works in you as "children of disobedience." Until now, you have "been foolish and disobedient, deceived, serving divers lusts and pleasures; living in malice and envy, hateful and hating one another," speaking and doing any evil you could. What innumerable, dreadful curses of Almighty God are inseparable from all your sinful thoughts, words, and actions! Alas; all things, Christ and His Gospel not excepted, are rendered the "savour of death unto death" unto you. What a dreadful thought: eternal destruction is ready at your side. God is angry with you every day; His wrath rests on you; His sword is drawn and His arrows are set to destroy you. The sound of your approaching condemnation roars loudly in every warning of His Word, if you only had ears to hear it. Even while you read this, hell stands open to receive you, and devils stand ready to drag you into everlasting fire. Why then are you not afraid to think another careless thought? Why are you not afraid to shut your eyes, even in necessary sleep, lest you should open them in hell?

My dear friends, think with grief, with shame, and with trembling; think with perseverance and deep concern. Think how criminal your sins are before the Lord, which you think are mere trifles, mere fun and sport. They are the cursed product of your inward, original, and increased ignorance, pride, deceit, and enmity against God. They are the most treacherous rebellion against His law, which is "holy, just, and good." They are committed against His authority over you and against all His warnings, counsels, promises, threatenings, mercies, and judgments. They are ungratefully committed against all His special favors in preserving and providing for you while you could not help yourselves. They are committed against all His special calls, invitations, promises, and encouragements for young people. They are a complete misuse of the excellent talents, enjoyments, and energy He has given you in your youth. They are a vicious abuse of this uniquely precious season of life, in which you should be preparing for future usefulness and happiness. They strengthen the original habits of corruption in you, and form many bad habits of vanity and lust. They deprave your tender affections to oppose God and His ways. And they are committed at the smallest temptations! They entice others around you to sin, or harden them in it. They fling reproach on God, your Maker, Preserver, and Savior, as if He, His promises, laws, mercies, and judgments, were unworthy of your attention, and instead encourage you in sin. They offend your parents and ministers, as if they had agreed to train you up for the devil. They draw down reproach on yourselves, which you must bear either in deep convictions or in everlasting punishment. They deprive you of the most pleasant and profitable fellowship with God. They forfeit the precious promises of long life and prosperity, and expose you to judgment in this life and to hell in the next. Are these light matters? Will you think such things are unimportant when you arrive at the agonies of death, at the tribunal of Christ, or amid the flames of hell?

Alas! Why do you, by your unconcern and wickedness, take such early pains to become fuel for the "everlasting fire prepared for the devil and his angels"! If God gives you repentance, how it will sting to remember what earnest offers and opportunities for grace you have neglected and abused; what infinite kindness, condescension, and love you have trampled under your feet; what fellowship with Christ, His Father, and His blessed Spirit, you have despised and refused! What ravishing views of His glory and of all the perfections of God in Him, manifested forever in your eternal salvation; what delightful tastes of His goodness; and what enriching acceptance of His fullness you have rejected, for the sake of vulgar and petty pleasure or profit on earth, which will entail grief and shame on you while you live and draw others around you to hell before and after you die! If God gave you up to your own heart's desires, provoked with your perseverance in folly and guilt, alas! Your wickedness will rob Him and His Christ of His place in our land and nation, and consign yourselves, your friends and family, and even the church and nation, the whole management of which will quickly be in the hands of the rising generation into the power of the devil and the hand of an angry God!

My dear young people, know the God of your fathers—the God who preserved, guided, blessed, and saved many of your ancestors; the God to whom your fathers dedicated you; the God "whom to know is life eternal, and this life is in his Son." We parents tell you, our children, that this God is our God forever, and that He "will be our guide even unto death." We never found Him a barren wilderness or a land of drought. We have found infinitely more satisfaction in this God, given to us in His Word, than could balance all the pleasures, all the wealth, all the honor of ten thousand worlds. These words—"your God" and "my God"—have been the "joy and rejoicing of our heart." There is none like the God of Jeshurun, who pardons iniquity, transgression, and sin, and who delights in mercy. How our hearts are enflamed when we think how this God, this "fountain of living waters," will be our eternal all-in-all, the strength of our heart and portion forever! If wisdom's ways are so pleasant even on this sinful earth, what will it be like to enter the joy of our Lord forever! "We shall be like him, for we shall see him as he is." "Come, taste and see that our God is good" and that they who trust in Him are blessed. Consider the Apostle and High Priest of our profession, Christ Jesus. Behold our Surety, our Savior, whom our souls love, our King, "meek and lowly," bringing salvation. Behold our God-man, "the chief among ten thousand; fair, pleasant, most sweet, and altogether lovely." This is our Beloved, our Friend, our Mediator, our God.

Sons and daughters of Jerusalem, looking away from all the vanities of creation, consider Him, the only begotten Son of God in our nature; in His saving offices, His endearing love, His incomparable excellencies, sufferings and glories; His unbounded fullness of grace and truth, offering every good thing in time and eternity—and then tell us what you think of our Christ.

My dear boys and girls, do you believe that there is a God who made you, who gave you a law for your heart and life, and who will quickly call you to an account of every thought, word, and deed? And yet, do you never think of your appearance before His throne, or of your being forever under His infinite wrath? Have you not seen, tasted, and felt that God is good? Have you not heard, have you not known, what He has done for the eternal salvation of sinful men? And will you give Him contempt and hatred for all His bounty and love? You have a natural interest in your own life and well-being; will you counteract it by a malicious and obstinate refusal of our Lord Jesus and His everlasting righteousness, mercy, and grace? Has God implanted in you a tender compassion towards animals, and will you still be so inhumanly cruel as to break the hearts of your godly parents, pastors, or friends—and, if possible, break the heart of our infinitely gracious Redeemer and His Father and blessed Spirit—by crucifying Him afresh, trampling His covenant and blood under your feet, and murdering your own soul? Will you use your minds to think and learn about everything except Jesus Christ and what relates to Him? Will you easily believe everything except the gracious words of a God who cannot lie? His "faithful saying" is "worthy of all acceptation, that Jesus Christ came into the world to save sinners." In His Son, there is eternal life prepared for and given to you. Will you pursue everything except Jesus, the "pearl of great price," the "unspeakable gift" of God, and His great and everlasting salvation? Will you give in to everything except the offers of the glorious gospel? Will you thankfully receive everything except God Himself, the true bread of life, which the Lord your God gives you from heaven? Are you fond of all beauties except that of gracious conformity to God? Why are you fond of every pleasure, every joy, except the joy of rejoicing in God through our Lord Jesus Christ, which is "joy unspeakable and full of glory"?

Allow me to argue with you on God's behalf—and on your own soul's behalf. Why, in your special day of grace, do you indulge such ignorance of Jehovah and His law, of Jesus and His salvation, and of their necessity and usefulness for you? Why do you have such contempt and unbelief for the gospel of the grace of God? Why encourage and promote such desperate hardness of heart? Why cherish such attachment to the perishing pleasures and profits of sin and sense? Why cultivate such malice and enmity against Jesus Christ, the Father, and the Holy Spirit, as to neglect His precious salvation? Oh, that you only felt the Word of God, "quick and powerful, sharper than a two-edged sword, piercing even to the dividing asunder of your soul and spirit," "discerner of the thoughts and intents of your heart"! If you only knew the depth of the sin in you and the everlasting misery that awaits you! If you would only believe God's admonition of the necessity of His supernatural change in your life and nature: "Except you be converted, and become as little children, you shall not enter into the kingdom of heaven"; "Except a man be born again he cannot see the kingdom of God"; "Except a man be born of the Spirit he cannot enter into the kingdom of God"; "If any man be in Christ Jesus, he is a new creature: old things are passed away, and all things are become new"; putting off the "old man" and putting on the "new man," you must as "new-born babes, desire the sincere milk of the word, that you may grow thereby"; or, "if any man have not the Spirit of Christ, he is none of his."

Oh, if you only knew the "riches of the glory of the gospel, which is Christ in you, the hope of glory," in these days of youth, while your minds are fresh and alive, while your affections are tender, while your lusts are less powerful, your hearts less hardened, and your worldly cares less embarrassing. If only you knew that fellowship with the Father in His redeeming love, which you so carelessly neglect; with the Son in His blood and grace, which you so madly resist! If you could only understand with all saints, "what is the breadth, and length, and depth, and height" of the power and the "love of Christ, which passeth knowledge, that you might be filled with all the fullness of God."

Think what kind of preparations God has made for your everlasting salvation—how He "so loved the world, that he gave his only begotten Son, that whosoever believeth on him shall not perish, but have everlasting life"! He set Him "up from everlasting" as our Surety, who engaged His heart to delight to do His Father's will in ransoming and saving us. In His incarnation, He was brought into this world "in the likeness of sinful flesh." The Father "made him under the law," and exacted from Him all the infinite debt of obedience and suffering due from us. All this, "that he might redeem us that were under the law"! "He made him to be sin for us, who knew no sin," that we who knew nothing but sin "might be made the righteousness of God in him." The Father made Him a curse for us so that we could be "blessed in him with all spiritual blessings in heavenly places." His Father put Him to grief and to death for us so that we might live through Him in the joy of the Lord. He delivered Him to the cross for our offenses, and raised Him from the dead for our justification. He gave Him glory for Himself and unbounded fullness of gifts for men, "for the rebellious, that our faith and hope might be in God." He made Him "wisdom, and righteousness, and sanctification, and redemption" for us! And think with what honesty and compassionate earnestness Jehovah, the Son, and the Holy Spirit call you. By all His words, invitations, commands, promises, and warnings; by all His works; by all His mercies and judgments; by all His ordinances and ministers; by all your needs in time and eternity; by all your desires and enjoyments—in all of these, He speaks to you and entreats you to receive Himself and all His full and everlasting salvation, offered to you in the gospel "freely, without money and without price."

My dear young men and women, why are you so prone to listen to and comply with every temptation of Satan, your destroyer; every enticement of your worldly friends; every suggestion of your own foolish and wicked heart, to your temporal and eternal ruin? And yet, you are so deaf and averse to the most earnest entreaties of the great God, your Savior! Do others love you more, or will they do more for your everlasting welfare, than He? Why do you work so hard to pull down everlasting destruction on yourselves by your quick compliance with everything hurtful and your obstinate resistance of all attempts to promote your true holiness and happiness? Why do you try to extract your own ruin from all the perfections of a gracious God; from all the Persons of the Godhead; from all His purposes, covenants, words, and works?

My beloved children, I wish for my "joy and crown in the day of the Lord." When so much of the best of your life is already spent in uselessness and wrath; when death, judgment, and eternity hurry to meet you; when your judgment does not linger—why should you put aside for one more moment your deepest concern about your eternal salvation? Why wait to come to an infinitely gracious Redeemer, to the "Lord God, merciful and gracious, longsuffering, and abundant in goodness and truth, keeping mercy for thousands, and forgiving iniquity, transgression and sin"? Why delay when you are called from darkness to God's "marvellous light"—called to receive redemption through Jesus' blood, to receive out of His fullness grace for grace, to the fellowship of God's Son, to be "heirs of God and joint heirs with Christ"? Why lose another year, another month, another hour, another moment, without the sweet joy of God in Christ as your Father, Husband, Friend, and Portion? Why hide among the vain or earthly cares, when a "kingdom which cannot be moved" is offered to you? Why, to render your eternal damnation more certain and more dreadful every moment, and your way of escape more difficult, should you remain among worldly companions and selfish lust, when Jesus is lifting up His voice and crying, "Whosoever will let him come unto me"?

"Come unto me all ye that labour and are heavy laden, and I will give you rest." "Him that cometh unto me I will in no wise cast out." "Come ye to the waters; come, buy wine and milk, without money and without price. Incline your ear, and come unto me; hear and your soul shall live; and I will make an everlasting covenant with you, even the sure mercies of David." "Behold I stand at the door [of your heart] and knock." You run from storms, from trouble, from outward danger; why not make haste to Jesus, the refuge, the hope, set before you? When He says, "Today if you will hear my voice," do not harden "your hearts...now is the accepted time; now is the day of salvation," why should you say, "Tomorrow"? When He waits to be gracious and show mercy, why tire out His patience until He "shuts up all his tender mercies in his wrath"? Does it mean nothing to you to weary your parents and ministers? And will you weary God also?

Lord Jesus, make haste to convince, to convert, and to save the rising generation. They perish, they perish! O Redeemer, do not tarry. Let now be an accepted time; let now be a day of salvation. Save now, O Lord, we beseech thee; send now prosperity!

Synopsis of the Shorter Catechism

To manifest the importance, fullness, and order of that system of divinity laid down in the Assembly's Shorter Catechism, it is observable that it contains:

    I. The Great End of all Religion: Question 1

    II. The Unerring Standard of it: Question 2

    III. The Sum and Principal Parts of it: Question 3, which are three:

        1. The Doctrinal Part, Questions 4-38

        2. The Practical Part, Questions 39-81

        3. The Application of Both Conjointly, Questions 82-107

First, the doctrinal part, which describes what we are to believe concerning God and man.

    First, concerning God; wherein view:

    (1) The perfections of His nature, Questions 4-5

    (2) The persons in His essence, Question 6

    (3) The purposes of His will, Question 7

    (4) The productions of His power, Question 8; in the work of creation, Question 9; and the work of providence, Question 11

    Second, concerning man, in:

    (1) His state of innocency, which consisted in his:

        1. Likeness to God, Question 10

        2. Covenant alliance with God, Question 12

    (2) His fallen state, in

        1. Its sinful cause, Question 13; where we have the nature of sin in general, Question 14; and the particular sin by which man fell, Question 15

        2. Its extent over all mankind by that sin, Question 16

        3. Its fearful ingredients, Question 17; of sinfulness, Question 18; and misery, Question 19

    (3) His state of salvation, in which is represented:

        1. Its causes and means; the electing and covenanting love of God the Father, Question 20; the

redeeming grace of the Son, manifested in His incarnation, Questions 21-22; offices of prophet, priest and king, Questions 23-26; states of humiliation and exaltation, Questions 27-28; and the applying work of the Holy Ghost, Questions 29-30

2. The blessings thereof; as union to Christ in effectual calling, Questions 30-31; justification, adoption, sanctification, and their attendant comforts, Questions 32-36; a happy death, Question 37; and complete and everlasting glory, Question 38

Second, the practical part, which represents our duty in:

(1.) Its nature, Question 39

(2) Its rule, Questions 40-41

(3) Its substance, Question 42

(4) The reasons of and obligations to it, Questions 43-44

(5) Its particular parts and branches, that is:

1. Duty to God; with respect to the nature and object of worship, first commandment, Questions 45-48; the ordinances of worship, second commandment, Questions 49-52; manner of worship, third commandment, Questions 53-56; and times of worship, fourth commandment, Questions 57-62

2. Duty to man; respecting our own and our neighbor's relations, fifth commandment, Questions 63-66; life, sixth commandment, Questions 67-69; chastity, seventh commandment, Questions 70-72; civil property, eighth commandment, Questions 73-75; reputation, ninth commandment, Questions 76-78; contentment and charitableness, tenth commandment, Questions 79-81

Third, the application, serving:

(1) For conviction of our weakness, and of the

number, aggravations, and desert of our sins, Questions 82-84

(2) For direction, how to receive and improve the redemption prepared for us in Christ, Question 85; by faith, Question 86; by repentance unto life, Question 87; by a diligent use of God's instituted means of salvation, Question 88; and especially:

1. His Word, Questions 89-90
2. Sacraments; whose efficacy, nature, number, and different forms of baptism and Lord's Supper, and the proper subjects of which are represented, Questions 91-97
3. Prayer; the nature and rule of which, particularly the Lord's Prayer in its preface and petitions relative to God's glory and our happiness, and its conclusion, are explained, Questions 98-107

In order to avoid repetition, and to render the following explication at once low priced, abundant in matter, as well as practical, plain, and brief in its answers, some more important questions of the *Shorter Catechism* are more largely handled, while others, especially toward the end, are more briefly reviewed, their subject matter being considered under some other head. It is therefore hoped that the reader will compare Questions 9, 11, 46, 54-55 with Question 4; Question 31 with Questions 14-28; Question 33 with Questions 14, 18-20, 25; Question 35 with Questions 46-81; Question 50 with Questions 26, 54-55, 88, 102; Question 84 with Questions 14, 19; and Questions 86-87 with Questions 18, 31, 35, etc.

The author has been at no small pains to correct, enlarge, and improve this new edition of his Catechism, particularly by adding a great number of Scripture texts, in order more clearly to elucidate and confirm the different points of doctrine advanced herein.

— John Brown

CATECHISM.

QUEST. I. *What is the chief end of man?*
ANSW. Man's chief end is to glorify God, and to enjoy him for ever.

Q. What do you mean by that *end* which all men propose in their actions?—A. That which they seek to obtain in and by their actions.

Q. What ought man to make his *chief* or *highest* end?—A. The glorifying and enjoying of God, Rom. ix. 36.

Q. Why ought man to make the glory of God his *chief* end?—A. Because it was God's chief end in making, preserving, and redeeming man, Prov. xvi. 4.

Q. May man have no other end in any of his actions?—A. Yes; but it must be a subordinate end, which tends to obtain the chief end, 1 Cor. x. 31.

Q. What may be some of men's subordinate ends?—A. To provide food and raiment, and procure health, peace, liberty, and safety to themselves or others.

Q. How many parts doth man's chief end consist of?—A. Two; his chief duty, which is to *glorify* God; and his chief happiness, which is to *enjoy* God.

Q. How is the glory of God usually distinguished?—A. Into his essential and declarative glory.

Q. What is the essential glory of God?—A. That which he is and hath in himself, Exod. xiii. 14.

Q. What is God's declarative glory?—A. The shewing forth of his glory in and by his creatures, Isa. v. 16.

Q. Can we add any thing to that glory which God hath in himself?—A. No; for it is infinite, Job xi. 7.

Q. How then do creatures glorify God?—A. By shewing forth or declaring that he is glorious.

Q. How do beasts and lifeless creatures glorify God?—A. God shews forth his glory in and by them.

Q. How do devils and wicked men glorify God?—A. Not willingly; but God over-rules their works, however sinful, to his own glory, Psalm lxxvi. 10.

Q. How ought angels and men to glorify God?—A. By

2

doing all things with a view to shew forth and declare his glory, Psalm xcvi. 7, and cvii. 8, 15, 21.

Q. With what ought we to glorify God?—A. With our hearts, lips, and lives, Psalm ciii. 1.

Q. How should we glorify God with our hearts?—A. By knowing, trusting in, loving, admiring, adoring, and remembering him, 1 Chron. xxivii. 9, Psalm ciii. 1.

Q. How should we glorify him with our lips?—A. By praying to, praising, and commending him.

How should we glorify him with our lives?—A. By doing every thing which he commands out of love to him, Deut. x. 12, Matth. xvii. 37, 38.

Q. How did Adam in innocency glorify God?—A. By giving perfect obedience to his law, Eccl. vii. 29.

Q. Do men still answer their chief end in glorifying God?—A. No; All men have sinned, and come short of the glory of God, Rom. iii. 9—23.

Q. Hath God then lost his end in making man?—A. No; he will glorify his justice in damning some men, and his mercy in saving others, Rom. ix. 22, 23.

Q. Who hath most eminently glorified God?—A. Christ.

Q. Where hath Christ glorified God?—A. Both on earth and in heaven, Heb. i. 3.

Q. How did Christ glorify God on earth?—A. By obeying his law, and suffering his wrath, in the room of elect sinners, John xvii. 4, Matth. xx. 28.

Q. How doth Christ glorify God in heaven?—A. By pleading for his elect, and sending his Spirit to apply his purchased redemption to them, John xiv. 16, 17.

Q. When doth a sinner begin to glorify God aright?—A. When he first believeth in Christ, 1 John v. 10.

Q. How doth faith or believing glorify God?—A. It credits his word, unites us to Christ, and so makes us fruitful in good works, Rom. v. 20, John xv. 5.

Q. What is a good work?—A. A work commanded by God's law, performed in his strength, from a love to, and with a view of glorifying him.

Q. Doth faith make us glorify God in all our works?—A. Yes; 1 Cor. x. 31, Psalm cxv. 1, 2, Rom. xiv. 8.

Q. How doth faith make us glorify God in our natural actions, as eating or drinking, &c.?—A. By making us seek and receive a covenant-right to, and thank God for our food and raiment; and use them to fit our bodies for the service of God, Rom. viii. 32, Deut. viii. 10.

Q. How doth faith make us glorify God in our civil business?—A. By making us diligent in our trades and callings, from a regard to God's command; and causing us to use the gains of them to his glory, Isa. xxiii. 18.

Q. How doth faith make us glorify God in religious services?—A. It makes us perform them in the strength of Christ's Spirit, and look for acceptance of them only through his merit and intercession, 1 Peter ii. 5.

Q. What should we aim at next to the glorifying of God?—A. The enjoying of him, Psalm xliii. 4.

Q. What is meant by the enjoying of God?—A. The receiving, living on, and rejoicing in him as our portion, Psalm xvi. 5, 6, Isa. lx. 19, 20.

Q. Why should we seek to enjoy God?—A. Because he only is a suitable and sufficient person for our souls, Hab. iii. 17, 18, Psalm cxlii. 4, 5, lxxiii. 25, 26.

Q. Why cannot the riches, honours, and pleasures of this world be a satisfying portion to our souls?—A. Because they are vain and empty, unsuited to the spiritual nature, and disproportionate to the boundless desires of our immortal souls, Matth. xvi. 26, Psalm lxxiii. 25.

Q. How did Adam in innocency enjoy God?—A. By perfect friendship and fellowship. But sin quickly broke up that, Isa. lix. 2, Rom. v. 11, Gen. iii.

Q. What do all men now by nature enjoy instead of God?—A. Sin, Satan, and the world, 1 John ii. 16.

Q. How do they enjoy these?—A. They have sin as their pleasure, Satan as their prince and father, and the world as their portion, Heb. xi. 25, John viii. 44.

Q. Can we enjoy God in our natural estate?—A. No; for *what communion hath light with darkness, or Christ with Belial?* 2 Cor. vi. 14, 15.

Q. Is there any way to recover the lost enjoyment of God?—A. Yes, by Christ alone, Acts iv. 12, Eph. ii. 18.

Q. When doth a sinner first begin to enjoy God?—A. When he first receives Christ, and rests on him.

Q. In what means and ordinances is God to be enjoyed?—A. In prayer, reading or hearing God's word, meditation, fasting, receiving the sacraments, &c.

Q. Do the saints often enjoy God in these ordinances?—A. Yes; for these are their great delight, and they are much engaged in them, Psalm xxvii. 4, and lxxxiv. 10.

Q. What satisfaction doth a soul find in the enjoyment

of God ?—A. Unspeakably more than in the abundance of
all worldly good things, Psalm iv. 6—8.

Q. Where and when do the saints enjoy God ?—A. On
earth in this life, and in heaven hereafter.

Q. How is God enjoyed in this life on earth ?—A. By
our receiving the influences of his grace, and having his
love shed abroad in our hearts, 1 John i. 3. 7.

Q. How is God enjoyed in heaven ?—A. By our being
ever with him, and receiving that fulness of joy which is at
his right hand, Psalm xvi. 11, and xvii. 15.

Q. Wherein doth the enjoyment of God on earth, and
that in heaven agree ?—A. It is the same God who is enjoyed; and the enjoyment of him here as truly humbles
and satisfies the heart, as that in heaven.

Q. In what do they differ ?—A. In the manner and measure of enjoyment.

Q. How do they differ in the *manner* of enjoyment ?—
A. Here God often hides himself, and we enjoy him through
means and ordinances as through a glass darkly; but in
heaven we will enjoy him uninterruptedly and immediately,
and see him face to face, 1 Cor. xiii. 12.

Q. How do they differ in the *measure* of enjoyment ?—
A. Here we enjoy God only in part; but hereafter we shall
enjoy him fully, 1 Cor. xiii. 12, 1 John iii. 2.

Q. Shall the saints in heaven receive into their souls all
the infinite fulness and sweetness that is in God ?—A. No;
but their finite souls shall be filled with as much of it as they
can hold, Eph. iii. 19, Psalm xvii. 15.

Q. What is the sure pledge and earnest of our enjoying
God in heaven ?—A. Our enjoyment of him here, Psalm
lxxiii. 24. 26.

Q. Why is the glorifying of God placed before the enjoyment of him ?—A. Because the glory of God is of more
value than our happiness, Isa. xl. 17.

Q. Whether is our glorifying or enjoying of God first in
order ?—A. We must first enjoy God in his gracious influences, and then glorify him; and this leads on to further
enjoyment of him, Psalm cxix. 32.

Q. Is our delight in the glory or glorious excellencies of
God as satisfying to us, to be our chief end or motive in our
actions, religious or moral ?—A. No; but our shewing forth
the honour of these glorious excellencies, Isa. ii. 11, Psal.
xvi. 4, Isa. xliii. 21.

Q. Why may we not make our own delight in the glory

of God as satisfying to our desires, our chief end and motive?—A. Because this would be a setting up of our own happiness above the glory of God.

Q. Who alone may expect to enjoy God in heaven?—A. Only such as glorify him on earth, Heb. xii. 14.

Q. Why are the glorifying and enjoying of God joined as one chief end?—A. Because none can obtain or rightly seek the one without the other, 1 Cor. xv. 58.

Q. How do we most highly glorify God?—A. By receiving and enjoying him most fully.

Q. What chiefly secures our enjoyment of God?—A. The concern of the glory of God in it.

Q. How is the glory of God concerned in our enjoyment of him?—A. All his attributes are in Christ engaged for our enjoyment of him; and their glory shines brightly in fulfilling these engagements, Isa. xxx. 18.

Q. How long shall the saints glorify and enjoy God?—A. To all eternity; for *we shall ever be with the Lord*, 1 Thess. iv. 17, Isa. lx. 19, 20.

Q. What are the grounds which secure the eternal enjoyment of God to believers?—A. The infinite and eternal love of God; the extent of his promise; and the infinite merit, and eternal intercession of Christ.

QUEST. 2. *What rule hath God given to direct us, how we may glorify and enjoy him?*

ANSW. The word of God, which is contained in the scriptures of the Old and New Testament, is the only rule to direct us how we may glorify and enjoy him.

Q. Whence is it that we need a rule to direct us how to glorify and enjoy God?—A. Because God is our sovereign, and being infinite, is so much unknown to us.

Q. Who alone can give us a *rule* for these ends?—A. God only; for he only hath sufficient wisdom and authority to prescribe a sufficient rule, 2 Tim. iii. 16, 17.

Q. What is the rule which God hath given for man's direction?—A. The declaration of his own will.

Q. How did God shew this rule to Adam before the fall?—A. Mostly by the light of nature within him, and the works of creation and providence without him.

Q. Did he not shew his will wholly to Adam by these means?—A. No; the time of the Sabbath, and the prohi-

2*

bition to eat of the tree of knowledge, were made known to him by immediate revelation, Gen. ii.

Q. How far are the light of nature, and works of creation and providence, now of use as a rule to men?—A. They so far make known the perfections of God, and part of our duty, as renders us inexcusable when we disobey him, Rom. i. 20, and ii. 14, 15.

Q. Are these things now a sufficient rule to lead us to happiness?—A. No; for sin hath made us blind and foolish in the matters of God, 1 Cor. ii. 14.

Q. If our reason were as extensive as ever Adam's was, could it now lead us to holiness or happiness?—A. No; for sin hath fixed a gulf between God and us, through which our reason, however extensive, could never shew us a passage, Isa. xlix. 24.

Q. Hath God given us any rule that can direct sinful men to holiness and happiness?—A. Yes; the Bible, or holy scriptures, 2 Peter i. 19—21.

Q. Why is that rule called the Bible or Book?—A. Because it is far better than all other books.

Q. What makes it so?—A. It is the *word of God*, the testament of Christ, and of the greatest use to men.

Q. Why are the scriptures called the word of God?—A. Because they were given by the inspiration of his Spirit, 2 Peter i. 21, Heb. i. 1, 2 Tim. iii. 15, 16, 17.

Q. How do you prove the scriptures to be the word of God?—A. By the stamp of God that is to be seen upon them; for none can speak like him, John vi. 63.

Q. What is that stamp of God which is imprinted upon the scriptures?—A. That majesty, holiness, light, and efficacy which appear in them, Psalm xiv. 7, 8, 9.

Q. Wherein doth the majesty of the scriptures appear? —A. God therein is described, and speaks in the most lofty manner: therein sins are forbidden which God only can know or condemn; duties required that God only can command; and promises and threatenings are made which God only can accomplish, Isa. lvii. 15, 16.

Q. What divine holiness appears in the scriptures?—A. There every holy thing is strictly required, and every unholy thing is forbidden; and all the means and motives to perform duty, and avoid sin, are clearly shown, and warmly pressed, 1 Pet. i. 13—23.

Q. What divine light appears in the scriptures?—A.

There mysteries are revealed which God only knew, or can comprehend, Col. i. 26, 1 Tim. iii. 16.

Q. What are some of those mysteries?—A. The mystery of the persons in one Godhead; of Christ, the Son of God, his becoming man; and our union with him, &c. 1 John v. 8, Isa. vii. 14, Eph. v. 30, 32.

Q. What divine efficacy or power have the scriptures?— A. They are the means of convincing, converting, and quickening dead and obstinate sinners; and of comforting those that are cast down, Psal. xix. 7, 8.

Q. By what other arguments may we be convinced that the scriptures are the word of God?—A. By their antiquity, harmony, scope, success, accomplishment of prophecies, and confirmation by miracles and the blood of martyrs.

Q. What is their *antiquity*?—A. Their being written in part before all other books; and giving us the only rational account of ancient things, such as the creation, the fall, flood, and dispersion of men at Babel.

Q. What do you call the *harmony* of the scriptures?— A. The agreement of every part one with another.

Q. How is this a proof of their being the word of God?— A. Because it is impossible that such a number of writers, in so many different ages and places, could ever of themselves so agree, in opposition to the common inclinations of men.

Q. Doth no part of scripture really contradict another?— A. No; though some parts seem to contradict others, as John x. 30, with xiv. 28.

Q. How may seemingly contradictory scriptures be reconciled?—A. By considering that these different scriptures either speak of different things, or of different views of the same thing, Rom. i. 3, 4, and ix. 6.

Q. What is the *scope* and *design* of the scriptures?—A. To humble all men, and give all the glory to God.

Q. What success have the scriptures had?—A. The gross manners of many nations have been reformed; and multitudes of most wicked men have been gained to deny ungodliness and worldly lusts, and to live soberly, righteously, and godly, by means of the scriptures, though published by the meanest instruments, notwithstanding the combined opposition of hell and earth against them, Acts i—xx.

Q. Of what *prophecies* doth the accomplishment prove the scriptures to be the word of God?—A. The prophecies of Israel's entrance into, and deliverance from Egypt and

Babylon; and of the destruction of Chaldea, Egypt and Tyre; and of the rise and fall of the Persian, Grecian, and Roman Empires; and of the birth and death of Christ, &c.

Q. How doth the accomplishment of such prophecies prove the divinity of the scriptures?—A. Because none but God could foretell future events, depending on a multitude of second causes, in so particular a manner, and at such a distant time, before they took place.

Q. What *miracles* have been wrought to confirm the scriptures?—A. The plagues of Egypt; the dividing of the Red Sea; causing the sun to stand still; raising the dead; giving sight to such as were blind, &c.

Q. How do miracles confirm the divinity of the scriptures?—A. Because God would never work miracles to confirm any imposture, Heb. ii. 3, 4.

Q. But may not Satan, &c. work miracles?—A. He may work counterfeit, but no true miracles.

Q. Wherein doth a counterfeit miracle differ from a true one?—A. Besides a difference in their natures, all true miracles confirm doctrines leading to a virtuous and holy life; but counterfeit miracles always confirm falsehoods and wicked practices, Deut. xiii. 5, 2 Thess. ii.

Q. Why doth not God still work miracles for the confirmation of the scriptures?—A. Because they are only necessary to establish truth at first, and to awaken the world to consider and receive it; and if always wrought, be esteemed common things, and make no impression on the minds of men, Exod. iv.—xiv, &c.

Q. How do the sufferings of martyrs prove the divinity of the scriptures?—A. So many millions could never have borne such cruel torments for their adherence to the scriptures, with such calmness, patience, and joy, if God had not assisted them, Heb. xi. 35—39.

Q. Why might not good angels be the authors of the scriptures?—A. Because these could never pretend to be God; nor speak without his commission, Psal. ciii. 20.

Q. Why might not Satan have been their author?—A. Because they wholly tend to the ruin of his kingdom and interest in the world, 2 Tim. iii. 15.

Q. How do you prove that the scriptures cannot be a forgery and imposture of the writers?—A. Because the writers candidly relate their own failings; and the tendency of the scriptures to condemn all deceits, and sinful inclinations and practices, under the severest penalties, exposed the penman to the rage and hatred of the world; whereas impostors conceal their own vices, and flatter men's corruptions, in order to procure carnal pleasures, honours, or riches to themselves.

Q. Can an unbeliever discern the stamp of God in the scriptures, or be by the above arguments savingly convinced that they are the word of God?—A. No; but he may be rationally convinced that they are so, Acts xxvi. 28.

Q. What hinders unbelievers from discerning the stamp of God in the scriptures when they read them?—A. Satan hath blinded their minds, 2 Cor. iv. 3.

Q. How may we attain to a saving persuasion that the scriptures are the word of God.—A. Only by the Spirit's powerful application of them to our heart, 1 Cor. ii.

Q. What is the formal reason and ground of a saving faith of what the scriptures teach?—A. The authority and faithfulness of God therein spiritually discerned, 2 Thess. ii. 13. 2 Chron. xx. 20.

Q. Doth the authority of the scriptures depend on the church?—A. No; for the church is founded on, and derives all her authority from them, Eph. ii. 20.

Q. Why then is the church called *the pillar and ground of truth?*—A. Because the church keeps and publishes the scripture, Rom. iii. 2. Isa. ii. 3.

Q. Do the scriptures derive any authority from man's reason?—A. No: they derive it from God only.

Q. If we find in them any thing which we reckon contrary to reason, may we reject it?—A. No; for as the heavens are higher than the earth, so are God's thoughts, the scriptures, higher than our thoughts, Isa. lv. 9.

Q. Why is the Bible called the *scriptures* or *writings?* A. Because of its distinguished excellency above all other writings, 2 Tim. iii. 15—17. Psal. xix. 7—10.

Q. Why was the word of God committed to writing?——A. For the better preserving and spreading of it.

Q. Why would God have his word preserved?—A. For the comfort and establishment of his church.

Q. Why would he have his word propagated and spread? —A. For the increase and enlargement of his church.

Q. Would it have been safe to have still trusted revelation to the memoirs of men?—A. No: for these are very weak and deceitful, Jer. ii. 32. Psal. cvi. 13.

Q. Did not God preserve his church for 2500 years,

from Adam to Moses, without the writing of his word ?—A. Yes; (though he revealed his will by visions, &c.)

Q. Why might he not as yet do so still ?—A. Because all that God had revealed of his will before Moses was safely remembered ; men lived then so long, that a few persons conveyed revelation pure and uncorrupted to the church till that time, Gen. i. to xlix.

Q. Why are the scriptures called a *testament?*—A. Because therein Christ bequeathes his rich legacies and blessings to sinful men, Luke xxii. 29. Heb. ii. 3.

Q. Whereby is this testament confirmed?—A. By the death of Christ the testator, Heb. ix. 15, 16.

Q. Into how many testaments is the Bible divided ?—A. Into two, the Old and the New, Heb. viii. and ix.

Q. Which is the Old Testament ?—A. That which begins with Genesis, and ends with Malachi.

Q. Why is it called the Old Testament ?—A. Because it was first published; and contains the dispensation of the covenant of grace,which is now ceased.

Q. By what death of Christ was the Old Testament confirmed?—A. By his typical death in the ancient sacrifices, Rev. xiii. 8. Heb. ix. 18—20.

Q. Which is the New Testament ?—A. That which begins with Matthew, and ends with the Revelation.

Q. Why is it called the New Testament ?—A. Because it was last published; and it contains that more perfect dispensation of the covenant of grace which is still present, Heb. viii. 6—13. and ix. 15.

Q. By what death of Christ was this Testament confirmed ?—A. By his actual death in his own person.

Q. In what do the Old and New Testament agree ?—A. God in Christ is the author of both ; all the blessings of the new covenant are bequeathed in both ; and the glory of God, and salvation of men, is the end of both.

Q. In what doth the Old and New Testament differ?— A. In duration and excellency, Heb. viii. 6. 13.

Q. How do they differ in duration ?—A. The Old continued from Adam's fall till Christ's coming and death ; and the New from thence continues till the end of the world, Gen. iii., Mat. xxvii., Rev. xx.

Q, Is the Old Testament scripture now of no force ?— A. Its truths are still of as much force as ever, but its types are ceased, Heb. x. 1, 2. Col. ii. 14—20.

Q. How do these Testaments differ in excellency ?—A. The New excels the Old in many things.

Q. Wherein doth the New Testament excel the Old?— **A.** In evidence, extent, gifts, and worship.

Q. How doth the New Testament excel in *evidence* ?— **A.** The Old Testament darkly pointed out Christ as to come; but the New points him out as already come, 2 Cor. iii. 14, Col. ii. 17, Heb. v.—x.

Q. How doth the New Testament excel in *extent?*—A. The Old Testament was mostly confined to the Jews ; but the New extends to all nations; and many more are by it converted to Christ, Rev. vii. 9.

Q. How doth the New Testament excel in *gifts?*—A. The gifts of the Spirit are more plentiful and powerful under the New than under the Old, Acts ii.

Q. How doth the New Testament excel in *worship?*— **A.** The Old Testament worship was more carnal and burdensome ; but the worship under the New is more free, spiritual, and easy, Gal. v. 7, John iv. 22—24.

Q. For what end hath God given us the scriptures ?—A. To be a rule to direct us how to glorify and enjoy him, 2 Tim. iii. 15—17, John v. 39.

Q. What kind of a rule is the holy scripture ?—A. A perfect, plain, absolute, infallible, and only rule.

Q. How is the scripture a *perfect* rule ?—A. As all we are bound to believe or do, in order to salvation, is therein revealed, either in express words, or by necessary consequence, 2 Tim. iii. 15—17.

Q. How do you prove, that plain and necessary consequences, drawn from the express words of scripture, are a part of our rule ?—A. Because Christ proved the resurrection against the Sadducees by a scripture consequence: and the apostles often reasoned in this manner, Matth. xxii. 31, Heb. i. and ii., &c.

Q. How is the scripture a *plain* rule ?—A. Because all things necessary to be believed and done, in order to salvation, and so clearly revealed in some place thereof, as every man who hath the exercise of reason, by a diligent use of the scripture may know them, Psalm cxix. 105. 130, and xix. 7. 8.

Q. What should we do that we may rightly understand the scripture when we read, hear, or think of it ?—A. We should cry to God to *open our eyes, that we may behold the wonders of his law*, Psalm cxix. 18.

Q. How are the scriptures an *absolute* rule?—**A.** Because the Spirit of God speaking in them is the supreme judge of all controversies, decrees, and doctrines of men, Mat. xxii. 29, Isa. viii. 20, Luke xvi. 29. 31.

Q. May not the scriptures be tried and judged by other rules?—**A.** No; every thing is to be tried by them; but they are to be tried by no standard rule, Isa. viii. 20.

Q. How are the scriptures an *infallible* rule?—**A.** Because they contain the mind and will of the God who cannot lie, Tit. i. 2, 2 Tim. iii. 16, 17.

Q. How are the scriptures the *only* rule? **A.** Because nothing else can direct us aright how to glorify and enjoy God, Prov. xxix. 18, Isa. viii. 20.

Q. Why may not unwritten traditions be received as a part of our rule?—**A.** Because they are cursed that add to, or take from the word of God; and such as speak not according to it, have no light in them, Rev. xxii. 18.

Q. Why may not the spirit or light within men be a part of our rule?—**A.** Because every spirit and light that is without the word is darkness, and a spirit of error, 1 John iv. 1 6, Mat. xxii. 29.

Q. In what language were the scriptures first written?—**A.** The Old Testament in Hebrew, and the New in Greek.

Q. Why must they be translated *into the languages* of every nation whither they come?—**A.** That all may have opportunity to read them, John xv. 39, Acts xvii. 11.

Q. Why ought all men to read the scriptures?—**A.** Because God often commands it, and the knowledge of the scriptures is very excellent and useful, John v. 39, 2 Tim. iii. 15, 16, 17, 2 Pet. i. 19.

Q. How doth it appear that the scripture is so excellent and useful?—**A.** It contains all sovereign remedies against distress, and all true comfort under it; all spiritual armour for defence of our souls; and is an unerring guide to glory, 2 Tim. iii. 15, 16, 17.

Q. Are the apocryphal books, as Tobit, Judith, &c. any part of the word of God?—**A.** No.

Q. How prove you that?—**A.** Because the Jewish church, to which the oracles of God were then committed, never acknowledged them as the word of God; nor have they the stamp of God upon them, but contain several things false, and disagreeable to the word of God.

Q. How may the scriptures be more generally distinguished?—**A.** Into the Law and the Gospel.

Q. What is the *Law* of God?—A. It is that declaration of his will to reasonable creatures, whereby he shows them their duty, and binds them to it, Exod. xx.

Q. What parts of scripture belong to the law?—A. All these that require any duty to be performed by men, Exod. xx. 3—17. 1 John iii. 23, Isa. lv. 6, 7.

Q. How are scripture laws usually distinguished?—A. Into the ceremonial, judicial, and moral.

Q. Which are the *ceremonial* laws?—Those that directed the Old Testament church, concerning the types and ceremonies used in their religious worship.

Q. Which are the *judicial* laws?—A. Those which directed the Jews concerning the affairs of their state, as a nation, separated to the Lord, Exod. xxi. 22, &c.

Q. Which is the *moral* law?—A. That which equally and always binds all men to the whole of their duty.

Q. How is the *Gospel* usually distinguished?—A. Into the *gospel largely taken*, and the *gospel strictly taken*, Acts xvi. 31, Isa. lv. 4.

Q. What is the *gospel strictly taken*?—A. It is the glad tidings of salvation to lost sinners through Christ.

Q. What parts of scripture belong to this?—A. All these that offer Christ, or promise any good thing through him to sinful men, Rev. xxii. 17.

Q. Wherein do the law and the gospel *strictly taken* agree?—A. God is the Author; his glory is the end; and Christ is the confirmer of both, Psalm cxlvii. 19, 20.

Q. Wherein do they differ?—A. The law requires good in and from us; but the gospel declares Christ hath done, and will do all for and in us, and freely brings all good things to us, Rom. x. 4, 5.

Q. Do not the law and gospel concur with, and promote the honour of one another?—A. Yes, Luke ii. 14.

Q. How doth the law concur with the gospel?—A. It drives men to embrace the grace of the gospel, and teaches them how to improve it; and it condemns them to more dreadful wrath if they slight it, Rom. iii. 20.

Q. How doth the gospel honour the law?—A. It brings in Christ as perfectly fulfilling it as a covenant; and it strengthens and encourages us to obey it as a rule.

Q. If the law and gospel so well agree, how is it that men, by cleaving to the law as a covenant, slight the grace of the gospel?—A. Because they abuse the law, in seeking justification by the works of it, Rom. ix. 31, 32.

3

Q. Are not both law and gospel sometimes contained in one and the same sentence of scripture?—A. Yes, as Gen. iii. 15.

Q. What is the *gospel largely taken?*—A. The whole word of God, 1 Cor. ix. 14.

Q. How can the whole word of God be called *gospel* or *good tidings*, since it brings many sad tidings to sinners, in requiring duties which they cannot perform, and threatening wrath which they cannot bear?—A. Because all these tend to promote and maintain the honour of the free grace of the gospel, Heb. x. 29, and ii. 3, 2 Thess. i. 7—9.

Q. How may the scriptures be more particularly divided?—A. Into histories, prophecies, threatenings, promises, commands, and doctrines.

Q. Which are the histories of scripture?—A. Such as record the facts and events which have come to pass.

Q. Which are the *prophecies* of scripture?—A. Such as foretell what hath or shall come to pass.

Q. What are the *threatenings?*—A. All such scriptures as denounce God's wrath against men for their sins.

Q. What are the *promises?*—A. All such scriptures as signify God's will to bestow any good thing on us.

Q. May the same sentence be both a promise and threatening?—A. Yes; every threatening to destroy a believer's enemies is a promise to him, Gen. iii. 14, 15.

Q. How are the promises usually distinguished?—A. Into absolute and conditional.

Q. What is a *conditional* promise?—A. That in which God engages to do us some good if we have some good quality, or do some good work, Acts xvi. 31.

Q. What is an *absolute* promise?—A. It is that wherein God engages to bestow good upon us, without requiring any condition in or from us, Isa. xlv. 24, Heb. viii. 12.

Q. Which scriptures are *commands* or *precepts?*—A. Such as require us to be, do, or avoid any thing.

Q. What call you *doctrines?*—A. All such scriptures as show us the nature, qualities, and connections between persons and things; as what God, Christ, man, &c., are; and how they stand related to one another.

Q. Is every word of scripture equally true, and of divine authority?—A. Yes; but every word is not of equal weight and importance, Matth. xxiii. 23, Hos. viii. 12.

Q. How are the truths of scripture distinguished with respect to their weight and importance?—A. Into fundamental, and not fundamental truths. Q. What mean you by *fundamental* truths?—A. Such truths, as we cannot be saved without the knowledge, belief, and improvement them, John xvii. 3.

Q. What are some of these truths?—A. That there is one God in three persons; that man is fallen, and cannot recover himself; that Christ hath assumed our nature, and paid our debt; that we are justified only by faith in his righteousness; that being born again, and made holy, are necessary to our entrance into heaven, &c.

Q. Why call you these fundamental truths?—A. Because other divine truths are built upon them.

Quest. 3. *What do the scriptures principally teach?*

Answ. The scriptures principally teach what man is to believe concerning God, and what duty God requires of man.

Q. What things do the scriptures chiefly teach?—A. Matters of faith and practice, 2 Tim. iii. 16.

Q. What doth *faith* or *believing* mean?—A. An assenting to the testimony of another.

Q. How may faith, as to the authority on which it depends, be distinguished?—A. Into human and divine.

Q. Wherein do human and divine faith differ?—A. In their foundation and firmness.

Q. How do they differ as to their *foundation?*—A. Human faith believes a report upon the testimony of man; but divine faith believes it upon the footing of God's testimony, Exod. iv. 30, 31. Psalm iv. 20.

Q. How do they differ in their firmness of assent?—A. Human faith admits, that the report which it credits may possibly be false; but divine doth not, Tit. i. 2.

Q. With what faith ought we to believe the whole scriptures, and them only?—A. With a divine faith.

Q. How may faith, as to its *effects*, be distinguished? —A. Into historical faith; the faith of miracles; temporary faith, and saving faith.

Q. What is *historical* faith?—A. The believing scripture-truths as we do historical reports, in which our own welfare is not deeply concerned, Exod. iv. 31.

Q. What is the *faith of miracles?*—A. The believing that God will work such a miracle upon, or for us.

Q. What is *temporary* faith?—A. An affecting persuasion of divine truths, and presumptuous leaning on the promises for a time, without receiving Christ as our only Saviour, Matth. xiii. 20—22. Acts. viii. 13.

Q. What is *saving* faith?—A. That by which we credit the whole word of God, and receive Christ in it, to the saving of our souls, Rom. x. 10.

Q. What call you matters of *practice* or *duty* required of man?—A. Whatever man owes to God, to himself, or to others, Mic. vi. 8.

Q. Whether must duty or faith be first in order?—A. Faith: for till we believe the love of God, and receive Christ as our strength, it is impossible for us to please God, Luke i. 74, 75, Heb. xi. 6.

Q. Will true faith produce true obedience?—A. Yes; *faith worketh by love*, Gal. v. 6. 22, 23.

Q. Who then shine most in holy obedience?—A. Those who are strongest in faith, Rom. iv. 20.

Quest. 4. *What is God?*
Answ. God is a Spirit, infinite, eternal, and unchangeable, in his being, wisdom, power, holiness, justice, goodness, and truth.

Q. What doth the name of God properly signify?—A. A being of infinite perfection, Job xi. 7.

Q. What are we to believe concerning God?—A. That he is, what he is, and what he hath done.

Q. What religious principle must we first in order believe? —A. That there is a God, Heb. xi. 6.

Q. What things teach us that there is a God?—A. Both scripture and reason, Mal. iii. 6.

Q. In what are all men taught that there is a God?—A. In the works of creation and providence.

Q. How doth creation-work prove that there must be a God?—A. Because nothing can make itself; and so there must be a God who hath made all things, Rom. i. 20.

Q. How do the works of providence prove that there must be a God?—A. Because so many, so vast and unruly things, could never be preserved and guided to one common end, if there were not a God to over-rule them.

Q. How doth our own being prove that there is a God?— A. The curious frame of our bodies, the noble powers of our souls; our consciences daily accusing or excusing us, together with our inability to live, move, or do any thing of ourselves, clearly prove it, Psal. cxxxix. 16, &c.

Q. Can the works of nature now teach us what God is?
—A. They may teach us some things darkly concerning God, but nothing savingly, Acts xvii. 27, Rom. ii. 14, 15.

Q. What do the works of nature more darkly shew God to be?—A. They shew that he is holy, just, wise, good, eternal, &c., Rom. i. 20—32.

Q. Who alone can teach us the saving knowledge of God?
—A. Christ by his word and Spirit, Isa. xlviii. 17.

Q. What doth the scripture or word of Christ declare God to be?—A. Light, love, and a spirit, 1 John i. 4.

Q. Why is God called *light?*—A. Because of his purity, knowledge, and being the Father of light.

Q. Why is God called *love?*—A. Because in Christ all his other attributes are employed to exalt his *love.*

Q. Why is God called a *spirit?*—A. Because his nature and attributes are spiritual, John iv. 24.

Q. What is a spirit?—A. It is a living, thinking, and invisible substance, without any matter or bodily parts.

Q. If God be a *spirit*, how are eyes, ears, arms, feet, face, fingers, mouth, lips, &c., ascribed to him in scripture?
—A. God, in condescension to our weakness, doth by these bodily members point out some property in himself, the work of which some way resembleth the use of such members in man, Hos. xii. 13, and xi. 8.

Q. What is meant by eyes and ears when ascribed to God?—A. His knowledge, care, and pity, Psal. xxxiv. 17.

Q. What do *face, nose,* and *nostrils,* mean, when ascribed to God?—A. His knowledge, favour, or wrath, Psal. xlviii. 8; and *face* also signifies his glory.

Q. What is meant by *mouth* or *lips,* when ascribed to God?—A. His truth, word, authority, or love.

Q. What is meant by *arms, hands,* and *fingers,* when ascribed to God?—A. His power; and sometimes *arms* and *hands* signify his mercy and love, Deut. xxxiii. 27.

Q. What doth *heart* mean when ascribed to God?—A. His love, approbation, or purpose.

Q. What doth *bosom,* when ascribed to God, mean?—A. His love, care, and protection, Isa. xl. 11.

Q. What do *feet,* when ascribed to God, mean?—A. His power, and providential works, Hab. iii. 5.

Q. What is meant by God's *sitting?*—A. His authority and undisturbed happiness, Psalm xxix. 10.

3*

Q. What is meant by his *standing ?*—A. His readiness to help his people, and destroy their enemies.

Q. What is meant by *walking*, *running*, *riding*, or *flying*, when ascribed to God ?—A. The calm, speedy, or kind manner of his working, Psal. xviii. 9, 10.

Q. Are there any other spirits besides God ?—A. Yes; angels, and souls of men, Psal. civ. 4.

Q. How do these differ from God ?—A. These are finite, created, and changeable spirits; but God is an infinite, eternal, and unchangeable spirit, Psal. ciii.

Q. What is meant by the attributes of God ?—A. The properties or perfections of his nature.

Q. Are all the properties of God the very same with his nature, and with one another ?—A. Yes; and so one cannot be separated from another, as the divine nature is most simple and uncompounded, Exod. iii. 14.

Q. Why then are they represented to us as different ?—A. Because of their different respects to the creatures, and because we cannot take them up as they are in God.

Q. How may the attributes of God be distinguished ?—A. Into *communicable*, which may be some way resembled by creatures ; and *incommunicable*, which can no way be resembled by creatures.

Q. Which are the communicable attributes of God ?—A. Being, wisdom, power, holiness, justice, &c.

Q. Which are his incommunicable properties ?—A. His independency, infinity, eternity, and unchangeableness, and his subsisting in three persons.

Q. What is proper *independency ?*—A. It is to have in and of one's self whatever is necessary for being, happiness, and work, Psal. cxv. 3, Exod. iii. 14.

Q. How do you prove that God is independent ?—A. The scripture affirms that *he needs nothing from, nor can be profited by any creature*, Acts xvii. 25.

Q. Do all other things depend on God in being and acts?—A. Yes; and cannot do otherways, Rom. xi. 36.

Q. What is meant by God's being *infinite ?*—A. His being without bounds or limits, Job. xi. 7.

Q. How do you prove that God is infinite ?—A. Because he cannot by searching be found out to perfection, Job. xi. 7, 1 Tim. vi. 15, 16.

Q. Wherein is God infinite ?—A. In being, perfection, and presence, Exod. iii. 14, Psal. cxlvii. 5.

Q. How is God infinite in perfection ?—A. The glory

of his perfections can admit of no addition or increase, Job xxii. 2. xxxv. 6, 7.

Q. How may God be said to be infinite in presence ?—A. He is present in all his works ; nay, *the heaven of heavens cannot contain him*, 1 Kings viii. 27, Jer. xxiii. 24.

Q. How may the presence of God be distinguished ?—A. Into his essential and operative presence.

Q. Is God's essential presence partly in heaven and partly in earth ; or partly within and partly without the limits of creation?—A. No ; the whole being of God is equally every where, Jer. xxiii. 23, 24.

Q. How may the *operative* presence of God be distinguished ?—A. Into his *natural* presence with all creatures, in preserving and governing them ; his *symbolical* presence in the ordinances of his grace ; his *gracious* presence with his saints on earth, by the indwelling and influence of his spirit ; his *glorious* presence in heaven, as the blessed portion of angels and saints ; and his *vindictive* presence in hell, by taking vengeance on devils and wicked men.

Q. Is there not, besides all these, a *singular* presence of God with the man Christ?—A. Yes ; *the fulness of the Godhead dwells in him bodily*, Col. ii. 9, 2 Col. v. 19.

Q. How is God's infinity terrible to the wicked?—A. Their loss of him, as a portion, is unspeakable ; and his treasures of wrath against them cannot be exhausted.

Q. How is it sweet to believers ?—A. Because God is their boundless portion and joy.

Q. What is meant by the *eternity* of God ?—A. His being without beginning, end, or succession of duration.

Q. How do you prove that God is without beginning or end ?—A. He is said to be *from everlasting to everlasting God*, Psal. xc. 2. 1 Tim. vi. 15, Jer x. 10.

Q. How prove you that God is without succession of duration ?—A. Because *one day is with* him *as a thousand years, and a thousand years as one day*, 2 Pet. iii. 8.

Q. How doth eternity differ from time ?—A. Time can be measured by days and years, and one part of it follows another ; but it is not so with eternity.

Q. Is any besides God *eternal?*—A. Angels and souls of men have a sort of eternity as they live for ever, Matth. x. 28, and xxv. 41.

Q. How doth their eternity differ from that of God?—A. Angels and souls of men have a beginning and succession of duration, which God hath not, Gen. i.

Q. How is the eternity of God terrible to the wicked?—
A. It secures the eternal duration of their torments.

Q. How is eternity sweet to believers?—**A.** It secures his being their everlasting portion and joy.

Q. What is meant by God's being *immutable* or *unchangeable?*—**A.** His being always the same. Mal. iii. 6.

Q. How prove you that God is unchangeable?—**A.** Himself says, *I am the Lord, I change not.*

Q. Can nothing be added to, or taken from the glorious perfections of God?—**A.** No; their glory cannot be diminished, because it is essential to God; nor can it be increased, because it is infinite, Psal. cii. 26, 27.

Q. Did not God change when he became a Creator, or when the Son of God became man?—**A.** No; the change only respected the creature, Rom. viii. 3. Heb. ii. 14.

Q. Were God's power and will to create, or become man, the same from all eternity?—**A.** Yes.

Q. If God change not, how is he said to *repent?*—**A.** His repenting means only a change of his work, but it means no change of his will, Gen. vi. 6, 7.

Q. Why is the change of work called a *repenting?*—**A.** In allusion to the case of men, whose change of work shows a change of their will, Acts iii. 19.

Q. Can a creature be by nature unchangeable?—**A.** No; for as they have their being from the will of God, they may be changed as he seeth meet, Dan. iv. 35.

Q. Are not holy angels, and glorified saints, unchangeable?—**A.** Yes; but they are so by the gracious will of God, not by nature, Heb. i. 14. Jude 1.

Q. How is God's unchangeableness terrible to the wicked?—**A.** It secures the full execution of all his threatenings upon them, 1 Sam. xv. 28, 29.

Q. How is it sweet to believers?—**A.** It secures God's resting in his love to them, fulfilling all his promises, and finishing the work of grace in them, Mal. iii. 6.

Q. Wherein is God independent, infinite, eternal, and unchangeable?—**A.** In his being, wisdom, power, holiness, justice, goodness, and truth.

Q. What is meant by the *essence* or *being* of God?—**A.** His very nature or Godhead, Exod. iii. 14.

Q. What is the highest perfection of being?—**A.** To depend on nothing, and have all other beings dependent on it, Exod. iii. 14. Dan. iv. 34, 35. Psalm cxv. 3.

Q. Is God happy only in himself, and *all in all* to himself and others?—A. Yes; he is God all-sufficient, Gen. xvii. 1, and every being is from him, Gen. i.

Q. Are they not then fools and brutish, who prefer created beings to God?—A. Yes, Jer. ii. 13.

Q. Doth not the very being of God secure the accomplishment of all his promises?—A. Yes, Exod. vi. 3.

Q. Wherein doth the being of God differ from that of creatures?—A. The being of God is independent, infinite, eternal, and unchangeable; but that of creatures is dependent, finite, created, and changeable.

Q. How may the *wisdom* of God be distinguished?—A. Into his omniscience and wisdom strictly so called.

Q. What is the *omniscience* of God?—A. That essential attribute whereby he knows all things.

Q. How do you prove that God knows all things?—A. Reason shews, and the scriptures expressly affirm it, John xxi. 17. 1 John iii. 20. Heb. iv. 13.

Q. Doth God learn anything by experience, information, observation, or reasoning, as we do?—A. No; he knows all things by the simple glance of his eye.

Q. What is the object of the knowledge of God?—A. Himself, and all things possible, or real.

Q. What doth God know of himself?—A. He knows his own nature, perfections, and decrees.

Q. How prove you that?—A. Because his understanding is infinite, cxlvii. 5. John xxi. 17.

Q. What things doth God know?—A. All past, present, future, and possible things.

Q. How prove you that God knows all past things?—A. Because he never forgets any thing, Amos viii. 7.

Q. How prove you that God knows all present things?—Because nothing can be hid from him, and he searches our very hearts, Heb. iv. 13. Rev. ii. 23.

Q. How prove you that God knows all things that are to come?—A. Because *known to God are all works from the beginning of the world;* and he hath often foretold the most accidental of them, Acts xv. 18.

Q. How prove you that God knows all possible things?—A. Because he knows his own power, and what it can do.

Q. Doth God know all things, particularly in all their properties, relations, circumstances, &c.—A. Yes.

Q. What is the *wisdom* of God?—A. His skill in directing and ordering all things to proper ends.

Q. Wherein doth wisdom and knowledge differ?—A.

Knowledge views things in their natures, qualities, &c., but wisdom directs things to their proper ends.

Q. Wherein doth God's wisdom appear?—A. In the works of creation, providence, and redemption.

Q. How doth God's wisdom appear in creation?—A. In his framing so many creatures, so fit for shewing forth his own glory, and promoting their own and one another's good, Psalm civ. 24, Gen. i.

Q. How doth it appear in the works of providence?—A. In God's directing all the motions of his creatures, however opposite, to one common end, his own glory, the good of his people, and of one another, Rom. viii. 28.

Q. In what of redemption is the wisdom of God displayed?—A. In the contrivance, purchase, and application thereof.

Q. How is the wisdom of God displayed in the contrivance of redemption?—A. In choosing a most fit Redeemer and ransom, and most suitable objects and means of receiving redemption, Psalm lxxxix. 19, 1 Cor. i. 24.

Q. How is Christ a most fit person to be our Redeemer? —A. He being the second person in the Godhead, the Son of God is most fit to be sent by the Father, and the Spirit, and make us the Sons of God, Gal. iv.

Q. How is Christ's righteousness a most fit ransom or price of redemption?—A. It at once brings the highest glory to God, and the greatest good to men, Luke ii. 14.

Q. How are the elect most suitable objects of redemption?—A. They being not angels, but men, and these commonly the meanest or worst, the choice of them pours contempt on worldly greatness, and highly exalts God's free grace, 1 Cor. 24—29, Rom. v. 21.

Q. How is faith a most fit means of receiving redemption?—A. It most highly exalts the free grace, and other attributes of God; most deeply humbles man, and yet best secures his happiness, Rom. iv. 16—20.

Q. How is the wisdom of God evidenced in the purchase of redemption?—A. Sin at once slays, and is slain by Christ; and God's strict justice and free grace therein meet together, and exalt one another, Dan. ix. 34.

Q. How is the wisdom of God displayed in the application of redemption?—A. As, by occasion of our sin and misery, we are made to give most glory to God, and receive most good to ourselves; and are made glorious, in the way of debasing all our self-righteousness, wisdom, and strength, Rom. v. 20, 21, Eph. ii. 1—8.

Q. Wherein doth the knowledge and wisdom of God differ from that of creatures?—A. The knowledge and wisdom of God are independent, infinite, eternal, and unchangeable; but that of creatures is dependent, finite, created and changeable.

Q. How are the knowledge and wisdom of God sweet to believers—A. As God knows all their concerns, and will make all things work for their good, Rom. viii. 28.

Q. How are they terrible to the wicked?—A. As none of their sins can be hid from God's sight, and as he makes all things work for their ruin, Deut. xxviii.

Q. What is the *power* of God?—A. That attribute by which he can do all things, Gen. xvii. 1.

Q. Can God repent, lie, or do any thing sinful?—A. No; for to be capable of such things would evince imperfection and weakness, 1 Sam. xv. 29.

Q. Could God's power do more than ever he will do?—A. Yes; nothing is too hard for him, Jer. xxxii. 17.

Q. Wherein is the power of God manifested?—A. In creation, providence, and redemption.

Q. How doth God's power appear in creation?—A. In his bringing so many powerful creatures out of nothing, in so quick and easy a manner, by a word.

Q. How doth it appear in common providence?—A. In his upholding all things, and ordering all their motions, Heb. i. 3, Psalm cxxxvi. cvii., &c.

Q. How doth God's power appear in his special providence?—A. In his working so many miracles for, and protecting his church amidst so many dangers and enemies, and at last making her to triumph over them all.

Q. In what of redemption-work is the power of God manifested?—A. In the constitution of Christ's person; in his sufferings, resurrection, and coming to judgment; and in calling, justifying, adopting, sanctifying his people, &c.

Q. How is God's power manifested in the constitution of Christ's person?—A. In so closely uniting his two natures, though in themselves at an infinite distance from one another, 1 Tim. iii. 16, Isa. vii. 14, and ix. 6.

Q. How is it manifested in the sufferings of Christ?—A. In laying such a load of wrath on him, supporting him under it, and making him victorious over it, and all his enemies, Isa. liii. 11, 12, Psal. xxii. and cx.

Q. How is it manifested in Christ's resurrection?—**A.** God thereby broke open the prison of death, and exalted him to glory in name of his elect seed, Isa. liii. 8.

Q. How will it appear in Christ's judging the world?—**A.** In his raising the dead, sifting men and devils at his bar, driving all his enemies at once to hell, and perfecting the happiness of his people, Matth. xxv. Rev. xx.

Q. How doth God's power appear in calling and converting sinners?—**A.** In turning them from enmity to love, from filth to holiness, from darkness to light, from death to life, by the word of his grace, Acts xxvi. 18.

Q. How doth God's power appear in our justification?—**A.** In his ready and full forgiveness of so many and great offences, Numb. xiv. 17—20, Psal. xxv. 11.

Q. How doth it appear in our sanctification?—**A.** In keeping alive weak grace in the midst of so many corruptions and temptations, and making it at last victorious over them all, 1 Pet. i. 5, Rom. vii. 14—25.

Q. What are some of the more open displays of the power of God in favour of his church?—**A.** Israel's dedeliverance from Egypt, and entrance into Canaan; the destruction of the Assyrian army, Chaldean, Syrian, and Roman empires; the overthrow of Pagan idolatry, destruction of Antichrist, &c. Exod. xii. Josh. i—xii.

Q. How is the power of God sweet to believers?—**A.** As it is easy with God to perform all his promises, and supply all their wants, Gen. xvii. 1 and xviii. 14.

Q. How is it terrible to the wicked?—**A.** As it is to be glorified in their everlasting destruction, 2 Thess. i. 9.

Q. What is the *holiness* of God?—**A.** It is the purity of his nature, whereby he delights in whatever is pure and holy, and abhors every thing sinful, Hab. i. 13.

Q. What peculiar honor doth God put upon his holiness? —**A.** He swears by it; he calls every thing pertaining to him by its name; and he counts it the beauty and glory of his other perfections, Psal. lxxxix. 35.

Q. What things pertaining to God are called *holy*?— **A.** His name, work, word, covenant, promise, dwelling-place, angels, people, and service, Psal. cxi. 9, &c.

Q. How is God's holiness the *beauty* of his other perfections?—**A.** As thereby they are all pure, glorious, and lovely, Exod. xv. 11, Psal. xxvii. 4.

Q. Can any creature behold the full brightness of this beauty of God's holiness?—**A.** No: Isa. vi. 2.

Q. Wherein does the holiness of God appear?—A. In creation, providence and redemption.

Q. How did it appear in creation?—A. In God's enduing all reasonable creatures with perfect holiness.

Q. How doth it appear in providence?—A. In God's giving holy laws, and strong encouragements to keep them; and in his severely punishing angels and men for sin.

Q. How doth God's holiness appear in redemption?—A. In his setting up Christ as a perfect pattern of holiness; in his making vile sinners holy by conversion and sanctification; and especially in his smiting, and hiding his face from his own Son, when bearing our iniquities.

Q. In what manner doth God hate sin?—A. With a boundless hatred, as a thing most abominable to him.

Q. How then is God in scripture said to *bid* men sin, and to *harden* them in it?—A. The meaning only is, that he permits, and punishes men by sin, 2 Sam. xvi. 10.

Q. If God hate sin so much, how can he permit it?—A. His permission doth not in the least effect or encourage sin; nor would he have permitted it, but to display his holiness by occasion thereof, especially in punishing it upon Christ, and saving men from it through him.

Q. How doth the power and holiness of God differ from that of creatures?—A. The power and holiness of God are independent, infinite, eternal, and unchangeable; but the power and holiness of creatures are dependent, finite, created and changeable.

Q. How is God's holiness sweet to believers?—A. It secures the complete destruction of sin, and perfection of grace in them, 2 Cor. iii. 18, Lev. xx. 7, 8.

Q. How is it terrible to the wicked?—A. It secures God's most fierce indignation against them for ever.

Q. What is the *justice* of God—A. It is that attribute of his nature, whereby he is disposed to give himself and all creatures their proper due, Deut. xxxii. 4.

Q. What doth God render to himself as his own due?—A. He makes his own glory his chief end and motive, and his will his rule in all his works, Prov. xvi. 4.

Q. What is the common justice or due that God renders to all creatures?—A. His governing them according to their natures, and the law he hath given them, Psalm cxlviii.

Q. How may God's special justice, which respects reasonable creatures, be distinguished?—A. Into his legislative and distributive justice.

4

Q. What do you mean by *legislative* justice?—**A.** The giving to rational creatures holy and good laws, suited to their natures, powers, and circumstances.

Q. Is it just to require obedience to these laws from creatures whom sin has disabled for it?—**A.** Yes; for such have lost their power to obey by their own fault; and so God must not lose his due, Gen. iii. Rom. iii.

Q. What is the *distributive* justice of God?—**A.** It is his rendering to rational creatures the due wages of their works, 2 Thess. i. 6, 7. Rom. ii. 5—12.

Q. How is distributive justice usually distinguished?—**A.** Into remunerative or *vindictive* justice.

Q. What is God's remunerative or *rewarding* justice?—**A.** That which gives rewards for keeping his law.

Q. What is God's vindictive or *revenging* justice?—**A.** That which renders punishment for breaking his law, Psal. xi. 6, 7. Mal. iii. 5. Rev. ii. 23.

Q. According to what law doth God distribute justice to men?—**A.** According to the law of works, and the law of faith, Rom. iii. 26, 27.

Q. What is the due of a sinner, according to the law or covenant of works?—**A.** The eternal wrath of God.

Q. What is his due according to the law of faith, or covenant of grace?—**A.** Eternal life through Christ.

Q. Can God pardon sin without satisfaction to his justice?—**A.** No; for God cannot but hate sin with an infinite hatred; and as ruler of the world, must punish what disturbs it: and if he could have pardoned sin without a satisfaction, he would not have exposed his only beloved Son, as our surety, to his most fierce wrath, Psal. xi. 6, 7. Rom. viii. 32. Isa. liii. 10. Zech. xiii. 7.

Q. Wherein doth God's rewarding justice appear?—**A.** In rewarding men's external obedience with temporal rewards, and believers' gracious obedience with gracious rewards; and in rewarding Christ's righteousness with his own exaltation, and his people's salvation, Isa. liii. 10.

Q. Wherein doth God's revenging justice appear?—**A.** In the punishment of sinners here and hereafter; and especially in laying upon Christ all the wrath due to an elect world, Isa. liii. 4, 5, 6. 11. Rom. viii. 32.

Q. How is the justice of God sweet to believers?—**A.** It secures to them, however unworthy, all the blessings which Christ hath purchased for them, 1 John i. 9.

Q. How is it terrible to the wicked?—A. It binds God to pursue them with his everlasting wrath, Psal. xi. 5. 7.

Q. What is the *goodness* of God?—A. It is that attribute whereby he is good to himself, and the giver of all good, Psal. cxix. 68. and lxxxvi. 5—15. Isa. lxiii. 7.

Q. How is the goodness of God usually distinguished? —A. Into his absolute and relative goodness.

Q. Wherein do these differ?—A. His absolute goodness is an essential property in himself, and is the fountain; but his relative goodness is that kindness which flows out from that fountain upon his creatures.

Q. How is God's relative goodness distinguished?—A. Into his *common* goodness, which he exerciseth towards all his creatures good and bad, and his *special* goodness, which he exerciseth towards his elect only, Ps. cxlv.

Q. What are some branches of God's common goodness?—A. The exercise of his long-suffering patience towards sinful men, his giving them the offers of salvation and space to repent of their sin, with corn, wine, oil, fruitful seasons, and other temporal blessings, Rom. ii. 4.

Q. What are the branches of God's special goodness? —A. Saving grace, and eternal glory, Psal. xxiv. 11.

Q. What are the properties of God's special goodness? —A. It is unspeakably great, sweet, satisfying, seasonable, unchangeable, and everlasting, Psal. xxxi. 19.

Q. Where is this goodness laid up for the elect?—A. In Christ, in whom all fulness dwells, Col. i. 19.

Q. How is it brought near to us sinners?—A. In the promise and offer of the gospel, Isa. lv. 7.

Q. How doth it all become our own?—A. By our receiving Christ, in whom it is laid up, 1 Cor. iii. 22.

Q. What are the fruits and effects of our receiving it?— A. Wonder, joy, delight, satisfaction, self-abasement, and love to God, Christ, and the souls of men.

Q. F om what fountain doth this special goodness flow? —A. From God's love, grace, and mercy in Christ.

Q. Wherein do love, grace, and mercy differ?—A. They are much the same; only love views the elect as creatures; grace views them as unworthy; and mercy views them as in misery.

Q. What are the different actings of God's love towards the elect?—A. Choosing, blessing, and delighting in them, Eph. i. v., Zeph. iii. 17.

Q. Wherein doth God's absolute goodness appear ?—A. In creation, providence, and redemption.

Q. How doth the goodness of God appear in creation ?—A. In his making all things *very good*, Gen. i. 31.

Q. How doth it appear in the works of providence ?—A. In God's preserving, and making plentiful provision for his creatures, Psalm cxlv. 9. 16, and civ. and cvii.

Q. How doth it appear in redemption-work ?—A. In the gracious contrivance and execution of it.

Q. How doth God's goodness appear in the contrivance of redemption?—A. In his so early, freely, and kindly, remembering elect sinners, and laying their help upon one mighty to save, Psalm cxxxvi. 23, Eph. i. 3—11.

Q. How doth God's goodness appear in the execution of redemption ?—A. In sending his son to assume our nature, and pay our debt ; and in bestowing all his purchased blessings upon us, John iii. 14—17.

Q. Is not mercy or goodness, as employed in redemption, God's darling attribute?—A. Yes ; for God oftener ascribes mercy to himself than any other attribute : all the divine persons, perfections, operations, and relations, and all the servants of God, are employed in promoting the work of mercy ; and the greatest price was laid out in shewing mercy, Exod. xxxiv. 6, 7.

Q. How is God's goodness terrible to impenitent sinners ?—A. Their contempt of it heaps up for them wrath against the day of wrath, Rom. ii. 4, 5, Heb. ii. 3.

Q. How is it sweet to believers ?—A. Because they shall be for ever filled and satisfied with its ravishing pleasures, Psal. xvi. 11. Jer. xxxi. 12.

Q. Is it not very encouraging to such as desire to believe? —A. Yes ; for it runs to meet such with mercy and kindness, Luke xv. 17. 20, Jer. xxxi. 18—20.

Q. What is the *truth* of God ?—A. It is that perfection whereby he cannot but hate all deceit and falsehood.

Q. How may the *truth* of God be distinguished ?—A. Into his sincerity and his faithfulness.

Q. What is the *sincerity* or *uprightness* of God ?—A. His speaking and acting as he thinks and designs.

Q. How is God sincere when he offers his eternal life to such as are in his decree appointed to wrath ?—A. He is really willing to give salvation to all men to whom it is offered, if they would receive it; and his decree no way necessitates them to refuse it, John v. 40.

Q. How can he be sincere in offering reprobates a salvation which was never purchased for them?—A. The purchased salvation, and price thereof in itself, are equally applicable to every gospel hearer: and therefore believe the gospel promise and offer who will, he shall be saved, John iii. 16, Mark xvi. 15, 16.

Q. What is the *veracity* and *faithfulness* of God?—A. That whereby he cannot but do as he hath said.

Q. Wherein is God's faithfulness manifested?—A. In the exact accomplishment of all his promises, prophecies, and threatenings, Josh. xxiii. 14, Zech. i. 6.

Q. Did not God's word fail of accomplishment, when Saul came not down to Keilah, and Nineveh was not destroyed in forty days, as he had said?—A. No; for God's word bore no more than, that if David staid at Keilah, Saul should come down; and if Nineveh did not repent, it should be destroyed, 1 Sam. xxiii., Jonah iii.

Q. Do not unbelievers make God a liar, in stopping the fulfilment of the gospel promises?—A. They indeed call him a liar, and refuse the benefit of the promise to themselves; but their unbelief cannot make the faith of God of none effect, Rom. iv. 4, and ix. 6.

Q. Wherein is God's faithfulness most brightly manifested?—A. In his fulfilling the most improbable promises and threatenings, though long suspended.

Q. What was the most improbable promise?—A. That of Christ's coming to die for us, Gen. iii. 15.

Q. What made this promise appear difficult?—A. It was astonishing that God should stoop so low; it required great power to unite our nature to his; and infinite provocation had been given to cause him refuse such kindness, Jer. xxxiii. 22.

Q. What appeared the most improbable threatening?— A. The threatening of God's wrath upon Christ as our surety, Zech. xiii. 7, Dan. ix. 24, Isa. liii.

Q. What made this threatening appear difficult?—A. God's infinite love to Christ his beloved Son.

Q. How doth the accomplishment of such promises or threatenings, after being long suspended, shew the faithfulness of God?—A. As it shews that God cannot forget his word or change his mind, Mal. i. 6.

Q. When will God's truth (as well as his other perfections) be most openly manifested?—A. In the day of judgment, 1 Tim. vi. 15, 16, 2 Thess. i. 6—10.

4*

Q. How will God's truth be then manifested?—A. In his rendering rewards and punishments exactly according to his promises and threatenings, Rom. ii. 16.

Q. Wherein do God's justice, goodness, and truth differ from that justice, goodness, and truth which are in creatures?—A. God's justice, goodness and truth, are independent, infinite, eternal, and unchangeable; but those of creatures are dependent, finite, created, and changeable.

Q. How is God's truth sweet to believers?—A. It secures God's fulfilling of all promises to them.

Q. How is it terrible to the wicked?—A. It secures God's execution of all his threatenings upon them.

Q. How doth faith improve all the attributes of God?—A. It takes his wisdom for its guide; his power for its strength; his holiness for its pattern; his justice for its advocate; his goodness for its portion; his truth for its security; and all to be its plea before God, and the ground of its expectation of grace and glory.

QUEST. 5. *Are there more Gods than one?*

ANSW. There is but one only, the living and true God.

Q. Whence do ye prove that there is *but one* God?—A. —From reason and scripture.

Q. How doth reason prove that there is but one God?—A. It shews, that if there were more Gods than one, God could not be independent, infinite, almighty, &c. and so not God at all.

Q. Why might not God be independent, though there were more Gods than one?—A. Because if there were more Gods than one, each behoved to depend on, and be bounded by the will of another.

Q. Why might not God be infinite, though there were more Gods than one?—A. Because one infinite Being, possessing all divine perfections, sets limits to the perfection of every other being, and excludes them from the possession of divine perfections.

Q. Why might not God be almighty, though there were more Gods than one?—A. Because each could oppose and hinder the designs of another.

Q. Could the world be governed, if there were more Gods than one?—A. No: for all things would be directed to different and opposite ends at once.

Q. Why might not there be three Gods, as well as three persons in one Godhead?—A. Because three Gods could not be one and the same in substance, as the three divine persons are, John x. 30, 1 John v. 7.

Q. How doth the scripture prove there is but one God? —A. It expressly affirms, *the Lord our God is one Lord :* and *there is no other God but one,* Deut. vi. 4, 1 Cor. viii. 4.

Q. Are there no others, besides the true God called gods in scripture?—A. Yes; angels, magistrates, idols, men's belly, and the devil are so called.

Q. Why are angels called *gods?*—A. Because they are most like God in spirituality, wisdom, and power.

Q. Why are magistrates called *gods?*—A. Because, as God's deputies, they rule over others.

Q Why are heathen idols called *gods?*—A. Because blinded sinners worship and honour them as gods.

Q. Why is men's belly called *a god?*—A. Because many are chiefly careful to satisfy and please it, Phil. iii. 19.

Q. Why is the devil called the *god of this world?*—A. Because he rules over, and is honoured and worshipped as a god by the most part of mankind, 2 Cor. iv. 4.

Q. Is not God sufficiently distinguished from these gods? —A. Yes: for he is the only living and true God, Jer. lxv. 22, and x. 10, John xvii. 3, 1 John v. 22.

Q. Why is he called *the living God?*—A. Because he *hath life in himself,* and gives to others whatever life they have, natural, spiritual or eternal, John v. 26.

Q. From whom doth this character, *living God,* especially distinguish him?—A. From dead idols.

Q. Why is he called the *true God?*—A. Because he is possessed of all perfections in an infinite degree, which distinguishes him from all others who are called gods.

QUEST. 6. *How many persons are there in the Godhead?*

ANSW. There are three persons in the Godhead; the Father, the Son, and the Holy Ghost : and these three are one God, the same in substance, equal in power and glory.

Q. What is meant by the *Godhead?*—A. The divine nature or essence, whereby God is what he is.

Q. What is a *person?*—A. A complete substance, which can think and act by itself.

Q. Are then irrational creatures persons ?—**A.** No ; for they cannot properly think.

Q. Is the human nature of Christ a person ?—**A.** No ; for it never thought or acted but in union to his divine person, Isa. ix. 6, 7. 14, John i. 14.

Q. Are men and angels persons, notwithstanding their dependence on God ?—**A.** Yes ; for though they think and act dependently on God ; yet their thoughts and actions can not be properly called his but their own.

Q. What is a person in the Godhead ?—**A.** It is the divine nature, as subsisting with a particular personal property.

Q. What is the difference between a created and a divine person ?—**A.** Besides other differences, every created person has a different substance ; but all the three divine persons are the *same in substance.*

Q. How is this distinguishing perfection of God, relative to persons in the Godhead, ordinarily called ?—**A.** TRINITY ; which signifies *three in one.*

Q. Who are these three persons in the Godhead ?—**A.** The Father, the Son, and the Holy Ghost.

Q. Is the residing or subsisting of the same divine nature in three distinct persons, as *natural* and *necessary* to it, as the very existence of it ?—**A.** Yes ; it is altogether *as natural* and *necessary*, Exod. iii. 14.

Q. Is it *natural* and *necessary* to the divine nature, to reside in the first person as a father ; in the second as a Son ; and the third as one proceeding from the Father and Son ?—**A.** Yes ; there is nothing in the Godhead or any person in it, which is not *natural* and *necessary* in the highest sense, Exod. iii. 14.

Q. Are then these three divine persons equally independent upon one another ?—**A.** Yes, Phil. ii. 6.

Q. Doth the light of nature discover that the one divine nature subsists in three distinct persons ?—**A.** No ; the uncorrupted light of nature discovers no more of God's perfection than is necessary to our giving him that honour we owe him as the author of our being, if so much.

Q. Can the reason of creatures comprehend the substance of one divine nature in three persons ?—**A.** No ; no more than it can comprehend the infinity, eternity, &c., of God, Job xi. 7, and xxvi. 14.

Q. Why have Satan and his instruments so much opposed the doctrine of he Trinity ?—**A.** Because it is a *fundamental truth*, upon which the whole work of redemption, and all revealed religion, are founded, John xvii. 3.

Q. How is the whole work of redemption founded on it?—A. Because if there had not been one divine person to send, and be the exacting judge, another to be sent as atoning surety, and a third to apply his purchase, we could not have been saved, 2 Cor. xiii. 14.

Q. How is the whole of revealed religion founded on the doctrine of the Trinity?—A. Because we must worship the Father, in the Son, and by the Spirit.

Q. Is the knowledge of the doctrine of the Trinity necessary to salvation?—A. Yes, John xvii. 3.

Q. How can that be, when it is so mysterious?—A. So is every thing in God; and it is only necessary that we know and believe concerning it what the scripture plainly reveals in 1 John v. 7, 2 Cor. xiii. 14, &c.

Q. How prove you that there are three persons in the Godhead?—A. The scripture affirms, that in the name of three divine persons baptism is administered; and that these three bear witness to divine truths, bestow divine blessings, and acted different parts at Christ's baptism.

Q. What different parts did these persons act at Christ's baptism?—A. The Father from heaven gave testimony to Christ, the Son stood on Jordan's bank, and the Holy Ghost descending upon him like a dove, Mat. iii. 16, 17.

Q. How prove you that these three are *persons*, and not bare names or properties?—A. Because thinking, willing, and such acts and relations as are proper only to persons, are in scripture ascribed to each of them.

Q. How do you prove that they are *distinct* persons from one another?—A. Because they have distinct offices in the work of redemption, and distinct personal properties, John xvi. 7. 15. Eph, i. 3—22.

Q. What distinct office or agency have they in the work of redemption?—A. The Father proposeth, the Son purchaseth, and the Holy Ghost applieth it, Eph. i. 3. 22.

Q. Whereby are these divine persons properly distinguished?—A. By their distinct personal properties.

Q. What is the personal property of the Father?—A. To beget the Son, Psal. ii. 7.

Q. What is the personal property of the Son?—A. To be begotten of the Father, John i. 14.

Q. What is the personal property of the Holy Ghost?—A. To proceed from the Father and Son, John xv. 26.

Q. How prove you that the Holy Ghost proceeds from the Son as well as from the Father?—**A.** Because he is called *the Spirit of the Son,* and is sent by him as well as by the Father, Gal. iv. 6. John xvii. 7. and xv. 26.

Q. When did the Father beget the Son, and the Spirit proceed from both?—**A.** From all eternity, Psal, ii. 7.

Q. Is it the divine nature or substance, absolutely considered, that begets, is begotten, or proceeds?—**A.** No; it is a divine person: the person of the Father begets, the person of the Son is begotten, and the person of the Holy Ghost proceeds from both, John i. 15. xv. 26.

Q. Wherein doth a personal and an essential property differ?—**A.** An essential property is common to all the divine persons; but a personal property is peculiar to one person, and incommunicable to another.

Q. Are the properties of absolute independency, necessary existence, most high, and only true God, equally applicable to all the divine persons?—**A.** Yes; for these are absolute and essential, not personal properties.

Q. Is it then safe to call the Father *the fountain of the Godhead,* or *of the Trinity?*—**A.** No, John x. 30.

Q. Is it not a preferring of one person to another, to call the Father the first, the Son the second, and the Holy Ghost the third?—**A.** No; it only says they subsist and act in that order, Mat. xxviii. 19. Eph. i. 3—23.

Q. Is it safe to say the Father begets the Son by knowing himself, and that the Holy Ghost proceeds from the mutual love of Father and Son?—**A.** No; for God's knowledge and love, as in himself, are the very same.

Q. How prove you that these three persons are one God?—**A.** There is but *one God;* and all these three are in scripture called *God* and *one,* 1 John v. 7. John x. 30.

Q. How can these three persons be *one God?*—**A.** By their being the very same in substance, 1 John v. 7.

Q. Has each of these persons only a part of the divine nature, and a substance perfectly like to one another?—**A.** No; they have the very same divine substance, and each the whole of it; for the divine essence is simple, and cannot be divided, John x. 30. 1 John v. 7.

Q. If these persons be the same, how are they said to be equal?—**A.** They are the same *in substance and nature,* but they are equal *as persons,* 1 John v. 7.

Q. Wherein are they as persons equal?—**A.** In all divine perfections and glory, 2 Cor. xiii. 14.

Q. How prove you that the Father is God?—**A.** The scripture often affirms him to be God; and none but Atheists ever doubted of it, Eph. i. 3. 17.

Q. Is the father *only* God?—**A.** No.

Q. How then is he called *the only true God?* John xvii. 3. —**A.** Though he be the only true God, so as to exclude all false gods; yet that does not infer that *he only* is the true God, so as to exclude the Son and Holy Ghost from being the only true God, 1 John v. 7—20.

Q. How do you prove that the Son is God?—**A.** Because the names, attributes, works, and worship proper to God, are given to him as well as the Father in scripture.

Q. What divine names are given to the Son?—**A.** He is called *Jehovah* the *great God*, the *God of Glory*, &c. Isa. xlv. 24. Tit. ii. 13. Acts vii. 2, &c.

Q. What divine attributes are ascribed to the Son?—**A.** Eternity, unchangeableness, almighty power, knowledge of all things, and being every where present.

Q. What divine works are ascribed to the Son?—**A.** Creating and upholding all things, redeeming sinners, forgiving sins, raising the dead, judging the world, &c. John i. 2, Col. i. 17, Tit. ii. 14, Acts v. 31, &c.

Q. What divine worship is required and ascribed to the Son?—**A.** Honouring him even as the Father, believing, and being baptized in, and calling on his name.

Q. How then is the Son called the Father's *servant;* and himself says, *The Father is greater than I?*—**A.** The meaning is only, that the Son, (not as Son, but) as man and Mediator, is inferior to the Father.

Q. How do you prove that the Holy Ghost is God?— **A.** Because the same divine names, attributes, works, and worship, are ascribed to him in scripture as to the Father and Son.

Q. What divine names are given to the Holy Ghost?— **A.** He is called *Jehovah, God, &c.* Acts v. 4.

Q. What divine attributes are ascribed to him?—**A.** Eternity, knowledge of all things, and being every where present, Heb. xi 14, 1 Cor. ii. 10.

Q. What divine works are ascribed to him?—**A.** Creation, formation of Christ's human nature, regeneration, and sanctification of sinners, &c. Gen i. &c.

Q. What divine worship is ascribed to the Spirit?—**A.** Prayer, praise, baptism in his name, &c. Rev. i. 4.

Q. Can the mystery of the Trinity be illustrated by

similitudes ?—A. No ; whatever similitudes men have used
to this purpose, have rather clouded than cast light upon it.

Q. What doth the denial of any of the divine perfections,
or of the divinity of any of the persons in the Godhead,
amount to ?—A. To blasphemy and heresy.

Q. What is blasphemy ?—A. A reviling of God.

Q. What is heresy ?—A. The denial of a fundamental
truth by a professed church-member, especially if obstinately persisted in, 2 Tim. ii. 18, Tit. iii. 10.

Q. How is the mystery of the Trinity terrible to the
wicked ?—A. Because the wrath of all the three divine persons shall be eternally poured out upon them.

Q. How is it sweet to believers ?—A. Because these
three persons do attest the gospel truths the saints believe ;
and shall be their infinite and eternal portion.

QUEST. 7. *What are the decrees of God?*

ANSW. The decrees of God are, his eternal purpose, according to the counsel of his will, whereby,
for his own glory, he hath fore-ordained whatsoever
comes to pass.

Q. What are these acts of God which we must know and
believe ?—A. His decree and the execution of it.

Q. Wherein do these differ ?—A. His decree is his
agency within himself before time ; but the execution of it
is his work without himself, begun in time.

Q. What is a decree ?—A. Fore-ordaining what, and in
what manner, things shall come to pass.

Q. What hath God decreed and fore-ordained ?—A. All
things that come to pass, Acts xv. 18.

Q. When did God decree all things ?—A. From all eternity, Acts xv. 18, Eph. i. 4.

Q. According to what rule hath God decreed all things?
—According to the counsel of his own will.

Q. For what end hath God decreed all things ?—A. For
his own glory, and his people's good.

Q. Are the decrees of God one or many ?—A. The decreeing act of God is one, but the things decreed are many.

Q. How is God's decree called in scripture ?—A. A
counsel, purpose, appointment, or determination.

Q. Why is it called a *counsel* ?—A. Not as if God needed to deliberate ; but because of the great wisdom that is in
it, Rom. xi. 33, 34, Eph. i. 11.

Q. Why is the decree called a *purpose?*—A. Because God is fully resolved to execute it, Isa. xlv. 10.

Q. Why is it called an *appointment* or determination?—A. Because it is fixed by the highest authority.

Q. What are the properties of the decrees of God?—A. They are eternal, holy, wise, absolute, and unchangeable.

Q. How do you prove that God's decrees are eternal?—A. The decree of our salvation was *before the foundation of the world; all the works of God were* then *known to him,* and are connected with our salvation, Eph. i. 4.

Q. How do you prove that God's decrees are holy and wise?—A. Because the holy and wise God is the author of them ; and holiness and wisdom shine in the execution of them, Mark vii. 37, Psalm cxlv. 17.

Q. What do you mean by the decrees of God being *absolute?*—A. That they are fixed by the will of God, without any dependence on the creature, Isa. lv. 9.

Q. How do you prove God's decrees are absolute?—A. Because God cannot but foreknow all events, cannot want power to perform his designs ; nor can he subject his own will to a dependence on that of his creature.

Q. Though the decreeing act depend not on any thing done by the creature, yet has not God in the decree fixed an inseparable dependence of the end upon the means, in the execution of the decrees?—A. Yes ; he at once so fixed the end, and the means of obtaining it, that if men neglect the means, they must come short of the end, Acts xxvii. 24. 31, Mark xvi. 16, John iii. 36.

Q. Ought we then to be as diligent in using the means of happiness for our souls and bodies, as if there were no decree?—A. Yes, Deut. xxix. 39, Phil. ii. 12, 13.

Q. What mean you by God's decree being *unchangeable?*—A. That nothing can fall out, either as to means or end, otherwise than as settled in the decree.

Q. How prove you that God's decree is unchangeable?—A. Because God himself is unchangeable ; and has said his counsel shall stand, Isa. xlvi. 10, Psalm xxxiii. 9. 11.

Q. Doth not this force the will of creatures, and cause them to act contrary to it?—A. No ; the decree is so wisely laid as it cannot be frustrated, and yet as full scope allowed to the will of the creature, as if there were no decree, Acts xxvii. 27, 28, John vi. 37. 44, 45.

Q. Are the most casual events, and the precise term of every man's life, immutably decreed?—A. Yes.

5

Q. How prove you that?—**A.** Because such events have been often foretold; and man's days and number of his months, are determined by God, *and his bounds appointed that he cannot pass*, 1 Kings xxii. 34, Job xiv. 5.

Q. How then is God said to *shorten* men's lives?—**A.** Not by taking them away sooner than the appointed time, but by cutting them off sooner than the constitution of their bodies seemed to presage, Psalm lv. 23.

Q. Did not God add to Hezekiah's life after the appointed time of his death was come?—**A.** No; he only added fifteen years to his life after he was struck with a disease that threatened sudden death, Isa. xxxviii.

Q. How may the decrees of God as to their objects be distinguished?—**A.** Into common and special.

Q. What is God's *common* decree?—**A.** That which equally extends to all things, Eph. i. 11.

Q. What did God decree about creatures themselves?—**A.** To create, uphold, and govern them.

Q. What did he decree about the matter and goodness of actions?—**A.** To effect that matter and goodness.

Q. What did he decree with regard to the sinfulness of actions?—**A.** To permit, bound, and over-rule it to his own glory, Acts iv. 17. 28. and xiv. 16.

Q. What is *predestination*, or God's great and special decree?—**A.** It is the decree which unalterably settles the eternal state of angels and men, and the means thereof, Rom. ix. 22, 23, 1 Tim. v. 21.

Q. If the eternal state of every man and angel be unalterably settled, why need we pray, read, hear, &c., to make sure our eternal happiness?—**A.** Because the right use of these means is the decreed way of receiving Christ, in whom we obtain happiness; even as eating and drinking are the necessary means of our living a natural life.

Q. What are the two branches of predestination?—**A.** Election and reprobation, Rom. ix. 22, 23.

Q. What is the election of angels?—**A.** God's decree to continue and establish such particular angels in eternal holiness and happiness, 1 Tim. v. 21.

Q. What is God's election of men?—**A.** His choosing certain persons of mankind from among the rest, and giving them to Christ to be redeemed from wrath, 1 Thess. v. 9.

Q. Who are the elect of mankind?—**A.** Those that were chosen by God from all eternity to everlasting life, 1 Thess. i. 4. and v. 9, 2 Thess. ii. 13.

Q. For what end were they chosen?—A. For the praise of the glory of God's free grace, Rom. ix. 23.

Q. What reason or motive made God to choose any?—A. His own free love, Deut. vii. 7, 8, Eph. i. 4—7.

Q. What made him choose some rather than others?—A. His mere good pleasure, Exod. xxxiii. 19.

Q. How prove you that we were not elected upon account of our foreseen faith and holiness?—A. Because *it is not in him that willeth, or of him that runneth, but in God that sheweth mercy;* and faith and holiness are the fruits of election ; and so cannot be the cause of God's choosing us, Rom. ix. 16, 2 Thess. ii. 13.

Q. Is Christ as Mediator the cause of election, or electing love?—A. No; the Father himself loved us.

Q. What relation then hath Christ to our election?—A. He is the head of it, in whom we are chosen, and the great mean of accomplishing that purpose, Eph. i. 4.

Q. How do you prove that men are elected?—A. The scripture speaks of some as *vessels of mercy, afore prepared to* glory *ordained to eternal* life, *appointed* and *chosen to salvation,* Rom. ix. 23.

Q. How prove you that particular persons are elected?—A. Because otherwise Christ as an head might have for ever been wholly without members, Rom. ix. 13. 23.

Q. How ought we to improve the decree of election?—A. By taking encouragement to believe from the sovereignty of God's love, and studying to have our election evidenced by our effectual calling and sanctification.

Q. What is reprobation?—A. It is God's decree to permit unelected angels and men to fall into, and continue in sin, and to punish them for the same.

Q. Is sin the cause of reprobation?—A. Sin is the cause of damnation ; but God's sovereign will is the cause of reprobation, Rom. ix. 11—23.

Q. Is not God partial, in appointing some to wrath, and others to happiness?—A. No; for though he give the elect what they deserve not, yet he inflicts nothing upon reprobates, but what they well deserve.

Q. Doth reprobation oblige any to sin?—A. No; sin is wholly the creature's voluntary choice, Jam. i. 13.

Q. What is the end of reprobation?—A. The glory of God's sovereignty and justice, Rom. ix. 22.

Q. How should we improve this awful decree of reprobation?—A. By flying speedily to Christ, that we may see that we are not included in it, Isa. lv. 1—3.

QUEST. 8. *How doth God execute his decrees?*
ANSW. God executeth his decrees in the works of creation and providence.

Q. What do you mean by God's *executing* his decrees?—A. His doing what he purposed in the decree.

Q. When doth God execute his decrees?—A. He begins the execution in time, and continues it through all eternity, Gen. 1. Matth. xxv. 46.

Q. Doth God fully execute his decrees?—A. Yes; he *worketh all things according to the counsel of his will.*

Q. In what are God's decrees executed?—A. In the works of creation and providence.

Q. To which of these doth redemption-work belong?—A. To providence, as the principal part thereof.

Q. Wherein doth creation and providence differ?—A. In creation God gives a being to creatures, and works without means; in providence he upholds and directs his creatures, and ordinarily works by means.

Q. Can the execution of God's decrees be hindered?—A. No; the frequent essays of devils and men to hinder it, are made means of promoting it, Psal. lxxvi. 10.

QUEST. 9. *What is the work of creation?*
ANSW. The work of creation is, God's making all things of nothing, by the word of his power, in the space of six days, and all very good.

Q. In what did God begin the execution of his decree?—A. In the creation of the world, Gen. i.

Q. When did God create all things?—A. In the beginning of time, Gen. i. 1.

Q. Was there no matter, or any thing else besides God, before the creation?—A. No. Heb. xi. 3.

Q. How prove you that the world had a beginning?—A. Reason shews, and the scripture asserts it, Gen. i.

Q. How do you prove *from* reason, that the world did not exist from eternity?—A. Because it is finite and changeable; history reacheth but a few thousand years backward; arts, sciences, and many other discoveries, are but very late, &c.

Q. Why might not the world come into being by mere chance?—*A. Because chance, being the mere want of design, (or nothing) can produce nothing.

Q. Why might not creatures make themselves?—A. Because that which makes a thing, must be before it.

Q. Who then is the alone Creator of all things?—A. God; Father, Son, and Holy Ghost, Psal. xxxiii. 6.

Q. How do you prove, that no creature did or could assist God in creation-work?—A. Because, as there is an infinite distance between nothing and being, creation-work requires infinite power, which no creature can have.

Q. What is meant by God's *creating* of things?—A. His making them out of nothing, Gen. i. 1.

Q. What different kinds of creation are there?—A Two, viz. creation out of mere nothing, and creation out of unfit matter, Gen. i. 1—31.

Q. What was created immediately out of mere nothing? —A. Heaven, earth, light, angels, and the souls of men.

Q. What did God create out of unfit matter?—A. Fishes, fowls, cattle, the body of man, &c.

Q. Out of what were the fishes and fowls made?—A. —Out of the waters, Gen. i. 20.

Q. Of what were cattle and creeping things made?—A. Of earth, Gen. i. 24.

Q. In what space of time did God create all things?—A. In the space of six days, Exod. xx. 11.

Q. Could not God have created all things in a moment? —A. Yes; *there is nothing too hard for the Lord.*

Q. Why then took he up six days in creation-work?— A. That we might the better see the wise order of his work; and might imitate him in working six days, and resting on the seventh, Exod. ii. 9—11.

Q. What was God's work on the first day?—A. He made the heavens, the earth, the light, and probably also the angels, Gen. i. 1. 3.

Q. How does it seem probable that the angels were created on the first day?—A. Because it is said, they shouted for joy, when God laid the corner-stone of the earth, Job xxviii. 6, 7.

Q. What manner of creatures are angels?—A. Spirits, who have great wisdom and strength.

Q. Of what use are angels?—A. To attend God in heaven, guard his people on earth, and destroy their enemies, Matth. xviii. 10. Psal. xxxiv. 7. and xxxv. 5, 6.

5*

Q. In what estate were angels created?—**A.** In a most holy and happy estate, 2 Pet. ii. 4.

Q. Did they all abide in that estate?—**A.** No; many of them sinned and became devils, Jude vi.

Q. What did God upon the second day?—**A.** He made the air and firmament, Gen. i. 6.

Q. What did God upon the third day?—**A.** He sepaated the water from the earth, and made the herbs, grass, and trees, Gen. i. 9. 11.

Q. What did God upon the fourth day?—**A.** He made the sun, moon, and stars, and appointed them their motions and use, Gen. i. 14.

Q. What did God upon the fifth day?—**A.** He made the fishes and the fowls, Gen. i. 20.

Q. What did God upon the sixth day?—**A.** He made cattle, creeping things, and man, Gen. i. 25, 26.

Q. For what end did God make all things?—**A.** For the glory of his own perfections, Prov. xvi. 4.

Q. What perfections of God were especially glorified in creation?—**A.** His eternity, independence, wisdom, power, holiness, goodness, &c. Psal. civ. 24.

Q. How was God's *eternity* manifested in creation?—**A.** His making all things, shewed that he was before all things, John i. 1, 2. Psal. cii. 25. 27.

Q. How was God's *independence* manifested in creation? —**A.** His giving a being to all things shews, that all things depend on him; and that he is self-sufficient, and depends upon none, Rom. xi. 36.

Q. By what did God make all things?—**A.** By the word of his power, Gen. i. 3. 6. &c.

Q. What was that word?—**A.** LET THEM BE.

Q. In what condition did God make all things?—**A.** He made all things very good; that is, they were perfect in their kind, and fit to answer the ends for which they were made, Gen. i. 31.

Q. How then are many things now very hurtful?—**A.** Sin hath made them hurtful, Lam. iii. 33. 39.

Q. How hath sin made irrational creatures hurtful?—**A.** Sin made man a rebel against God; and therefore God hath made sundry creatures to hurt him, or what belongs to him, Deut. xxviii. 15. 68.

Q. What *evil* is it that God is said to create?—**A.** The evil of punishment, but not the evil of sin.

Q. Who created sin?—A. It cannot be created, as it hath no being; but the devil brought it into the world.

Q. What did God upon the seventh day?—A. He thereon rested from all his work, Gen. ii. 2.

Q. Was God wearied with his working six days?—A. No; *he fainteth not, neither is weary*, Isa. xl. 28.

Q. What then doth his *resting* signify?—A. His ceasing from creation-work, and rejoicing in it, Gen. ii. 1, 2.

Q. Hath God created nothing since the first six days?—A. Though he still immediately creates the souls of infants, yet he has made no new species of creatures.

Q. What may we learn from creation?—A. To humble ourselves before God, and to trust in his power.

QUEST. 10. *How did God create man?*

ANSW. God created man male and female, after his own image, in knowledge, righteousness, and holiness, with dominion over the creatures.

Q. Which was the best and last creature which God made on earth?—A. Man, who was to govern the rest, Gen. i. 26, Matth. xvi. 26.

Q. Why did God defer the creation of man till all other things were made?—A. That man might be brought into the world as a well-furnished habitation.

Q. What peculiar solemnity did God use in making man?—A. A council of the divine persons was held for that purpose, Gen. i. 26.

Q. Why was this solemnity used in making man?—A. Because he only was to bear God's image, and be God's deputy on earth; and in his nature the Son of God was to appear, Gen. i. 26. 28, Isa. vii. 14.

Q. In what sexes did God create man?—A. God created man male and female, Gen. i. 27.

Q. Why was man so made?—A. For the propagation of mankind, and their mutual helpfulness, Gen. ii.

Q. Of what parts doth the nature of man consist?—A. Of two, a body and a soul, Eccl. xii. 7.

Q. Wherein do a body and a soul differ?—A. A body is an unthinking substance, which may be seen, felt, and divided into parts; but a soul is a thinking substance, which cannot be seen, felt, divided into parts, or die.

Q. Of what was the body of man created?—A. Of the dust of the ground; to teach us to be humble and mindful of death, Gen. ii. 7, and iii. 19.

Q. Of what was the body of the woman formed?—**A.** Of a rib taken out of the man; to teach us the great love and *near* equality that should take place between married persons, Gen. ii. 22. 24.

Q. Of what were their souls made?—**A.** Of nothing; God breathed them into their bodies, Gen. ii. 7.

Q What doth that teach us?—**A.** How easily God createth, and that with the same ease he can call back our souls by death, Zech. xii. 1.

Q. In what doth the soul of a man and that of a beast, differ?—**A.** Beasts have no proper soul, and their spirit perisheth at death; but man's soul can subsist when separated from the body, and liveth for ever.

Q. How prove you that man's soul liveth for ever?—**A.** Christ paid an infinite price for its ransom; to it is made the promise of eternal life, or threatening of eternal death; it cannot be killed with the body, but in death returns to God, Matth. x. 28. Eccl. xii. 7, &c.

Q. What doth this teach us?—**A.** To be much more careful for our souls than our bodies, Matth. xvi. 26.

Q. How is God as our Creator called in scripture?—**A.** The Potter, and the Father of spirits.

Q. Why is he called *the Potter?* Isa. lxiv. 8.—**A.** Because he forms our bodies out of clay, and can dispose of us as he pleases, Jer. xviii. 6.

Q. Why is he called the *Father of Spirits?* Heb. xii. 9. —**A.** Because he creates angels and the souls of men.

Q. How did God call the first man and woman when he had made them?—**A.** *Adam;* which signifies either *red earth,* or *beautiful,* or *joined in love.*

Q. Why did God call them both by this name?—**A.** That they might continually remember their low original, their near relation, and duty of love to one another; and their duty to God, to shew themselves the beauty of this lower world, Gen. ii. 7. 22.

Q. How were they the beauty of this lower world?—**A.** In them the beauty of the heavenly and earthly creation, a most elegant body, and a rational spirit, were united into one person, Gen. i. 27, and ii. 7.

Q. After whose image was man created?—**A.** After the image of God, Gen. i. 27.

Q. Whether was man's soul or body properly made after the image of God?—**A.** His soul, Col. iii. 10.

Q. How prove you that his body was not properly made

after the image of God ?—A. Because God hath no body, but is a most pure spirit, John xi. 24.

Q. Wherein was man's soul made like unto God ?—A. In its substance and qualities.

Q. How was man's soul made like unto God in its substance ?—A. God is a Spirit, and it was made a spiritual substance, John iv. 24, Matth x. 28.

Q. In what qualities was man's soul made like unto God? —A. In knowledge, righteousness, and holiness.

Q. What knowledge had man at his creation ?—A. Such a perfect knowledge of God, his will and works, as rendered him happy, and perfectly fit for his duty, Gen. iii. 22. Eccl. vii. 29.

Q. What righteousness had man when created ?—A. He was sweetly disposed, and perfectly able to render to God, and to others, what was their due.

Q. What holiness had man at his creation ?—A. He was perfectly free from sin, loved and delighted in the holiness, worship, and service of God, Eccl. vii. 29.

Q. What flowed from Adam's likeness to God in knowledge, righteousness, and holiness ?—A. A likeness to God in honour and happiness.

Q. How was man like God in honour ?—As God's deputy he had dominion over the creatures, Psal. viii. 6.

Q. Over what creatures had man dominion ?—A. Only over the creatures on earth, as fishes, fowls, cattle, creeping things, &c. Gen. i. 28, Psal. viii. 6—8.

Q. What happiness had man at his creation ?—A. He was free from all sorrow and death, and had sweet communion with God, as his father and friend.

Q. Where was man placed when created ?—A. In the pleasant garden of Eden, which God planted, Gen. ii.

Q. Why put he man into it ?—A. To heighten his earthly happiness, and that he might keep and dress it.

Q. Did not God allow them to be idle in that estate ?— A. No ; all idleness is of the devil, 1 Tim. v. 13.

Q. Was man's work then a toil to him ?—A. No ; it did not fatigue him, but was his pleasure and happiness, as he saw and enjoyed God in every thing.

Q. What influence should the view of that holy and happy estate now have upon us ?—A. It should make us cry out with grief, *Wo to us that we have sinned.*

Q. 11. *What are God's works of providence?*
A. God's works of providence, are his most holy, wise, and powerful preserving and governing all his creatures, and all their actions.

Q. Wherein doth God still continue to execute his decrees?—**A.** In the works of providence.

What call you the *providence* of God?—**A.** It is that care he taketh of his creatures.

Q. What are the properties of God's care or providence? —**A.** It is most holy, wise, and powerful.

Q. Wherein doth the *holiness* of God's providence appear?—**A.** In its tendency to encourage holiness, discourage sin, and bring glory to God out of it.

Q. How doth God bring glory to himself out of sin?— **A.** In punishing it in some, forgiving it in others, and making the chief of sinners sometimes become the chief of saints, 2 Chron. xxxviii. 11, 12, 13, Acts ix.

Q. How doth the wisdom of God's providence appear? —**A.** In his making all, even the worst things, tend to his own glory, and the good of his people; and in causing one thing answer many ends at once, Rom. viii. 28.

Q. Wherein doth the powerfulness of God's providence appear?—**A.** In his irresistibly bringing about great events by weak or no means, or in opposition to them, Dan. iv. 34, Isa. xli. 14—16.

Q. What are the parts or branches of God's providential care?—**A.** Preserving and governing his creatures.

Q. What mean you by God's *preserving* his creatures? —**A.** His upholding them in their being and works.

Q. What need is there of God's preserving his creatures? —**A.** Because otherwise they would return to nothing.

Q. What is meant by God's governing his creatures?— **A.** Directing them to the ends he hath appointed them.

Q. What need is there of God's governing all things?— **A.** Because otherwise they would run into confusion.

Q. Whence do you prove, that God preserves and governs all things?—**A.** From the scripture and reason.

Q. How doth the scripture prove it?—**A.** It declares that God *upholds all things* and *directs our steps*, and that *we live and move in him:* and it foretold a multitude of events before they took place, Heb. i. 3, &c.

Q. How doth reason prove it?—**A.** It shews, that without God, so many jarring creatures could never be preserved in such order, or directed to one common end : nor could sun, moon, stars, &c., observe such exact order and revolutions, nor any miraculous event happen.

Q. What is the object of God's providence?—A. All his creatures, and all their actions, Psalm ciii. 19.

Q. How is God's providence exercised about angels?—A. In permitting some to sin, and lie therein; establishing the rest in holiness and happiness, and employing them in the administration of his mercy and justice.

Q. How is God's providence peculiarly exercised about men?—A. In giving or withholding from them the ordinary means of salvation, and enabling them to improve, or suffering them to abuse these means, as he sees meet, Psal. cxlvii. 19, 20. Rom. ix.

Q. About whom is God's providence especially exercised?—A. About his church, especially about Christ her head, and his real members, Isa. xliii. 1, &c.

Q. How prove you that God's providence extends to the meanest creatures?—A. Because the hairs of our heads are numbered; and sparrows cannot fall to the ground without him, Matth. x. 29, 30.

Q. Is it not mean for God to care for such inconsiderable things?—A. No; whatever he hath made, is not below his care: his care of high creatures shews his majesty, and his care of the meanest creature shews his great condescension, Matth. vi. 30, Psalm civ.

Q. Are not all creatures equally mean when compared with God?—A. Yes; for he is infinite, and they are all finite; and so equally at an infinite distance from him.

Q. What actions of creatures are the objects of God's providence?—A. All their actions, whether natural, accidental, or moral, Col. i. 17, Job xxxviii—xli.

Q. How is God's providence exercised about natural actions?—A. In exciting the natural instinct of creatures, and giving them power and opportunity to follow it.

Q. How is God's providence exercised about casual or accidental actions, as killing a man with a bow-shot at a venture, &c.?—A. In joining or disjoining the circumstances of these actions otherwise than the actors thereof intended, Exod. xxi. 13, 2 Kings xxii. 34.

Q. How is God's providence more generally exercised about moral and reasonable actions?—A. In prescribing a law to be the rule of them, and in annexing rewards and punishments to them, Exod. xx., Deut. xxviii.

Q. How may moral actions be distinguished?—**A** Into good and evil, Deut. xxviii. 1. 15.

Q. Are no reasonable actions indifferent, that is neither good nor evil?—**A.** They may be indifferent in their nature ; but with respect to their manner and end, they must be either good or evil, 1 Tim. i. 5, 6.

Q. How is God's providence specially exercised about good actions?—**A.** In stirring up to, directing in, and giving power and opportunity for them, Phil. ii. 12, 13.

Q. How is God's providence exercised about sinful actions?—**A.** In concurring to the substance of the act; and in permitting, bounding, and over-ruling to his own glory the sinfulness of it, Isa. xxxvii. 29.

Q. Doth not this way make God the author of sin?—**A.** No; when God so hates and punishes sin, he can never in any respect be the author of it, Zeph. iii. 6.

Q. Doth God's exciting or concurring in actions any way check the free will of creatures?—**A.** No.

Q. Whence is it then that men raise an outcry against God's providential concurrence with all, especially sinful actions, as if that and his decree put a farce upon the will of creatures?—**A.** It arises from their great pride and ignorance, in measuring God by themselves; for, because they could not effect the matter of a sinful action, and not its sinfulness, neither absolutely decree, nor infallibly determine another to an action, without forcing his will, they conclude that God is incapable to do it; forgetting that as the heavens are high above the earth, so are God's ways above our ways, Isa. lv. 9.

Q. How is God's providence with respect to actions ordinarily called?—**A.** His providence about moral actions is called *his moral government;* and his providence about all other motions or actions, is called *his natural government.*

Q. How may the providence of God with respect to its effects be distinguished?—**A.** Into ordinary and extraordinary, Gen. xxix. and xix.

Q. What call you *ordinary* providence?—**A.** That which produces common events by ordinary means.

Q. What call you God's *extraordinary* providence?—**A.** That which produceth miracles, Exod. vii.—xiv.

Q. What is a miracle?—**A.** An event beyond or contrary to the power of second causes, as raising the dead, healing the sick, by a word, &c. 2 Kings iv. &c.

Q. In what is God's providence often dark and mysterious ?—A. In its secret track and outward appearance.

Q. How is it mysterious in its secret track?—A. In bringing about the most glorious events by the most improbable means, Esther i.—x. Acts ii. &c.

Q. What are some instances of this ?—A. Joseph's dignity in Egypt was brought about by hatred, slavery, and imprisonment; and Christ's exaltation, and his people's salvation, by his cursed and shameful death.

Q. What doth this teach us?—A. To believe always that God is taking the best way to accomplish his promise though providence seem to contradict it.

Q. How is God's providence mysterious in its outward appearance ?—A. In the temporal prosperity of the wicked, and the adversity of God's dearest saints, Psal. lxxiii.

Q. Why doth God take this course ?—A. To shew his own contempt of worldly things, wean his people's hearts from the world, and gain them to himself.

Q. Whether are saints losers or gainers, when God emptieth them of worldly good things, in order to gain them to himself?—A. They are the greatest gainers.

Q. When shall all dark providences be cleared up ?—A. When we enter on the state of glory in heaven.

Q. What will the saints then think and say of all providences ?—A. They will admire the love, grace, and wisdom that ran through them all ; and with joy and thanksgiving cry out, *He hath done all things well.*

Q. What attributes of God are manifested in the works of providence?—A. His independency, infinity, wisdom, power, holiness, justice, goodness, truth, &c.

Q. 12. *What special act of providence did God exercise toward man in the estate wherein he was created?*

A. When God had created man, he entered into a covenant of life with him upon condition of perfect obedience ; forbidding him to eat of the tree of knowledge of good and evil upon the pain of death.

Q. What part of God's providence should we chiefly consider ?—A. His providence towards man.

Q. In what different estates is God's providence exercised towards man?—A. In his primitive, his fallen, his recovered, and his eternal estate.

Q. What providence did God exercise towards man in

his *primitive* estate?—A. He instituted the Sabbath for his rest, appointed marriage, and put him into the garden of Eden; and *especially he entered into a covenant with him,* Gen. ii.

Q. What is a covenant?—A. It is an agreement between two or more parties upon certain terms.

Q. What is requisite to the making of a covenant?—A. That there be parties, a condition, and a promise; and also a penalty, if any of the parties be fallible.

Q. What understand you by the *parties?*—A. The persons who make the agreement with one another.

Q. What is the *condition* of a covenant?—A. That which, when performed, doth, according to paction, give right to claim the reward.

Q. What call you the *promise* of it?—A. The engagement to reward the fulfilment of the condition.

Q. What is the *penalty?*—A. That which is agreed shall be inflicted upon the breaker of the covenant.

Q. Why hath God all along dealt with men by covenant?—A. To shew his own condescension, and how ready he is to bestow favours upon men; and to encourage a willing obedience, by promising to reward it.

Q. How many covenants hath God made for the eternal happiness of men?—A. Two; the covenant of works, and the covenant of grace, Gal. iv. 24. Heb. viii.

Q. How prove you that there are only two covenants respecting man's eternal happiness?—A. The scripture mentions only two such covenants; and represents all men as under the one or the other, Gal. iv. 24—31.

Q. How prove you that there was a covenant made with Adam in his innocent estate?—A. In Gen. ii. 16, 17, we have all the requisites of a covenant, *viz.* parties, condition, and penalty, which includes the promise: and Hos. vi. 7, *margin,* it is said, *They, like Adam, transgressed the covenant:* nor could Adam's sin be charged on his posterity, if no covenant had been made with him.

Q. Was Adam, by virtue of his creation, under this covenant?—A. No; he was only under the *law* of God.

Q. Wherein did that law, and the covenant made with him, differ?—A. The law made him God's servant, and required perfect obedience, without promising any reward; but this covenant made him God's friend and ally, and promised a glorious reward to his obedience to which himself had engaged.

Q. How is this covenant made with Adam ordinarily called ?—A. The covenant of works or life, the *law* or legal covenant, and the first covenant.

Q. Why is it called *the covenant of works?*—A. Because man's good works was the condition of it.

Q. Why is it called *a covenant of life?*—A. Because life was the reward promised for keeping it.

Q. Why is it called *the law* or *legal covenant?*—A. Because it was not made between equals, but enjoined by the great Lawgiver to his subject.

Q. Why is it called *the first covenant?*—A. Because, though *last made*, it was *first made known* to man.

Q. Who were the parties in this covenant?—A. God and Adam, Gen. ii. 16, 17.

Q. What moved God to enter into this covenant ?—A. His own free favour and bounty, Job. vii. 17.

Q. How doth that appear ?—A. Because God as a Creator might justly have exacted all the service man was capable of, without giving him any reward ; and, notwithstanding, punished him for disobedience, Luke xvii. 10.

Q. Was very much grace manifested in the covenant of works ?—A. Yes, very much free favour and bounty.

Q. How so ?—A. In God's not only promising to reward man's obedience ; but also in so framing this covenant, as to admit a covenant of grace, if it was broken.

Q. Why then is it not called *a covenant of grace ?*—A. Because there was far less grace manifested in it than is in the second covenant, Rom. v. 20, 21.

Q. How could Adam be bound by this covenant, when we never read of his consenting to the terms of it ?

A. Being made perfectly holy, he could not withhold his consent from any terms which God proposed to him.

Q. For whom did Adam stand bound in this covenant ? —A. For himself and all his *natural* posterity, Rom. v.

Q. Who are Adam's *natural* posterity ?—A. All mankind descending from him by ordinary generation.

Q. Did Adam stand bound for Christ *as man?*—A. No ; for Christ descended not from him by ordinary generation, and had not the person of a man, Isa. vii. 14.

Q. How doth it appear that Adam stood bound for all his natural seed ?—A. They are often called by his name *Adam ;* and his breach of covenant is charged upon them all, Rom. v. 12, 1 Cor. xv. 22.

Q. Why did God make Adam to stand bound for all his

posterity ?—A. Because this was a shorter and safer way of securing their happiness than if each man had stood bound for himself.

Q. How was it a shorter way of securing their happiness ?—A. Because if Adam's obedience had been once finished, none of his posterity could have ever fallen.

Q. How was it a safer way of securing their happiness ? —A. Adam was formed in an adult state, fully capable of perfect obedience ; and had not only a proper regard to his own happiness, but a fatherly concern for his whole natural seed, to engage him to obedience.

Q. How could Adam be justly bound for persons who never chose, nor consented to his being their covenant-head ?—A. He was the common father of them all ; and God, who is wiser than they, chose him ; and therefore they could not, without sin, have refused their consent.

Q. For what was Adam bound in the covenant of works ? —A. For performing the condition of it.

Q. What was the condition of the covenant of works ?— A. Personal and perfect obedience to God's law.

Q. How was this obedience to be *personal ?*—A. It was to be performed by Adam himself in his own proper person, Gen. ii. 16, 17, Gal. iii. 12.

Q. In what was Adam's obedience to be perfect ?—A. In extent, degrees, and duration.

Q. How was his obedience to be perfect in *extent ?*—A. His whole man, soul and body, was to obey the whole of God's law, Gal. iii. 10. 12, Matth. iii. 12.

Q. How was it to be perfect in *degrees ?*—A. He was to love and obey the Lord with *all his heart and strength.*

Q. How was his obedience to be perfect in *duration ?*— A. It was to be constantly continued in till his time of trial was over, Gal. iii. 10.

Q. Would Adam have ever been freed from obedience to God ?—A. He would have been free from obedience to the law as a covenant, but never from obedience to the law as an eternal rule of righteousness, Matth. v. 48.

Q. What command, besides the law of nature, did God require Adam to obey ?—A. The command of not eating the fruit of the tree of knowledge, which grew in the midst of the garden of Eden, Gen. ii. 16, 17.

Q. Why was this tree called *the tree of knowledge of good and evil?*—A. Because God thereby tried Adam's obedience : and he, by eating it, knew experimentally the good which he fell from, and the evil he fell into.

Q. Why did God forbid Adam to eat of this fruit ?—A. To manifest his own absolute dominion over, and interest in all things; and to try whether man would obey out of regard to his mere will and authority, or not.

Q. Was there no other reason against man's eating of this fruit, but merely God's forbidding it ?—A. No; the thing was quite indifferent in itself.

Q. Was God's forbidding Adam to eat of this fruit a snare to entrap him ?—A. No ; it was, in itself, a means to secure him in holiness and happiness.

Q. How did it secure him in holiness and happiness ?—A. It shewed him, that he was but a subject, and in danger of falling into sin ; and that his true happiness was in God himself.

Q. Would any other sin, besides eating this fruit, have broken the covenant of works ?—A. Yes, Gal. iii. 10.

Q. For what was God bound in this covenant ?—A. To fulfil the promise, if man kept it ; and to execute the threatening, if he should break it.

Q. What was promised to man in this covenant ?—A. Life temporal, spiritual and eternal, Gal. iii. 12.

Q. What was this *temporal* life ?—A. The happy union and communion of soul and body in this world.

Q. Wherein did that *spiritual* life consist ?—A. In union to, and perfect fellowship with God in this world.

Q. Wherein doth *eternal* life consist ?—A. In the full enjoyment of God in heaven for ever, Psal. xvi. 11.

Q. How could temporal and spiritual life be promised to Adam when he had it already ?—A. The continuance of this life was promised to him while he did his duty, and the bestowing of it promised to his seed.

Q. How prove you that eternal life was promised in the covenant of works ?—A. Because eternal death was included in the threatening : and Christ shews that according to the law of works, men would enter into eternal life by keeping the commandments, Matth. xix. 16, 17.

Q. What was the penalty of the covenant of works ?—A. Death *legal*, or being laid under a sentence of condemnation ; and death *real*, which includes death temporal, spiritual and eternal, Rom. v. 12, and vi. 23.

Q. What is that temporal death ?—A. The wrathful separation of the soul from the body, with much sorrow and trouble, while united together in this world.

Q. What is death spiritual?—A. An accursed separation of the soul from God, and loss of his favour and image.

Q. What is death eternal?—A. The accursed separation of the whole man from God, and lying under his wrath in hell for ever, Matth. xxv. 46.

Q. Did Adam die that very day in which he ate the forbidden fruit?—A. He died spiritually that very moment, and fell under the sentence of temporal and eternal death.

Q. Why was his natural and eternal death suspended?— A. That the seed whom he represented might be born, and many of the human race saved by the covenant of grace.

Q. Would Adam's sin have been punished with death, though no covenant had been made with him?—A. Yes; the law of nature being connected with God's vindictive justice, requires that every sin be punished with eternal death, Rom. vi. 23, Psalm xi. 6, 7.

Q. Did then his obedience in itself deserve any reward? —A. No; *man in his best estate is but vanity.*

Q. By what charter then had man his happiness secured?—A. Only by the promise of the covenant of works.

Q. By what sacramental seal was this promise to be confirmed?—A. By the tree of life, Gen. iii. 22.

Q. How was this a sacramental seal?—A. The eating of its fruit was a pledge of eternal life.

Q. In what manner did this fruit seal that promise?— A. Only *conditionally*, if Adam continued in perfect obedience till his time of trial was over, Gal. iii. 10.

Q. If Adam had perfectly fulfilled the condition of this covenant, what title would he have had to the reward?— A. A mere pactional title, secured by the promise of God.

Q. Why might not Adam's obedience have strictly merited or deserved a reward from God?—A. Because he owed it wholly to God as the author of his being; and when he had done all, he would have been an *unprofitable servant*, Luke xvii. 10, Job xxii. 3.

Q. Was the obtaining of the reward to be Adam's chief end or motive in his obedience?—A. No; but the glory of God, Prov. xvi. 4, 1 Cor. x. 31, Isa. xliii. 21.

Q. Is the covenant of works still binding?—A. Yes; it is still binding upon all that are out of Christ.

Q. Doth not man's breach of it disannul its binding

force?—A. No; it still continues to demand *perfect obedi-ence*, and has a new claim of *infinite satisfaction* for offences committed, Gal. iii. 10. 12, Heb. ix. 22.

Q. Doth not Christ by his obedience and suffering, or believers by receiving that as their righteousness, injure or destroy this covenant?—A. No; they fulfil, establish, and exalt it, Rom. x. 4—iii. 31.

Q. 13. *Did our first parents continue in the estate wherein they were created?*

A. Our first parents being left to the freedom of their own will, fell from the estate wherein they were created, by sinning against God.

Q. Did the making of the covenant of works with Adam infallibly secure him in the favour of God?—A. No; it left him in a state of probation.

Q. What mean you by Adam's *estate of probation?*—A. His being left to the freedom of his own will, and having it in his power to lose or gain happiness.

Q. Is any man since the fall properly in a state of pro-bation or trial?—A. No.

Q. How prove you that believers are not in such a state of trial?—A. Because their happy estate is infallibly se-cured in Christ, Rom. viii. 1, Jude 1, 1 Pet. i. 5.

Q. How then are believers' good works rewarded?—A. That reward is entirely of free grace, Rom. v.

Q. How prove you that unbelievers are not in such a state of trial?—A. Because they have destroyed themselves, and can do nothing for their own relief, Eph. ii. 1. Rom. viii. 8.

Q. How then are unbelievers punished for their sin?—A. Because though in our fallen estate sin is our necessary plague, yet we make it the object of our choice and de-light, Rom. iii. 12. 15.

Q. What understand you by *freedom of will?*—A. A power to act or not to act, to choose or refuse, without force from any other, Deut. xxx. 19.

Q. How many kinds of freedom of will are there?—A. Three; freedom only to good; freedom only to evil; and freedom to do both good and evil.

Q. Whose will is freely inclined only to good?—A. The will of God is *necessarily* inclined to good; and the will of holy angels and glorified saints is *infallibly* determined to good, by the will of God, Zeph. iii. 6. Rev. xxi. 27.

Q. Whose will is free only to evil?—**A.** The will of devils and unregenerate men, Rom. viii. 7, 8.

Q. What freedom of will have believers in this world?—**A.** Their new nature is free only to good, and their old nature free only to evil, Rom. vii. 14. 24.

Q. Whose will was free both to good and evil?—**A.** The will of Adam before the fall, Eccl. vii. 29.

Q. Was Adam's will *then* equally inclined to good and evil?—**A.** No; it was inclined only to good, Gen. i. 27.

Q. How was his will free to do evil?—**A.** Its inclination to good was not confirmed.

Q. Why might not God have made man by nature immutably good?—**A.** Because immutable goodness is contrary to the very nature of a creature, Mal. i. 6.

Q. Why might not God have confirmed Adam's will, that he could not have biassed it to evil?—**A.** Because that would have been inconsistent with his estate of probation, and the nature of the covenant made with him.

Q. How so?—**A.** that covenant required, that Adam's right improvement of his original righteousness should be the condition of his confirmation in holiness and happiness, Rom. x. 5. Gal. iii. 12.

Q. Did God give Adam full ability to keep this covenant?—**A.** Yes; he *made him upright,* and wrote his most perfect law in his heart, Eccl. vii. 29.

Q. How long did God continue this ability with Adam?—**A.** Till Adam, by abusing the fredom of his will, did forfeit it, Gen. iii. 6. Psal. xlix. 12.

Q. Did God any way influence Adam to abuse the freedom of his will?—**A.** No, not in the least, Jam. i. 13.

Q. What then is meant by God's *leaving man* to the freedom of his own will?—**A.** His withholding that further grace which would have confirmed him in holiness.

Q. How did Adam abuse the freedom of his will?—**A.** By sinning against God, Gen. ii. 6. 12.

Q. 14. *What is sin?*

A. Sin is any want of conformity unto, or transgression of, the law of God.

Q. How do you prove that there is any sin in the world?—**A.** The scriptures, our consciences, and the outward calamities of life, clearly prove it.

Q. How doth the scripture prove it?—**A.** It declares that *all men have sinned*, Rom. iii. 10. 23.

Q. How does our conscience prove it?—**A.** By often filling us with shame and dread of God's vengeance when we break his law, Gen. iii. and iv. Rom. ii. 14.

Q. How do the outward calamities of life prove it?—**A.** An infinitely good God would not afflict the work of his hands, if he was not offended by sin, Lam. iii. 33.

Q. By what rule and standard must we judge of the sinfulness of qualities and actions?—**A.** By the law of God.

Q. Can irrational creatures, who are under no law, sin? —**A.** No; *where no law is there is no transgression.*

Q. How many ways do irrational creatures sin?—**A.** By want of conformity to, or transgression of God's law.

Q. What mean you by want of conformity to God's law?—**A.** Our not having that purity of heart, and holiness of life, the law requires, Rom. vii. 14. Isa. lxiv. 6.

Q. What mean you by transgression of God's law?—**A.** The doing what it forbids, 1 John iii. 4. Isa. lix. 13.

Q. Why is it called *transgression of the law?*—**A.** Because hereby we *pass over* the limits which God hath fixed for our conduct in his law, Ezek. xx. Dan. ix.

Q. How many things are considerable in every sin?—**A.** Four; its filth, demerit, guilt, and strength.

Q. What is the *filth* of sin?—**A.** Its contrariety to the holiness of God's nature and law, by which it renders the sinner ugly and abominable in his sight, Hab. i. 13

Q. What is the demerit of sin;—**A.** Its deserving infinite wrath at the hand of God, Isa. iii. 11.

Q. Can the demerit and filth of sin ever be separated? —**A.** No; the wages of sin is death, Rom. vi. 23.

Q. What is the guilt of sin?—**A.** The chargeableness of it, in order to punishing one for it.

Q. Are the filth and guilt of sin naturally connected?— **A.** Yes; every blot of sin naturally binds over to wrath, Ezek. xviii. 4. Rom. ii. 8, 9. and iii. 19, 20.

Q. Whence doth that proceed?—**A.** From the justice of God, and sentence of his law, Psal. xi. 6, 7. Gal. iii. 10.

Q. Can the free grace of God separate the filth and guilt of sin?—**A.** Yes, with respect to the *persons* on whom they are found, Rom. viii. 1. 2 Cor. v. 21.

Q. Who ever had guilt lying on him without being polluted?—**A.** Christ, when our sins were laid on him.

Q. Who are polluted with sin's filth, without being bound over to *punishment?*—A. Believers, Rom. viii. 1.

Q. How was this separation of sin's filth and guilt effected?—A. Christ and his elect being made one in law, all their guilt was laid over on him, Isa. liii. 4, 5, 6.

Q. For what end was this separation made?—A. For the speedy and full destruction of sin.

Q. How is sin destroyed by this means?—A. In order of nature Christ taketh away the guilt of sin by his satisfaction of his own person and then by his Spirit purgeth away its filth in us, Dan. ix. 24. 1 Cor. vi. 11.

Q. What is the strength of sin?—A. Though sin, in respect of its guilt, hath a condemning strength; yet the strength of sin most properly consists in that mighty force which our indwelling lusts have to push us on to actual transgressions, notwithstanding great opposition from conscience, and the Spirit, word, and providence of God.

Q. To what issue doth this activity of sin tend?—A. To fix and bring forth more sin, and increase our bondage to it, Rom. vii, Psalm lxxxi. 12.

Q. What is the principal means of the strength of sin?—A. The *pure* and *holy* law of God, 1 Cor. xv. 56.

Q. How can the law be the means of sin's defiling strength?—A. Sin is irritated, and occasionally stirred up by its precepts; but especially its curse fixes sinners under the dominion of sin, as the principal branch of their punishment, Rom. vii. 5. 8—13, 1 Cor. xv. 56.

Q. 15. *What was the sin whereby our first parents fell from the estate wherein they were created?*

A. The sin whereby our first parents fell from the estate wherein they were created, was their eating the forbidden fruit.

Q. What was the cause of Adam's abusing his freedom of will?—A. The temptation of Satan, 2 Cor. xi. 3.

Q. Whom call you *Satan?*—A. The prince of fallen angels or devils, Matth. xxv. 41, Rev. xx. 2.

Q. When did Satan tempt our first parents?—A. Soon after they were created, and perhaps that very same day.

Q. Why did the devil tempt them so soon?—A. He is full of malice, set upon mischief, and will lose no opportunities of committing it, 1 Pet. i. 8, Job i. and ii.

Q. What moved Satan to tempt man?—A. His enmity against God, and envy at man's happiness.

Q. Whether did he first tempt the man or the woman?—A. The woman in her husband's absence, Gen. iii. 2.

Q. Why so?—A. Because she was the weaker vessel.

Q. By what instrument did Satan tempt the woman?—A. By a serpent, Gen. iii. 1, 2 Cor. xi. 3.

Q. Why made he use of a serpent as his instrument?—A. Because the serpent being naturally subtile, and perhaps beautiful, the woman might not suspect any thing uncommon in its speech, 2 Cor. xi. 3, Gen. iii. 1.

Q. To what did Satan tempt our first parents?—A. To eat of the forbidden fruit, Gen. iii. 1—5.

Q. How did he tempt him to eat of this fruit?—A. He suggested that there was reason to question God's command; and promised safety and advantage in eating it, Gen. iii.

Q. What advantage did he promise to them in eating this fruit?—A. He said they would be as Gods, knowing good and evil, Gen. iii. 5.

Q. How did he confirm this false promise of advantage?—A. By declaring that God knew the truth of what he said, Gen. iii. 5.

Q. What success had the devil in this temptation?—A. The woman coveted, took, and ate of this fruit; and gave to her husband also, and he did eat, Gen. iii. 6.

Q. Was the eating of this fruit a great sin?—A. Yes; for it broke all the commandments of God, and was attended with many grievous aggravations.

Q. How did our first parents eating the forbidden fruit break the first commandment?—A. By unthankfulness, and unbelief, in distrusting and discrediting God, and believing the devil; by making a god of their belly; and by pride, in seeking to render themselves as wise as God.

Q. How did it break the second commandment?—A. God's ordinance of abstaining from that fruit was not observed, and kept pure and entire, Gen. ii. 17.

Q. How did it break the third commandment?—A. God's attributes were hereby profaned; his truth called a liar, his majesty and holiness affronted, his power and justice contemned, and Satan's profane appeal to him approved, Gen. iii. 5, 6.

Q. How did this sin break the fourth commandment?—

A. It corrupted all the powers of their nature, and rendered them incapable to keep holy the Sabbath.

Q. How did this sin break the fifth commandment?—A. The wife tempted her husband to sin, and he, by yielding, encouraged her in wickedness; both rebelled against their only parent, God, and squandered away the eternal happiness of their children which was intrusted to them.

Q. How did the eating of this fruit break the sixth commandment?—A. Hereby our first parents murdered themselves and all their posterity, soul and body, Rom. v. 12.

Q. How did it break the seventh commandment?—A. The luxurious desire of this fruit begot in our first parents every unclean lust, Gen. iii. 6. Matth. xv. 19.

Q. How did it break the eighth commandment?—A. It was a sacrilegious theft and robbery of what was the sole property of God, Gen. iii. 11.

Q. How did it break the ninth commandment?—A. The eating of this fruit, to render themselves happy, falsely witnessed that God had envied their happiness; and brought the infamous character of covenant-breakers upon themselves and all their posterity, Gen. iii. 1. 4, 5.

Q. How did it break the tenth commandment?—A. They were discontent with their lot, and coveted that which God had denied to them, Gen. iii. 6—11.

Q. How was this sin of eating the forbidden fruit highly aggravated?—A. It was committed upon a small temptation; by a man lately made after the image of God, and endued with sufficient strength to resist temptations, expressly warned to avoid this sin, and honourably admitted into covenant with God; and in Paradise, where he had great abundance of pleasant fruits and other delights, Gen. i. ii. and iii.

Q. Wherein did man's sin first begin?—A. In Eve's listening to Satan as a teacher, Gen. iii. 1—6.

Q. What should this teach us?—A. To resist the first motions of lust and temptation; and to go out against them only in the strength of Christ, Eph. vi.

Q. Did this sin of eating the forbidden fruit deserve the temporal, spiritual, and eternal death of Adam, and all his natural seed?—A. Yes; being infinitely evil, it well deserved infinite punishment, Rom. vi. 23.

Q. What makes sin infinitely evil?—A. Its being committed against an infinitely great and holy God, Isa. lix. 13.

Q. 16. *Did all mankind fall in Adam's first transgression?*

A. The covenant being made with Adam, not only for himself, but for his posterity, all mankind, descending from him by ordinary generation, sinned in him, and fell with him, in his first transgression.

Q. What was the effect of Adam's eating the forbidden fruit?—A. He fell by it, Rom. v. 12. 19. 1 Cor. v. 22.

Q. Who fell with him?—A. All his natural posterity.

Q. Why fell they with him?—A. Because they sinned in him in his first transgression, Rom. v. 12—19.

Q. How were they in him when he sinned?—A. As their natural parent, and as their covenant head.

Q. If Adam had stood, would all his natural posterity have stood with him?—A. Yes, Rom. v. 12.

Q. Whether would Adam's obedience, or their own, have found their legal claim to eternal life?—A. Adam's obedience; and their own obedience to the law as a rule, would have been part of their happiness.

Q. Why did not Christ as a man, being a son of Adam, fall with him?—A. Christ was none of Adam's *natural* seed, descending from him by ordinary generation, nor represented by him as his covenant head, Isa. vii. 14.

Q. Wherein did the first Adam, and Christ the second Adam, agree?—A. Both represented men in a covenant with God, Rom. v. 12—19. 1 Cor. xv. 22. 45.

Q. Wherein did the first and second Adam differ?—A. In dignity of persons, the covenant they pertained to, and number and nature of those whom they represented.

Q. How did they differ in dignity of person?—A. The first Adam was a living soul, a mere man, and fallible creature; but the second Adam is a quickening head, a God-man, eternal, almighty, and unchangeable, 1 Cor. xv. 21, 22. 45. 47.

Q. How do they differ in the covenant to which they pertain?—A. Adam was representative in the covenant of works; but Christ is representative in the covenant of grace.

Q. How do they differ in the number they represented?—A. Adam represented all mere men; Christ represents only elect men, Rom. v. 12. 19.

Q. How do they differ as to the condition of those whom they represented?—A. Adam engaged only for innocent persons; Christ engaged for dead and guilty sinners, Isa. liii. 6.

7

Q. 17. *Into what estate did the fall bring mankind?*
A. The fall brought mankind into an estate of sin
and misery.

Q. Why is man's apostacy from God called *the fall?*—
A. Because man is debased, bruised, and ruined by it.

Q. From what have all mankind fallen in Adam?—A.
From a state of perfect holiness and happiness.

Q. Into what have they fallen?—A. Into an estate of
sin and misery, Eph ii. 1—3, Rom. v. 12—19.

Q. Why is man's fallen condition called an *estate* of sin
and misery?—A. Because sin and misery abound with
him, and he fixed in both, Zech. ix. 11.

Q. How are men fixed in actual sins?—A. The guilt
and stain which they leave behind them is abiding.

Q. What fixeth man in this state of sin and misery?—
A. The threatening of the broken covenant of works, and
the nature of sin, Gal. iii. 10, Eph. ii. 1.

Q. How doth the threatening of the broken covenant of
works fix men in an estate of sin and misery?—A. It engageth the justice of God to lay them under the threefold
death threatened in that covenant, Ezek. xviii. 4.

Q. How doth the nature of sin fix men in that estate?—
A. Wherever it reigns, it renders the person altogether incapable of delivering himself, and unwilling to be delivered
by another, Rom. viii. 7, Eph. ii. 1, 2.

Q. How is our fallen estate described in scripture?—A.
As a state of distance from God, of condemnation, pollution,
bondage, darkness, and death, Eph. ii. 12.

Q. Whether is our sin or our misery worst?—A. Sin :
for it immediately strikes against God, and is the cause of
misery ; whereas misery only strikes against sinners.

Q. Is not sin a misery to man, as well as an offence to
God?—A. Yes ; to be under the reigning power of sin is
the greatest misery, Eph. ii. 1—4. 12.

Q. 18. *Wherein consists the sinfulness of that estate whereinto man fell?*
A. The sinfulness of that estate whereinto man
fell, consists in the guilt of Adam's first sin, the
want of original righteousness, and the corruption
of his whole nature, which is commonly called original sin, together with all actual transgressions
which proceed from it.

Q. How many kinds of sin are there among men?—A. Two; original and actual, Matth. xv. 19.

Q. In what do these differ?—A. Original sin is the *sin of our natures*, and actual is the *sin of our lives*.

Q. What is original sin?—A. The sin which is conveyed to us by our parents from Adam, Rom. v., Psal. li.

Q. Why is this called *original sin?*—A. Because we have it from our conception and birth; and it is the fountain of all our actual sin, Psal. li. 5, Matth. xv. 19.

Q. Of how many parts doth original sin consist?—A. Of three; the guilt of Adam's first sin, the want of original righteousness, and the corruption of the whole nature; the first is called *orignal sin imputed*, and the two last *original sin inherent*.

Q. Of what sin of Adam's are we guilty?—A. Only his first sin; for he committed *it only* as our covenant-head and representative, Rom. v. 26.

Q. How are we reckoned guilty of Adam's first sin?—A. By God's imputing it to us, or his accounting it ours in law, Rom. v. 12. 19, 1 Cor. xv. 22.

Q. Why is it *in law* accounted our sin?—A. Adam, our representative, is one with us in the eye of the law.

Q. How prove you that Adam's first sin is imputed to his posterity?—A. The scripture declares that *by one man's disobedience many were made sinners*, Rom. v. 12. 19.

Q. Doth the justice of God require the imputation of Adam's first sin to his posterity?—A. Yes; as well as the imputation of Christ's righteousness to believers.

Q. Why are not Adam's other sins, as well as his first, imputed to us?—A. Because after he had broken the covenant of works by his first sin, he ceased to be our covenant-head, having become unfit for that station.

Q. How then did the broken covenant of works bind mankind after the fall?—A. Every man stood bound for himself, Gal. iii. 10. 12.

Q. What is the second part of original sin?—A. The want of *original righteousness*, Psal. xiv. 1, 2, 3.

Q. What do you understand by *original righteousness?* —A. That spiritual knowledge, righteousness, and holiness with which man was created, Eccl. vii. 29, Col. iii. 9.

Q. How do you prove that we naturally want this original righteousness?—A. The scripture affirms that there is no man *righteous, no not one*, Rom. iii. 10, 11, Isaiah lxiv. 6.

Q. Why doth God withhold this original righteousness when he createth our souls ?—**A.** He as a righteous Judge withholds it as the punishment of Adam's first sin imputed to us, Isa. lix. 2, Rom. iii. 23.

Q. Why might not God create our souls holy under that guilt ?—**A.** Because the guilt of Adam's first sin necessarily subjects us to the punishment of spiritual death.

Q. Why might not God have left them uncreated, rather than form them without original righteousness ?—**A.** Besides other reasons, men must be brought into being, either to be saved by Christ, or to beget, or be useful to such as shall be saved, Isa. liii. 10—12.

Q. Doth God then make any man from an inclination to damn him ?—**A.** No; God makes all things for his own glory; and when man will not glorify God by obedience, it is necessary that God glorify himself in man's punishment, Prov. xvi. 4, Psalm xi. 6, 7, Rom. xi. 36.

Q. How prove you that the want of original righteousness is a sin ?—**A.** It is a want of conformity to God's law.

Q. Under what penalty doth God's law demand original righteousness ?—**A.** Under the penalty of his eternal wrath, Gal. iii. 10, Ezek. xviii. 4.

Q. Is it not hard that God's law should so demand original righteousness, when men cannot afford it ?—**A.** No ; for man lost it by his own fault, Rom. iii. 23.

Q. What is the third branch of man's original sin ?—**A.** The corruption of our whole nature, Isa. i. 5, 6.

Q. What do you understand by the *corruption of nature ?*—**A.** It is that whereby all the powers of our soul, and members of our body, are indisposed to good, and defiled with, and disposed to evil, Isa. lxiv. 6, and i. 6.

Q. Whence do ye prove that men's nature is originally corrupted ?—**A.** From scripture and experience.

Q. How doth scripture prove it ?—**A.** It declares that being brought out of unclean things, we must be unclean ; that *of flesh* we are born *flesh ;* that we are begotten in the image of fallen Adam, and are *shapen* and *conceived in sin,* and *by nature the children of wrath,* Job xiv. 4, John iii. 6, Gen. v. 3, Psalm li. 5, Eph. ii. 3.

Q. How doth experience prove our natures to be corrupted ?—**A.** The flood of miseries upon infants, our universal and early inclinations to evil, and their breaking forth in opposition to the severest laws of God and men ; and even to the strongest resolutions, and largest measures of grace here, and our natural readiness to imitate Adam in his first sin, shew that our nature is corrupted.

Q. Wherein do we naturally imitate Adam in his first sin?—A. In our being more curious to know new things, than to practise known duty; in our bias to evil because forbidden; in our inclination to hear what is vain or wicked; and easy following of evil counsel rather than good.

Q. In what other things do we imitate Adam's sinful conduct?—A. In our anxious care for what is pleasant to our eyes, or other senses, at the expense of our souls; in our discontentment with our lot; and hiding, excusing, extenuating, or laying the blame of our sin upon others, &c., Ezek. xvi. xx. xxiii., Isa. lix.

Q. What about every man is corrupted with sin?—A. His whole man, soul and body, Isa. i. 6, Jer. xvii. 9.

Q. In what is our soul naturally corrupted?—A. In its understanding, will, conscience, affections, and memory, Isa. i. 6, Psal. xiv., Jer. xvii. 9.

Q. With what is our understanding or mind corrupted? —A. With ignorance of, and opposition to spiritual truths; and with proneness to vanity, pride, and lies.

Q. Of what things is our mind naturally ignorant?—A. Of God, of Christ, and the way of salvation; and of the wickedness of our own heart and life, and our danger on account of it, Isa. i. 3, Eph. iv. 18.

Q. Wherein doth the darkness, blindness, and ignorance of men's minds appear?—A. Few have sound notions of divine truths, and fewer the saving knowledge of them; but the most part, even of such as have gospel light, are like blind men daily stumbling into sin, John i. 5.

Q. How doth the natural opposition of our mind to divine truths appear?—A. In the difficulty there is to teach many the principles of religion, who quickly learn other things; and in men's frequent apostacy from the truth, or living in such a manner as shews they do not believe what they know, Isa. xxviii. 9, 10.

Q. How doth the natural vanity of our mind appear?— A. In our early and general delight in folly, and in our thinking on vain notions or projects, especially when we are engaged in the worship of God, Prov. xxii. 15.

Q. How doth the natural pride of man's mind appear?— A. In men's fondness of what makes them appear great or gay; and in their self-conceit, and unwillingness to believe what they really are, especially before God.

7*

Q. Wherein doth the natural proneness of our mind to lies and falsehood appear?—**A.** In our early and artfully devising lies; and loving to read, hear, or think of romances and fables, rather than the truths of God.

Q. How is our conscience naturally corrupted?—**A.** It is so blind as not duly to perceive God's challenges and commands; and is easily bribed by carnal advantage, to call good evil, and evil good, 1 Tim. iv. 2.

Q. With what is our will naturally corrupted?—**A.** With a bias to every thing sinful, enmity against every thing good, and a perverseness with respect to our chief end, Rom. vii. 19, and viii. 7.

Q. In what doth our natural bias, or strong inclination to evil appear?—**A.** In our early going astray from the path of duty; in the sudden expiry of our good motions and resolutions; and in the faint and imperfect religious service of believers themselves, Psal. lviii. 3.

Q. Wherein doth our natural averseness and enmity against that which is good appear?—**A.** In the frowardness of children; the backwardness of our hearts to religious, and especially more secret and spiritual duties; and our frequent sinning over the belly of our convictions and conscience, Deut. xxix. 19, Heb. x. 26. 29.

Q. To what is our will naturally an enemy?—**A.** To God, to Christ, and the Holy Spirit.

Q. To what of God is our will naturally an enemy?— To his being, perfections, word, worship, &c.

Q. How doth men's natural enmity against the being and perfections of God appear?—**A.** In their secret wishing that there were no God to give laws, or to punish for sin; and in their profaning and accusing his name when in passion, and often deliberately, without any provocation.

Q. How doth our natural enmity against the word of God appear?—**A.** In our perverting and opposing it; and improving its laws as irritations, and the gospel as an encouragement to sin, Jude 4, Gal. i. 7, 8.

Q. How doth our natural enmity against the worship of God appear?—**A.** In our universal and early inclination to shift it, or to disturb others in it; and in our encouraging drowsiness, vain and unseasonable thoughts, when we are engaged in it, 1 Sam. xxi. 7, Mal. i. 13.

Q. To what of Christ as Mediator is our will naturally an enemy?—**A.** To all of Christ, particularly his offices of prophet, priest, and king, 1 Cor. i. 23.

Q. How doth our enmity against the prophetical office of Christ appear?—A. In our conceit of our own wisdom, however brutish we be; and in our shifting and despising the instructions of Christ, 1 Cor. i. 23, Heb. iii. 10.

Q. Wherein doth our natural enmity against the priestly office of Christ appear?—A. In our high esteem of our own righteousness, and seeking salvation by it in whole or in part; in men's strong opposition to the doctrine of God's free grace, and refusing to receive Christ as their only righteousness; and frequent rushing themselves upon eternal damnation, rather than be saved by him *alone*, Rom. x. 3, and ix. 31, 32.

Q. Wherein doth our natural enmity against Christ's kingly office appear?—A. In our readiness to model his ordinances to our own taste, to rebel against his laws, and to censure or oppose the discipline of his church.

Q. Against which of Christ's offices have we the most open enmity?—A. Against his kingly office, Psal. ii. 1, 2.

Q. Against which of Christ's offices have we the strongest secret enmity?—A. Against his priestly office.

Q. How doth that appear?—A. In our frequent resting in duties when we will not omit them, Rom. x. 3.

Q. Why have we the strongest enmity against the priestly office of Christ?—A. It is no way discovered by the light of our natural conscience; it most clearly displays the glory of God, and the vileness of our own righteousness; and is the foundation of the other two offices.

Q. Do not many desire salvation by Christ as a priest, who refuse obedience to him as a king?—A. The salvation which such desire is not the salvation of Christ, but a salvation in sin, and through their own good works.

Q. Wherein lieth the evil of desiring such a salvation? —A. It chiefly dishonours God, and debaseth the priestly office of Christ, by attempting to render it needless, nay, the strongest encouragement to sin, Jude 4.

Q. How doth our natural enmity against the Spirit of God appear?—A. In our violent resistance of his kind motions and operations on our heart and conscience, before or after conversion, Acts vii. 51, Heb. x. 29.

Q. Wherein doth our natural perverseness with respect to our chief end appear?—A. In our making our own interests, real or imaginary, our chief end, rather than the glory of God, Zech. vii. 5, Phil. ii. 21.

Q. How are our affections naturally corrupted?—**A.** They are wrong placed, and in a wrong bent.

Q. How are they wrong placed on God, as love, joy, &c. are placed upon sin?—**A.** Those that should be turned against sin, are turned against God, Rom. viii. 7.

Q. How are our affections naturally wrong bended?—**A.** Our right-placed affections, as love of parents, &c., are always either too strong, or too weak.

Q. How is our memory naturally corrupted?—**A.** It readily forgets what is good, while it firmly remembers what is wicked or trifling, Jer. ii. 32.

Q. How are our bodily members corrupted with sin?—**A.** They are *ready instruments of unrighteousness.*

Q. What are our feet swift to?—**A.** To run Satan's errands, and mischief, Rom. ii. 15.

Q. With what is our mouth naturally filled?—**A.** With cursing and bitterness, Rom. iii. 14.

Q. What are our eyes most ready to behold?—**A.** Objects of vanity, wickedness, and lust.

Q. What are our ears most disposed to hear?—**A.** Error, folly, and filthiness, Prov. xix. 27.

Q. How doth it appear that original sin is very heinous?—**A.** From the death of so many infants; from believers' deep grief on account of it; and from its more lasting and extensive nature than other sins, being the fountain of all actual guilt, Exod. xii., Rom. vii. 14—24.

Q. Doth God implant original sin inherent in us?—**A.** No; it flows from original sin imputed.

Q. How then is original sin conveyed to us?—**A.** By natural generation; we being *degenerate plants of a strange vine,* Psal. li. 5, Jer. ii. 21.

Q. Do the saints, who are in part sanctified, convey as much natural corruption to their children as others?—**A** Yes; for they beget children according to nature, not according to their grace, 1 Sam. ii. 12, and viii. 3.

Q. How should parents begetting their children such monsters of sin, and heirs of wrath, affect them?—**A.** It should stir them up to cry earnestly to God for early regenerating grace to their children, and to use all appointed means for their salvation, Mark x. 14.

Q. Whether do we make ourselves better or worse after our birth?—**A.** Much worse by our actual sin.

Q. What is actual sin?—**A.** The sin which we daily commit in thought, word, and deed, Rom. iii. 9—21.

Q. How may actual sin be distinguished ?—**A.** Into sins of omission and of commission.

Q. What understand you by a sin of omission ?—**A.** Our neglecting to perform what God's law requires.

Q. What mean you by a sin of commission ?—**A.** Our doing that which God's law forbids, Hos. iv. 2.

Q What connection hath actual sin with original?—**A.** Original sin is the accursed root and fountain ; and actual sin the branches, fruit and stream, Rom. vii.

Q. How may our lusts, by which our original sin worketh towards actual, be distinguished?—**A.** Into the lusts of our flesh, and the lusts of our spirit, 2 Cor. vii. 1.

Q. Which are the lusts of the flesh?—**A.** Those to which we are excited by the members of our body, as gluttony, drunkenness, uncleanness, &c.

Q. Which are the lusts of the mind or spirit ?—**A.** Those that have their principal seat in our souls, as pride, ambition, envy, malice, &c., Tit. iii. 3.

Q. How may our lusts, in respect of our power and influence, be distinguished?—**A.** Into subordinate and predominant lusts, Heb. xii. 1, Matth. v. 29, 30.

Q. What is a predominant lust ?—**A.** That which chiefly rules over, and sways a person to sin, Heb. xii. 1.

Q. Have all men, or the same men at all times, the same lust predominant in them ?—**A.** No.

Q. Whence doth that proceed ?—**A.** It proceeds from the different constitutions of their bodies, different ages, callings, opportunities, &c.

Q. By what marks may we know our predominant lust?—**A.** That sin which we most delight in, and are most ready to excuse, or most easily tempted to, and into which we most frequently fall, is our beloved lust.

Q. What may we learn from the sinfulness of our natural estate ?—**A.** That our best works, while we continue unregenerate, are filthy rags before God ; that it is a wonder God spareth us a moment out of hell ; and that except we be born again, we cannot enter into the kingdom of God, Isa. lxiv. 6. Lam. iii. 22. John iii. 3. 5.

Q. 19. *What is the misery of that estate whereinto man fell?*

A. All mankind, by their fall, lost communion with God, under his wrath and curse, and so made liable to all miseries in this life, to death itself, and to the pains of hell for ever.

Q. What mean you by man's *misery?*—**A.** That which distresseth and hurts him, Rom. ii. 8, 9. Deut. xxviii.

Q. Wherein do sin and misery *as such* differ?—**A.** Sin is the cause; misery is the effect: sin is odious to God, and pleasant to sinners; misery is disagreeable to sinners, and agreeable to the justice of God, Rom. vi.

Q. Doth God take pleasure in the misery of man?—**A.** He takes no pleasure in it as distressing to man; but he takes pleasure in it as the just punishment of man's sin, Gen. iii. 17, 18, 19. Lam. iii. 33. 39. Jer. v. 9. 29.

Q. Of how many parts does the misery of our natural estate consist?—**A.** Of three; what we have lost; what we are brought under; and what we are liable to.

Q. What have we lost by the fall?—**A.** The glorious image of God, and most sweet communion with him.

Q. How prove you that the loss of God's image is a misery as well as a sin?—**A.** Because to be like God is our highest honour, and to be unlike him is our greatest ignominy, Hab. i. 13. John viii. 44.

Q. Hath man lost his likeness to God in the spiritual nature and substance of his soul?—**A.** No; but the image of the devil is drawn upon it; it is become a slave to our body, and a resting place for God's wrath, Jer. xvii. 9.

Q. How do you prove man has lost communion with God?—**A.** The scripture testifies, that God hates the wicked, and will not suffer them to dwell in his presence, or stand in his sight: and that men are naturally without God, and estranged from him, Psalm v. 4, 5. Eph. ii. 12.

Q. How can the loss of communion with God be a misery, when we naturally contemn and shun it?—**A.** Because God is the only sufficient portion of our souls; and nothing can supply the want of him, Jer. ii. 13.

Q. Why then do we slight and shun communion with God?—**A.** Because we are distracted fools, who forsake our own mercy, Jonah ii. 8. Jer. viii. 9.

Q. Shall all men at length know the value of communion and fellowship with God?—**A.** Yes; either when they are converted, or when they are cast into hell.

Q. Under what hath the fall brought mankind?—**A.** Under the wrath and curse of God, Psalm vii. 11.

Q. How prove you that?—**A.** The scripture affirms,

that we are *by nature children of wrath;* that *he that be-lieveth not, is condemned already, and the wrath of God abideth on him,* John iii. 18. 36.

Q. What are we to understand by the *wrath* of God?—A. His holy displeasure with sin, Hab. i. 13.

Q. Why is this called *wrath?*—A. Because it produceth the most terrible effects, Deut. xxxii. 22.

Q. Wherein is the wrath of God against the wicked?—A. In his heart, face, mouth, and hand.

Q. How is wrath against them *in the heart* of God?—A. His soul despises, loathes, and abhors them, and all their works, Psalm cxxxviii. 6. xi. 5. and vii. 11.

Q. How is wrath in *the face* of God against them?—A. In wrath he hides his gracious countenance from them, he frowns on them, and sets his eyes upon them for evil, Isa. lix. 2. Psalm xxxiv. 16. Amos viii. 4.

Q. How is wrath in his *mouth* or *lips,* against them?—A. His word condemns and curses them, and all their works; his breath slays them, and kindles Tophet for them, Gal. iii. 10. Rev. ii. 16. Isa. xi. 4. and xxx. 33.

Q. How is wrath in his *hand* against the wicked?—A. In the hand of the Lord there is a cup of unmixed wrath for them; and his power is engaged in smiting them with more secret or more sensible strokes of wrath.

Q. What are the properties of God's wrath?—A. It is irresistible, insupportable, unavoidable, powerful, constant, eternal, and most just wrath.

Q. How is God's wrath *irresistible?*—A. There is no prevailing against the force of it.

Q. How is it *insupportable?*—A. No creature is able to stand under it without sinking, Isa. xxxiii. 14.

Q. How is it *unavoidable?*—A. There is no flying from it, if we continue without Christ, Heb. ii. 3.

Q. How is this wrath *powerful?*—A. It reaches both soul and body, and destroys to the uttermost.

Q. How is it *constant?*—A. It lieth on the wicked without interruption, Psal. vii. 11, John iii. 36.

Q. How is the wrath of God *eternal?*—A. It shall *never, never* have an end, 2 Thess. i. 9.

Q. How is it most *just* wrath?—A. Our sins well deserve it, Psal. xi. 5, 6, 7, Jer. ii. 19.

Q. Upon what of the sinner doth God's wrath lie?—A. Upon his person, name, estate, actions, and relations.

Q. What is the curse of God ?—A. The threatening or sentence of his law denouncing wrath against sinners.

Q. Hath God set up any glasses in this world for displaying the terrible nature of his wrath and curse ?—A. Yes ; such as, the drowning of the old world, raining fire and brimstone upon Sodom and Gomorrha, &c. but especially the death of Christ, Gen. vii. and xix.

Q. How is the death of Christ the clearest glass for displaying the wrath of God ?—A. In it we behold God bruising the only Son of his love, and executing upon him the fierceness of his wrath, till his soul was exceeding sorrowful even unto death, Rom. viii. 32.

Q. To what is man by the fall liable ?—A. To all the effects of God's wrath and curse.

Q. In what different periods are we liable to these ?—A. In this life, at the end of it, and through eternity.

Q. To what are we by sin liable in this life ?—A. To all the miseries of this life, whether on our soul, body, name, estate, or relations, Deut. xxviii.

Q. To what spiritual miseries is man liable in this life ? —A. To judicial blindness of mind, hardness of heart, searedness and horror of conscience, vile affections, slavery to Satan, weakness of memory. &c. Eph. iv. 19, &c.

Q. What is *judicial blindness* of mind ?—A. It consists in God's giving up men to ignorance and delusion, and blasting the means of instruction to them, Eph. iv.

Q. What is *judicial hardness* of heart ?—A. It is when our heart is neither awakened by judgments, nor moved by mercies to repent of sin, but emboldened in it.

Q. What is *searedness* of conscience ?—A. It is to be without fear or shame in committing known sin.

Q. What is *horror* of conscience ?—A. It consists in our being terrified with apprehensions of God's wrath.

Q. What call you *vile affections ?*—A. Strong inclinations to unnatural wickedness, especially such as respects fleshly lusts, Rom. i. 26, 27, Eph. iv. 19.

Q. What is meant by the *thraldom* or slavery of Satan ? —A. Our want of ability to oppose, and ready compliance with Satan's vilest temptations, 2 Tim. ii. 26.

Q. Wherein do the blindness of mind, hardness of heart, searedness of conscience, vile affections, and slavery of Satan in reprobates, differ from the resemblances of these plagues and maladies in believers ?—A. In reprobates these plagues are their pleasure, but they are the believer's heavy burden, Rom. vii. 14. 24.

Q. Wherein doth a wicked man's horror of conscience differ from that of a believer?—A. Apprehensions of God's positive wrath, are the spring of the wicked man's horror; but sin, and dread of separation from God, are the chief spring of a believer's terror, Gen. iv. 13, Psal. lxxxviii.

Q. To what bodily miseries is man liable by sin?—A. To desolation, captivity, sword, famine, pestilence, persecution, sickness, infirmity, and toil, &c.

Q. To what misery on his name is man liable by sin?—A. To infamy and reproach, Deut. xxviii. 37.

Q. What misery is man by sin liable to, in his estate?—A. To poverty; or to have his riches turned into a curse, or a mean of fattening him for the slaughter of eternal wrath, Psal. xxxvii. 20, Prov. i. 32.

Q. To what misery is man liable, in his relations?—A. To lose them, or to be afflicted by them.

Q. Wherein do the afflictions of the godly and the wicked in this life differ?—A. The afflictions of the godly proceed from God's love, and promote their interest; but those of the wicked flow from God's wrath, and are their punishment, Heb. xii. 6—11, Psal. xi. 6.

Q. To what is man by sin liable at the end of this life?—A. To death itself; for the scripture saith, *The wages of sin is death; The soul that sinneth shall die;* and, *It is appointed for men once to die,* &c.

Q. How can it be appointed for all men to die, when Enoch, Elias, and those found alive at Christ's second coming, die not?—A. Those did, or shall undergo a change equivalent to death, 1 Cor. xv. 52.

Q. What is death to a wicked man?—A. A passage from all his joy and happiness to eternal misery.

Q. What makes death terrible to a wicked man?—A. It robs him of all his beloved enjoyments, tears his soul from his body, drags it to God's tribunal, and casts it into the prison of hell, Prov. xiv. 32.

Q. What is the sting of death?—A. Sin.

Q. How is sin the sting of death?—A. It renders death irresistibly powerful, and infinitely agonizing and ruinous, Prov. xiv. 32. Job xviii. 7—18.

Q. What is the grave to a wicked man?—A. It is a prison to retain his body till the judgment of the great day, Rev. xx. 13. Psalm xlix. 14.

Q. To what is man, by sin, liable after his death?—A. To the pains of hell for ever, Luke xvi. 22, 23.

Q. How is hell called in Scripture?—A. *Tophet, a prison, a lake of fire and brimstone, a bottomless pit, utter darkness,* &c. Isa. xxx. 33. Rev. xx. 3. 10.

Q. For whom was hell originally prepared?—A. For the devil and his angels, Matth. xxv. 41.

Q. Why then are men cast into it?—A. They joined with the devil and his angels in rebellion against God.

Q. How may the pains or punishments of hell be distinguished?—A. Into the punishment of loss and of sense.

Q. What do those in hell lose?—A. The enjoyment of God and Christ, the fellowship of holy angels and saints, the happiness of their soul, and every good thing.

Q. How are the damned affected with this loss?—A. They are filled with anguish and grief, Matt. xiii. 42.

Q. What is the punishment of sense in hell?—A. The most terrible torments in soul and body.

Q. Who torments the damned in hell?—A. God, the devil, and their own conscience.

Q. How doth God torment them?—A. By making all the arrows of his wrath stick fast in them, 2 Thess. i. 9.

Q. How doth Satan torment them?—A. His presence is a burden, and he insults them in their misery, &c.

Q. How doth the gnawing worm of conscience torment them?—A. It presents the eternity and justice of their misery, lashes them for their former sins, and especially gospel-hearers, for refusing Christ, Mark ix. 43—49.

Q. What are the properties of hell-torments?—A. They are inconceivably severe, constant, and eternal.

Q. How prove you that they are eternal?—A. The scripture calls them *everlasting punishment* and *destruction*.

Q. Why must the punishments of the wicked be eternal? —A. Because their sin is infinitely evil, Hab. i. 13.

Q. Why might not God lay all the infinite wrath which their sins deserve upon them at once?—A. It is impossible for creatures to bear it, and therefore it must be continued upon sinners through all eternity, Psal. xc. 11.

Q. What attributes of God are chiefly glorified in hell-torments?—A. His holiness, justice, and power.

Q. How is God's holiness glorified in hell-torments?— A. In casting the wicked out of his gracious presence.

Q. How is God's justice glorified in hell-torments?—A. In rendering to sinners according to their crimes.

Q. How is God's power glorified in hell-torments?—A. It upholds the damned in being with one hand, and lashes them with the other, 2 Thess. i. 8, 9.

Q. What doth this view of our misery teach us?—A. To fly speedily out of our natural estate to Christ, if in it; and if delivered, to extol the Lord who plucked us as brands out of the burning, Heb. vi. 19. Zech. iii.

Q. 20. *Did God leave all mankind to perish in the estate of sin and misery?*

A. God, having out of his mere good pleasure, from all eternity, elected some to everlasting life, did enter into a covenant of grace, to deliver them out of the estate of sin and misery, and to bring them into an estate of salvation by a Redeemer.

Q. What became of the angels that sinned?—A. God left them to perish in their sin and misery.

Q. Do any of mankind, by their prayers, sincere resolutions, or blameless lives, deserve more pity at the hand of God than fallen angels?—A. No; the best works of unregenerate men deserve hell; for *the prayer of the wicked is an abomination to the Lord*, and their *plowing is sin*, Prov. xv. 8. xxi. 4. and xxviii. 9.

Q. Hath God then left all men to perish in their state of sin and misery?—A. No; he delivers some, Zech. ix.

Q. Whom doth he deliver?—A. The elect only.

Q. What moved God to deliver these elect men?—A. His own free love, John iii. 16, 1 John iv. 10.

Q. What moved God to deliver men rather than fallen angels?—A. His sovereign good pleasure, Rom. ix. 16.

Q. By what means doth God deliver the elect?—A. By the covenant of grace, Zech. ix. 11.

Q. Might not the broken covenant of works have been renewed?—A. No; it was a covenant of friendship, and could never reconcile enemies.

Q. How is the covenant by which sinful men are delivered, called?—A. The covenant of grace, of promise, peace, of reconciliation, or redemption, and the second or new covenant.

Q. Why is it called the *covenant of grace?*—A. Because

free grace moved God to make it; and all the blessings thereof are freely bestowed upon unworthy sinners.

Q. What is meant by *grace?*—A. Either the undeserved love and good-will of God; or the effects of that good-will bestowed on undeserving creatures, Rom. v. 21.

Q. How is God's free grace manifested in this covenant? —A. In his freely providing and furnishing his own Son to be our Mediator, accepting his righteousness in our stead, and sending the Spirit to apply his purchase to us.

Q. Why is it called a *covenant of promise?*—A. Because it is dispensed to us in free promises.

Q. Why is it called a *covenant of peace?*—A. Because it brings about peace and reconciliation between God and rebellious sinners, 2 Cor. v. 19.

Q. Why is it called the *covenant of redemption?*—A. Because thereby lost and enslaved sinners are brought back, and delivered from their bondage, Zech. ix. 11.

Q. Is the covenant of grace, and that of redemption, one and the same covenant?—A. Yes; the scripture mentions only *two covenants* that regards man's eternal state, of which the covenant of works is one, and therefore the covenant of grace must be the other: and the blood of Christ is in scripture called the blood of *the covenant*, but never of *the covenants*, Gal. iv. 24. 30.

Q. How do you further prove that what some call the covenant of grace made with believers, and distinct from the covenant of redemption, is no proper covenant?—A. Because it hath no proper condition, faith being as much promised as any other blessing, Psal. cx. 3.

Q. Why is the covenant of grace called the *second* and *new* covenant?—A. Because, though it was first made, it was last executed, and is everlasting, 2 Sam. xxiii. 5.

Q. Did the covenant of grace disannul the covenant of works?—A. No; it honoured and established it.

Q. How did it honour and establish it?—A. As the condition of the broken covenant of works was made the condition of the covenant of grace, Gal. iii. 10, and iv. 21.

Q. What was the condition of the broken covenant of works?—A. Perfect obedience to its precepts, and suffering the infinite wrath contained in its penalty.

Q. Why was the condition of the broken covenant of works made the condition of the covenant of grace?—A. Because God's holiness, justice and truth, were concerned in the honour of the broken covenant of works.

Q. How were God's holiness and justice concerned in the honour of the covenant of works?—A. They required that the breaker of so just and holy a law should be exposed to infinite wrath, Psal. xi. 6, 7, Ezek. xviii. 4.

Q. How was his truth concerned?—A. It had engaged that the breaker of the precept should *surely die.*

Q. How many things are in general considered with respect to the covenant of grace?—A. Two; the making, and the administration of it.

Q. Is the making of it the same which some divines call the covenant of redemption?—A. Yes, Psal. lxxxix. 3.

Q. Is the administration of it, which some call the covenant of grace, made with believers?—A. Yes.

Q. Why was the covenant of grace made from all eternity?—A. Because of God's eternal and infinite love to elect sinners, Jer. xxxi. 3, 1 John iv. 9, 10. 16. 19.

Q. Who are the parties in the covenant of grace?—A. God and Christ, Psalm lxxxix. 3, Zech. vi. 13.

Q. Whether did God, essentially considered, or the person of the Father, make this covenant with Christ?—A. God essentially considered in the person of the Father.

Q. Under what view doth God appear in the making of this covenant?—A. As most high, holy, and just; offended with sin, and yet most merciful to sinners.

Q. How prove you that the covenant of grace was made with Christ?—A. The scripture affirms it; and he is called the covenant himself, Psalm lxxxix. 3, Isa. xliii. 6.

Q. Why is Christ called *the covenant* itself?—A. He is the matter of it, and stands in manifold relations to it.

Q. In what relations doth Christ stand to the covenant of grace, as to the making of it?—A. He is the surety, and sacrificing priest of the covenant, Heb. vii.

Q. In what relations doth he stand with respect to the administration of the covenant?—A. He is the trustee; testator, prophet, interceding priest, and king of the covenant, Col. i. 19. Heb. ix. 16, &c.

Q. In what relations doth he stand with respect to both the making and administration of the covenant?—A. In the relation of mediator and Redeemer, Heb. ix. 15.

Q. Did Christ in this covenant stand bound for himself?—A. Not for himself, but only for others, Isa. liii. 4.

Q. What was the necessity that this covenant should be made with a representative?—A. The persons chosen to salvation could do nothing for themselves, Eph. ii. 1—5.

8*

Q. How do you prove that Christ represented others in this covenant?—A. Because to him the promises thereof were first made; and he is called the Surety of it.

Q. What is in general meant by a *Surety?*—A. One who engageth to pay debt, or perform duty, in the stead of another; or to secure the other's paying or performing it himself, Prov. xxii. 26. and xx. 26.

Q. What for a Surety is Christ?—A. One who engageth to pay all the elect's debt to God himself.

Q. What debt did the elect owe to God?—A. Perfect obedience to his law, and infinite satisfaction for sin to his justice, Gal. iii. 10. 12. Matth. iii. 15.

Q. Is Christ surety for his people's faith and repentance?—A. No; for Christ's suretiship belongs to the condition of the covenant; whereas his people's faith and repentance belong to the promise of it, Psalm xxii.

Q. Is Christ properly a Surety for God's performing the promises to us?—A. No: though Christ as a prophet attest the promises, yet the all-sufficiency and unchangeableness of God exclude any surety for him.

Q. Why is the covenant of grace made with such an infinitely strong Surety?—A. That he might not fail in performing its infinitely high condition, Isa. xlii. 4.

Q. In what manner did Christ engage in this covenant? —A. With full knowledge of his undertaking, and yet with the utmost cheerfulness and resolution, Jer. xxx. 21.

Q. Whom did Christ represent or stand bound for in the covenant of grace?—A. The elect *only;* for they *only* bear his name and image; they *only* are called his seed; and they *only* partake of the saving blessings of his covenant, 1 Cor. xv. Rom. v. and ix. Eph. i. 1 Pet. i. 2.

Q. Why are the elect called Christ's *seed?*—A. Because in regeneration he begets them again by his word and Spirit, 1 Pet. i. 3. 23. James i. 18.

Q. Why is Christ said to take hold of the *seed of Abraham*, and not of the seed of Adam?—A. To show that he represented only a part of Adam's seed, Heb. ii. 16.

Q. Is it any dishonour to Christ to represent a lesser number than Adam?—A. No; for Christ had infinitely more to do for the salvation of *one sinner*, than Adam had to do for the happiness of *innocent mankind*.

Q. How are the elect considered in the making of this covenant?—A. As lost sinners, wholly unable to help themselves, and yet as objects of·the free and sovereign will of God, 1 John iv. 9, 10. 19. John iii. 16.

Q. Wherein doth the freedom of this love appear?—A. In pitching upon objects altogether unlovely.

Q. In what doth the sovereignty of the Father's love appear?—A. In choosing some, while others no worse are left to perish in their sin, Rom. ix. 22.

Q. How did God make this covenant with Christ?—A. He proposed to him the persons to be saved, together with the parts of the covenant; and Christ accepted of them, Zech. vi. 13. John xvii. 6.

Q. What are the parts of the covenant of grace?—A. The condition, and the promise of it.

Q. How can this covenant have a condition, when it is a covenant of grace?—A. Though it be absolutely of free grace to the elect, yet it is strictly conditional to Christ, Matth. iii. 15, Isa. liii. 10, 11, 12.

Q. What is the condition of the covenant of grace?—A. Christ's Surety-righteousness, Dan. ix. 24, Rom. v. 19.

Q. What do you mean by the *righteousness* of Christ?— A. The holiness of his human nature, the righteousness of his life, and his satisfactory death, Phil. ii. 8.

Q. Why was *satisfaction* required from Christ, when it was not required from Adam as our public head?—A. Because Adam engaged only for an *innocent* seed ; but Christ engaged for *guilty* sinners, Rom. v. 12—19.

Q. Why was the perfect holiness of Christ's human nature necessary?—A. To answer for the original righteousness demanded of us by the law of God, Rom. v. 19.

Q. Why was his righteousness of life necessary?—A. To answer for that perfect righteousness of life demanded from us by the law, Rom. x. 4, Matth. xix. 17.

Q. Why was his satisfactory death necessary?—A. To atone and satisfy the justice of God for our sin.

Q. For what was Christ to satisfy the justice of God?— A. For all the sins of an elect world, Isa. liii. 4, 5, 6.

Q. How was he to make satisfaction?—A. By suffering the very same infinite punishment which we deserved.

Q. How prove you that Christ fulfilled the whole condition of the covenant of grace?—A. He *was holy, harmless ; became obedient unto death ; and gave himself to be a sacrifice of a sweet-smelling savour unto God.*

Q. How do you prove Christ's righteousness to be the only proper condition of the covenant of grace?—A. Because it is the only pleadable ground of the believer's title to eternal life, Rom. v. 21 and vi. 23.

Q. Is not faith the proper condition of this covenant?—A. No; for it can no way answer the demands of the broken law; and it is a blessing promised in the covenant of grace, Gal. iii. 17, Phil. i. 29.

Q. Were then these godly divines in an error, who called faith the *condition* of the covenant of grace?—A. No; for they only meant, that it was the instrument by which we are personally interested in that covenant, and receive the blessings of it, Acts xvi. 31.

Q. What is the promise of the covenant of grace?—A. It is the Father's engagement to bestow good things upon Christ, and his elect-seed, Isa. liii. 11, 12.

Q. Is the promise of the covenant of great importance?—A. Yes; for it is confirmed by the oath of God; and his glory, the honour of Christ, and the happiness of the elect, depend upon fulfilling of it.

Q. How many kinds of promises are there in the covenant of grace?—A. Two kinds, *viz.* such as directly respect Christ's person, and such as relate to his people.

Q. How may the promises *respecting Christ's person* be distinguished?—A. Into absolute and conditional.

Q. What are the *absolute* promises respecting Christ?—A. The promises of furniture for, and assistance in his work, Isa. xi. 2, 3, and xlii. 1, and lxi. 1, 2, 3.

Q. What is the only cause of the fulfilment of these promises?—A. The infinite sovereign love of God.

Q. What furniture was promised to Christ?—A. A human nature, filled with the Holy Ghost, and united to his divine person, Heb. x. 5, Isa. xi. 2, 3.

Q. What assistance was promised to Christ?—A. The continual influence of the Spirit, and the ministration of angels, &c. Isa. xi. 2, Psal. xci. 11.

Q. What are the promises respecting Christ's person, which depend upon the condition of his righteousness?—A. The promises of acceptance, and reward for his work.

Q. What acceptance was promised to Christ?—A. That God should declare himself well pleased for his righteousness' sake, and with him as Mediator, and believers in him for it, Isa. liii. 8, 12, 2 Cor. v. 18—21.

Q. What reward was promised to Christ?—A. The highest exaltation of his person, *as God man*, and a numerous seed to serve and praise him, Psal. cx. 1, Isa. liii. 10.

Q. What is the promise immediately respecting the elect?
—A. The promise of eternal life, Tit. i. 2, John ii. 25.

Q. What is included in this eternal life?—A. All true
happiness in this life, and that which is to come; or the life
of *grace* here, and of *glory* hereafter, Psal. lxxxiv. 11.

Q. What is one of the most comprehensive promises of
the covenant of grace made to the elect in Christ?—A. *I
will be your God, and ye shall be my people.*

Q. What doth that part of the promise, *I will be your
God*, mean?—A. That God himself shall be their everlasting portion, his perfections exerted for their interest, and all
his works tend to their eternal advantage.

Q. What doth that part of it, *Ye shall be my people*,
mean?—A. That all grace and glory suiting to the dignity
of God's people shall be given them, 1 Cor. iii. 22.

Q. To whom were the promises of our eternal life made?
A. Primarily to Christ as our head, and to us in him.

Q. How prove you they were primarily made to Christ?
—A. The promise of eternal life was made *before the world
began*, when it could not be made to any but Christ.

Q. Is not this very comfortable to believers?—A. Yes;
for whatever cause we may give God to deny his promised
blessings; yet Christ, to whom they were originally promised, never gave him any cause for it.

Q. What are the properties of the promises of the covenant of grace?—A. They are *exceeding great and precious*, well-ordered, free, and sure, 2 Pet. i. 4.

Q. How are they *great*?—A. They are the promises of
the great God; and pregnant with boundless blessings to
man, Isa. liv. lv. and lx. &c., Jer. xxxi. &c.

Q. How are they *precious?*—A. The good which they
contain is purchased with the precious blood of Christ.

Q. How are they *well-ordered?*—A. They are beautifully connected with one another, and suited to our many and
various needs, Ezek. xxxiv. and xxxvi. &c.

Q. How are they *free?*—A. They flow from free grace,
and are freely made out to believers, Hos. xiv. 4.

Q. How can they be absolutely free, when many of them
require some condition to be performed by us?—A. Nothing
is required as a condition in one promise, but what is absolutely promised in another.

Q. Why then hath God made many of his promises to
run in a conditional form?—A. To excite us to holiness,
and to teach us to apply sundry promises at once.

Q. How are the promises *sure ?*—A. They are confirmed by the oath of God, and blood of Christ.

Q. Hath the covenant of grace any penalty?—A. No; for both parties are infallible, Psalm lxxxix. 19.

Q. Are not believers, the representees, fallible?—A. They are fallible in their actions ; but their gracious state is infallibly secured in Christ, Rom. viii. 39.

Q. Are not their afflictions a proper penalty?—A. No ; they are a privilege promised in the new covenant, and to tend to their good, Heb. xii. 6. 11.

Q. What security have believers from any proper penalty for sin ?—A. Christ's everlasting righteousness.

Q. What is the administration of the covenant of grace ? —A. The dispensing and applying of it to men for the purposes for which it was made, Isa. lv. 3. 11.

Q. Who is the administrator of it?—A. Christ was appointed administrator of it by God, Isa. xlix. 6.

Q. Wherein do Christ's relations of surety, and of administrator, differ?—A. Christ, *as our surety*, served in our law-stead ; *as administrator*, he only acts for our good : the work of suretiship was his humiliation, but the work of administration is his honour and reward.

Q. Where doth Christ administer the new covenant?—A. Both on earth and in Heaven, Rev. iii. 20. xxii. 2.

Q. Wherein doth Christ's administration of it on earth and that in Heaven differ?—A. In heaven, Christ administers it personally, without ordinances, and to the elect only ; but on earth he administers it in ordinances, and partly by instruments, and partly to reprobates.

Q. To whom doth Christ administer the covenant on earth ?—A. To sinners of mankind in general, Isa. lv.

Q. Wherein doth he administer the covenant to these ? A. In the general offer of the gospel, Rev. xxii. 17.

Q. Why is the covenant of grace administered to sinful men in general, when the elect only are represented in it ? —A. Because Christ's righteousness, the only price of salvation, is in itself equally sufficient and suitable to purchase salvation for all men, Acts xx. 28, Matth. xviii. 28.

Q. How is it sufficient to purchase salvation for all men ? —A. Its infinite intrinsic worth renders it of sufficient value to purchase salvation for millions of worlds.

Q. How is it suitable to purchase salvation for all men ? A. It is a righteousness fulfilled in the human nature, which is common to all men, Heb. ii. 14. v. 2.

Q. How long will Christ continue to administer the covenant of grace?—A. For ever; for he shall *reign for ever;* and *he ever liveth to make intercession,* and *save to the uttermost,* Luke i. 33, Heb. vii. 25.

Q. How will Christ administer the covenant through eternity?—A. He will be the eternal bond of union, and medium of communion between God and the saints, and *will lead them to living fountains of waters,* Rev. vii. 17.

Q. What is Christ's primary relation as administrator of the covenant?—A. He is the trustee of it.

Q. What is his office as trustee of the covenant?—A. To be the repositary or storehouse of all the blessings of it for the good of his people, Col. i. 19.

Q. Who lodged all the blessings of it in Christ's hand?—A. God the Father, John iii. 35. Col. i. 19.

Q. Why did he so?—A. To exalt Christ, and prevent the elect from losing these blessings, Isa. liii. 10, 11, 12.

Q. In what relation doth Christ give us these blessings?—A. As the Testator, and the Executor of his testament.

Q. How doth Christ administer the new covenant as a Testator?—A. He dispones and bequeathes all the blessings of it in the way of legacy to men, Luke xxii. 29.

Q. Wherein do a testament and a covenant differ?—A. In a covenant good things are bestowed on account of some price or valuable consideration; but in a testament, good things are dispensed freely.

Q. When was the new covenant first clothed with the form of a testament?—A. That very day in which Adam fell.

Q. Why was it not clothed with a testamentatary form from eternity?—A. Because till Adam fell, no man needed the legacies of it, Gen. iii. 15. 1 Tim. i. 15.

Q. How could Christ's testament be of force before his death?—A. He was the *Lamb slain from the foundation of the world,* and in the ancient sacrifices confirmed his testament, Rev. xiii. 8. Heb. ix. and x.

Q. What legacies doth Christ dispone in his testament?—A. Himself, and all things in and with him, Rev. xxi.

Q. What are some of these things which Christ dispones?—A. Conviction, conversion, pardon, peace, acceptance, adoption, sanctification, and glorification, &c.

Q. To whom doth Christ bequeath these blessings?—A. To sinful men in general as his legatees, Prov. viii. 4.

Q. Wherein doth Christ bequeath these blessings to all men?—**A.** In the promises and offers of the gospel.

Q. Have all Christ's legatees an equal title to his promises and legacies?—**A.** No; all men in general have a *right of access* to them, but believers have *also a right of possession*, Prov. ix. 4, 5. Zech. xiii. 9.

Q. What do you mean by a *right access* to Christ's promises and learning?—**A.** A full warrant to take hold of them as our own, Isa. lv. 1, 2, 3. i Tim. i. 15.

Q. What do you mean by a *right of interest*, or possession?—**A.** The actual having of Christ, and all things in him as our own, Song ii. 16. 1 Cor. iii. 22, 23.

Q. Who is the executor of Christ's Testament?—**A.** Christ himself, John xiv. 4. Isa. lii. 12—15.

Q. May not the Holy Ghost also be called the Executor of Christ's testament?—**A.** Christ executes it by the Holy Ghost, John xvi. 13, 14.

Q. How can Christ be the Executor of his own testament?—**A.** Because though he died to confirm it, yet he rose again, and lives for evermore to execute it.

Q. In what relations doth Christ execute his own testament?—**A.** As a prophet, interceding priest, and king.

Q. For what end is the covenant of grace made and administered?—**A.** For the glory of God, and for bringing elect sinners out of an estate of sin and misery, into an estate of salvation, Isa. xlii. 4—16.

Q. What is meant by salvation?—**A.** A deliverance from sin, and all its fatal effects, and a possession of the utmost happiness to all eternity, Isa. xlv. 17. Rom. v. 21,

Q. How are sinners brought into an estate of salvation? —**A.** By their being personally and savingly brought into the bond of the new covenant, 2 Sam. xxiii. 5.

Q. What is the mean and instrument of interesting sinners in the covenant of grace?—**A.** Faith, or believing in the Lord Jesus, Acts xvi. 31.

Q. Why hath God appointed faith the instrument of interesting us in the new covenant?—**A.** Because it most illustrates the free grace of the covenant, and best insures the promises of it, Rom. iv. 16.

Q. How doth faith illustrate the grace of the covenant? —**A.** By receiving all blessings as God's *free gifts*.

Q. How doth faith insure the promises of the covenant? —**A.** It employs God's power and grace to perform them, 2 Chron. xx. 20. Psalm. xl. 11. and cxxxviii. 8.

Q. In what do the covenant of works and of grace agree?
—A. God was the maker; his glory and the happiness of man, are the end; and eternal life the thing promised in both, Psalm lxxxix. 3, 4.

Q. In what do the covenant of works and of grace differ?—A. In the party contracted with, the administrator, nature, properties, conditions, promises, order of obedience and execution, ends and effects.

Q. How do they differ with respect to the *party contracted with?*—A. The covenant of works was made with Adam, a mere man, and all his natural seed in him; but the covenant of grace was made with Christ, who is God man, as head of his elect seed, 1 Cor. xv. 47.

Q. How do they differ with respect to their *administrator?*—A. The covenant of works was administered by an absolute God; but the covenant of grace is administered by Christ as Mediator, Gal. iii. 10. 16. 19.

Q. How do they differ in their *nature?*—A. The covenant of works was a covenant of friendship; but the covenant of grace is a covenant of reconciliation.

Q. How do they differ in their *properties?*—A. The covenant of works was easily broken, and is now a cursing and condemning covenant; but the covenant of grace cannot be broken, and is still pregnant with blessings and salvation to men, Gal. iii. 13, 14.

Q. How do these covenants differ in their *condition?*—A. The original condition of the covenant of works was the perfect obedience of a mere man; but the condition of the covenant of grace is the perfect obedience, and full satisfaction of a God-man, Matth. iii. 15.

Q. How do they differ in their *promises?*—A. In the covenant of works all the promises were conditional to Adam; but in the covenant of grace the promises are absolutely free to man, Rom. iv. 4. 16.

Q. How do they differ in the required *order of obedience?*—A. In the covenant of works duty went before privilege, and acceptance of the work before the acceptance of the person; but in the covenant of grace, privilege goes before duty, and acceptance of the person before acceptance of his work, Gal. iii. 12, Eph. i. 6.

Q. How do they differ in their *order of execution?*—A. The covenant of works was made in time, and first executed; but the covenant of grace was made from eternity, and is last executed, Gen. ii. Tit. i. 2.

9

Q. How do they differ in their *end* and *design?*—A. The end of the covenant of works was to show man his duty to God ; but the great end of the covenant of grace is to show the greatness of God's grace to man.

Q. How do they differ in their *effects?*—A. The cove-. nant of works terrifies a guilty sinner, and binds him over to hell; but the new covenant comforts and strengthens him, by opening the gates of heaven to him.

Q. How may we know if we are savingly interested in the covenant of grace ?—A. If we have seen ourselves wholly ruined by the covenant of works, and are content to be entirely indebted to the free grace of God for our salvation, Phil. iii. 8, 9, Hos. xiv. 3.

Q. What should we do if we find ourselves without this covenant?—A. Cry earnestly to Christ to bring us into it, and essay to take hold of the promises of it.

Q. What is our duty, if we find ourselves in this covenant?—A. To admire and adore God's free grace which brought us in ; and to improve the fulness of the covenant, in living like the children of God, 2 Sam. vii.

Q. 21. *Who is the Redeemer of God's elect?*

A. The only Redeemer of God's elect is the Lord Jesus Christ, who, being the eternal Son of God, became man, and so was and continueth to be God and man, in two distinct natures, and one person for ever.

Q. 22. *How did Christ, being the Son of God, become man ?*

A. Christ the Son of God became man by taking to himself a true body and a reasonable soul, being conceived by the power of the Holy Ghost, in the womb of the Virgin Mary, and born of her, yet without sin.

Q. By whom doth God bring his elect into a state of salvation ?—A. By the Redeemer with whom the covenant of grace was made, Isa. xlii. 6, 7, Mat. i. 21.

Q. Who is the only Redeemer of God's elect?—A. Christ the eternal and only begotten Son of God.

Q. Hath God any other who are called his sons besides Christ ?—A. Yes : angels and believers.

Q. Wherein do their sonship differ from that of Christ ? —A. Christ is God's eternal, necessary, and natural Son;

but angels and believers are only made the sons of God in time, by a mere act of his will.

Q. How are angels the sons of God?—A. By immediate creation, Psalm civ. 4. Job xxxviii. 6, 7.

Q. How are believers the sons of God?—A. By regeneration and adoption, 1 John iii. 1. 9.

Q. How is Christ the Son of God?—A. By necessary, natural, and eternal generation, and therefore called his *only* Son, John i. 14. and iii. 16.

Q. Is Christ the Son of God only by office and exaltaon?—A. No; he is the Son of God by nature.

Q. How prove you that?—A. Christ says, *I and my father are one*, John x. 30.

Q. Why may we not say, that Christ is the Son of God, by virtue of his mediatory office and exaltation?—A. Because that would make Christ's proper sonship and personality dependent on the Father's will, as his mediatory office and exaltation are.

Q. Doth Christ distinguish his sonship from his mediatory mission?—A. Yes: for he says, *I am from him (viz.* the Father, by eternal generation;) *and he hath sent me*, (with respect to office,) John vii. 29.

Q. What did the eternal Son of God become, that he might redeem man?—A. He became man; which was the greatest wonder that the world ever saw, 1 Tim. iii. 16.

Q. Of what was Christ's becoming man a wonder?—A. A wonder of love, wisdom, power, faithfulness, &c.

Q. How was it a wonder of love?—A. As God took on him the likeness of sinful flesh, out of infinite pity to poor, vile, rebellious men, John iii. 16. Rom. viii. 3.

Q. How was it a wonder of wisdom?—A. It was the most curious work of God, and a proper mean of bringing the highest glory to God, and greatest good to men, out of sin the greatest evil, Jer. xxxi. 22.

Q. How was it a wonder of power?—A. Herein the most distant natures were closely joined together.

Q. How was it a wonder of divine faithfulness?—A. Herein the most difficult like promise was fulfilled.

Q. Did Christ cease to be God when he became man? —A. No; but he became *Immanuel, God man*, Isa. vii. 14.

Q. Was Christ, *as God*, in the least changed when he became man?—A. No; neither in person nor in nature.

Q. How many natures hath Christ?—A. Two; the nature of God, and the nature of man, Rom. ix. 5.

Q. Are these two natures in Christ mixed together, or turned into one another?—**A.** No; they are distinct natures, 1 Pet. iii. 18. Rom. ix. 5. Isa. ix. 6.

Q. What do you understand by their being distinct natures?—**A.** That each of them still retains its own essential properties.

Q. Is Christ's divine nature, by its union with the human, become finite, dependent, or subject to suffering or motion?—**A.** No; John iii. 13. Isa. xl. 28.

Q. Is the human nature of Christ, by its exaltation and union to the divine, infinite, independent, almighty, knowing all things, or every where present?—**A.** By no means; for that would infer, that a creature might be made God; than which nothing can be more absurd.

Q. Why was it necessary that our Saviour should be both God and man?—**A.** That he might be qualified for executing his general and particular offices, Isa. ix. 6.

Q. Why was his being God and man necessary to his being our *Mediator?*—**A.** That he might be nearly interested in, and have due zeal for the rights of both parties, 1 Tim. ii. 5, 6. Heb. ii. 17.

Q. Why was his being God and man necessary to his being our *Redeemer?*—**A.** That he might have a sufficient price to give, and almighty power to exert for our deliverance, Heb. vii. 25. and ix. 14.

Q. Why was it necessary that he should be God to execute his prophetical office?—**A.** That he might at once know the whole will of God, be present with his disciples every where, and teach them to profit, John i. 18.

Q. Why was Christ's being man necessary to his being our prophet?—**A.** That he might teach us in a way adapted to our weakness, and exemplify the truths which he taught in his own life, John xiii. 15.

Q. Why was it necessary that Christ should be God to execute his priestly office?—**A.** That he might bear infinite wrath, *give worth and efficacy to his obedience and suffering*, and render his intercession ever prevalent.

Q. Why was it necessary that he should be man to execute his priestly office?—**A.** That in his obedience and suffering he might pay that very debt which we owed to God; might in our nature appear in the presence of God for us; and experimentally sympathize with us in trouble.

Q. Why was it necessary that he should be God to execute his kingly office?—**A.** That he might know the cases, ånd subdue the hearts of his subjects; rule, defénd, and highly exalt them ; and conquer all théir enemies.

Q. Why was it necessary that Christ should be man to execute his kingly office ?—A. That he might enforce obedience to his laws by his own example, and have a tender regard for his subjects.

Q. In what are Christ's divine and human nature united ? —A. In his divine person, Isa. ix. 6.

Q. How many persons hath Christ ?—A. One only, and which is a divine person, Isa. ix. 6.

Q What is the difference between a human nature and a human person ?—A. A human person subsists by itself; but a human nature subsists in a person.

Q. How can Christ have the nature of man without the person of man ?—A. Because his human nature never subsisted by itself, but was, in its very formation, assumed into his divine person, John i. 14.

Q. Is not Christ's human nature, by the want of its proper personality, rendered more imperfect than the human nature in other men ?—A. No ; it is hereby highly dignified, as the place of a *human* is supplied with a *divine* personality, Isa. vii. 14. and ix. 6, John i. 14.

Q. Is Christ then the same person he was from eternity ?—A. Yes; though a human nature is united to that person.

Q. Whether is Christ's human nature united immediately to his person, or to the divine nature ?—A. It is united immediately to his person, and to the divine nature, as subsisting in his person, John i. 14, Isa. ix. 6.

Q. How prove you that ?—A. If it were united immediately to the divine nature, it would be equally united to the Father and Holy Ghost with the Son, since the nature is the same in all the divine persons, 1 John i. 7.

Q. How was the union between Christ's two natures constituted ?—A. By Christ's assuming the human nature into his divine person, Heb. ii. 14. 16, John i. 14.

Q. Wherein did Christ's assumption of the human nature differ from the union of his two natures ?—A. Assumption is a transient act of his divine nature *only*, and is the cause of union ; but this union is the *effect*, and is an eternal mutual relation of both his natures.

Q. How can the human nature be united to the divine, which exists every where ?—A. Though Christ's divine nature transcends his human nature, in respect of its infinity ;

9*

yet it wholly dwells in it, in respect of its spirituality, Col. ii. 9, John. i. 14, 1 Tim. iii. 16.

Q. How do you prove that Christ's two natures are united, and do subsist *in one person*?—A. Because the same person is called the *child born*, and the *mighty God*, Isa. ix. 6. See also Luke i. 35, Rom. ix. 5.

Q. Why was it necessary that our redeemer should be God and man *in one person*?—A. That the works of each nature might be accepted of God, and relied on by us, *as the works of his whole person*, Heb. ix. 14.

Q. What are the properties of the union betwixt Christ's two natures?—A. It is an incomprehensible, personal, everlasting, and indissoluble union.

Q. How is it *incomprehensible*?—A. No man or angel can fully understand the mysteries of it, 1 Tim. iii. 16.

Q. How is it a *personal* union?—A. The two distinct natures are united and subsist in one person, Isa. ix. 6.

Q. How is this union everlasting and indissoluble?—A. As Christ's natures never will, nor can be separated.

Q. How prove you that?—A. From the eternity of Christ's priesthood, which requires the eternal union of his two natures to appear with, in the presence of God for us, Heb. vii. 25, Rev. i. 18.

Q. What other wonderful unions besides this are there? —A. There is the union of the three persons in the Godhead; the natural union of our soul and body; and the mystical union of believers with Christ.

Q. How doth the union of Christ's two natures differ from the union of the persons in the Godhead?—A. The union of persons in the Godhead is an *uncreated* and *necessary* union of distinct persons in one nature and substance; but this in Christ is a created union of distinct natures in one person, Exod. iii. 14. Jer. xxxi. 22.

Q. How doth the union of Christ's natures differ from the union of our soul and body?—A. The union of our soul and body is *natural*, and can be *broken;* but this union of Christ's natures is *supernatural* and *inseparable*.

Q. How doth the union of Christ's natures differ from the union of believers to Christ?—A. Notwithstanding believers union to Christ, he and they remain *distinct persons;* but the union of Christ's natures makes both *one person*, John xv. 1—5. Isa. ix. 6. and vii. 14.

Q. What follows upon the union of these two natures in the person of Christ?—A. That the properties and works of both natures may be ascribed to his person: so we may say, the son of David or Mary, *is God, infinite, eternal,* &c.; and that *God,* or *the Son of God,* is *man, was born, died, shed his blood, rose again,* &c.

Q. May we say, Christ *as God* is man, was born, died, &c.; or that Christ *as man* is God, infinite, &c.?—A. No; this would confound the properties of Christ's nature.

Q. When did the Son of God assume our nature, and become man?—A. About 1794 years ago.

Q. How prove you that Christ is already come?—A. Because sundry events have happened which God declared should not take place till his Son became man.

Q. What are some of these events?—A. The departure of the sceptre from Judah, the destruction of the second temple, the loss of David's line, the end of Daniel's seventy weeks, and ceasing of the daily sacrifice, &c.

Q. Who is the promised Messiah, or incarnate God?— A. *Jesus of Nazareth,* the son of Mary, John i. 45.

Q. How prove you that?—A. All things foretold concerning the Messiah, were exactly fulfilled in him.

Q. What was foretold concerning the Messiah?—A. That before the church and second temple of the Jews should be destroyed, or their nation dispersed, he should spring out of the family of David; be born at Bethlehem of a virgin, in a low condition; work many miracles; be despised, crucified and buried; rise again and erect a glorious church among the Gentile nations, &c.

Q. How is the time of Christ's coming designated in scripture?—A. It is called *the fulness of time,* Gal. iv. 4.

Q. Why is it called *the fulness of time?*—A. It was the time fixed in God's decree, foretold by the prophets, and when the world was in the most proper condition for his coming into it, Hag. ii. 6—9.

Q. When was the world in the most proper condition for Christ's coming?—A. When it had been sufficiently warned of, and strongly expected his coming; and when Satan's power over it was at its height, ignorance and knowledge jointly subserving his interests.

Q. Why was it necessary that the world should be well warned concerning Christ before he came?—A. That he might come with due honour; and that many signs of his coming might be understood, whereby it might be tried whether he was the true Messiah, and no impostor.

Q. Why was it necessary that the world should be in

great expectation of Christ when he came?—A. That all
might be ready to examine his character and conduct, and
be rendered inexcusable, if they did not receive him.

Q. Why was it necessary that Satan's power over the
world should be very strong when Christ came?—A. That
the love of God in sending him, the need of his coming,
and its powerful influence in destroying Satan's kingdom
when at its height, might be the more visibly displayed,
1 John iv. 9, 10. and iii. 8. John iii. 16.

Q. How did Christ the Son of God become man?—A.
By taking to himself a true body, and a reasonable soul;
which are the two parts of a human nature.

Q. How prove you that Christ took on himself a true
body, and not the mere shape of the human body?—A.
Christ says, *A spirit hath not flesh and bones, as ye see me
have;* neither could he have been born, hungered, thirsted,
or died, &c., without having a true body.

Q. Was Christ's body framed in heaven, or created immediately out of dust?—A. No; it was made of the substance *of a woman;* and so he was *the seed of the woman,*
Gal. iv. 4. Gen. ii. 15.

Q. Why was it necessary it should be made of the substance of mankind?—A. That he might be our brother
and kinsman, and the right of our redemption be his.

Q. Of whom was he born?—A. Of the Virgin Mary.

Q. Why was Christ born of a virgin?—A. That he
might be free from original sin, Luke i. 35.

Q. Why behoved Christ's human nature to be free from
sin?—A. Because it was so closely united to his divine nature; and because otherwise he could not have been a propitiation for our sins, Heb. vii. 26, 2 Cor. v. 21.

Q. How could Christ be born of a virgin?—A. He was
conceived by the power of the Holy Ghost.

Q. Why is this work of the Holy Ghost called an *over-
shadowing* of the virgin?—A. Because of the great myste-
riousness of it, Luke i. 35.

Q. How prove you that Christ assumed a reasonable
soul?—A. He cried out, *My soul is troubled and exceeding
sorrowful;* and God made *his soul an offering for sin.*

Q. Had all the three persons of the Godhead an active
concern in the Son's becoming man?—A. Yes.

Q. What distinct concern had they in it?—A. The Father prepared this human nature, the Spirit formed, and
the Son assumed or put it on, and wears it for ever.

Q. What were the Old Testament names of our Redeemer?—A. Shiloh, Messiah, Immanuel, David, the Branch, the Messenger or Angel, &c. Gen. xlix. 10, &c.

Q. Why is he called *Shiloh?*—A. Properly because he is our peace, salvation, and rest, Micah v. Isa. xi.

Q. Why is he called *Messiah?*—A. Because he is the anointed of God, Psalm lxxxix. 20, Isa. lxi. 1, 2, 3.

Q. Why is he called *Immanuel?*—A. Because he is God with us in our nature, and on our side, Isa. ix. 6.

Q. Why is he called *David?*—A. Because he is a man after God's heart, and king of his true Israel, Hos. iii. 5.

Q. Why is he called *the Branch?*—A. Because in our nature he is a stem growing out of the root of Jesse, which bears fruit of glory to God, and good to men, Isa. iv. 2, and xi. 1, Zech. iii. 8, and vi. 12.

Q. Why is he called *the Angel and Messenger of the covenant?*—A. Because God sent him on the errand of our redemption, and he proclaims his covenant to us, Mal. iii. 1.

Q. What is our Redeemer's most ordinary New Testament name?—A. The Lord Jesus Christ, 2 Tim. iv. 1.

Q. Why is he called *Lord?*—A. Because he is the true God, and rules over all, Acts x. 36, Matth. xxviii. 18.

Q. Why is he called *Jesus?*—A. Because he saves his people from their sin and misery, Matth. i. 21, and xviii. 11.

Q. Why is he called *Christ?*—A. Because he was anointed by God to his mediatory offices, John x. 36.

Q. Wherewith was Christ anointed by God?—A. With the oil of the Holy Ghost, Isa. lxi. 1, 2.

Q. In what proportion was Christ anointed?—A. He had the Spirit given him above measure, John iii. 34.

Q. Is his human nature filled with an *infinite* fulness of the Spirit?—A. No; but he is anointed with it far above the measure of believers who are his fellows, Psalm xlv. 7.

Q. What do you understand by the anointing of Christ? —A. God's giving him a commission and call to his offices, with proper furniture for the execution of them.

Q. When did God first call Christ to his offices?—A. From all eternity, Prov. viii. 23, 1 Pet. i. 20.

Q. When did God first furnish Christ for executing his offices?—A. In his incarnation, Luke i. 35.

Q. When did God publicly install Christ in his offices? —A. At his baptism, Matth. iii. 16, 17.

Q. How was Christ then installed in his offices?—A.

The Father solemnly attested him, and the Spirit descended on him, to furnish him further for his work.

Q. Why are New Testament believers called Christians? —A. Because they follow Christ, and are anointed with his Spirit, 1 Cor. xii. 12, 13, 1 John ii. 20.

Q. What improvement should we make of Christ's incarnation and unction?—A. We should admire, love, adore, marry, and trust in the person of Christ as our near kinsman; and cry for his Spirit to anoint us.

Q. 23. *What Offices doth Christ execute as our Redeemer?*

A. Christ, as our Redeemer, executeth the office of a prophet, of a priest, and of a king, both in his estate of humiliation and exaltation.

Q. To what different kinds of offices was Christ anointed?—A. To general and particular offices.

Q. Wherein do Christ's general and particular offices differ?—A. Christ's general offices are executed in every thing which he doth for our salvation; but his several particular offices are executed only in part of his work.

Q. To what general offices was Christ anointed?—A. To that of Mediator and Redeemer.

Q. What is the business of a Mediator?—A. It is to reconcile parties at variance, Job ix. 33.

Q. Between whom is Christ a Mediator?—A. Between God and sinful men, 1 Tim. ii. 5.

Q. Can there be any other Mediator between God and man?—A. No; for none other has a proper interest in both parties; nor can any lay his hand upon them both for their reconciliation, Job ix. 33, 1 Tim. ii. 5, 6.

Q. How hath Christ a proper interest in both parties?—A. He is God's son, and our brother and kinsman.

Q. By what doth Christ remove God's *legal* enmity against us?—A. By his righteousness and intercession.

Q. How doth Christ stay our *real* enmity against God? —A. By enlightening our minds and subduing our wills.

Q. What do you mean by a Redeemer?—A. One who recovers back that which is forfeited and enslaved.

Q. From what doth Christ redeem us sinful men?—A. From our spiritual slavery and bondage, Tit. ii. 14.

Q. To whom are we naturally in spiritual bondage?—A. To law and justice, to sin and Satan, Isa. xlix. 24.

Q. By what means doth Christ redeem sinners?—A. By price and power, or by purchase and conquest.

Q. How doth he redeem us from the law and justice of God?—A. By the infinite price of his blood, 1 Peter i. 19·

Q. How doth Christ redeem us from sin and Satan?—A. By the infinite power of his Spirit, in teaching, subduing, ruling and defending us, Psalm cx. 2, 3.

Q. Why is not a price given to sin and Satan, as well as to the law and justice of God?—A. Because sin and Satan have no *just right* to enslave sinners, except what depends upon the law and justice of God, 1 Cor. xv. 56.

Q. Who typified Christ *as our Redeemer?*—A. The kinsman redeemer under the law, in his redeeming his brother, or near kinsman, Ruth iv., Lev. xxvii.

Q. In what doth our redemption by Christ resemble that?—A. Christ buys back our persons from slavery, and our inheritance from mortgage; he avengeth our blood upon Satan our murderer; and, by marriage with our nature and persons, he raiseth up a seed of saints, and fruits of good works, Rev. v., Isa. lxiii., John xv.

Q. To what particular offices was Christ anointed?—A. To the offices of prophet, priest, and king.

Q. Did ever these three offices properly meet in any other?—A. No; but Christ is *the way* to God as a priest, *the truth* as a prophet, *and the life* as a king, John xiv. 6.

Q. How do you prove that Christ is a prophet?—A. The scriptures call him *a prophet like to Moses.*

Q. How do you prove that Christ is a priest?—A. He is often so called in scripture, and God swears that he is *a priest for ever*, Psalm cx. 4, Heb. v. vii.

Q. How do you prove that Christ is a king?—A. The scripture often affirms it, and God calls him his *king set upon his holy hill of Zion*, Psalm ii. 6.

Q. Why behoved Christ to have all these three offices?—A. To cure our threefold misery of ignorance, guilt, and bondage, Acts xxvi. 18, Col. i. 13, Titus ii. 14.

Q. How doth Christ cure our ignorance?—A. By becoming the *wisdom of God* to us as a prophet.

Q. How doth Christ cure our guilt?—A. By becoming *the Lord our righteousness* as a priest. 1 Cor. i. 30.

Q. How doth Christ deliver us from bondage?—A. By becoming our *sanctification* and *redemption* as a king.

Q. What connection hath our salvation with these offices

of Christ ?—A. He purchased our salvation as a priest, reveals it as a prophet, and applieth it as a king.

Q. What connection have the gospel promises in general with these three offices of Christ ?—A. Christ reveals the promises as a prophet, confirms them by his blood as a priest, and applieth them as a king.

Q. Are Christ's offices the *proper fountain* of the gospel-promises in the original making of them ?—A. No ; in that respect they flow from the infinite, free, and sovereign love of God, Jer. xxxi. 3.

Q. Doth not the accomplishment of the promises on us flow from the offices of Christ ?—A. Yes ; 2 Cor. i. 20.

Q. What promises are accomplished by Christ's executing the office of a prophet ?—A. The promises of light, leading knowledge, and instruction, Isa. xlviii. 17.

Q. What promises stand immediately connected with Christ's priestly office ?—A. The promises of pardon, peace, reconciliation, acceptance, &c. Isa. liii. 5. 11.

Q. What promises are accomplished by Christ's executing his kingly office ?—A. The promises of regeneration, sanctification, defence, and preservation from enemies, and victory over them, &c. Psalm cx. 2—6.

Q. In what different orders do Christ's offices stand related to one another ?—A. In their natural order of dependence upon one another, and in their order of execution upon the hearts of sinners.

Q. How do they stand in their *natural order* ?—A. The *priestly* office possesses the first place, the *prophetical* the second, and the *kingly* the last, Psalm xxii.

Q. Why must Christ's priestly office stand first in the natural order ?—A. Because divine justice cannot admit of our being blessed with instruction or deliverance, till first in order of nature our sins be atoned for ; and God, as reconciled through Christ's death, must be the matter which he as a prophet doth teach ; and his blood must be the price of his kingdom, Isa. liii. 2—12, Psalm ii. 8—11.

Q. Why must Christ's prophetical office stand before his kingly ?—A. Because his saving instructions are the means of our subjection to him as our king, Isa. liv. 13.

Q. Where is this natural order of Christ's offices clearly represented ?—A. In the 22d Psalm ; where Christ first suffers as a priest, then declares God's name to his brethren as a prophet, and at last becomes governor among the nations as a king.

Q. What is the order of Christ's offices in their execution upon us?—A. The prophetical office possesseth the first place, the priestly the second, and the kingly the last.

Q. Why must his prophetical office be first executed on us?—A. Because till we are savingly taught by him as our prophet, we can neither know, nor believe in him as our priest for remission and acceptance, Gal. i. 15, 16.

Q. Why must the priestly office stand before the kingly in this order of execution upon us?—A. Because till the death of Christ as a priest be applied to our conscience, for removing our guilt, and staying our enmity against God, there can be no deliverance from the bondage of sin, or subjection to Christ as a king, Heb. ix. 22, &c.

Q. Is it very dangerous to invert the true order of Christ's offices?—A. Yes; it is ruining to our souls.

Q. Who invert this order?—A. Such as place Christ's kingly office before his priestly, by teaching, that Christ in the gospel has given us a new law of sincere obedience, by observance of which, we become entitled to Christ and his righteousness, Rom. ix. 31, 32.

Q. What is the danger of that doctrine?—A. It makes our justification to depend on the works of the law.

Q. Do sinners close with all Christ's offices at once?—A. Yes; Christ cannot be divided, 1 Cor. i. 13.

Q. To which of these offices must we fly for justifying righteousness?—A. Only to the priestly, Rom. iii. 24.

Q. Doth Christ fully execute all his offices?—A. Yes.

Q. What mean you by Christ's *executing* his offices?—A. His doing the work which belongs to each of them.

Q. In what estates doth Christ execute his offices?—A. In his estate of humiliation, and of exaltation.

Q. Why did he first in order of nature execute them in an estate of humiliation?—A. Because by his humiliation he procured to himself the honour of executing them in an estate of exaltation, Phil. ii. 7—10, Isa. liii.

Q. How long shall Christ continue to execute his offices?—A. To all eternity, Heb. xiii. 8.

Q. How prove you that Christ will be a prophet for ever?—A. From the Lamb's (or Christ's) being called the light of heaven, which is *everlasting*, Isa. lx. 19.

Q. How prove you that Christ will be a priest forever?—A. God sware to him, *Thou art a priest for ever*, Psalm cx. 4, Heb. vii. 3. 16. 24, 25. 28.

Q. How prove you that Christ will be a king for ever?

10

—A. *Of his kingdom there shall be no end; and he shall reign for ever*, Isa. ix. 7, Luke i. 35, Psalm xlv. 6.

Q. How should we improve these offices of Christ?—A. By receiving and employing him in them all in their due order, for wisdom, righteousness, and sanctification.

Q. 24. *How doth Christ execute the office of a prophet?*

A. Christ executeth the office of a prophet, in revealing to us, by his word and Spirit, the will of God for our salvation.

Q. Why is Christ called a *prophet?*—A. Because he reveals and teacheth men the will of God, Deut. xviii. 18.

Q. Hath Christ any other names relating to this work and office?—A. Yes; he is also called an apostle, interpreter, witness, and the Word of God, Heb. iii. &c.

Q. Why is Christ called an *apostle?*—A. Because he is sent of God to make a perfect revelation of his will, and to erect his church on earth, Heb. i. 1. and iii. 1.

Q. Why is Christ called an *Interpreter?*—A. Because he explains the mysteries, or hidden things of God, Job xxxiii. 23.

Q. Why is Christ called a *Witness?*—A. Because he attests the truths of God, John xviii. 37.

Q. By what doth he attest them?—A. In his person, and by his declarations, miracles, death, and sacraments.

Q. How doth Christ attest divine truths in his *person?*— A. The great truths of God are clearly represented, and have their certainty evidenced in the *constitution of his person as God-man*, 1 Tim. iii. 16, John i. 14.

Q. How doth Christ attest divine truth by his *declarations?*—A. He affirms them by his word, and confirms them by his oath, 2 Cor. i. 22, Heb. vi. 17.

Q. How doth Christ attest divine truths by his death?— A. He suffered it from men for his adherence to truth; and the leading truths of God are clearly exemplified and displayed in his death, Rom. viii. 32, 33. and iii. 24—26.

Q. How doth Christ attest them by his *sacraments?*—A. The sacraments represent the doctrines, seal the promises, and bind us to obey the commands of God.

Q. Why doth Christ attest divine truths?—A. They are wonderful; and sinners are slow of heart to believe them, 1 Tim. iii. 16, Luke xxiv. 25.

Q. Why is Christ called *the word of God?*—A. Because by him the mind of God is made known ; and he is the matter of his word, 2 Cor. i. 20, Heb. i. 1.

Q. Why was Christ made a prophet ?—A. Because none else could teach sinners *to profit*, John i. 18, Isaiah xlviii. 17.

Q. What'doth Christ teach us ?—A. The will of God.

Q. What of God's will doth Christ teach us ?—A. Whatever is needful for our salvation, Isa. xlviii. 17.

Q. In what periods doth Christ teach men the will of God ?—A. Both under the Old and the New Testament.

Q. How prove you that he taught it under the Old Testament ?—A. The scripture affirms he preached to the old world, and spake to Moses in Mount Sinai, 1 Peter iii. 19.

Q. How prove you that Christ continued to teach it under the New Testament ?—A. The scriptures represent him as *yet* speaking from heaven, Heb. xii. 25, and i. 1.

Q. By whom hath Christ revealed the will of God to men ?—A. By himself, and by others, Luke xx. 9. 13.

Q. How hath he revealed it by himself?—A. In voices, visions, dreams, and his personal ministry on earth.

Q. How hath he revealed the will of God by others ?—A. By qualifying and sending angels, prophets, apostles, and ordinary pastors and teachers, to declare it.

Q. In what doth Christ as a prophet excel all these ?—A. Christ is their Lord, hath all furniture in himself, and teacheth effectually : others are servants, receive their furniture from him, and cannot teach *to profit*, John vi. 63.

Q. By what means doth Christ reveal the will of God to men ?—A. By his word and Spirit, Luke v. 17.

Q. Is the word alone sufficient to teach us the will of God ?—A. No; for it cannot give the blind their sight to discern the glory of divine truths, Isa. vi. 9, 10.

Q. May men have the gospel faithfully preached to them, and yet not profit thereby?—A. Yes; Nothing is more common : *Many are called but few chosen.*

Q. Whence doth this proceed?—A. From men's not mixing faith with the word when they hear it, Heb. iv. 2.

Q. When God's word doth not profit hearers, what effect hath it on them?—A. It hardens their hearts, and becomes the savour of death to them, Isa. vi. 10.

Q. What then can make the teaching of the word effectual to salvation ?—A. Only the teaching of the Spirit.

Q. How doth Christ teach us by his Spirit?—**A.** He opens our understanding by the word, and makes us see the beauty of divine things, and fall in love with them.

Q. Doth ever the Spirit teach men without the word?—**A.** No; in such as are capable to hear it, Rom. x. 14.

Q. Can then such as want the word of God be saved by the light of nature?—**A.** No; *where no vision is, the people perish,* Prov. xxix. 18. Acts iv. 12. Rom. x. 14.

Q. Why will not Christ's Spirit teach men without the word?—**A.** To put honour upon the word, Psal. cxxxviii. 2.

Q. At what schools doth Christ teach men?—**A.** At the schools of the law, of the gospel, and of affliction.

Q. What doth Christ teach us at the school of the law?—**A.** The great evil and danger of sin, Rom. iii. 20.

Q. What doth he teach us at the school of the gospel?—**A.** That our salvation is wholly in Christ, and freely offered to us, Hos. i. 7. Rom. v. 21.

Q. What doth he teach us at the school of affliction?—**A.** The bitterness of sin, the vanity of this world, and the exercise of justifying God, resignation to his will, and desire to be with him, Hos. ii. 6—16.

Q. In what doth Christ's saving teaching and all other teaching differ?—**A.** Christ's saving teaching discovers to us our vileness and ignorance, humbles us in the dust, and makes us desire to be like Christ in holiness, and with him in glory, Job xl. 4. and xliii. 50. Isa. vi. 5.

Q. Doth Christ make all men welcome to him for instruction?—**A.** Yes; Prov. viii. 4. and ix. 4.

Q. For what end doth Christ teach sinful men?—**A.** For their salvation, Isa. liv. 13, 14. and xlv. 17. 22.

Q. Are then all those saved who are taught by Christ's word and Spirit?—**A.** Yes; John xvii. 3. 1 John v. 20.

Q. What shall become of such as refuse to hear Christ's word and Spirit?—**A.** They *shall be destroyed.*

Q. How should we improve Christ as a prophet?—**A.** By believing our own ignorance, and applying to him for instruction, Psalm cxix. 18.

Q. 25. *How doth Christ execute the office of a priest?*

A. Christ executeth the office of a priest, in his once offering up of himself a sacrifice, to satisfy divine justice, and reconcile us to God; and in making continual intercession for us.

Q. What do you mean by a priest?—A. One who, by virtue of God's appointment, offers up sacrifice to him, in the room of guilty sinners, Heb. viii. 3.

Q. What is a proper sacrifice?—A. A holy offering up of some life to God in the stead of guilty men, upon an altar, and by a priest of his appointment, Heb. v. 8.

Q. Why call you it *a holy offering*?—A. Because it was to be made to a *holy* God, in a *holy* and reverend manner, Lev. x. 3.

Q. Why call you it *the offering of a life*?—A. Because the life of the thing offered was to be taken from it in the sacrifice of it, Lev. xvii. 11.

Q. Why was the life of the thing offered to be taken from it?—A. Because without shedding of blood there can be no remission of sin, Heb. ix. 22.

Q. Why so?—A. Because man's sin is an attack upon the life of the most high God, Job xv. 25, 26.

Q. In what doth Christ's priestly office differ from his prophetical and kingly offices?—A. Christ, in the execution of his prophetical and kingly offices, deals with creatures; but in the execution of his priestly, he deals immediately with God, Heb. ii. 17. ix. 14, vii. 27.

Q. What are the two parts of Christ's priestly office?—A. His offering sacrifice, and making intercession.

Q. What sacrifice did Christ offer up?—A. He offered up himself, both soul and body, Heb. ix. 14.

Q. How prove you that he offered his soul?—A. It is said, *Thou shalt make his soul an offering for sin :* his soul was *troubled* and *sorrowful :* nor could he have atoned for the sin of our souls, if he had not offered his own in sacrifice, Isa. liii. 10. &c. John xii. 27.

Q. How prove you that Christ's divine nature was not properly offered in sacrifice?—A. Because his divine nature cannot suffer, 1 Tim. vi. 16.

Q. How is it then said, *He gave himself for us*?—A Because his divine person gave *infinite worth* to the offering of his human nature, Acts xx. 28. Titus ii. 14.

Q. On what altar did Christ offer his sacrifice?—A. On the altar of his divine nature, Heb. ix. 14.

Q. Of what use was the altar in sacrifices?—A. It supported, sanctified, and made valuable the gift.

Q. How prove you that the cross could not *properly* be the altar on which Christ offered his sacrifice?—A. Because it could not give value to his offering.

10*

Q. How long did Christ continue in offering himself?—
A. He began his offering in his incarnation, continued it through his life, and completed it in his death and burial.

Q. When did he most remarkably offer himself?—**A** In his agony in the garden and on the cross.

Q. What was the sword which killed, and fire which consumed this sacrifice?—**A.** The justice and wrath of God.

Q. Did not divine justice make use of men and devils as instruments in slaying this sacrifice?—**A.** Yes; but not in the severest part of its work, Zech. xiii. 7. Isa. liii. 10.

Q. Why did not an angry God make use of them in the whole of that work?—**A.** Because they could not afflict Christ with such severity as his justice required.

Q. Who was the priest that offered up Christ in sacrifice?—**A.** It was himself, Heb. ix. 14. Tit. ii. 14.

Q. Why was it necessary that Christ should offer himself?—**A.** Because a voluntary death was essentially necessary to the acceptance of this sacrifice: and none else could present this offering to God, John x. 17. Phil. ii. 7, 8.

Q. Where did Christ offer himself?—**A.** On earth.

Q. Why upon earth?—**A.** Because the earth is the theatre of that rebellion of man against God for which he atoned; and it was necessary that God should be glorified by Christ's death, where sin had dishonoured him.

Q. How often did Christ offer himself a sacrifice?—**A.** Only once, Heb. ix. 28. Rev. i. 18.

Q. Why not oftener than once?—**A.** Because his once offering, which comprehends his whole surety-righteousness, fully satisfied the law and justice of God.

Q. In whose stead did Christ offer himself?—**A.** In stead of *the elect only,* and for no other.

Q. How prove you that Christ died in the room of the elect?—**A.** The scripture affirms that their sin was *laid upon him,* and *he bare* it, and *laid down his life for them.*

Q. How prove you that he died in the room of the *elect only?*—**A.** Because he prayed for, and saves the elect only, John xvii. 9. and x. 15. Rom. xi. 7. Acts xiii. 48.

Q. Why then do other men share of gospel offers, common operations of the Spirit, and much temporal happiness?—**A.** Though Christ represented the *person of the elect only* in his death; yet others, for the elect's sake, receive these good things as the consequence of his death, Matth. xxiv. 22. Isa. lii. 15. and liii. 12.

Q. To whom did Christ offer himself?—A. To God.

Q. For what end did Christ offer himself?—A. To satisfy divine justice, and reconcile us to God, Eph. v. 2.

Q. Why did divine justice require a satisfaction?—A. Because the elect had dishonoured God, and broken his law, Isa. liii. 6. Rom. iii. 9—26

Q. What did divine justice require as a satisfaction?—A. That the curse of God's law should be executed, either upon the elect themselves, or a surety in their room.

Q. Why might they not have satisfied for themselves?—A. Because they were wicked, and could not cease from sin; and were finite, and could not give the infinite satisfaction which divine justice required, Micah vi. 6, 7.

Q. Why did divine justice require an infinite satisfaction for the sin of finite creatures?—A. Because sin had given infinite offence to God, Jer. xliv. 4. 1 John iii. 4.

Q. How could divine justice demand that satisfaction from Christ?—A. Because he had engaged to pay all the debt of the elect world, Psalm xl. 6, 7. Isa. liii. 6.

Q. How could Christ lawfully give away his life for others?—A. He was God, and his life was wholly his own, which he might dispose of as he pleased, John x. 18.

Q. Hath Christ fully satisfied God's justice for our sins?—A. Yes; his sacrifice was to God of a *sweet-smelling savour*, and *savour of rest*, Eph. v. 2. Heb. ix. 12.

Q. Why is Christ's sacrifice so called?—A. Because it entirely overcame the abominable savour of sin, and gave God's justice the sweetest rest, Isa. xlii. 21.

Q. How do you further prove that Christ *satisfied* God's justice?—A. From his saying on the cross, *It is finished;* and from his Father's raising him from the dead, and exalting him to his right hand, John xix. 30.

Q. What is the effect of Christ's satisfying divine justice?—A. Our reconciliation to God, Rom. v. 10.

Q. Did Christ's offering himself change God's dispositions towards us?—A. No; but it removed out of the way whatever hindered the manifesting of his love to us.

Q. How doth the death of Christ reconcile men's hearts to God?—A. When it is applied to their conscience, the love of God shines so brightly in it, that it slays their *enmity against God*, 1 John iv. 9, 10. 19.

Q. Is not the shedding of Christ's blood sufficient to save us?—A. No; it must also be applied to, or sprinkled on our consciences; and hence it is called, the *blood of sprinkling*, Ezek. xxxvi. 25. 1 Peter i. 2.

Q. When are we actually reconciled to God?—A. When Christ's blood is sprinkled on our consciences.

Q. How may we know that we are reconciled to God?—A. If we are made heart enemies to all sin, Ps. cxix. 104.

Q. What is the second part of Christ's priestly work?—A. His making intercession for us, Heb. ix. 24, and vii. 25.

Q. What do you understand by Christ's intercession?—A. His willing the application of his purchased redemption to his people, John xvii. Heb. vii. 25.

Q. Is Christ's intercession in heaven any part of his surety righteousness?—A. No; it is a part of his glorious reward, Heb. i. 3. and ix. 24.

Q. Might not his intercession alone have saved sinners?—A. No; for it could not satisfy God's justice, Rom. iii. 25.

Q. If God's justice be satisfied, and all blessings purchased by his sacrifice, what need is there of Christ's intercession?—A. That he may procure the possession of these blessings to the elect in such a way as best secures the glory of God, his own honour, and our welfare.

Q. How doth Christ's intercession secure the glory of God?—A. As by this means God hath no gracious dealings with sinners but through a Mediator, 2 Cor. v. 19.

Q. How doth it honour Christ?—A. In this way believers have immediate dependence on Christ for ever.

Q. How doth Christ's intercession secure the welfare of his people?—A. It renders them bold before God; and secures their grace and glory, notwithstanding their great carelessness and folly, Heb. iv. 14, 15, 16.

Q. For whom doth Christ make intercession?—A. For the elect only, John xvii. 9.

Q. For what doth he intercede to them, in their unconverted state?—A. For their preservation from hell, and in bringing into the bond of the new covenant.

Q. What intercedes he for, to them, after their conversion?—A. For their continuance in the covenant, and the constant communication of its blessings to them.

Q. How doth he obtain this?—A. By answering all accusations against them, by removing new differences between God and them, and by procuring the acceptance of what service they perform in faith, 1 John ii. 1.

Q. Who accuses believers before God?—A. Satan and their own consciences, Rev. xii. 10.

Q. Of what do they accuse believers?—A. Of continual departures from God, Zech. iii. 1.

Q. How doth Christ answer these accusations?—A. By continually presenting his righteousness as theirs before God, Heb. ix. 24.

Q. How doth he take up the new differences which sin makes between God and them?—A. By procuring new application of his blood to their consciences, 1 John ii. 1, 2.

Q. What in believers' worship tends to render it unacceptable to God?—A. The unworthiness of their persons, and the sin and weakness that attend their worship.

Q. How doth Christ cure these defects?—A. By appearing in their name, and presenting his atoning blood to God for the perfuming of their services, Rev. viii. 4.

Q. What doth Christ by his intercession procure to his people at death?—A. Abundant admission to glory.

Q. For what doth Christ intercede after their death?—A. For their resurrection and eternal continuance in glory, John xvii. 24.

Q. How long will Christ intercede for his people?—A. For ever: *He ever liveth to make intercession.*

Q. Upon what plea or ground does Christ intercede?—A. Upon the footing of his own merit or blood, which purchased *eternal redemption* for us, Heb. ix. 12. 24.

Q. Where doth Christ now intercede?—A. Within the vail in heaven, the true holy of holies, Heb. ix. 24.

Q. In what manner doth Christ intercede for us?—A. Continually, distinctly, carefully, and successfully.

Q. How is Christ's intercession *continual?*—A. He never ceases from his interceding work, Rom. viii. 34.

Q. How is it *distinct?*—A. He represents his people's case precisely as it is, Zech. i. 12, John xvii.

Q. How is it *careful?*—A. He intercedes with the greatest earnestness and zeal for our good, John xviii.

Q. How is Christ's intercession *successful?*—The Father heareth him always, John xi. 42.

Q. Can angels, or saints departed, assist Christ in his intercession?—A. No; Christ is the only *Advocate with the Father*, 1 John ii. 1, 2, Eph. ii. 18.

Q. Wherein do the intercession of Christ and of the Holy Ghost differ?—A. The Holy Ghost intercedes within us on earth by stirring us up, and directing us how to plead with our God for ourselves; but Christ intercedes without us, and presents our petitions to God, Rom. viii. 26, 27. 34, John xviii. Heb. ix. 24 and vii. 25.

Q. What singular honour hath God put upon the priesthood of Christ?—A. He made him priest *with an oath ;* and appointed more types to represent his priesthood than any of his other two offices, Psalm cx. 4, Heb. v. ix. x.

Q. Why was this peculiar honour put upon Christ's priesthood?—A. Because it is most above the light of nature, most opposed by carnal men; it gives the brightest view of the perfections of God ; it is the foundation of the other two offices, and hath the most difficult work belonging to it, 1 Peter i. 10, 11, Isa. liii.

Q. What types under the Old Testament represented Christ's priesthood?—A. The most of the types; but especially the sacrifices, altars, and priests.

Q. What was typified by all the *proper* sacrifices ?—A. The suffering of the Lord Jesus Christ, Heb. ix. 10.

Q. What was typified by the *pouring out* of the blood of the sacrifice, *burning* the fat, and sometimes the whole beast? —A. The severity of Christ's sufferings, Isa. liii. 10.

Q. What was signified by the *blood* of the sacrifice being *sprinkled* both on the altar, and on the person for whom it was offered?—A. That Christ's sufferings should both appease God and purify sinners, Heb. ix. x.

Q. What was signified by the *feasting* on the flesh of sacrifices after the fat was burnt?—A. That the sacrifice of Christ is the most proper, quickening, and nourishing entertainment for our souls, John vi. 53, Isa. xxv. 6.

Q. What did the *salting* of the sacrifice typify ?—A. The everlasting sweet savour, reconciling, and sin-killing influence of Christ's death, Eph. v. 2.

Q. What did the offering of sacrifices *every day* signify ? —A. The constant virtue of Christ's blood, and our daily need of applying it, Gal. ii. 20, John vi. 56.

Q. What were some of the most distinguished typical sacrifices ?—A. The sacrifice of the birds for the leper, of the red heifer, and especially that of universal atonement, on the tenth day of the seventh month.

Q. What did the sacrifice of the *birds* typify ?—A. The bird slain over running water, typified God's holy child Je, sus dying for our sins; and the living bird flying away after it had been dipped in the blood of the slain bird, typified his rising and ascending to glory, to present his blood before God for our justification, Rom. iv. 25.

Q. What did the burning, &c. of the *red heifer* signify?
—A. That Christ's sufferings should perfume and purify all his people in every generation, Heb. xiii. 12.

Q. What did the sacrifice of *universal atonement* signify?
—A. The slaying of one goat for all Israel typified Christ bearing all the sins of the elect in his death : and the sending the other goat into the wilderness, signified Christ's taking away, and making an end of our sins by it.

Q. What did the burning of sacrifices with *holy fire* typify?—A. That Christ as a sacrifice offered through the eternal Spirit, should be scorched and melted in the fire of the Father's wrath, Psalm xxii. 14. and lxix.

Q. What did the *altar* typify?—A. Christ's divine nature as supporting and sanctifying the human in its obedience and suffering, Heb. ix. and xiii. 10.

Q. What did the altar's being made of *stone, brass,* &c. typify?—A. The sufficiency of Christ's divine nature to support the human in his sufferings.

Q. What did the *priests,* and especially the *high priests,* typify?—A. The person of Christ as our priest.

Q. What did the washings and freedom from blemishes in priests and sacrifices, typify?—A. The perfection and purity of Christ and his righteousness, Heb. vii. 26.

Q. What was typified by the *vast number* of priests?—A. The great extent and importance of Christ's work as our great High Priest, Heb. vii. viii. ix.

Q. What did their *robes,* especially those of the high priest, typify?—A. Christ's *glorious* righteousness.

Q. What did the high priest's *mitre* typify?—A. That Christ is both king and priest, Heb. i. and v.

Q. What did his *Urim* and *Thummim* signify?—A. The infinite knowledge and perfection of Christ.

Q. What did the high priest's bearing the names of all the tribes of Israel *on his breast plate* signify?—A. That Christ has all the elect's names engraven on his heart, and continually represents them before God.

Q. What did the high priest's *going in once a year to the holy of holies,* to present the blood of atonement, typify?
—A. Christ's ascending once for all into heaven, to present his sacrifice to God in the name of his people.

Q. Why might not one type have sufficed to represent Christ?—A. All types were created and imperfect things, whereas Christ's person and work was divine.

Q. In what did Christ resemble the Old Testament

priests ?—A. He, like them, had God's call; was taken from among, and represented his guilty brethren.

Q. In what did Christ excel the Old Testament priests ? —A. In his person, instalment, order and duration of office; and in the nature, extent, and efficacy of his work.

Q. How doth Christ excel them in his *person ?*—A. He is *Immanuel, God man ;* and they were but sinful men, Isa. ix. 6, Heb. vii. 27.

Q. How doth he excel them in his *instalment* into his office?—A. He was installed by God, *with an oath ;* but they by men, *without an oath,* Heb. vii. 21.

Q. How doth Christ excel them in his *order* of office ? —A. They were priests after the *order of Aaron ;* but he is a priest after the *order of Melchizedek,* Heb. vii.

Q. In what did Melchizedek typify Christ ?—A. In the dignity and eternity of his priesthood.

Q. How doth Christ excel the Old Testament priests in duration of office ?—A. They did not continue *by reason of death,*and their priesthood is now abolished ; but Christ's priesthood is eternal and *unchangeable.*

Q. How doth he excel them in the nature of his work ? —A. They offered *beasts,* &c.; Christ offered *himself.*

Q. How doth he excel them in the extent of his work ? —A. They were many, and each had but a small share of work ; but Christ *alone* performs the whole works of the priesthood for all the elect, Heb. x. 14, and ix. 12. 14.

Q. Why then are believers called *priests unto God ?*— A. Because they are clothed with Christ's righteousness ; and in his name offer sacrifice, *not of atonement,* but of praise and thanksgiving to God, Rev. i. iv. and v.

Q. How doth Christ excel the Old Testament priests in the *efficacy* of his sacrifice ?—A. Their sacrifices in themselves never pleased God nor took away sin ; but his sacrifice perfectly satisfied divine justice, and made an end of our sin, Heb. x. 1. 14.

Q. How should we improve the priesthood of Christ ?— A. By making his righteousness and intercession the only ground of our confidence before God ; and by boldly asking in his name whatever blessings we need.

Q. 26. *How doth Christ execute the office of a King?*
A. Christ executeth the office of a king, in subduing us to himself, in ruling and defending us, and in restraining and conquering all his and our enemies.

Q. Why is Christ called a *king*?—**A.** Because he gives law to, and rules over many subjects, Psalm cx.

Q. What different kingdoms hath Christ?—**A.** An essential and mediatorial kingdom.

Q. What is the essential kingdom of Christ?—**A.** That dominion which he, *as God*, hath over all things.

Q. What is his mediatorial kingdom?—**A.** That dominion which he hath over the Church, and all the concerns of it.

Q. In what do these two kingdoms differ?—**A.** He hath the essential kingdom by nature ; but he hath the mediatorial kingdom by his own purchase, and his Father's gift, Phil. ii. 7—10, Matth. xxviii. 18.

Q. What ensigns of royalty or kingly honour are ascribed to Christ in scripture?—**A.** A palace, throne, sceptre, ambassadors, armies, tribute, and laws, &c.

Q. What is Christ's *palace*?—**A.** Heaven.

Q. What *thrones* hath Christ, and where do they stand? —**A.** Christ hath a throne of grace in his church on earth, a throne of glory in heaven, and a throne of judgment, probably in the air at the last day, Heb. iv. 16.

Q. What *sceptre* hath Christ?—**A.** The golden sceptre of the gospel, and the iron sceptre of his wrath, Psalm cx.

Q. Of what use is his golden sceptre?—**A.** To gather, subdue, strengthen, and comfort his people, Psalm cx. 3.

Q. Of what use is his iron sceptre?—**A.** To punish and destroy his incorrigible enemies, Psalm ii. 9.

Q. Who are Christ's *ambassadors*?—**A.** Sometimes angels, but especially gospel-ministers, 2 Cor. v. 20.

Q. Is it not high treason for any to intrude themselves into this office without Christ's call?—**A.** Yes.

Q. What *armies* hath Christ?—**A.** The heavenly armies of angels, saints, stars, &c. and the armies of hell and earth, Rev. xix. 14, and xii. 16.

Q. What is Christ's *tribute* or revenue?—**A.** All the service and praise of angels and saints ; and he makes even his enemies' wrath to praise him, Psalm lxxvi. 10.

Q. Of what nature is Christ's mediatorial kingdom?— **A.** Of a spiritual nature, and *not of this world*.

Q. Do civil magistrates derive their authority from Christ as Mediator?—**A.** No ; for God acknowledgeth the authority of *Pagan* magistrates, Jer. xxvii. 17.

Q. How may Christ's mediatorial kingdom be distinguished?—**A.** Into his kingdoms of grace and of glory.

Q. How do these differ?—**A.** His kingdom of grace is

11

on earth, amidst enemies, and consists of imperfect subjects; but his kingdom of glory is in heaven, and consists only of perfect subjects, Psalm cx. 2, 3, &c.

Q. For what different ends hath Christ erected his kingdoms of grace and glory?—A. His kingdom of grace is erected for gathering and gaining subjects to him; but his kingdom of glory is for making them fully happy.

Q. How is Christ's kingdom of grace distinguished?—A. Into his visible and invisible kingdom.

Q. What is Christ's visible kingdom or church?—A. The society of them who, in all ages and places, do profess the true religion, and their children.

Q. What is Christ's invisible kingdom of grace?—A. True believers, in the hidden man of whose heart Christ reigns, Luke xxvii. 20, 21, Rom. xiv. 17.

Q. Are not the unconverted elect members of this invisible kingdom of grace?—A. They are intended, but not actual members of it, Col. i. 13.

Q. Why is Christ's church on earth called *militant?*—A. Because the members of it are daily called to fight with sin, Satan, and the world, Eph. vi. 10—20.

Q. Why is his church in heaven called triumphant?—A. Because their only work is to sing and share of Christ's victories, Rev. vii. and xv. Isa. li. 11. and xxxv. 10.

Q. When did Christ enter on the execution of his kingly office?—A. When he published the first promise.

Q. When was he most solemnly installed in this office?—A. When he ascended into heaven, Dan. vii. 13, 14.

Q. When will he most fully display his royal power?—A. At the last day, 1. Tim. iv. 14, 15, 16. Rev. 20

Q. Over whom doth Christ exercise his kingly office?—A. Over his people, and over his and their enemies.

Q. How doth he exercise it over his people?—A. In subduing, ruling, and defending them.

Q. How doth he deliver them from bondage by these acts?—A. He brings them out of bondage by subduing them? he prevents their voluntary return to bondage by ruling them; and saves them from being driven back to bondage by defending them, Psalm cx. Jer. xxxiv.

Q. Why must Christ first in order subdue his people?—A. Because by nature they are his enemies, Rom. viii. 7.

Q. By what means doth Christ subdue us to himself?—A. By his word and Spirit, Psalm cx. 3. Acts xxvi. 18.

Q. How do these subdue us to Christ?—A. The Spirit

by the word, applies the blood of Christ and love of God to our consciences, renews our hearts, slays our enmity, and constrains us to yield ourselves to Christ.

Q. What is the language of the soul, when thus melted and overcome by the love of Christ?—A. It is, *Truly I am thy seraant: thou hast loosed my bonds*, Psalm cxvi. 16.

Q. From what bonds doth Christ loose us?—A. From the bonds of the guilt, filth, and power of sin, which bind us in the kingdom and prison of Satan, Zech. ix. 11.

Q. How doth he loose the bond of sin's guilt?—A. By applying his blood to our conscience for justification.

Q. How doth he loose the bonds of sin's filth and reigning power?—A. By shedding abroad the love of God in our hearts, for melting, purging, and renewing it.

Q. What is the effect of this loosing of bonds?—A. We are hereby translated from the kingdom of Satan, to the kingdom of Christ, Col. i. 13. Acts xxvi. 18.

Q. How doth Christ exercise his dominion over those whom he hath subdued?—A. He rules in and over them.

Q. Doth he free them from their obligations to magistrates, masters, and other superiors?—A. No; he requires that such be obeyed in all things lawful, Titus iii. 1.

Q. By what doth Christ rule his people?—A. By his word and Spirit, Jer. xxxi. 33.

Q. How doth he rule them by his word?—A. By giving them laws to direct their conversation.

Q. What laws doth he give them?—A. The law of the ten commandments as a rule of life, 1 Cor. ix. 21.

Q. By what motive doth he excite them to obedience? —A. By the motives of gracious rewards when they obey, and of heavy chastisements when they offend.

Q. How doth Christ rule his people by his Spirit?—A. He thereby gradually writes his law upon their hearts, and excites and enables them to keep it.

Q. Doth not he sometimes make providence a mean of ruling them?—A. Yes; he thereby often hedgeth them in to their duty, Hos. ii. 6, 7.

Q. How are believers safe in the paths of duty?—A. By Christ defending them, Psalm xci. Isa. xxxi. 5.

Q. From whom doth Christ defend his people?—A. From all their enemies, Psalm xci. 10. 1 Pet. iii. 13.

Q. Who are their enemies?—A. Sin, Satan, the world, and death; the worst of which is indwelling sin.

Q. How doth Christ defend believers from sin?—A. By

keping alive the spark of their grace in an ocean of corruption, till it be quite dried up, Rom. vii.

Q. How doth he defend them from Satan?—A. By a close application of his own blood to their consciences for the quenchiug of his fiery darts, and by strengthening their grace in oposition to his temptations.

Q. How doth he defend them from the world?—A By outward dispensation of providence, and such powerful impressions of his love on their hearts, as overbalance the influence of the smiles or frowns of the world.

Q. How doth he defend them from the hurt and fear of death?—A. By securing their eternal life, and giving them comfortable views of it, 2 Cor. v., 1 Cor. xv. 57.

Q. How doth Christ exercise his dominion over his and our enemies?—A. In restraining and conquering them.

Q. Whence is it that Christ and his people's enemies are the same?—A. He and his people are one, John xvii. 26.

Q. How doth Christ restrain his and our enemies?—A. By hindering them, even while their strength remains, to execute their attempts any further than he seeth meet for his glory and our good, Psalm lxxvi. 10.

Q. In what doth Christ limit the attacks of his enemies? A. In their kind, number, degree, and duration.

Q. How doth Christ conquer his and our enemies?—A. By taking away their power and strength; and in punishing them, if reasonable creatures, Dan. vii. 12.

Q. In what different ways doth Christ conquer his enemies? —A. Two ways: in his own person, and in the persons of his people, Psalm cx. and lxviii.

Q. In what periods are they especially conquered in his own person?—A. At his death, and at the last day.

Q. How doth Christ in his own person conquer sin?—A. By fulfilling the law, and so removing the curse, which is the strength of sin; and by condemning sin publicly at the last day, Rom. viii. 3, Matth. xxv.

. How doth Christ in his own person conquer Satan? —A. He in his death spoiled him of his warrant to be the executioner of God's justice; and he will condemn him to hell at the last day, Heb. ii. 14, Matth. xxv.

Q. How doth Christ in his own person conquer the world? A. In his life he despiseth it; in his death he crucified it to us, and delivered us from it; and he will condemn the men of it to hell at the last day.

Q. How doth Christ in his own person conquer death?—
A. In his death he unstinged it; and in his resurrection
he opened the gates of its prison, Hos. xiii. 14.

Q. Shall all his people also conquer these enemies?—A.
Yes; in him they shall be *more than conquerors.*

Q. Why say you they are conquerors *in him?*—A. Because it is only in a state of union to Christ, and in his
strength that they conquer, Rom. viii. 1. 37.

Q. How are they *more than conquerors in him?*—A.
They lose nothing, their conquest is easy and complete, and
they gain even when they seem to be conquered.

Q. How doth Christ conquer Satan in his people?—A.
By enabling them to oppose and baffle his temptations, Rom.
xvi. 20, Eph. vi. 10—16.

Q. How doth Christ conquer sin in his people?—A. By
pardoning their guilt, and making grace in their hearts
prevalent over all their lusts, Micah vii. 18, 19.

Q. How doth Christ conquer the world in his people?—
A. By raising their affections above it, and fixing them on
heavenly things, Psalm iv. 6, 7, Col. iii. 1—4.

Q. How doth Christ conquer death in his people?—A.
By making it a great gain to them, enabling them to triumph
over it, and freeing them from its bonds at the resurrection,
1 Cor. xv. 54, 55, Phil. i. 21

Q. How should we improve Christ as a king?—A. By
submitting to, loving, glorying, and trusting in him; zealously maintaining his rights of government, and fighting under his banner against his enemies.

Q. 27. Wherein did Christ's humiliation consist?
A. Christ's humiliation consisted in his being
born, and that in a low condition, made under the
law, undergoing the miseries of this life, the wrath
of God, and the cursed death of the cross; in being
buried, and continuing under the power of death for
a time.

Q. What is Christ's estate of humiliation?—A. The veil-
ing of his divine glory for a time, and appearing in this
world as *a man of sorrows* and suffering.

Q. What moved Christ to humble himself?—A. His
great love to elect sinners, Gal. ii. 20.

Q. In what did Christ humble himself?—A. In his birth,
life, death, and after his death.

11*

Q. How did he humble himself *in his birth?*—**A.** In his being conceived and born in a low condition.

Q. Was it great humiliation in Christ to be thus born? —**A.** Yes; how wonderful for the great God to become man! the Father of eternity, a creature of time! the Ancient of days, an infant! and the Holy One of Israel, to assume the likeness of sinful flesh! Jer. xxxi. 22, Isaiah vii. 14.

Q. In what low condition was Christ born?—**A.** He was born of a mean woman, in Bethlehem, a mean place, in a stable, and laid in a manger, Luke ii.

Q. Was he not descended of the family of David king of Israel?—**A.** Yes; and to shew this, the evangelists give us the history of his pedigree, Matth. i., Luke iii.

Q. How then was he born in such a low condition?—**A.** At that time the family of David had lost its lustre, and was sunk into a very low state, Isa. liii. 2, and xi. 1.

Q. How was Christ humbled *in his life?*—**A.** In being made under the law, and undergoing the miseries of this life, Gal. iv. 4, Isa. liii. 3.

Q. Under what law was Christ made?—**A.** Under the ceremonial and judicial, but *especially* under the moral law, Matth. iii. 15, Gal. iv. 4, 5.

Q. Why was he especially made under the *moral* law? —**A.** Because this was the *matter* of the covenant which Adam broke, and we in him, Gal. iii. 10 and iv. 4.

Q. For what end was he made under the law?—**A.** *To redeem them that were under the law*, Gal. iv.

Q. Are then believers not bound to obey God's law?— **A.** They are bound to obey it *as a rule ;* but *not as a covenant*, to procure life by it, Gal. ii. 19—21.

Q. Whether was Christ made under the law as a covenant, or as a rule of life?—**A.** As a covenant of works; for he was made under that same law from which he intended to redeem his people, Gal. iv. 4, 5.

Q. Why might he not intend to redeem us from the law as a rule?—**A.** Because that would make his righteousness the price of licentiousness, Jude iv. Titus ii. 14, and iii. 8.

Q. Under what of the law as a covenant was Christ made?—**A.** Under the command and the curse of it.

Q. Why was he made under the command of it?—**A.** That he might perfectly obey it in our stead.

Q. Why was he at the same time made under the curse

of it?—A. That he might satisfy the justice of God, for
our disobedience, Dan. ix. 23, 1 John ii. 2.

Q. If Christ was made under the curse, how is it that
he was not brought under the defiling strength of sin?—A.
The infinite holiness of his person prevented it.

Q. Was it not great humiliation in Christ to be made
under the law?—A. Yes; it was astonishing for the great
Lawgiver to become the law's bond-servant; and for God,
blessed for ever, to be made a curse for us, Phil. ii. 8.

Q. What miseries of this life did Christ undergo?—A.
Such as were sinless and common, Matth. viii. 27.

Q. If Christ did not undergo sinful plagues how did he
suffer the *same* punishment which we deserved?—A. Sinful plagues are not of the essence of punishment, but only
spring from the curse as it lies on a sinner.

Q. How then was Christ *made sin for us?*—A. All the
sin of an elect world was laid on, and punished in him.

Q. Did Christ undergo the sinless infirmities of deafness,
blindness, &c.?—A. No; they are not common, and would
have hindered him from duly executing his office.

Q. In what did Christ undergo the miseries of this life?
—A. In his soul, body, reputation, estate, and relations.

Q. What miseries did he undergo in his soul?—A. The
temptations of Satan, with much grief and sorrow from the
world, Matt. iv. Isa. liii.

Q. What chiefly occasioned this grief and sorrow?—A.
The wikedness of men, and their opposition to his ministry, Heb. xii. 3, Luke xix. 41, 42.

Q. What bodily miseries did he undergo?—A. Cold,
hunger, thirst, weariness, sweating, bleeding, &c., Matth.
xxi. John iv. Luke xxii.

Q. What misery did he undergo in his reputation?—A.
The vilest calumny and reproach, Luke xxiii. 2.

Q. How was he reproached?—A. He was called a
glutton, drunkard, blasphemer, Sabbath-breaker, a seditious
person, a companion of profligates, and one in compact
with the devil, Matth. xi. 19, &c.

Q. How did he undergo misery in his estate?–A. Though
the foxes have holes, and the birds of the air have nests,
yet he *had not where to lay his head.*

Q. What misery did he undergo in his relations?—A.
His own friends and countrymen disbelieved, despised, hated, and otherwise injured him, Luke iv. 28.

Q. Was it astonishing humiliation for God, infinitely

rich, glorious, and happy, to become thus poor, reproached, and miserable?—A. Yes; 2 Cor. viii. 9.

Q. Why did Christ undergo these miseries of this life?—
A. That he might unsting them to his people, and the better sympathize with us in trouble, Heb. ii. 17, 18.

Q. How was Christ humbled at his death?—A. By undergoing the wrath of God, and the cursed death of the
cross, Isa. liii. 10, Phil. ii. 8, Luke xxii. xxiii.

Q. Had not Christ undergone the wrath of God all his
life time?—A. Yes; but he suffered it more severely at
his death, Phil. ii. 8, Matth. xxvi. and xxvii.

Q. From whom did he suffer it at his death?—A. From
devils, disciples, malicious men; and from an angry God.

Q. What did he suffer from devils?—A. Great harass-
ment of his sinless soul, John xiv. 30, Luke xxii. 53.

Q. What did he suffer from his disciples?—A. Judas
betrayed, Peter thrice denied, and they all forsook him,
Matth. xxvi.

Q. What did he suffer from malicious men?—A. They
preferred a thief and a murderer to him; crowned him
with thorns; reviled, buffetted, scourged, condemned, and
crucified him, Matth. xxvi. and xxvii.

Q. What did he suffer from God?—A. The hiding of
his face, and the direful effects of his wrath, Psal. xxii.

Q. Where did he especially suffer the wrath of God?—
A. In the garden, and on the cross, Mark xiv. xv.

Q. How know you that he then suffered the wrath of
God?—A. By his bloody sweat, and the words which he
spake at these times, Luke xxii. 44, Psal. xxii.

Q. What did the pressure of God's wrath make Christ
cry out in the garden?—A. He cried out in an agony, *My
soul is exceeding sorrowful even unto death;* and *if it be
possible, let this cup pass from me,* Matth. xxvi.

Q. Why did it make him cry out upon the cross?—A.
My God, my God, why hast thou forsaken me?

Q. How could God thus lay his wrath upon Christ, his
holy and well beloved Son?—A. Because he was now
standing in the law-room of elect sinners, 2 Cor. v. 21.

Q. Did God spare Christ any more than he would have
done sinners?—A. No, not in the least; *but delivered him
up to the death for us all,* Rom. viii. 32.

Q. To what death did God deliver Christ up?—A. To
the death of the cross, Gal. iii. 13.

Q. What kind of death was that?—**A.** A cursed, shameful, and painful death, Gal. iii. 13.

Q. How was the death of Christ a *cursed* death?—**A.** God, to testify his displeasure of man's sin by the fruit of a tree, had said *Cursed is every one that hangeth on a tree,* Gal. iii. 13, Deut. xxii. 23.

Q. How was it a *shameful* death?—**A.** He was hung up naked, as a vile slave and malefactor, Luke xxiii.

Q. How was it a *painful* death?—**A.** His hands and feet were nailed to the cross, his bones drawn out of joint, and he expired, in a lingering manner, in these tortures, Psal. xxii. 14—21, Matth. xxvii. John xix.

Q. What was the type of Christ's death on the cross?—**A.** Moses lifting up the brazen serpent in the wilderness, John iii. 14, and xii. 32, 33, Num. xxi. 4. 9.

Q. How did this typify his death?—**A.** This symbol of the serpent, a cursed creature, was lifted upon a pole for the healing of Israel; so Christ, made a curse, was lifted upon the cross for the healing of sinners.

Q. Why did Christ die a cursed death?—**A.** To redeem them that were under the curse, Gal. iii. 13.

Q. Did Christ's death separate his soul or body from his divine nature?—**A.** No; Rev. i. 18, 1 Pet. iii. 18.

Q. What became of his soul when it was by death separated from his body?—**A.** It went to heaven.

Q. Why did not Christ suffer eternal wrath?—**A.** The divinity of his person gave infinite value to what he suffered; and therefore the law could not require the eternity of suffering, Acts xx. 28, Eph. v. Heb. ix. 12. 14.

Q. How was Christ humbled after his death?—**A.** In his being buried, and continuing under the power of death for a time, Psalm xvi. 10.

Q. How could Christ say on the cross, *It is finished,* when he was humbled after his death?—**A.** His meaning was, that his sensible and soul sufferings were just then finishing.

Q. Why was Christ buried?—**A.** To show that he was really dead, and to perfume the grave for his people.

Q. Who buried Christ's body?—**A.** Joseph of Arimathea, and Nicodemus, John xix. 38. 42.

Q. Where did they bury him?—**A.** In Joseph's new grave in his garden near Mount Calvary, John xix. 41.

Q. Why did God so order it, that Christ was buried

where never man was laid?—A. That there might be no room to say, another had risen in his stead.

Q. Why did he suffer his agony, and was buried in a garden?—A. Man first sinned in a garden, Gen. iii.

Q. What gave death and the grave dominion over Christ?—A. His being made sin for us, 2 Cor. v. 21.

Q. How long did Christ's body continue in the grave?—A. Till the third day after his death, 1 Cor. xv. 3, 4.

Q. What was the type of Christ's lying so long in the grave?—Jonah's being three days and three nights in the whale's belly, Matt. xii. 40, Jon. i. 17, and ii. 10.

Q. How can it be said, Christ was *three days* and *three nights* in the grave, when he lay only about thirty-four hours in it?—He was in it a part of three natural days.

Q. Did he see corruption in the grave?—No; for he had never sinned, and his body was still *closely* united to his divine nature, 2 Cor. v. 21, Psalm xvi. 10.

Q. What are the glorious properties of this infinitely amazing humiliation and death of Christ?—A. It was voluntary, acceptable, meritorious, and victorious.

Q. How was it *voluntary?*—A. Christ undertook and underwent it with the utmost cheerfulness, Psal. xl. 7, 8.

Q. How was it *acceptable?*—God took infinite pleasure and delight in this service of Christ, Eph. v. 2.

Q. Whence did the acceptableness of Christ's death flow?—From its being infinitely valuable and voluntary; and its being commanded of God, John x.

Q. How was it *strictly meritorious?*—A. He never owed it for himself; and it was as valuable as the reward of our eternal life, and his own glorious exaltation, Acts xx. 28.

Q. How was it *victorious?*—A. Christ hereby vanquished and triumphed over sin, devils, and death; and opened an abundant vent for God's love to us, Dan. ix. 24.

Q. How should we improve the humiliation of Christ?—A. By believing and admiring his love; by humility and contentment under the heaviest afflictions; and by boldly craving and expecting the blessings which our brother Christ hath, by his humiliation, purchased for us.

Q. 28. *Wherein consisteth Christ's exaltation?*

A. Christ's exaltation consisteth in his rising again from the dead on the third day, in ascending up into heaven, in sitting at the right hand of God the Father, and in coming to judge the world at the last day.

Q. Did Christ always continue in his estate of humiliation ?—A. No ; having suffered, he entered into his glory, or estate of exaltation, Luke xxiv. 26.

Q. Is, or can Christ's divine nature be exalted in itself ? —A. No ; for it is infinite, Acts vii. 2.

Q. How then is Christ exalted ?—A. His person as *God-man* is highly glorified by the shining forth of the glory of his divine nature in a new manner, through his human nature, whereby great glory is added unto his human nature, Phil. ii. 9, John xvii. 5.

Q. Why was Christ exalted ?—A. That God might be honoured, Christ rewarded, and his people saved.

Q. How doth the exaltation of Christ honour God ?—A. It shows his infinite love, justice, faithfulness, and bounty to Christ, *as Mediator*, and to his people in him.

Q. How is it a reward to Christ ?—A. Hereby the ignominy of his cross is wiped off, the fulness of his satisfaction evidenced, and he is filled with joy, and crowned with glory and honour, Hab. ii. 7, xii. 2, Phil. ii.

Q. How is Christ's exaltation a reward to him, when his human nature had a natural right to it, by virtue of its union with the divine ?—A. The human nature of Christ enjoys its exaltation, both as a reward and in the way of natural right, Phil. ii. 8, 9, Col. i. 16. 18.

Q. How doth Christ's exaltation render his people happy ?—A. He was exalted *on high to give gifts to men ; and that our faith and hope might be in God*, Acts v. 31.

Q. Of how many steps does Christ's exaltation consist ? —A. Four ; his resurrection, ascension, sitting at the right hand of God, and coming to judge the world.

Q. Why could not death and the grave detain Christ ?— A. Because he had perfectly satisfied for our sins, Heb. x.

Q. How prove you that Christ rose from the dead ?—A. His resurrection was prefigured and foretold, and attested by many credible witnesses, 1 Cor. xv. 3—23.

Q. How was Christ's resurrection prefigured ?—A. By the types of Isaac's escape from death, Jonah's coming out of the whale's belly, &c. Gen. xx. Jon. ii. 10.

Q. By whom was it foretold ?—A. By himself and by the prophets, David, Isaiah, and Jeremiah, &c.

Q. How did the prophets foretell it ?—A. David said, *Thou wilt not suffer thine holy One to see corruption ;* and Isaiah, *He was taken from prison,* &c.

Q. How did Christ himself foretell it ?—A. He declared

that he would raise up the temple of his body in three days ; and that he should be killed and rise again on the third day, John ii. 19. 21, Matthew xvi. 21.

Q. By what witnesses was Christ's resurrection attested ? —A. By angels, by disciples, and by his enemies.

Q. How did the angels attest it ?—A. They said to the women who came to see his sepulchre, *He is not here, he is risen, as he has said*, Matth. xxviii. 6.

Q. How did the disciples attest it ?—A. They affirmed Christ was risen, and had often appeared to them alive.

Q. To whom only did Christ shew himself after his resurrection ?—A. To his followers, Acts i. 3.

Q. Why did not Christ shew himself to the priests, &c. ? —A. To punish them for their former unbelief; and especially, that the report of his resurrection might not be supported by the countenance of worldly power.

Q. How often did he shew himself after his resurrection ? —A. We read of ten or eleven several appearances.

Q. To whom did he first appear ?—A. To the women.

Q. Why did he first appear to women ?—A. That as sin had entered by a woman, the first news of a finished salvation might be reported by women.

Q. Of how many was ever Christ seen at once after his resurrection ?—A. Of above five hundred, 1 Cor. xv. 6.

Q. How long did Christ continue on earth after his resurrection ?—A. Forty days, Acts i. 3.

Q. How was he employed during that time ?—A. In giving proofs of his resurrection, and instructing his disciples in things pertaining to the kingdom of God, Luke xiv. Matth. 27, John xx. and xxi. Acts i.

Q. How doth it appear, that Christ's disciples' testimony of his resurrection deserved the fullest credit?—A. They had the fullest proof of what they attested ; did openly declare it amidst his enemies, in the place where, and within a few days after the event happened ; and had no temptation for carnal advantage, but were hereby exposed to the severest sufferings and death.

Q. What enemies of Christ attested his resurrection ?— A. The band of soldiers that were set to guard his sepulchre, at first attested it, Matth. xxviii. 11.

Q. Why do you say, they at *first* attested it ?—A. Because afterwards the priests and elders hired them to say, that his disciples stole him away while they slept.

Q. Could any reasonable man believe this forged story ?

—A. No : for, how could the whole watch sleep, when it was death for Roman soldiers to sleep on guard ? and if asleep, how could they tell who stole away his body ?

Q. By whose power did Christ rise ?—A. By his own, and by that of the Father and Holy Ghost; Rom. vi. and viii.

Q. How prove you that he rose by his own power ?—A. He declared that he had *power to take* his life *again ; and by his resurrection from the dead*, he was *declared to be the Son of God with power*, John x. 18, Rom. i. 4.

Q. What solemnities attended Christ's resurrection?—A. A great earthquake, appearance of angels, &c.

Q. Why did God send an angel to roll away the stone from the grave's mouth ?—A. To show that Christ was solemnly released from prison, as one who had fully satisfied law and justice, Isa. liii. 8, and xlii. 21, Eph. v. 2.

Q. Why were Christ's grave clothes left in the grave, and why in such order ?—A. To shew that he should die no more ; and that he rose with great deliberation.

Q. On what day did Christ rise ?—A. On the third day after his death, and first day of the week ; which is since called *the Lord's day*, in honour of our Redeemer, who thereon entered on his glorious rest, and appointed it to be kept as a memorial of his resurrection.

Q. In what capacity did Christ rise from the dead ?—A. As the head of an elect world, 1 Cor. xv. 20—22.

Q. For what end did Christ rise ?—A. For God's glory, his own honour, and our advantage.

Q. How was it for the glory of God ?—A. That, being the God and Father of Christ, he might be the God, not of a dead, but living Redeemer, Matth. xxii. 32.

Q. How was it for Christ's own honour ?—A. That, having in his death paid his elect's debt, and purchased a kingdom, he might come out of prison to possess his kingdom, Phil. ii. 8, 9, 10.

Q. How was it for our advantage ?—A. Therein our debt is legally discharged, and Christ took possession of eternal life in our name, Rom. iv. 25.

Q. What are the necessary fruits of Christ's resurrection to the elect?—A. Their justification, quickening in grace, support against enemies, and glorious resurrection.

Q. What is the second step of Christ's exaltation ?—A. His ascending into heaven, Psalm xlvii. 5.

Q. According to what nature did Christ ascend ?—A.

12

According to his human nature ; for his divine, being every where at once, can neither ascend nor descend.

Q. How then is Christ, in respect of his divine nature, said to *descend into the lower parts of the earth?*—A. Descending there is only to be understood of his condescension in assuming our nature, Eph. iv. 9.

Q. To which of Christ's offices doth his ascension relate?—A. To all the three, Psalm lxviii. 18.

Q. How was it an act of his prophetical office?—A. It confirmed his doctrine ; and he ascended to send the Spirit to convince and instruct us, John xvi. 7—10.

Q. How was it an act of his priestly office?—A. He thus entered into the holy place to present his blood before God, Heb. i. 3. and ix. 24. Rom. viii. 34.

Q. How was it an act of his kingly office?—A. He triumphed over his enemies in it, Psalm xlvii. 5.

Q. Whence did Christ ascend?—A. From about mount Olivet, near, if not exactly from the place where he had his bitter agony, Acts i. 12.

Q. Whither did he ascend?—A. To heaven.

Q. Who saw him ascend?—A. His disciples.

Q. What was Christ doing when he ascended to heaven?—A. Blessing his disciples, who saw him ascend.

Q. What was one of his parting words?—A. *Lo, I am with you alway, even unto the end of the world*, Matth. xxviii. 20. Luke xxiv. 51.

Q. In what capacity did Christ ascend?—A. As head and forerunner of his people, Micah ii. 13. Heb. vi. 20.

Q. In what manner did he ascend?—A. In a most glorious and triumphant manner, leading captivity captive.

Q. What do you mean by his *leading captivity captive?*—A. That Christ, in his ascension, chained and triumphed over Satan, who had taken his elect captive, Psalm, lxviii. 18.

Q. Who attended Christ in his ascension to heaven?—A. Thousands of angels with shouts of praise, Dan. vii.

Q. Who welcomed him into heaven?—A. His Father and all the inhabitants of heaven, Dan. vii. 13.

Q. How did Christ prove his ascension?—A. By sending down the Holy Ghost a few days after, at Pentecost.

Q. Did this descent of the Spirit prove the perfection of Christ's righteousness?—A. Yes ; For if Christ had not been perfectly righteous in his person and office, he would never have been received up into heaven, nor exalted to such power and glory there, 1 John iii. 1. Psalm cx. 1.

Q. Why did Christ ascend to heaven?—A. To receive to himself a kingdom, prepare mansions for his people, and send his Spirit to fit them for these mansions.

Q. What is the third step of Christ's exaltation?—A. His sitting at the right hand of God the Father.

Q. What is meant by the right hand of God?—A. A state of the highest honour and authority.

Q. What is meant by sitting at God's right hand?—A. Christ's security and rest in that glorious state.

Q. For what end doth Christ sit at God's right hand?—A. To represent his people, and make his enemies his footstool, Heb. ix. 24. and i. 13. Psal. cx. xxi. lxxii.

Q. How prove you that he there represents his people?—A. Because while on earth they are said to *sit in heavenly places in Christ*, Eph. ii. 6.

Q. How shall he make all his enemies his footstool?—A. By covering them with shame and terror, and crushing them down to hell at the last day, Rev. xx.

Q. How long shall Christ sit at God's right hand?—A. For ever, Psalm cx. 4. Isa. ix. 7.

Q. What is the fourth step of Christ's exaltation?—A. His coming to judge the world at the last day.

Q. How do you prove that the world shall be judged?—A. From scripture and from reason.

Q. How doth scripture prove it?—A. It affirms, that *God has appointed a day* for judging the world : and that *every work shall be brought into judgment*, Acts xvii. 31, Eccl. xii. 14, 2 Cor. v. 10.

Q. How doth reason prove it?—A. It shews, that, since the wicked are now happy, and the godly in distress, the just and good God will at length call men to an account, and render the godly happy, and the wicked miserable.

Q. Who shall judge the world?—A. God shall judge it by Christ Jesus, Acts xvii. 31, John v. 22.

Q. Why is the judging of the world committed to Christ?—A. That we may have a visible Judge, who hath obeyed the law by which he will judge others ; that Christ may be honoured, his saints encouraged, and his enemies confounded, Rev. i. 7, John v. 27.

Q. What are Christ's qualities as a Judge?—A. He is a righteous, inexorable, all-seeing, and almighty Judge.

Q. When will Christ come to judge the world ?—**A.** At the last day, John xii. 48, Matth. xxv.

Q. Why is that time called the *last day* ?—**A.** Because after it the wicked shall have one everlasting night of darkness, and the saints one eternal day of glory.

Q. Hath God fixed the time of the last day ?—**A.** Yes; but no man knows when it shall be, Mark xii. 32.

Q. Why hath God so concealed the time of it from us ? —**A.** That we may be always watching and ready for it.

Q. What will be some of the forerunners of that day ?— **A.** The fall of Antichrist; the general conversion of the Jews and Gentiles to the Christian faith, followed with a general apostacy from the same, Rev. xiv.—xxii.

Q. In what manner will Christ come to judgment ?—**A.** In a most unexpected, sudden, and glorious manner.

Q. Wherein will his second coming differ from his first? —**A.** His first coming was obscure and debased, in the likeness of sinful flesh; but he will come again without sin, and with power and great glory, Heb. ix. 28.

Q. In what glory will Christ come to judgment?—**A.** In his own and his Father's glory, Matth. xvi. 27.

Q. Who will attend him as his retinue from heaven ?— **A.** All the holy angels, and glorified saints, Zech. xiv. 5.

Q. For what end will Christ come again ?—**A.** To judge the world, Matth. xxv. 31—46, Acts xvii. 31.

Q. Whom will he judge ?—**A.** Men and devils.

Q. How can all the dead be judged at that day ?—**A.** They shall be raised up out of their graves: *For we must all appear before the judgment-seat of Christ.*

Q. By what shall men be summoned to Christ's bar ?— **A.** By the voice of the archangel, and trump of God.

Q. Who will bring them to the bar ?—**A.** The angels.

Q. Shall the righteous be then fully and finally separated from the wicked ?—**A.** Yes, Matth. xxv. 32.

Q. How will all men be classed at Christ's bar ?—**A.** The saints or sheep shall be placed on his right hand, and the wicked or goats on his left, Matth. xxv. 33.

Q. Why are the wicked called *goats ?*—**A.** Because of their filthiness, ill-favour, and feeding on the poison of sin.

Q. Why are the righteous called *sheep ?*—**A.** Because of their innocence, purity, and having many enemies.

Q. Who will be counted righteous at that day ?—**A.** Only such as are clothed with the righteousness of Christ.

Q. What shall be judged at that day?—A. All our thoughts, words, and actions, Eccl. xii. 14, Matth. xii.

Q. In what manner shall these things be judged?—A. Most exactly, for *the books* shall be *opened.*

Q. What books shall be opened for judging the world?—A. The books of God's remembrance, of conscience, and of the law, and the book of life, Rev. xx. 12.

Q. What is the book of God's remembrance?—A. His infinite knowledge of all men's state, thoughts, words, and actions, Heb. iv. 13, Psalm cxlvii. 5.

Q. For what will this book serve?—A. As a libel of wicked men's bad works, and a memorial of saints' good works, Matth. xxv. 35, 36. 42, 43.

Q. What is the book of conscience?—A. Men's knowledge of their own state, thoughts, words, and deeds; accompanied with a self-condemnation of every bad, and approbation of every good thing about them, Rom. ii. 15.

Q. What will this book serve for?—A. It will fully attest the records of God's book of remembrance, confound the wicked, and comfort the saints, Rom. ii. 15.

Q. Why shall the book of the law, or covenant of works, be opened?—A. To be the standard of right and wrong, and of the sentence pronounced against the wicked.

Q. By what law shall the Heathen world be judged?—A. By the law manifested by the light of nature.

Q. By what law shall wicked Jews, and nominal Christians, be judged?—A. By the law revealed in the Bible.

Q. Will the righteous be judged by this law or covenant of works?—A. No; they shall be judged by the *Lamb's book of life*, Rev. xx. 12, Matth. xxv. 34.

Q. Why are they not judged by the law as a covenant?—A. Because they are not under it, Rom. ii. 14.

Q. Is not the sentence of the righteous, in respect of their oneness with Christ, according to the terms of the law?—A. Yes: and it greatly honours the law.

Q. What is the *book of life?*—A. It is God's eternal purpose to save the elect in Christ, Rom. ix. 23.

Q. Why is it called the book of life?—A. Because all they whose names are in it, are *ordained to eternal life.*

Q. Whose names are written in this book of life?—A. The name of all the elect, Rev. xx. 15.

Q. Why is it called *the Lamb's book?*—A. Because it is lodged in the hand of Christ *the Lamb of God,* Rev. xiii. 8.

Q. What do the righteous see by the opening of this

12*

book ?—A. That their eternal salvation flows through Christ from God's most ancient love, Jer. xxxi. 3.

Q. Who shall be first judged at the last day ?—A. The righteous, Matth. xxv. 34, with 41.

Q. Why shall they be first judged ?—A. To shew that God more delights in mercy than wrath ; and that they being openly acquitted, may, together with Christ, judge devils and wicked men, Isa. xxviii. 1 Cor. vi.

Q. What will be the sentence of the righteous ?—A. *Come, ye blessed of my Father, inherit the kingdom prepared for you from the foundation of the world.*

Q. Why calls he them *blessed of his Father*?—A. To refresh them with the views of his and their Father's early and everlasting love, John xvi. and xx.

Q. Why calls he them to *inherit* the kingdom ?—A. To shew, that they come to the kingdom of glory as *heirs*, not as *purchasers* of it, Rom. viii. 17.

Q. What is the ground or foundation of this happy sentence ?—A. God's free grace reigning through the righteousness of Christ, Rom. v. 21, and vi. 23.

Q. How then is *every man judged according to his works?*—A. The saints are judged according to the nature, but not according to the merit or desert of their works.

Q. How are the saints judged according to the nature of their works ?—A. As their works are gracious and holy; so they are adjudged, by a gracious sentence, to a holy kingdom, Rev. xx. xxi. Rom. v. 21.

Q. Why then are their good works mentioned, Matth. xxv. 35, 36, as if grounds of their sentence ?—A. These works are not mentioned as the foundation of their sentence, but as evidences of their union to Christ, and title to heaven, 1 John iii. 16, 17.

Q. Why are works of charity to the saints only mentioned?—A. God much regards these works ; and they shew a man to be born of God, Heb. vi. 9, 10.

Q. Why are the saints represented as not knowing of their good works?—A. To shew how much they are denied to them, Luke xvii. 10, Gen. xxxii. 10, Isa. lxiv. 6.

Q. What will be the sentence of the wicked?—A. *Depart from me, ye cursed, into everlasting fire, prepared for the devil and his angels,* Matth. xxv. 41.

Q. What is the ground of this sentence of the wicked ? —A. Their wicked state and works, Rom. ii. 8, 9.

Q. Why are sins of omission only mentioned as the

ground of the sentence of damnation ?—A. Because men generally esteem sins of omission as but *trifles*.

Q. Why is omission of charity to the saints particularly mentioned as the grounds of eternal damnation ?—A. To deter men from this great and common evil, which so clearly shews their hatred of Christ himself.

Q. Will the devils also be then judged ?—A. Yes ; and shall thenceforth be confined to hell, and have their torments increased, 2 Pet. ii. 4, Rev. xx. 10.

Q. How shall the righteous judge the world ?—A. By saying *Amen* to the sentences which Christ shall pass on devils and wicked men, 1 Cor. vi.

Q. What shall follow immediately after the judgment ?— A. The wicked *shall go away into everlasting punishment ; but the righteous into life eternal,* Matth. xxv. 46.

Q. What shall Christ do after the judgment ?—A. He shall *deliver the kingdom up to the Father,* and *be subject to God who put all things under* his feet.

Q. How shall he deliver up the kingdom to the Father ? —A. He shall lay aside all the ordinances of the militant church ; and present all the subjects of his invisible kingdom before his Father without spot, and with great joy, 1 Cor. xv. 24—27, Jude 24, Eph. v. 27.

Q. How will the Son then be *subject* to the Father ?— A. His subjection to him as a man and Mediator will be more clearly seen than before, 1 Cor. xv. 28.

Q. How should we improve the exaltation of Christ ?— A. By seeking after spiritual quickening and justification ; by honouring Christ, trusting in him, setting our affections on things above ; and in waiting, preparing, looking, and longing for his second coming.

Q. 29. *How are we made partakers of the redemption purchased by Christ?*

A. We are made partakers of the redemption purchased by Christ, by the effectual application of it to us by his Holy Spirit.

Q. 30. *How doth the Spirit apply to us the redemption purchased by Christ?*

A. The Spirit applieth to us the redemption purchased by Christ, by working faith in us, and thereby uniting us to Christ, in our effectual calling.

Q. What is the general end and fruit of Christ's undertaking, incarnation, offices, and states, with respect to his people ?—A. Their eternal redemption.

Q. What call you their redemption ?—A. Their deliverance from all evil, and possession of all happiness.

Q. Why is our redemption said to be *purchased*?—A. Because Christ gave the price of his blood for it.

Q. Have we by nature any interest in this redemption ? —A. No ; we are *without God in the world*, Eph. ii. 12.

Q. Are we by nature inclined, or able to receive an interest in it?—A. No ; we *forsake* our *own mercy*, Jonah ii. 8.

Q. How then do we become sharers of redemption ?— A. We are by God *made* partakers of it, Isa. lv. 3, 4.

Q. How are we made partakers of it?—A. By the application of it to us, Isa. lxi. 10, Ezek. xxxvi. 25—31.

Q. What do you understand by the application of redemption ?—A. The making of it ours in possession.

Q. In what do the purchase and application of redemption differ ?—A. The purchase is Christ's work without us, and is the cause ; the application takes place upon and in us, and is the effect of the purchase.

Q. When did Christ's redemption begin to be applied? —A. Soon after the fall of Adam, Gen. iii. 15.

Q. How was redemption applied before Christ purchased it by his death?—A. It was applied upon the credit of Christ's engagement to purchase it in due time.

Q. Can we profit by Christ's purchase, if it is not applied ?—A. No; no more than by buying food and clothes, &c., without using them, Heb. ii. 3, and iv. 2.

Q. How was the application of redemption typified of old ?—A. By the sprinkling of the blood of the sacrifice upon the people, Heb. ix. 13, 14, Exod. xxiv. &c.

Q. What are the different kinds of the application of redemption ?—A. An outward application of it in baptism, and an effectual application of it, 1 Peter iii. 21.

Q. Can the outward application alone do us good ?—A. No ; for it changeth not our nature or state.

Q. What is an effectual application of redemption ?—A. That which giveth us a real and actual share of it.

Q. Who is the effectual applier of redemption ?—A. The Holy Spirit, John xvi. 14.

Q. Do not the Father and Son also apply it ?—A. Yes ; but they do so by the Holy Ghost, John xvi.

Q. Why is the applier of redemption called *the holy*

Ghost?—A. He is holy in himself; and it is his office to make us holy in applying redemption to us.

Q. Why is he called the *Spirit of Christ?*—A. He proceeds from Christ; and Christ purchased his coming, and sends him to apply redemption to us, John xvi. 7.

Q. Did Christ purchase the Holy Spirit?—A. Christ purchased the Spirit's *gifts* and *influences* in applying redemption; but not his *being*, which is independent.

Q. To whom doth the Spirit apply redemption?—A. To the elect *only*, for whom *only* it was purchased.

Q. How doth he apply it to convert infants?—A. Immediately by himself, without the word.

Q. How doth he apply it to such as have the use of reason?—A. By means of the word of God, Psalm cx. 2, 3.

Q. What doth that teach us?—A. To cry, that God's word may, by his Spirit, be made effectual for our salvation, Psalm cxix. 18. 2 Thess. ii. 13. and iii. 1.

Q. How doth the Spirit apply redemption to us?—A. By uniting us to Christ, in whom it is lodged.

Q. To whom are we by nature united?—A. To the first Adam *as fallen*, Rom. v. 12. 1 Cor. xv. 22.

Q. By what bond are we united to him?—A. By the bond of the broken covenant of works.

Q. How is our union to fallen Adam, and to the law, the devil, the world, and our lust, dissolved?—A. By our spiritual marriage and union to Christ, Rom. vii. 4.

Q. To what of Christ doth the Spirit unite us?—A. To his person, Rom. vii. 4. Isa. liv. 5.

Q. Why cannot we share of redemption without union to Christ's person?—A. Because all the blessings of redemption are lodged in his person, and received with him.

Q. What do you understand by union to Christ?—A. Our being joined to, or made one with him.

Q. Doth this union make believers one essence or individual person with Christ?—A. No; Rev. iii. 20.

Q. How then doth it make Christ and believers ONE?—A. It makes them one body mystical, of which he is the head, and they are the members, 1 Cor. xii. 12.

Q. How can we be united to Christ, when his human nature is in heaven, and we on earth?—A. We are united to his person, which is every where.

Q. Doth this union unite us to the other persons in the Godhead?—A. Yes; in and through Christ, John xvii.

Q. Is there any other union between Christ and his people, besides this mystical union?—A. Yes; there is also a legal union, or union in law, Isa. liii. 4, 5, 6.

Q. What call you the *legal* union?—A. That which is between Christ as a surety and his elect seed.

Q. What is the connection of these two unions?—A. The legal union is the foundation of the mystical.

Q. Wherein doth this legal and mystical union differ? —A. In their order of nature and time, in relation of the parties united, and in the bonds of union.

Q. How do they differ in their *order* of nature and time? —A. The legal union is the cause, and was made up from all eternity; but the mystical is the effect, and is made up in the moment of conversion, Rom. vii. 4.

Q. How do they differ in the *relation* of the parties united?—A. In the legal union, the elect, *as bankrupt dyvours*, are united to Christ *as surety;* but in the mystical union, the elect, *as Christ's purchased bride*, are united to him *as their husband and head of influence.*

Q. What are the *bonds* of the legal union?—A. God's everlasting love, and covenant transaction with Christ.

Q. What are the *bonds* of the mystical union?—A. The Spirit on Christ's part, and faith on our part.

Q. Wherein doth Christ come near us, in order to make up the mystical union?—A. In the gospel, Rom. x. 8.

Q. On whose side doth the uniting work begin?—A. On Christ's side, not on ours, 1 John iv. 19.

Q. How doth it begin?—A. Christ's Spirit, by the word, enters into our heart, and takes hold of it in his name, Psalm cx. 2, 3. Acts xxvi. 17, 18.

Q. Can our soul give the Spirit any actual welcome when he first enters our heart?—A. No; our soul is then quite dead in sin, and can do no good thing, Eph. ii. 5.

Q. What is the immediate effect of the Spirit's entering into our soul?—A. He quickens us, forming faith, and all his other graces, in our heart, Eph. ii. 1—8, 22.

Q. How can the word be a mean of our first quickening in regeneration, when we have no faith to receive it?—A. The Spirit, as he in the word enters our heart, gives faith much in the same way as God created the world, by speaking to nothing, and calling it into being and existence, Eph. ii. 5. Rom. iv. 17.

Q. What is the immediate effect of the Spirit's quickening us?—A. We believe the quickening word of the Gospel-promise, and receive Christ in it, 1 Thess. ii. 13.

Q. At what time doth the Spirit enter into, and quicken the souls of the elect?—At the time fixed in the decree of election and covenant of grace, Ezek. xvi. 8.

Q. Whether are we united to Christ as saints or as sinners?—A. In the very uniting act we are changed from sinners to saints, Ezek. xxxvi. 26, 27.

Q. What of a believer is united to Christ?—A. His whole man, soul and body, 1 Cor. vi. 15, 19.

Q. What are the properties of this union which the Spirit makes up between Christ and his people?—A. It is a real, spiritual, mystical, close, and indissoluble union.

Q. Why call you it a *real union?*—A. Because believers are as truly united to Christ, as the members of our natural body to the head, 1 Cor. xii. 12, John xvii. 21.

Q. Why do you call it a *spiritual union?*—A. Because *he that is joined to* Christ *is one Spirit* with him, 1 Cor. vi. 17.

Q. How are believers *one spirit* with Christ?—A. The same Spirit dwells in both; and they have the *same mind in* them *that was in Christ Jesus,* Phil. ii. 5.

Q. Why is it called a *mystical union?*—A. Because it is so wonderful and full of mysteries.

Q. What are some of the mysteries in this union?—A. Hereby Christ lives and dwells in believers; and they live in, and on, and walk in Christ, and dwell in God, &c., Gal. ii. 20, John xv. and xvii.

Q. How is it a *close* and *intimate* union?—A. It is closer than all unions among natural things, and like the union of Christ with his Father, John xvii. 21.

Q. Why is it called an *indissoluble union?*—A. Christ and believers can never be separated, nor the bonds of their union be broken, John x. 28.

Q. How is the Spirit an inviolable bond of union?—A. He never departs from believers after his entrance into their hearts, John xiv. 16. Isa. lix. 21.

Q. How is our faith an inviolable bond of union?—A. The Spirit preserves its habit from ever failing, and influences it to acts in time of need, Luke xxii. 32.

Q. Whether does the habit or act of faith bind the soul to Christ?—Both; but chiefly the habit.

Q. What is the mystical union compared to in scripture? A. To the union between husband and wife, head and members, root and branches, foundation and building,

Q. How doth this mystical union resemble the union of husband and wife ?—**A.** The marriage union is voluntary, and gives each an interest in the other, and whatever belongs to them ; so is the union between Christ and believers, Isa. lxii. Ezek. xvi. Song ii. 16.

Q. How doth it resemble the union of root and branches ?—**A.** The root bears the weight of, and gives sap to the branches ; so doth Christ to believers, John xv.

Q. How doth it resemble the union between head and members ?—**A.** The head governs, and gives light and life to the body ; so doth Christ to believers.

Q. How doth it resemble the union of foundation and building ?—**A.** The foundation supports the building ; so doth Christ the believer, 1 Cor. iii. 11, Isa. xxviii. 16.

Q. How are those who are united to Christ ordinarily called ?—**A.** Believers, saints, godly, righteous, &c.

Q. Why are they called *believers?*—**A.** Because they credit or believe God's word, and live by faith, Gal. ii. 20.

Q, Why are they called *saints?*—**A.** Because they are made holy in heart and life, 2 Pet. i. 4, Isa. lxii. 12.

Q. Why are they called *godly ?*—**A.** Because they fear God, and study to be like him, Matt. v. 48.

Q. Why are they called *righteous?*—**A.** Because they are clothed with Christ's righteousness, and study to practise what is just and righteous, 1 John iii. 7.

Q. How ought saints to improve their union to Christ ?—**A.** In studying holiness and intimate fellowship with Christ, Rom. vii. 4. 6, John xvi.

Q. What ought sinners to do with respect to it ?—**A.** To lament over their union to Satan, the law, and their lusts, and seek after a speedy marriage with Christ.

Q. 31. *What is effectual calling ?*

A. Effectual calling is the work of God's Spirit, whereby convincing us of our sin and misery, enlightening our minds in the knowledge of Christ, and renewing our wills, he doth persuade and enable us to embrace Jesus Christ, freely offered to us in the Gospel.

Q. In what doth the Spirit apply the redemption purchased by Christ ?—**A.** In our effectual calling, justification, adoption, sanctification, and glorification.

Q. Wherein is the union between Christ and his people constituted ?—**A.** In their effectual calling.

Q. Whether is effectual calling a work or an act ?—**A.** It is a work, Eph. i. 18, 19.

Q. What is the difference between a work and an act ? —**A.** An act is done in a moment ; but a work often requires more time, and consists of sundry acts.

Q. Whose work is effectual calling ?—**A.** It is the work of God's spirit, John xvi. 8—14.

Q. Is it not also a work of the Father and Son ?—**A.** Yes; but they work it by the Spirit, John xvi.

Q. How doth the Spirit constitute the union between Christ and us in our effectual calling ?—**A.** By persuading and enabling us to embrace Christ, Psalm cx. 3.

Q. What do you mean by our embracing of Christ ?— **A.** Receiving him by faith, and with great delight.

Q. Into what do we by faith receive Christ ?—**A.** Into our heart, Prov. xxiii. 26, Eph. iii. 17.

Q. Wherein do we by faith receive Christ ?—**A.** In the promise of the gospel, Rom. x. 8, 9.

Q. Whether is it in the gospel strictly or largely taken ? —**A.** In the gospel strictly taken, Isa. lv. 1—7.

Q. What warrant have we to embrace Christ in the gospel ?—**A.** The Father's gift of Christ, and Christ's offer of himself to us, Isa. xlii. and lv.

Q. What do you understand by the Father's gift of Christ ?—**A.** His setting forth Christ as the great mean of salvation, which every one of mankind hath a right and welcome to receive, John iii. 16, Isa. xlii. 6, 7, and xlix. 6.

Q. Can any man receive Christ but upon the footing of this gift ?—**A.** No ; John iii. 16. 27.

Q. Doth God command every man that hears the gospel to take his gift *Christ* out of his hand ?—**A.** Yes ; under pain of his most dreadful wrath, 1 John iii. 23.

Q. What mean you by Christ's offer of himself ?—**A.** His holding forth himself as able and willing to save, and inviting sinners to receive salvation from him.

Q. To whom doth Christ offer himself?—**A.** To every one that hears the gospel, without exception, Prov. viii. 4.

Q. In what manner is Christ offered in the gospel?—**A.** Fully, freely, earnestly, and indefinitely, Isa. lv.

Q. How is he offered *fully* ?—**A.** He is offered in his whole person, offices, relations, righteousness, and blessings.

13

Q. How is he offered *freely?*—**A.** No condition is required from sinful men to give them a right to the offer.

Q. How is Christ offered *earnestly?*—All the divine persons do often, in the most engaging terms, and with the most powerful motives, beseech, intreat, and command us to embrace Christ, Isa. lv. 1—13, Rev. xxii.

Q. How is Christ offered *indefinitely?*—**A.** The gospel-offer of him suits every hearer's case as exactly as if he was named in it, Rev. iii. 17, 18.

Q. What do you understand by *embracing* of Christ as offered in the gospel?—**A.** A particular persuasion that Christ in the promise is *mine;* and made of God *to me* wisdom, righteousness, sanctification, and redemption; and trusting on his word, that he will act up to all his saving characters to me in order to promote my everlasting salvation.

Q. Are all the effectually called equally sensible of their embracing Christ?—**A.** No; sometimes Christ is embraced in the way of bold claiming of the promises; and sometimes in the way of desire, attended with much fear and doubting, Psalm xlii. 1, 2. 5. 8.

Q. How is Christ embraced by a bold claiming such a promise as that, *Though your sins be as scarlet, they shall be as snow, &c.?*—**A.** By replying with our heart, "Lord my sins are indeed as scarlet; but since thou hast thus promised, on the footing of thy word, I am verily persuaded, that thou shalt make them white as snow, by purging them away."

Q. How is Christ embraced in his promise, in the way of desire, attended with much fear and doubting?—**A.** By replying with our heart, "Lord, I prize this promise as infinitely suited to my monstrous guilt; and, oh! for Christ's sake, do as thou hast said."

Q. What is the principal thing of which we take hold, in embracing Christ?—**A.** His person, Acts xvi. 31.

Q. Have sinners always the person of Christ most directly in view when they first believe?—**A.** No; but often some particular blessing, as pardon of sin, a new heart, drawing grace, &c. Acts xvi. 30.

Q. How then do we principally receive the person of Christ?—**A.** As we only believe, expect, and desire that blessing in and through Christ, Acts xvi. 30, 31.

Q. In what manner do we receive Christ?—**A.** As he is offered in the gospel, John iii. 27.

Q. How do we receive Christ *fully?*—**A.** By embracing him in his whole person, offices, relations, and benefits, as our all, Song ii. 16 and v. 10—16.

Q. How do we receive him *freely* ?—A. By receiving him in the view of our being utterly unworthy of any good, and most worthy of eternal ruin, 1 Tim. i. 15.

Q. How do we receive him in agreeableness to his being *earnestly* offered ?—A. By receiving him with great earnestness, and most fervent desire, Prov. xxiii. 26.

Q. How do we receive him in agreeableness to his being *indefinitely* offered ?—A. By applying the offer as particularly to ourselves as if it had pointed us out by name, and were not to another, Gal. ii. 20.

Q. When is the word of the gospel thus believed ?—A. When Christ applies it by the power of his Spirit to our hearts, John v. 25, 1 Thess. ii. 13.

Q. How doth the Spirit make us to embrace Christ?—A. By persuading and enabling us to it, John vi.

Q. What need is there of his persuading us to embrace Christ ?—A. Because we are naturally averse to it.

Q. Cannot men effectually persuade us to embrace Christ ?—A. No ; not in the least, Heb. iv. 2.

Q. How doth the Spirit persuade us to embrace Christ ? —A. By shewing us strong reasons for it, and answering all our objections against it, Isa. lv. 1—13.

Q. What powerful motives, and strong reasons, for embracing Christ, does the Spirit shew us?—A. Our great need of him ; his infinite excellency, love, and earnestness to become ours ; the great advantage of receiving, and danger of refusing him, &c. Song v.

Q. How doth he reprove all our objections against our present receiving of Christ?—A. By convincing us that the least delay may ruin us for ever ; that fears of our day of grace being past, of our reprobation, or having committed the unpardonable sin, ought not to hinder, but to excite us to a present embracement of Christ.

Q. Why must the Spirit enable us to embrace Christ?—A. Because by nature we have no strength to do any thing spiritually good, Rom. v. 6, Eph. ii. 1, 1 Cor. ii. 14.

Q. How doth the Spirit enable us to embrace Christ?—A. He conveys strength into our hearts, by the persuasion of the word of the gospel, Isa. xl. 31.

Q. By what means does the Spirit persuade and enable us to embrace Christ ?—A. By convincing our consciences, enlightening our minds, and renewing our wills; which are the three parts of effectual calling.

Q. What is the first part of the Spirit's work upon us?—**A.** Conviction, John xvi. Rom. vii. 9.

Q. What is in general understood by conviction?—**A.** The presenting a thing so clearly to our view, that we must see, and be affected with it, John xvi. 8—11.

Q. Of what doth the Spirit convince us?—**A.** Of our sin and misery, Rom. iii. John xvi.

Q. Of what in sin doth he convince us?—**A.** Of the guilt, filth, strength, number, and aggravations of our sin.

Q. What do we think of ourselves when convinced of the guilt of sin?—**A.** We see that we are ruined for ever, if God's rich and free grace do not prevent it.

Q. What do we think of ourselves when convinced of the filth of sin?—**A.** We see ourselves, and our works, even the best, to be vile and abominable before God.

Q. What do we think of ourselves when convinced of the strength of our sin?—**A.** We see we can do nothing but sin, and cannot cease from sinning, Rom. vii. 8—13.

Q. What do we think of ourselves when we are convinced of the number of our sins?—**A.** We see that none *can understand our errors*, which *are more than the hairs of our head*, Psalm xix. 12, and xl. 12.

Q. What do we think of ourselves when we are convinced of the aggravations of our sins?—**A.** We look on ourselves as the very chief of sinners, 1 Tim. i. 15.

Q. With what sins do convictions ordinarily begin?—**A.** With outward acts of sin, chiefly those of the grosser kind, John iv. 16. Acts ix. 4. and ii. 36, 37.

Q. Do right convictions of sin stop there?—**A.** No; but proceed to more secret and refined sins, John iv. 29.

Q. How may we know if our convictions are carried to a proper length?—**A.** If we have been convinced of the great vileness of our unbelief, original sin, beloved lusts, and best duties, John xvi. 9. Psalm li. 5.

Q. Of what misery doth the Spirit chiefly convince us?—**A.** Of the spiritual misery which we are under, and the eternal misery to which we are liable, Eph. ii. 12.

Q. Of what concerning our misery doth the Spirit convince us?—**A.** Of the certainty, greatness, nearness, and justness thereof, Acts xvi. 30.

Q. By what doth the Spirit convince us of the filth of sin?—**A.** By the command of the law, Rom. iii. 20.

Q. By what doth the Spirit convince us of our guilt and misery ?—A. By the threatenings of the law, Rom. iii. 19.

Q. How doth he convince us of our sin by the law ?—A. He presents to our conscience the lay of God in its spirituality and breadth, and the contrariety of our heart and life to it, Rom. vii. 8. Matth. v. 18—48.

Q. What is the fruit and effect of these convictions ?—A. Great shame and fear, Acts ii. 37. and xvi. 30.

Q. Why cannot other men convince us of sin ?—A. Because they cannot awaken our conscience.

Q. Why cannot we convince ourselves?—A. Because by nature we are blind, and full of self-conceit.

Q. What effect hath this self-conceit upon our convictions ?—A. It tends to stifle them, Deut. xxix. 19.

Q. How do we often stifle our convictions ?—A By confining our thoughts to the badness of our actions, without impression of the badness of our state ; rebelling against convictions, or diverting them by vain projects or company ; or by bribing our conscience with duties, and legal resolutions, as an atonement for our faults, &c. Deut. xxix. 19. Acts xxiv. 25.

Q. Do convictions of themselves make us any better ?—A. Though they may produce outward reformation of life, yet our heart is occasionally made worse by them.

Q. How are convictions the occasion of our heart's becoming worse ?—A. This flows not from their own nature ; but sin taketh occasion thereby to fill us with wrath against God for the strictness of his law, and disposeth us to seek to establish our own righteousness, in opposition to the righteousness of Christ, Rom. vii. 8—13.

Q. Why is conviction necessary ?—A. To make us see our absolute need of Christ for salvation, Gal. iv. 24.

Q. What measure of conviction is necessary?—A. So much as to render us sensible, that we are utterly lost and undone without Christ, Acts ii. 37. and xvi. 30.

Q. Who have ordinarily the sharpest convictions?—A. Such as have been most hardened in sin, guilty of many gross sins, or are designed for special use in the church of God, Rom. vii. 8—13. Acts ii. 36, 37. and xvi. 30.

Q. Are convictions necessary to give us a title to Christ?—A. No ; but to stir us up to flee to Christ, Gal. iv. 24.

Q. May we have strong convictions, and yet be damned?—A. Yes ; as Cain, Judas, &c. were, Gen. iv.

Q. What more is then necessary to salvation ?—A. The

13*

enlightening of our mind, by enabling it to discern spiritual things, 2 Cor. iv. 6. Eph. i. 18, 19.

Q. In what doth the Spirit enlighten our mind ?—A. In the knowledge of Christ, Gal. i. 16. Eph. i. 17, 18.

Q. In the knowledge of what of Christ is our mind enlightened?—A. In the knowledge of his person, offices, relations, righteousness, fulness, love, &c.

Q. What are we made to know concerning his person ? —A. That he is infinitely glorious, and fit to be matched with us, as he is God's Son, and our near kinsman.

Q. What are we made to know concerning his offices and relations ?—A. That they are wonderful and excellent, suited to our case, and shall be infinitely well filled up and executed by Christ, Song v. 10—16.

Q. What are we made to know concerning his righteousness ?—A. That it is infinitely perfect, law-magnifying, and God exalting, suited to the chief of sinners, and to us in particular; that it merits all blessings, and endureth for ever, Isa. xlii. 21. Dan. ix. 24. Rom. v.

Q. What are we made to know concerning his fulness of grace and glory ?—A. That it is infinite, precious, and suitable; is lodged in our kind Brother, and brought near to us in the Gospel, Col. i. 19, Isa. xlvi. 12, 13.

Q. What are we made to know concerning his love ?— A. The antiquity, freedom, sovereignty, greatness, and everlasting duration of it, John iii. 1, and iv. 10. 19.

Q. Are we not then made to see all the attributes of God shining gloriously in Christ?—A. Yes, 2 Cor. iv. 6.

Q. What are the properties of the saving knowledge of Christ.—A. It is an humbling, sanctifying, and growing knowledge, Isa. vi. 5, 1 Pet. iii. 18.

Q. How is it humbling ?—A. It makes us then ever see ourselves and our sins to be vile and ugly, Job xlii. 5, 6.

Q. How doth the knowledge of Christ make us discern a greater ugliness in sin ?—Hereby we see how foolish it was to prefer other things to Christ; and that every act of our sin was a rebellion against a God of infinite love, Phil. iii. 8, 9, Zech. xii. 10, Job xlii. 5, 6.

Q. What effect hath this knowledge upon us with respect to Christ ?—A. Our souls wonder at and esteem him as the *chief among ten thousand, and altogether lovely.*

Q. What think we of the world when we thus discern Christ ?—A. We count all things but loss and dung to win Christ, Phil. ii. 8, 9, Psalm lxxiii. 25, 26.

Q. What do we think of our own righteousness when

we thus see Christ?—A. We count it abominable and filthy rags, Isa. lxiv. 6, Phil. iii. 9.

Q. For what end is this enlightening of our mind necessary?—A. To cure our natural blindness and ignorance, and to engage our souls to embrace Christ, Gal. i. 16.

Q. May one have pleasant views of Christ, and yet be damned?—A. Yes; it is the case with many gospel-hearers, Matth. xiii. 20, Heb. vi. 4, Num. xxiii. xxiv.

Q. What then, besides conviction and illumination, is necessary to salvation?—A. The renewing of our will.

Q. What do you mean by the renewing of our will?—A. The making it averse from evil, and inclined to good.

Q. Doth God renew our will by force?—A. No; he sweetly changes it, by means of the pleasant and attracting discoveries he makes of Christ, Psalm cx. 2, 3.

Q. What need is there of the renovation of our will?—A. Because our will is naturally full of *enmity against God*, and we cannot renew it ourselves, Rom. viii. 7, 8.

Q. Why then doth God call us to *make to ourselves a new heart and a new spirit?*—A. It is to shew us our duty, and convince us of our inability, that we may apply to Christ for the promised new heart, Ezek. xxxvi. 26.

Q. How is this work of God's spirit, in uniting us to Christ, ordinarily called?—A. A calling, regeneration, or new birth, conversion, resurrection, and new creation.

Q. Why is it termed a *calling?*—A. Because the work is performed by the invitation and voice of Christ in the gospel, Rev. iv. 17, Prov. viii. 4, Rev. xxii. 17.

Q. What are the properties of this calling?—A. It is an effectual, high, heavenly, and holy calling.

Q. Why is it termed an *effectual* calling?—A. Because our soul is made to answer the call, Psalm cx. 3.

Q. What makes our soul to answer the call?—A. The drawing power of Christ that attends it, John xii. 32.

Q. Is there any call that is not effectual?—A. Yes; the more outward call of the gospel.

Q. Whether is the least or greatest part of gospel-hearers effectually called?—A. The least part by far: *Many are called, but few are chosen*, Matt. xx. 16.

Q. Why is it termed a *high* calling?—A. It is of God; and calls us to high honour and happiness, Phil. iii. 14.

Q. Why is it termed a *heavenly* calling?—A. It is most glorious; it comes from heaven, and draws up our heart to heavenly things, Heb. xii. 25.

Q. Why is it termed a *holy* calling?—**A.** Because thereby we are made partakers of God's holiness, being made holy as he is holy, 2 Pet. i. 4. 2 Tim. i. 9.

Q. From and to what are we hereby called?—**A.** From the power of sin and Satan to God; from darkness to light; from death to life; from bondage to liberty, Acts xxvi. 18, Col. i. 13, 1 Pet. ii. 9.

Q. Why is this work called *a new birth* or *regeneration?*—**A.** Because therein, without our own agency, and with some pain, we are made partakers of *a divine nature*, imperfectly conformed to God as our Father in our whole man, and brought into a new world.

Q. Into what new world are we brought?—**A.** Into Christ's invisible church, the world of grace.

Q. Who are the inhabitants of this new world?—**A.** All saints, and none else, 1 Pet. ii. 9.

Q. By what door do men enter into this new world?—**A.** By Christ, *the door, the way, the truth, and the life.*

Q. What is the sun, light, food, raiment, &c. of this new world?—**A.** Christ is the *all and in all* of it.

Q. Why is this work of the Spirit called *conversion?*—**A.** Because therein we are turned from sin to God.

Q. Is not conversion often used to signify only the soul's actual motion towards God, after it is quickened or regenerated by him?—**A.** Yes; Isa. vi. 10.

Q. Why is this work called *a resurrection?*—**A.** Because therein we are brought out of the grave of sin to newness of life, Rom. vi. 4, 5.

Q. Why is it called *a creation?*—Because therein God forms (not new substance, but) new qualities in our heart by the word of his power, Eph. i. 19.

Q. Why is the person thus changed called *a new creature?*—**A.** Because *all things* in him *are made new.*

Q. What in us is made new in effectual calling?—**A.** Our mind, conscience, will, affections, memory, body, and conversation, 2 Cor. v. 17.

Q. Wherein is our mind made new?—**A.** In its apprehension, judgment, estimation, thoughts, devices, and designs, Micah vii. 18, Psalm. cxix. 128, &c.

Q. How is our mind made new *in its apprehension?*—**A.** It now apprehends a beauty, loveliness, honour, and advantage in spiritual things; and an ugliness and danger in sin, Song v. 10—16, Isa. vi. 5.

Q. How is our mind made new *in its judgment?*—**A.** It now assents to God's truths, and dissents from the suggestions of sin, Satan, and the world.

Q. How is our mind made new *in its thoughts?*—A. Now our meditation is in God's law; and our meditation of him is sweet, Psalm civ. 34.

Q. How is our mind made new in *its devices, designs,* and *inquiries?*—A. We now enquire what we shall do to be saved; when God will come to our soul; how sin may be effectually ruined in us, &c. Acts xvi. Psalm ci.

Q. How is our conscience made new?—A. It is softened by Christ's blood, enlightened by his Spirit, and stirs up against spiritual wickedness, and to spiritual duties.

Q. Wherein is our will made new in conversion?—A. In its inclination, aim, delight, choice, and purpose.

Q. How is it made new *in its inclinations?*—A. Our will is now freely, powerfully, and constantly inclined towards God in Christ, Psalm xviii. 1, and xli. 1.

Q. How is our will made new *with respect to aim?*—A. Now its chief aim is to be like God, and to be with him; and to promote his honour in the world.

Q. How is our will made new as to *delight and rest?*—A. Its chief delight is now in the law of God, and in fellowship with him; and not in worldly honours, riches, or pleasures, Psalm iv. 17, and cxix. 16.

Q. How is our will made new *in its choice?*—A. It now chooseth the reality of religion rather than the shew of it, and to enjoy and obey God rather than any other.

Q. How is our will made new *in its purposes?*—A. It now purposes to leave all, especially secret and beloved sins, and to practice every known duty, Psalm cxix. 106.

Q. How are our affections made new?—A. They are rightly placed and rightly bounded.

Q. How are our affections rightly placed?—A. Love is set upon God, and hatred against sin, &c.

Q. How are our lawful affections rightly bounded?—A. We are in some measure determined to love creatures in that degree God's law requires, and out of regard to his authority and honour, Matth. x. 37, Heb. xiii. 1.

Q. How is our *memory* made new?—A. It is weakened with respect to things sinful and trifling, and strengthened to remember the word and works of God.

Q. How is our *body* made new?—A. It is made new in its use, being dedicated to, and a ready instrument in the service of God, Rom. vi. 13.

Q. How is our *conversation* made new ?—**A.** We now choose the fearers of God for our companions, are concerned for the church of Christ, and *zealous in good works*, Psal. cxix. 63, and cxxxvii. 4, 5.

Q. What is the necessity of this great change ?—**A.** Except we be thus born again, we *cannot enter into the kingdom of God*, John iii. 3. 5, Rev. xxi.

Q. Can we have any communion with God, or receive any spiritual blessing without this change ?—**A.** No.

Q. What is all our religion, if we want this great change ? —**A.** An abomination to God, Prov. xv. 8.

Q. What would heaven be to us if we could get thither without this change—**A.** The holiness of it would make it nauseous, and a burden to us, Rom. viii. 7, 8.

Q. What is the best season for getting this great change wrought in us ?—**A.** The season of youth, Prov. viii. 17.

Q. How is youth the fittest season of conversation ?—**A.** Then our lusts are less strong, conscience more easily roused, affections more pliable, carnal cares less heavy; and God hath promised special encouragement to an early concern about our souls, Eccl. xii. 1, Psalm xxxiv. 11.

Q. What special encouragement has God promised to an early concern about our souls ?—**A.** He hath said, *They that seek me early shall find me ;* and *Suffer little children to come to me,* &c. Prov. viii. 17, Mark x. 14.

Q. Is any such promise made to such as wilfully delay seeking of God till old age ?—**A.** No ; God rather says of such, *They shall seek me, but they shall not find me*, Prov. i. 24—28.

Q. Hath not an early convert more time to get communion with God on earth, and is not early communion with him singularly sweet and pleasant ?—**A.** Yes ; Jer. ii. 2.

Q. Is it not great folly and madness to bestow the flower of youth upon the service of Satan ?—**A.** Yes.

Q. How may we know if we are effectually called ?—**A.** If we love all that bear Christ's image ; count ourselves vile and worthless before God ; and desire above all things to be like him, and with him, 1 John iii. 16.

Q. What is our duty if we find this change has not been wrought in us ?—**A.** Carefully to wait on the ordinances of God's grace, and cry for the Spirit to apply them with power unto our hearts, Prov. viii. 34, Isa. lv. 1—3.

Q. What is our duty if we are thus changed ?—**A.** Greatly to bless the Lord for it ; and to walk in holiness as the children of God, Psalm ciii. 1—6, and cxlv.

Q. 32. *What benefits do they that are effectually called partake of in this life?*

A. They that are effectually called, do, in this life, partake of justification, adoption, sanctification, and the several benefits which in this life do either accompany or flow from them.

Q. What is the fruit of our union with Christ in our effectual calling?—A. Communion with him.

Q. How may communion with Christ be distinguished? —A. Into communion of interest and of intercourse.

Q. What is the communion *of intercourse?*—A. That near intimacy and sweet freedom which Christ and his people have with one another, Isa. lviii. 9.

Q. What is the communion *of interest?*—A. Our actual title to, and possession of Christ himself, and his purchased blessings, Song ii. 16, 1 Cor. i. 30.

Q. In what periods are we made sharers of his blessings?—A. In this life, at death, and at the resurrection.

Q. What blessings do believers share of in this life?—A. Of justification, adoption, and sanctification, and such benefits as in this life flow from them, Rom. viii.

Q. How are the benefits which believers receive from Christ, connected with effectual calling?—A. They all flow from our union with Christ obtained in it, 1 Cor. i. 30.

Q. How doth justification flow from union to Christ?— A. By our union to Christ, *the Lord our righteousness*, we become *the righteousness of God in him*, 2 Cor. v. 21.

Q. How doth adoption flow from union to Christ?—A. By union to Christ, the Son of God, we are made the children of God in Christ Jesus, Gal. iii. 26.

Q. How doth sanctification flow from union to Christ?— A. By our union to Christ as a head of influence, he becomes our strength and satisfaction, 1 Cor. i. 30.

Q. How doth a happy death flow from this union?—A. This union draws our departing souls to Christ's presence, and renders the grave a perfumed bed for our bodies, Rev. xiv. 13, Isa. xxvi. 19, and lvii. 2.

Q. How doth our happy resurrection flow from this union?—A. Being one with Christ, *the resurrection and the life*, we must be raised as members of his body, Isa. xxvi.

Q. How doth our eternal happiness flow from this

union?—A Being one with Christ, the *eternal life*, we must live forever in and with him, Col. iii. 3, 4.

Q. 33. *What is justification?*

A. Justification is an act of God's free grace, wherein he pardoneth all our sins, and accepteth us as righteous in his sight, only for the righteousness of Christ, imputed to us, and received by faith alone.

Q. What benefit doth first in order flow from our union to Christ?—A. Justification, Rom. viii. 30.

Q. What in general is meant by Justification?—A. Not the making of our natures holy; but the holding and declaring of our persons righteous in law.

Q. To what is justification opposed in scripture?—A. To condemnation, Prov. viii. 15. Rom. viii. 1.

Q. Why is our justification called *an act?*—A. Because it is perfected in an instant.

Q. Who is the author of our justification?—A. God essentially in the person of the Father, Rom. viii. 33.

Q. How then doth Christ as a Prince exalted give remission of sins?—A. He issues forth the sentence in his Father's name, Acts v. 31. Mark ii. 5. 10. Isa. liii. 11.

Q. How doth the Spirit justify us?—A. He applieth the righteousness of Christ, and justification through it, to our conscience, 1 Cor. vi. 11. Luke xv. 22.

Q. In what state are the elect before justification?—A. Though God loves them with an everlasting love, and his providence secretly makes way for their union to Christ; yet, in respect of the law, and of God as a judge, they are in a state of wrath and condemnation, Eph. ii. 3.

Q. What moves God to justify such persons?—A. His own free grace, Rom. iii. 24. Eph. i. 7.

Q. What are the parts of our justification before God?—A. His pardon of sin, and accepting us as righteous.

Q. What is the pardon of sin?—A. God's taking away the guilt of sin, or removing our obligation to punishment for sin, Rom. viii. 1. Psalm xxxii. 1, 2.

Q. How is the pardon of sin described in scripture?—A. As a *blotting it out, forgiving, covering*, and *remission* of it, *purging* it away, *casting it behind God's back*, or *into the depths of the sea*, &c. Isa. xliv. 22.

Q. What sins are pardoned in justification?—A. All our sins, past, present, and to come.

Q. How are our past sins pardoned?—A. Their guilt is formally removed from off our conscience, Jer. xxxiii. 8.

Q. How is the sin of our nature, which is still present, pardoned?—A Justification translates us from under the law as a covenant, so that our indwelling sin, being no longer a breach of that covenant, it no more subjects us to eternal wrath, Rom. viii. 1. Jer. l. 20. Isa. liv. 9.

Q. How are our sins committed after justification pardoned in it?—A. Justification prevents the imputation of them as to the guilt of eternal wrath, Rom. viii. 1.

Q. Do not our sins after justification *deserve* eternal wrath, as well as those before it?—A. Yes; and more so.

Q. Can then these sins bring us under God's wrath?— A. No; *there is no condemnation to them who are in Christ;* and he has sworn he *will not be wroth* with them.

Q. Whence does this proceed?—A. From our being no more under *the law of works,* which denounceth wrath.

Q. To what then do believers' sins bind them over?—A. To fatherly chastisement, Psalm lxxxix. 32.

Q. Do believers need the pardon of indwelling and actual sin every day they live?—A. Yes; they daily need a fathely, but no new legal pardon, Matth. vi. 12.

Q. Wherein does a fatherly pardon, and the legal pardon in justification, differ?—A. A *Legal pardon* in justification is an act of God as a Judge, forgives sins as against the covenant of works, frees from obligation to eternal wrath, changeth our state, and is the source of gospel-repentance; but *fatherly pardon* is an act of God as a Father, forgives sins committed against the law as a rule of life, frees from chastisement, makes no change in our state, and is the consequence of gospel-repentance.

Q. How prove you that repentance for sin is not a condition of our pardon in justification?—A. Because repentance is a work of the law, by which none can be justified; nor can an unpardoned sinner perform gospel-repentance, 1 Cor. xv. 56, Rom. viii. 7, 8, Eph. ii. 1.

Q. Doth not a legal repentance often go before justification?—A. Yes; but that is an abomination to God, Isa. i.

Q. What scriptures prove, that gospel-repentance follows our legal pardon in justification?—A. Ezek. xvi. 62, 63, and xxxvi. 25, 31, Luke vii. 42, 47, &c.

Q. How do you prove it impossible to perform gospel-repentance before justification?—A. Till the curse be removed in justification, we continue under the reigning pow-

14

er of sin ; nor can we turn to, but flee from God as an enemy, till his pardoning love encourage and inflame our
heart, and melt it into godly sorrow for sin, 1 Cor. xv. 56.

Q. How then is repentance sometimes in scripture represented as going before pardon of sin ?—A. In these texts,
Repentance either means only legal repentance, or pardon
must be understood of fatherly pardon, or of the declaration of our pardon at the last day ; or the connection between pardon and repentance is *simply* affirmed.

Q. Can there be any pardon without true repentance ?—
A. No ; no more than the sun can rise without light.

Q. How is it that believers can repent before receiving
fatherly pardon ?—A. They are not under the curse,
which is the strength of sin ; nor are their chastisements
evidences of God's wrath, but of his love, Heb. xii. 6. 11.

Q. Can pardon of sin be the whole of our justification ?
—A. No ; for it includes not a title to eternal life.

Q. What then is the second part of justification ?—A.
God's accepting us as *perfectly righteous in law.*

Q. Wherein do pardon and acceptance differ ?—A.
Pardon sustains us as innocent in law, and frees us from
the sentence of death ; but acceptance sustains us as posi-
tively and *perfectly righteous* in law, and entitles us to eternal life, Eph. i. 6, 2 Cor. v. 21.

Q. In whose sight are we accepted as righteous ?—A.
In the sight of God as a just Judge, 2 Cor. v. 21.

Q. How can God sustain us as perfectly righteous in
law, when we are ungodly ?—A. He sustains us as righteous in law only as we are one with Christ, Isa. xlv. 24, 25.

Q. What about us is in justification accepted as truly
and perfectly righteous ?—A. Our persons.

Q. Is not a foundation laid for God's acceptance of our
good works ?—A. Yes ; for the acceptance of all the
works we perform in faith, which is the bond which unites
our persons to Christ, Isa. lvi. 7, 1 Cor. xv. 38.

Q. Upon what ground or cause doth God pardon all
our sins, and accept us as *perfectly* righteous ?—A. Only
for the righteousness of Christ, Rom. iii. 24.

Q. How then is justification an *act of free grace ?*—A.
God freely provides and bestows this righteousness of Christ
upon us, 2 Cor. v. 21, Isa. lxi. 10.

Q. How do you prove that we are justified *only* for the
righteousness of Christ ?—A. The scripture declares all

our own righteousness *filthy rags;* and that *by the deeds of the law, no flesh shall be justified in God's sight.*

Q. What is the righteousness of Christ?—A. His obedience and suffering, Phil. ii. 8.

Q. How is it ordinarily distinguished?—A. Into his obedience active and passive, Dan. ix. 4, &c.

Q. What is his active obedience?—A. His holiness of nature, and righteousness of life, Rom. v. 19.

Q. What is his passive obedience?—A. His satisfactory sufferings, which are a full compensation for all the injury done to the honour of God by our sin, Eph. v. 2.

Q. Why are Christ's sufferings called *obedience?*—A. Because he suffered willingly, out of regard to God's authority, and with a view to his glory, John xvii. 6.

Q. Why is our justifying righteousness called *the righteousness of God?*—A. Because God the Father devised, accepted, and bestows it; God the Son fulfilled it; and God the Holy Ghost applieth it, Isa. xlii. 21. and xlv. 24.

Q. Is Christ's righteousness merely the price, condition, and meritorious cause of our justification, as it is of our regeneration, sanctification, &c.—A. No; it is also *the matter* of our justification, which enters *into it,* as that very righteousness by which we are constituted perfectly righteous before God, and have the righteousness of the law fulfilled in us, Rom. v. 19. viii. 4. and x. 4.

Q. How is the righteousness of Christ applied to us?—A. God gives and imputes it to us, and we receive it by faith, Isa. xlv. 24, xlvi. 13, and lxi. 10.

Q. How doth faith give us an interest in the righteousness of Christ?—A. It receives it from God *as his free gift;* and by uniting us to Christ as our Husband, gives us an *interest in it as his,* Rom. v. 17, Phil. iii. 9.

Q. What mean you by God's imputing the righteousness of Christ?—A. His accounting it to us, as if we had obeyed the law, and satisfied the justice of God in our own persons, Rom. viii. 4, 2 Cor. v. 21.

Q. How prove you that Christ's righteousness is imputed to us?—A. The scripture declares, that it is *unto and upon all them that believe;* and that we are *made the righteousness of God in him,* Rom. iii. 22, 2 Cor. v. 21.

Q. How prove you, that Christ's active obedience is imputed to us?—A. Because otherwise the righteousness of the law could not be fulfilled in us; and it is by *the obedi-*

ence of one (Christ,) *many are made righteous*, Gal. iii. 12,
Rom. viii. 4, v. 19, and iii. 22. 24.

Q. How can Christ's active obedience be imputed, when
his human nature owed obedience for itself?—**A.** Adam's
owing his obedience for himself hindered not the imputation of it to his seed ; moreover, Christ's obedience imputed
to us, being an obedience to the law *as a broken covenant
of works*, is such as a human nature, united to a divine
person, *could never owe for itself,* Gal. iv. 4, 5.

Q. Is the righteousness of Christ itself, or only its effects,
imputed to us?—**A.** His righteousness itself is *imputed*, and
its effects are *imparted* to us, Rom. v. 19.

Q. For what end is the righteousness of Christ imputed
to us?—**A.** His passive obedience is imputed to found our
legal security from eternal death ; and his active to found
our legal title to eternal life, John x. 10, Rom. v. 19.

Q. Is Christ's righteousness imputed *partly to one and
partly to another ;* or his active and passive obedience *sepa-
rately* imputed, the one to procure pardon, and the other acceptance?—**A.** No ; his *whole undivided* righteousness is,
in both its parts, jointly imputed to every believer as one
complete righteousness, constituting him *perfectly* righteous
before God, Isa. lxi. 10, 2 Cor. v. 21.

Q. Upon what ground is the righteousness of Christ imputed to us?—**A.** Upon the footing of our union to him as
our surety and husband, Isa. liii. 4, 5, 6. 11, 12.

Q. In what do the imputation of our sins to Christ's, and
that of his righteousness to us, differ?—**A.** Our sin was imputed to him, that he, by bearing it for a time, might destroy it ; but his righteousness is imputed to us that he
might wear it for ever, Dan. ix. 24.

Q. What are the instrumental causes of justification?—
A. The gospel-promise on God's part, and faith on ours.

Q. How is the gospel an instrument in justification?—
A. It reveals, offers, and makes over to us Christ and his
righteousness, and justification through it, Isa. xlv. 24.

Q. How is faith an instrument in our justification?—**A.**
It receives Christ's person and righteousness, and justification through it, as offered in the gospel, Gal. ii. 16.

Q. Is the receiving act of faith, or our new obedience,
imputed to us as our gospel-righteousness, or condition of
right to Christ's righteousness?—**A.** No ; only the righteousness of Christ, which faith receives, is imputed in our
justification, Rom. iv. 5, Isa. xlv. 24, Phil. iii. 9.

Q. How then is it said, *Abraham believed God, and it was imputed to him for righteousness?*—A. The meaning is not, that Abraham's *act of faith*, but that *what he believed on* was imputed to him for righteousness.

Q. Is faith the alone instrument of justification on our side?—A. Yes; we are justified by faith, without the deeds of the law, Rom. iii. 28, and v. 1, Phil. iii. 8, 9.

Q. Are all our good works and resolutions deeds of the law?—A. Yes; for they are all obedience to it.

Q. How then is it said, James ii. 24. *By works a man is justified, and not by faith only?*—A. That is to be understood of the justification of our faith before men, and not that of our persons before God.

Q. Can we be justified, and yet neglect the study of good works?—A. No; *faith without works is dead.*

Q. If our good works are *no cause* of justification, what connection have they with it?—A. They flow from it, and evidence it, and testify our thankfulness to God for it, James ii. 18, Rom. vii. 4.

Q. Is not faith itself a good work?—A. Yes; but it justifies not as a good work, but only as an instrument, receiving Christ and his righteousness for justification of life, Acts xxvi. 18, Isa. xlv. 24, 25, Phil. iii. 9.

Q. Why hath God made faith alone the instrument on our part in justification?—A. That his free grace might clearly shine, and all pride and boasting of men be excluded.

Q. When are we justified?—A. The sentence of justification was conceived in the mind of God from eternity; but is not actually applied to our persons and conscience, till the moment in which we first believe in Christ.

Q. How doth God intimate the sentence of justification?—A. In the powerful application of his promise to our conscience; which is manifested in our good works: and he will publicly declare it at the last day.

Q. Were believers under the Old Testament justified in the same manner as we are now?—A. Yes, Isa. xlv. 24, 25.

Q. How should we improve the doctrine of justification?—A. By renouncing all dependence on our works, and leaning on Christ as our only righteousness, Phil. iii. 9.

14*

Q. 34. *What is adoption ?*

A. Adoption is an act of God's free grace, whereby we are received into the number, and have a right to all the privileges of the sons of God.

Q. What is in general meant by *adoption?*—A. The taking a stranger into our family, and dealing with him as a son born in it, Gen. xv. 3.

Q. Wherein doth adoption among men differ from God's adoption of children ?—A. Men adopt, because they want children, or see something lovely in the adopted ; but it is not so with God, 1 John iii. 1.

Q. How many kinds of adoption are ascribed to God ? —A. Two kinds, common and special.

Q. What is God's *common* or *general* adoption ?—A. His taking some part of mankind into his family of the visible church, Rom. ix. 4.

Q. What is the badge of this general adoption ?—A. Circumcision under the Old Testament, and baptism under the New, Gen. xvii. Matth. xxviii. 19.

Q. What is God's *special* adoption?—A. His bringing a child of the devil into his family of the invisible church, and giving him a right to all the privileges of the sons of God, Col. i. 13, Gal. iv. 5, 6, 2 Cor. vi. 18.

Q. Whether is adoption a *work* or an *act?*—A. An act.

Q. What moves God to adopt any of mankind ?—A. His own rich and free grace, 1 John iii. 1.

Q. Whose children are those, by nature, whom God adopts ?—A. The children of the devil, Eph. ii. 2, 3.

Q. Are these men, who are adopted by God any better in themselves than those who are not ?—A. No.

Q. What then moves God to adopt some, and pass by others no worse ?—A. His mere good pleasure, Jer. iii. 19.

Q. Whose act is adoption ?—A. It is an act of God the Father, Son, and Holy Ghost, Rom. viii. 33.

Q. How is it an act *of the Father?*—A. He predestinates us to the adoption of sons, Rom. viii. 29.

Q. How is adoption an act *of the Son?*—A. He gives us, whom he redeemed with his blood, power, or *privilege*, to become the sons of God, John i. 12.

Q. How is adoption an act *of the Holy Ghost?*—A. He enters into our souls as a spirit of adoption, and makes us cry, *Abba, Father*, Rom. viii. 15.

Q. What is the price or meritorious cause of our adoption?—A. The righteousness of Christ alone.

Q. What is the instrumental cause of our adoption?—A. We *are the children of God by faith in Christ Jesus.*

Q. How is faith the instrument of adoption?—A. It unites us to Christ, in whom we become heirs of God.

Q. To whom is adoption intimated?—A. To holy angels, and to the adopted persons themselves, Heb. i. 14.

Q. Why is it intimated to the angels?—A. That they may rejoice over, and minister to the new heirs of God.

Q. How is it intimated to the adopted persons themselves?—A. By the Spirit's bearing witness with their spirits that they are the children of God, Rom. viii. 16. 26.

Q. What honour have those whom God adopts?—A. They are received into the number of his children.

Q. What happiness have those whom God adopts?—A. They have a right to all the privileges of the sons of God, Rom. viii. 17, Rev. xxi. 7, 1 Cor. iii. 22.

Q. Wherein doth our right to these privileges given us in justification, and that given us in adoption, differ?—A. The right given us in justification is a law-right of purchase; but that in adoption is a right of inheritance.

Q. To what privileges have the sons of God a right?—A. A new name; new honour; a new spirit; God's fatherly protection, provision, correction, direction, and hearing their prayers; spiritual liberty; boldness and familiarity with God; and an everlasting inheritance.

Q. What was God's children's old and former name?—A. It was *rebellious, strangers, foreigners, unrighteous, children of wrath, of disobedience,* and of *the devil, having no hope, without God and Christ* in the world.

Q. What new name are God's children called by?—A. Christ's new name is written on them, Rev. iii.

Q. How is Christ's new name written on them?—A. They are called the *redeemed of the Lord,* and the *righteousness of God* in him; the *sister, spouse, love,* and *dove* of Christ, &c. Isa. lxii. 4. 12, Song v. 2.

Q. How is this new name put on them?—A. It is conveyed to them in the sentence of their pardon.

Q. Are we then quickened, united to Christ, justified, and adopted, in the same moment of time, and by means of the same word of promise?—A. Yes.

Q. What new honour do God's children receive?—A. They are made *kings and priests, unto God,* Rev. i. 6.

Q. What new spirit of adoption have they?—**A.** The spirit of Christ dwells in them, Rom. viii. 9.

Q. Whether does the Holy Ghost dwell in them in his person, or in his influence?—**A.** In both, 2 Tim. i. 14.

Q. How can the one person of the Spirit dwell in each believer?—**A.** His person is every where, and he dwells in all believers as the one mystical body of Christ.

Q. Of what use is the Spirit of adoption to believers?—**A.** To sanctify, direct, comfort, and assist them.

Q. What divine protection have God's children?—**A.** God's fatherly eye is still on them, his arms about them, and his angels surround them, Psalm xxxiv.

Q. Of what use are angels to the children of God?—**A.** They attend, guard, support, and direct them.

Q. What provision hath God made for his children?—**A.** All things necessary for their soul and body.

Q. What provision is secured by promise for their bodies?—**A.** Bread and water, Isa. xxxiii. 16.

Q. Why is no better provision secured for their bodies?—**A.** To wean them from this world, and make them feed more largely on their spiritual provision, 2 Cor. iv. 7.

Q. What is provided for the souls of God's children?—**A.** All the fulness of God, Eph. iii. 19, 1 Cor. xv. 28.

Q. What spiritual food is provided for believers' souls?—**A.** The flesh and blood of Christ, John vi. 53—57.

Q. What clothing is provided for believers' souls?—**A.** The righteousness and image of Christ, Rom. xiii. 14.

Q. What bed hath God provided for his children's souls?—**A.** His bosom of love, and covenant of grace, Song i. 15.

Q. What house is provided for their souls?—**A.** God in Christ, and the heavenly mansions.

Q. What teachers are assigned to their souls?—**A.** God their Father, Christ their brother, the Spirit their guest, and ministers their servants, Isa. xlviii. 17.

Q. What direction have God's children a right to?—**A.** To God's gracious leading and drawing of them in the paths of duty and happiness, Psalm lxxiii. 24.

Q. What correction have God's children a right to?—**A.** To the rod of both outward and spiritual troubles.

Q. What moves God to correct his children for their faults?—**A.** His great love to them, Heb. xii. 6—11.

Q. How may we know if our afflictions spring from God's love?—**A.** If they are attended with resignation to his will, and earnest desire after holiness, Heb. xii. 6. 10.

Q. For what end doth God correct his children ?—A. To drive folly out of their hearts, and make them partakers of his holiness, Heb. xii. 10, 11, Isa. xxvii. 9.

Q. How should believers behave when God corrects them ?—A. They should neither despise his chastening, nor faint under it, Heb. xii. 5, Job v. 17.

Q. What is meant by God's hearing of their prayers ?—A. His kindly accepting and answering of them.

Q. What spiritual liberty have the children of God ?—A. Freedom from the power of sin, Satan, death, and the law as a covenant; and sweet pleasure in running a course of obedience to the law as a rule, Psalm cxvi. 16.

Q. To what spiritual boldness have believers a right ?—A. They may boast in God as their own, and boldly seek, and firmly expect all his blessings, Psalm lxii.

Q. What is the ground of our holy boldness towards God?—A. Christ's righteousness and intercession.

Q. To what familiarity with God have believers a right? —A. They may freely represent their case to him as a Father, whose ear is open to hear, and his heart full of pity to them; and may take his word as a Father's language to them, Job xxiii. 3—6. Song ii. 8—13.

Q. Of what inheritance are God's children heirs ?—A. Of salvation, righteousness, GOD, and glory.

Q. By what marks are God's children distinguished ?—A. By a desire to be like God, their Father, in holiness, to be in his company, and hear his voice; zeal for his honour; and a love to all his children, ordinances, &c.

Q. How should we improve this benefit of adoption?—A. By refusing to be at ease till we possess it; and by wondering at the love of God manifested in it, &c.

Q. 35. *What is sanctification?*

A. Sanctification is the work of God's free grace, whereby we are renewed in the whole man, after the image of God, and are enabled more and more to die unto sin, and live unto righteousness.

Q. What doth our sanctification generally include ?—A. Our being made *holy* in nature, and separated from the world to the *holy* service of God, Ezek. xxxvi. 26, 27.

Q. Are our justification and sanctification inseparably linked together ?—A. Yes; Isa. lxii. 12. 1 Pet. i. 2.

Q. Wherein are justification and sanctification linked together?—A. In God's decree and promise, in the offices of Christ, and end of his death, in the gospel-offer, and the experience of all believers, 1 Cor. i. 30.

Q. Doth our sanctification depend on our justification and adoption?—A. Yes; as its root and spring.

Q. How doth sanctification depend on justification?—A. It is the native fruit of the removal of our guilt, and a necessary part of the happiness to which we are adjudged in justification, Acts xxvi. 18. Psalm cxvi. 16.

Q. How doth sanctification depend on adoption?—A. It is the natural fruit of God our Father his holy Spirit dwelling in us, 1 Cor. vi. 11. 2 Cor. vi. 18. and vii. 1.

Q. Wherein doth justification and sanctification differ?—A. In their nature, order, matter, form, properties, subject, extent, ingredients, evidence, relation to sin, to the law, to God, to the offices of Christ, and their use to believers.

Q. How do they differ in their *nature?*—A. Justification changes our law state; sanctification changes our heart and life, Ezek, xxxvi. 25, 26, 27.

Q. How do they differ in their *order?*—A. Justification is first; and sanctification follows as the fruit of it.

Q. How do they differ in their *matter?*—A. The righteousness of Christ imputed is the matter of justification; but the grace of Christ implanted in our heart is the matter of sanctification, John i. 16. 29.

Q. How do they differ in their *form?*—A. Justification is an act; but sanctification is a work.

Q. How do they differ in their *properties?*—A. Justification is constantly equal in all believers, and perfect at first; but sanctification is unequal in different believers, and in the same believers at different times, and is never perfect in any till death, Rom. viii. 1. 1 John ii. 13.

Q. How do they differ in their *subject?*—A. The righteousness of justification is subjectively in Christ, and on believers as a robe; but sanctification is in believers as a new nature, Rom. iii. 22. 2 Pet. i. 4.

Q. How do they differ in their *extent?*—A. Though justification respect our whole person, yet it especially affects our conscience; but sanctification equally affects our whole man, Heb. ix. 14. 1 Thess. v. 23.

Q. How do they differ in their *ingredients?*—A. In justification *only* the love of God is manifested to us; but in sanctification our love to God is also manifested.

Q. How do they differ in their *evidence?*—**A.** Justification is in itself a most secret act; but sanctification is an evidence of our justification.

Q. How do they differ in their *relation to sin?*—**A.** Justification removes the guilt of sin; but sanctification removes the filth, Ezek. xxxvi. 25, 26, 27.

Q. How do they differ in their *relation to the law?*—**A.** Justification *frees* us from the *law as a covenant;* sanctification *conforms* us to the *law as a rule.*

Q. How do they differ in their *relation to God?*—**A.** Justification instates us in God's favour; sanctification conforms us to his image, Rom. viii. 1, and xii. 2.

Q. How do they differ in their *relation to the offices of Christ?*—**A.** Justification is immediately founded on the righteousness of Christ as a priest; sanctification immediately flows from the subduing, ruling, and defending influence of Christ as a king, 2 Cor. v. 21, Psalm cx. 3.

Q. How do they differ in their *use to believers?*—**A.** Justification frees us from hell, and entitles us to heaven; sanctification makes us meet for heaven.

Q. Is it very dangerous to confound justification with sanctification?—**A.** Yes; for it either tempts them to turn the grace of God into sloth and licentiousness, or place their own holiness in the room of Christ's righteousness; and it leads believers into the practical error of judging their state by their frame, Jude 4, Rom. x. 3.

Q. Whose work is our sanctification?—**A.** It is the work of God's Spirit, 1 Cor. vi. 11.

Q. Is it not also the work of the Father and Son?—**A.** Yes; but they work it by the Spirit, Phil. ii. 13.

Q. Cannot believers, who have received grace, sanctify themselves?—**A.** No; *without Christ* they *can do nothing.*

Q. Do not believers' good works deserve God's sanctifying grace?—**A.** No; when we have done all we are but *unprofitable servants,* Luke xvii. 10.

Q. What then moves God to sanctify his people?—**A.** His own free grace, reigning through the righteousness of Christ, Titus iii. 5, Rom. v. 21.

Q. How may our sanctification be distinguished?—**A.** Into sanctification of nature, and sanctification of life, 2 Cor. vii. 1, Matth. v. 17, Ezek. xxxvi. 27.

Q. What is *sanctification of nature?*—**A.** The renewing of our whole man after the image of God.

Q. After what pattern is our whole man renewed in sanctification ?—**A.** After the image of God, Eph. iv.

Q. Whose image is defaced in our sanctification?—**A.** The image of the devil, and fallen Adam.

Q. Wherein doth the renewing of our whole man in sanctification differ from the renewing of it in effectual calling?—**A.** In effectual calling the renewing is begun, and the new creature is begotten and born in us; but in sanctification this renewing is carried on more and more, till our new nature become fully perfect, Prov. iv. 18.

Q. What is the fruit of sanctification of nature?—**A.** Sanctification of our life, Matt. v. 17, and vii. 17.

Q. What do you mean by sanctification of life?—**A.** Our being enabled more and more to die unto sin, and live unto righteousness, Rom. vi. 11, and viii. 13.

Q. Wherein do sanctification of nature and life differ ? —**A.** The *first* strengthens us in holy and gracious dispositions; but in the *last* we exert that strength in holy thoughts, words and actions, Matt. xii. 35.

Q. What are the parts of sanctification of life?—**A.** Our dying to sin, and living to righteousness.

Q. What is meant by our dying to sin?—**A.** Our ceasing more and more from the love and practice of it.

Q. Do not the remains of sin in our whole man oppose this death?—**A.** Yes; most vigorously, Rom. vii. 23.

Q. How do they oppose it?—**A.** By secret lusting, and violent fighting against grace in our heart, Gal. v. 17.

Q. Doth indwelling sin ever prevail against our grace ? —**A.** Yes; very often, and very far, Rom. vii. 19. 23.

Q. How far may indwelling sin prevail against our grace?—**A.** So far as to bring it to the brink of destruction, and keep it long so, Rom. vii. 23.

Q. Can indwelling sin utterly destroy our grace?—**A.** No; however small and weak it be, Job xvii. 9.

Q. Why so ?—**A.** Not because our grace itself is stronger than sin; but because God is the strength of our grace.

Q. If God be the strength of our grace, how can sin ever prevail against it?—**A.** God often hides himself: and we neglect to improve his strength for subduing sin.

Q. Whether doth sin or grace prevail at last?—**A.** Always grace, Rom. viii. 13. 37, Prov. iv. 18.

Q. Who assist sin in its opposition to implanted grace ? —**A.** Satan and the world, Eph. vi. 1 John v. 4.

Q. Who assists our new nature or grace in its exercise ?

—A. The Spirit of God, by whom we *mortify* and kill *the deeds of our body*, or remainders of lust, Rom. viii. 13.

Q. May there not be an inward struggle with sin, where there is no real grace?—A. Yes; it is often so.

Q. Wherein doth this differ from the struggle between sin and grace in believers?—A. In unbelievers the struggle about sin is only between the mind or conscience, and the will and affections ; but in believers the inclination to good in the will and affections strives against the inclination to evil in the same faculties.

Q. What is meant by our living to righteousness?—A. Our becoming more in love with it, and more constant and active in the practice of it, Job xvii. 9.

Q. To what righteousness do believers live?—A. To a continued obedience to all God's commands.

Q. In what manner do we die to sin and live to righteousness?—A. By degrees, or more and more.

Q. Can we die to sin or live to righteousness of ourselves?—A. No; the Spirit of God must enable us to do it, Ezek. xxxvii. 27, John xv. 5.

Q. How doth the Spirit enable us to die to sin, and live to righteousness?—A. By conveying new strength through the promise into our heart, and by stirring us up to the study of more holiness, 2 Cor. vii. 1, Rom. viii. 13.

Q. Is the work of our sanctification often interrupted?—A. Yes, in our apprehension ; but God still carries on his work, even by means of the prevalency of sin.

Q. When is our sanctification in heart and life completed?—A. At death, Heb. xii. 23, Eph. v. 27.

Q. Why doth God suffer sin to remain in his people till death?—A. To shew the riches of his grace in pardoning so much sin ; to try and exercise their grace ; to render heaven more sweet ; and that sin may die in them in a lingering manner, as Christ did, Rom. v. 20, 21.

Q. From what about Christ doth our sanctification flow?—A. From his death and resurrection, Rom. vi. 4.

Q. How doth it flow from his death?—A. His death purchased it ; and, when applied to our conscience, frees us from the curse of the law, which is the strength of sin, and stirs us up to the love of God, 2 Cor. v. 14, 15.

Q. How doth it flow from his resurrection?—A. In his resurrection he took possession of spiritual life for his people, to be bestowed on them, Rom. vi. 4, 5, 6.

15

Q. What is the instrument of our sanctification?—**A.** Faith in Christ Jesus, Acts xxvi. 18.

Q. How doth faith sanctify us?—**A.** By receiving the comfort and cleansing virtue of the promises into our hearts, 2 Cor. vii. 1, John xv. 4, and xvii. 17.

Q. What is the only rule of our sanctification?—**A.** The holy law of God, Psalm cxix. 1. 9.

Q. What pattern must we study to imitate in our sanctification?—**A.** The example of God and Christ.

Q. Why is our sanctification necessary?—**A.** Not to be a condition of our salvation; but to evidence our faith and union to Christ, glorify God, adorn our profession, promote our peace of conscience, make us meet for heaven, gain others to Christ, &c., Matth. v. 17.

Q. What are the chief motives to sanctification?—**A.** The holiness, command, and love of God; Christ's dying to save and sanctify us; and the great dignity of holiness, 1 Peter i. 16, 1 John iv. 19, Titus ii. 14.

Q. Is sanctification a great privilege, as well as duty?—**A.** Yes; it is a great duty as required from us by the law; and a rich privilege as promised in the gospel, and produced in us by the Holy Spirit, Phil. ii. 12, 13.

Q. How prove you, that sanctification is a most excellent privilege and duty?—**A.** It is the end of Christ's offices, death, and exaltation; and of our election, effectual calling, justification, and adoption; and of all the work of the Spirit; and of all the precepts, promises, and providences of God, Titus ii. 14, Heb. ii. 10, 11, &c.

Q. What are some marks of our sanctification?—**A.** A deep sense of our vileness, a love to God's law, and an earnest desire after growth in grace, Job xl., &c.

Q. How should we study sanctification?—**A.** By making sure our union to Christ; by watchfulness against sin; and a believing attendance on God's ordinances, in order to gain more near communion with Christ.

Q. 36. *What are the benefits which in this life do accompany or flow from justification, adoption and sanctification.*

A. The benefits which in this life do accompany or flow from justification, adoption, and sanctification, are assurance of God's love, peace of conscience, joy in the Holy Ghost, increase of grace, and perseverance therein to the end.

Q. Do justification, adoption, and sanctification come alone to the people of God ?—A. No; many rich blessings attend and flow from them, Rom. v. 1. 5.

Q. What benefits flow from the knowledge of our justification, adoption, and sanctification ?—A. Assurance of God's love, peace of conscience, and joy in the Holy Ghost, Rom. xiv. 17.

Q. What benefits flow from the being of our justification, adoption, and sanctification ?—A. Increase of grace, and perseverance in it, Prov. iv. 18.

Q. Have all believers always assurance of God's love, peace of conscience, and joy in the Holy Ghost ?—A. They have them always in the root, but often want the sensible experience of them, Isa. liv. 8. 13.

Q. How many kinds of assurance of God's love may believers have ?—A. Two; an assurance of faith, and an assurance of sense, Job xiii. 15, Song ii. 16.

Q. In what do the assurance of faith, and that of sense, differ ?—A. The assurance of faith is a firm persuasion of God's love to us, founded on his promise; the assurance of sense is a persuasion that we have already tasted of his love, Heb. xi. 1. 13, 1 John v. 9, 10. 20.

Q. Have all believers the assurance of faith ?—A. Yes; they all have it in some measure, Song viii. 5.

Q. Have all believers the assurance of sense ?—A. No; many want it; and such as have once obtained it, may again lose it for a time, Heb. ii. 15, Psal. lxxvii.

Q. Do assured believers see God's love in the whole benefits of justification, adoption, and sanctification ?—A. Yes; they see his love to be the source, matter, and end of these privileges, 1 John iii. 1, 2, Rev. i. 6.

Q. How prove you, that believers may attain sensible assurance of God's love ?—A. God commands us to seek it; hath given many marks to try ourselves by; and many saints, as David, &c. have attained it, 2 Pet. i. 10.

Q. By what means is assurance of sense maintained ?—A. By a holy walk, diligent self-examination; and especially by the Spirit's *bearing witness with our spirits, that we are the children of God*, Rom. viii. 13. 16.

Q. What may comfort believers when they have lost the

assurance of sense?—A. That God's love is unchangeable, and will again be manifested, Mal. iii. 6.

Q. Doth God always love believers alike?—A. He always loves their persons alike, but not their works.

Q. Why doth he not always love their works equally?—A. Because frequently their works are sinful; and such as are good, are not equally good, Gen. xxvii. and xxxii.

Q. Doth God always evidence his love to believers in the same manner?—A. No; he sometimes manifests his love in correcting, and sometimes in comforting them, Heb. xii. 6, Isa. liv. 11.

Q. How may sensible assurance of God's love be recovered when lost?—A. By the lively exercise of faith, by repentance of our sin, by justifying God's hiding, and by waiting and praying for new tokens of his love, Micah vii.

Q. What is the advantage of sensible assurance of God's love?—A. It stirs up to duty, comforts under trials, and fills our hearts with love to God, Rom. i. 1—5.

Q. May not men falsely persuade themselves that God loveth them when he doth not?—A. Yes; many do so.

Q. In what do true and false assurance differ?—A. True assurance humbles men, begets ardent desires after holiness and communion with God, stirs up to all known duty, and loveth to be tried; but false assurance encourageth pride, sloth, and sin, and shuns trial, Isa. vi. 5.

Q. What is *peace of conscience?*—A. A holy quiet of mind arising from the views of our being in favour with God, Rom. v. 1, Psalm cxiv. 7.

Q. Can unbelievers have true peace of conscience?—A. No; but many of them have a false peace, Isa. lvii. 21.

Q. In what do true and false peace of conscience differ?—A. True peace of conscience strongly stirs up against sin; false peace encourageth in sin, 2 Cor. i. 12.

Q. Doth all true peace of conscience flow from justification, adoption, and sanctification?—A. Yes, Rom. v. 1.

Q. When have we the peace which flows from justification?—A. When our conscience, sprinkled with the blood of Christ, is set free from the fears of God's revenging wrath, Heb. x. 22.

Q. When have we that peace which flows from adoption?—A. When we calmly view God as our Father in Christ.

Q. When have we that peace which flow from sanctification?—A. When our conscience bears witness to our sincerity and uprightness in the Lord's way, 1 Cor. i. 12.

Q. Whether is the peace of conscience flowing from justification, or that flowing from sanctification, most firm and lasting?—A. The peace flowing from justification.

Q. Why is this peace most firm and lasting?—A. It is immediately founded on Christ's perfect, eternal, and unchangeable righteousness, Rom. v. 1—10.

What is *joy in the Holy Ghost?*—A. A spiritual pleasure in feeding on, and walking with Christ.

Q. Why is this called *joy in the Holy Ghost?*—A. Because it flows from his presence and work in our heart.

Q. What is the matter and ground of this joy?—A. God in Christ as our eternal portion, Psalm xvi. 5.

Q. What are the properties of this joy?—A. It is a spiritual, hidden, abiding, and unspeakable joy.

Q. In what seasons do believers often receive this joy?—A. At conversion, after signal desertion, under heavy persecution, and about the time of their death.

Q. When have we the joy flowing from justification?—A. When we can come with boldness to God through the blood of Christ, Heb. iv. 16. Rom. v. 11.

Q. When have we the joy which flows from adoption?—A. When the Spirit enableth us to cry, *Abba, Father.*

Q. When have we the joy flowing from sanctification?—A. When the Holy Ghost makes every duty sweet and pleasant to us, Psalm cxix. 32.

Q. May not unbelievers have some kind of spiritual joy?—A. Yes; many have a false joy, Matth. xiii. 20.

Q. Wherein do false and true spiritual joy differ?—A. True joy in the Holy Ghost makes us holy and humble; but false joy encourageth pride and spiritual sloth.

Q. What is meant by *increase of grace?*—A. Receiving new measures of it, and more active exercise of it.

Q To what is growth in grace compared in scripture?—A. To *the light that shineth more and more unto the perfect day*, Prov. iv. 18. Job xvii. 9. 2 Pet. iii. 18.

Q. What is the spring of our growth in grace?—A. Union to Christ and influences from him, John xv.

Q. For what end must believers grow in grace?—A. That they may arrive at the fulness of the stature of perfect men in Christ, Eph. iv. 13. Phil. iii. 14.

Q. How doth growth in grace flow from justification?—

15*

A. As therein we receive a law-right to grace in its perfection, Rom. v. 1—5.

Q. How doth growth in grace flow from adoption?—**A.** Believers, as God's babes *suck the sincere milk of* his *word, that they may grow thereby*, 1 Peter ii. 2.

Q. How doth growth in grace flow from sanctification? —**A.** As therein we are renewed more and more.

Q. Do saints grow in grace at all times?—**A.** They have a constant disposition to grow, but do not always actually grow in grace, Psalm xxxii. 3, 4.

Q. In what graces do saints grow?—**A.** In all graces; such as faith, hope, love, repentance, zeal, patience, humility, brotherly kindness, &c. 2 Peter i. 5.

Q. Are these particular graces different parts of the new nature?—**A.** No; they are only the new nature exercised in different ways.

Q. By which of these graces is the growth of the rest chiefly promoted?—**A.** By faith, Psalm xxvii. 13, 14.

Q. How doth faith make our other graces to grow?— **A.** By drawing in virtue from Christ in the promise, and receiving *out of his fulness grace for grace*.

Q. What stops our growth in grace?—**A.** Our neglect of the exercise of faith on Christ our life, Heb. iii. 19.

Q. May not hypocrites grow in the appearance of grace? —**A.** Yes, Matth. xiii. 26. Isa. lviii. 2.

Q. In what doth the religious growth of hypocrites and of saints differ?—**A.** Hypocrites grow only in some things, as head knowledge, and external duties; but believers grow up in all good things in heart and life.

Q. In what different ways do believers grow in grace?— **A.** Inwardly, outwardly, upwards, and downwards.

Q. How do the saints grow *inwardly?*—**A.** By uniting more closely with Christ, and becoming more like him in their hearts, Eph. iv. 15. 2 Cor. iii. 18.

Q. How do they grow *outwardly?*—**A.** By abounding more and more in good works, Tit. iii. 8. 14.

Q. How do they grow *downwards?*—**A.** By becoming more humble and self-denied, Eph. iii. 8, Gen. xxxii. 10.

Q. How do they grow *upwards?*—**A.** By becoming less carnal, and more heavenly-minded, Phil. iii. 20.

Q. Do saints often mistake their growth?—**A.** Yes.

Q. In what manner do saints mistake their growth?—**A.** By thinking themselves growing when they are not, or not growing when they are; and in not regarding their downward growth, because they cannot perceive their upward growth, Psalm xxx. and xxxi.

Q. How may we know if we have grace, though of a small growth ?—A. If we desire growth in grace, and love all that have the appearance of it, 1 John iii. 14.

Q. What is perseverance in grace ?—A. Our constant continuance in it, John x. 28.

Q. May not believers fall from some degrees of grace which they once attained ?—A. Yes ; but they can neither fall totally nor finally, Jer. xxxii. 40, 1 Pet i. 5.

Q. What do you mean by falling *totally* from grace ?—A. The falling from every degree of grace.

Q. What do you mean by falling *finally* from grace ?—A. Falling so from grace as never to be recovered.

Q. What are the bonds that secure believers' perseverance in grace ?—A. The unchangeable love, covenant, promise, and infinite power of God ; Christ's infinite merit, and eternal intercession ; their union to him, and his Spirit dwelling in them, Jer. xxxi. 3, 1 Pet. i. 5.

Q. What hath God promised concerning the saints' perseverance ?—A. That he will never turn from them, and that they shall never depart from him, Jer. xxxii. 40.

Q. What is the meritorious cause of believers' perseverance in grace ?—A. Christ's perseverance in obedience and satisfaction till he finished his work, Isa. xlii. 4.

Q. Do not some, who once appeared to be saints, fall away totally and finally from their profession?—A. Yes ; but these are such as never had real grace.

Q. If believers cannot fall away from grace, why are they called to beware of falling ?—A. Because they may fall from many degrees of grace : and, if left of God to themselves, would totally fall away from it.

Q. How doth God preserve the saints in grace ?—A. By continued influences of his grace, and by continued pardon of their daily sins, Isa. xxvii. 3, Acts v. 31.

Q. Why are continued influences of grace necessary to believers ?—A. Because without these their stock of grace would soon waste and die, John xv. 6.

Q. Why is •continued pardon necessary to them ?—A. Because though their daily sins do not bind them over to God's judicial wrath, yet they much hinder the communications of his love and favour to them, Isa. lix. 2.

Q. When do believers receive God's fatherly pardon ?—

A. As often as they exert new acts of faith, on the blood of Christ, and repent of their sin, 1 John i. 7, and ii. 1, 2.

Q. How doth our perseverance in grace flow from justification?—**A.** As justification secures our eternal life, and is an act that can never be recalled, Rom. xi. 29.

Q. How doth our perseverance flow from adoption?—**A.** God, being our everlasting Father, we must abide in his house for ever, John viii. 35.

Q. How doth perseverance flow from sanctification?—**A.** As God's sanctifying Spirit is in us *a well of water springing up to everlasting life*, John iv. 14.

Q. How ought we to improve this variety and connection of benefits?—**A.** By studying to be among the happy number of saints; and admiring the wisdom and grace of God in linking so many privileges together.

Q. 37. *What benefits do believers receive from Christ at death?*

A. The souls of believers are, at their death, made perfect in holiness, and do immediately pass into glory; and their bodies being still united to Christ, do rest in their graves till the resurrection.

Q. What different kinds of benefits do believers receive from Christ at their death?—**A.** Benefits to their souls, and benefits to their bodies, Heb. xii. 23, Isa. lvii. 2.

Q. Do the souls of the saints die with their bodies?—**A.** No; they go to a house *eternal in the heavens*.

Q. How prove you that our souls cannot properly die? **A.** They are spiritual, and not constituted of parts; and so cannot be dissolved, Matt. x. 28.

Q. How prove you, that God will not suffer our souls to return to *nothing*?—**A.** He hath promised eternal life to saints, and threatened eternal death to the wicked.

Q. What benefits do believers' souls receive at death?—**A.** They are made perfect in holiness, and do immediately pass into glory, Heb. xii. 23, Phil. i. 23.

Q. What do you mean by being perfect in holiness?—**A.** Our being fully freed from all sin, and made perfectly like unto God, Rev. xxi. 4, 1 John iii. 2.

Q. Are the saints made infinitely holy, as God is?—**A.** No; but they are made as perfect in holiness as their finite natures are capable of, Jude 24, Eph. v. 27.

Q. Why are saints made perfect in holiness at death ?—
A. Because no unclean thing can enter into heaven.

Q. Into what do the souls of believers pass when they leave the body ?—A. Into glory, Jude 24, Psalm lxxiii. 24.

Q. Into what glory do they pass ?—A. Into a glorious place, a glorious company, and a glorious state.

Q. Into what glorious place do the souls of believers pass at death ?—A. Into the third heaven, 2 Cor. v. 1.

Q. How is that glorious place described in scripture ?—
A. As Christ's *palace, a house not made with hands, the better country, the New Jerusalem, the throne of God, Paradise, the inheritance of the saints in light, &c.*

Q. Why is it called Christ's *palace ?*—A. Because Christ there dwells and reigns in a glorious manner.

Q. Why is it called *a house not made with hands ?*—A. Because God himself built it for his own dwelling ; and it cannot be destroyed, Isa. lxvi. 1.

Q. Why is it called *a better country ?*—A. Because its inhabitants, manners, privileges, exercises, &c., are far better than those on earth, 1 Cor. xiii. 12.

Q. Why is it called *the New Jerusalem ?*—A. Because there all the holy tribes of God meet with him, and with one another, Heb. xii. 23, Psalm cxxii.

Q. Why is it called *the throne of God ?*—A. Because there God most brightly shews his glory and authority, Rev. xxii. 3, 4, Isa. lx. 19, 20.

Q. Why is it called *Paradise ?*—A. Because like *the garden of God,* it is full of pleasure, Psalm xvi. 11.

Q. What for an inheritance is that of the saints in light ?
—A. *An inheritance incorruptible, undefiled, and that fadeth not away,* 1 Peter i. 4.

Q. To what glorious company do believers go at death ?
—A. To the company of God, Father, Son, and Holy Ghost ; and of holy angels and glorified saints, Heb. xii. 22, 23, 24.

Q. From what company do believers go to these ?—A. From the company of a deceitful heart, devils, wicked men, imperfect saints, Rom. vii., Eph. i.

Q. To what glorious state do the souls of believers go at death ?—A. To a state of rest and royalty.

Q. From what do they rest ?—A. From sin's suggestions, Satan's temptations, the world's persecutions, and all the grief and sorrow arising therefrom, Isa. lvii. 1, 2.

Q. Where do believers' souls rest ?—**A.** In Christ's bosom of love, and on his throne of glory, Rev. iii. 21.

Q. How is their state a kingdom, or state of royalty ?——**A.** Because of their kingly honour and happiness.

Q. With what are they, as kings, crowned ?—**A.** With crowns of glory, life, and righteousness.

Q. When do believers' souls pass into this glory ?—**A.** They pass into it *immediately* after death.

Q. What do you mean by believers' souls passing *immediately* into glory ?—**A.** That they pass into it as soon as out of the body, without going through any middle state by the way, Phil. i. 23.

Q. How prove you there is no purgatory or middle state ? —**A.** The scripture speaks nothing of it ; but represents the rich glutton in hell, and the believing beggar and thief in heaven as soon as they died, Luke xvi. and xxiii.

Q. Why do believers' immediately pass into glory ?—**A.** Because heaven is fully ready for them, and they are made ready for it, and Christ longs for their coming thither.

Q. How doth Christ evidence his longing for them ?— **A.** In his constant pleading, that these whom the Father has given him may be with him, to behold his glory.

Q. Who carry the souls of believers into Abraham's bosom, or heaven ?—**A.** The holy angels, Luke xvi. 22.

Q. What benefits do believers' dead bodies share of ?— **A.** They are still united to Christ, and do rest in their graves till the resurrection, 1 Thess. iv. 14.

Q. How prove you that the dead bodies of believers are still united to Christ's ?—**A.** The scripture represents them as dying and sleeping in the Lord, and calls them *his dead body*, Rev. xiv. 13. 1 Thess. iv. 14.

Q. Is it not dishonourable for Christ to be united to bodies rotting in the dust ?—**A.** No ; it is an evidence of his glorious condescension and love, Rom. viii. 38.

Q. What is the grave to believers ?—**A.** A bed of rest, perfumed by Christ, Isa. lvii. 2.

Q. From what do their bodies rest in the grave ?—**A.** From all toil and trouble, Job iii. 17.

Q. How long shall the bodies of believers rest in their graves?—**A.** Till the resurrection, Job xiv. 12.

Q. May not the view of these benefits make believers greatly rejoice in the prospect of death?—**A.** Yes; and sing, *O death! where is thy sting! O Grave! where is thy victory?* 1 Cor. xv. 55.

Q. What disarms death of its sting to believers ?—A. Christ's suffering and vanquishing death.

Q. What secures believers' immediate passage into glory ?—A. Christ's being accepted of God after his death.

Q. What secures the perpetual union of the bodies of believers to Christ ?—A. The perpetual union of our nature to his divine person, Rev. i. 18.

Q. In what do the death of believers and of wicked men differ ?—A. The death of believers is unstinged ; is a promised blessing, translating them from misery to perfect happiness ; but that of the wicked is armed with the sting of sin ; is a dreadful punishment, forcibly carrying them from their present happiness to eternal wrath.

Q. What is the difference of the grave to believers and to the wicked ?—A. To believers the grave is a bed of sweet rest ; but to the wicked it is a prison, wherein their bodies are reserved for hell, Isa. lvii. 2. Psalm xlix. 14.

Q. 38. *What benefits do believers receive from Christ at the resurrection ?*

A. At the resurrection, believers being raised up in glory, shall be openly acknowledged and acquitted in the day of judgment, and made perfectly blessed in full enjoying of God to all eternity.

Q. When is the third period of believers receiving benefits from Christ ?—A. At the resurrection.

Q. What do you mean by the *resurrection ?*—A. The general rising of the dead from their graves.

Q. Who are the dead that shall be then raised ?—A. All men, good or bad, who are in the grave at Christ's second coming, Acts xxiv. 15. John v. 29.

Q. How prove you that all the dead shall be raised ?— A. God hath declared that he will raise them ; and he is able to perform his word, Matth. xxii. 23. 29.

Q. How prove you, that God can raise the dead ?—A. Because *nothing is too hard* for him ; he hath created all things, and raised sundry dead persons already.

Q. Who are the persons God has thus raised from death ? —A. The sons of the Shunamite, and of the widows of Sarepta and Nain, the man cast into Elisha's grave, Dorcas, Lazarus, the daughters of Jairus, and many saints about the time of Christ's death, 2 Kings iv. and xiii.

Q. When the bodies of men and beasts are mingled together, and have perhaps eaten one another, how can God restore to each man his own body?—A. God by his infinite power, wisdom, and knowledge, can easily separate these mixed particles of dust from one another.

Q. How prove you, that God *will* raise the dead?—A. The scriptures often affirm it, by declaring, that *all that are in the grave shall come forth*, &c. John v. 28. Dan. xii. 3. Luke xx. 37, 38. Acts xvii. 30.

Q. Will the same body which died be raised?—A. Yes; the same body in substance, though different in qualities.

Q. How prove you that?—A. Rising from the dead is called an *awakening* from sleep, and *rising again;* nor would it be just, that one body should sin, and another be eternally punished for that sin; nor meet, that one body should do and suffer for Christ, and another receive the glorious reward, 1 Cor. xv. 53. Ezek xii. 14.

Q. By what means shall the dead be raised?—A. By the power of God attending the voice of the archangel, and sound of the last trumpet, 1 Thess. iv. 16.

Q. What shall become of those who are alive when Christ comes to judgment?—A. They shall be changed in a moment, and have their bodies made like these that are raised from the grave, 1 Cor. xv. 51.

Q. Wherein will the resurrection of the saints, and that of the wicked differ?—A. In their cause, order, and manner.

Q. How will they differ in their *cause?*—A. Believers shall be raised by Christ's Spirit dwelling in them, and making them one with him; but the wicked shall be raised by him as an angry Judge, Rom. viii. 11, John v. 28.

Q. How will they differ in their *order?*—A. The righteous, *the dead in Christ, shall rise first*, and be caught up to meet the Lord in the air, 1 Thess. iv. 16.

Q. How will their resurrection differ in the *manner?*— A. The righteous shall be raised in glory and triumph, but the wicked with trembling and horror, Dan. xii. 2.

Q. With what honourable qualities shall the bodies of the saints be raised?—A. They shall be raised glorious, powerful, spiritual, and incorruptible bodies.

Q. What glory shall be then put on the bodies of saints? —A. They shall beautifully shine as the sun or stars.

Q. What power shall the saints' bodies be endued with? —A. They shall be able to bear up under the *exceeding and eternal weight of glory* bestowed on them, 2 Cor. v.

Q. How will the saints' bodies be spiritual?—A. Not that they shall be turned into spirits ; but that they shall be active *as angels*, and have no need of the natural supports of meat or drink, Matt. xxii. 30.

Q. How will the saints' bodies be incorruptible?—A. They shall be no ways liable to diseases or death.

Q. After what pattern shall believers' bodies be glorified?—A. After the pattern of Christ's *glorious body.*

Q. With what bodies will the wicked be raised from their graves?—A. With ugly and loathsome bodies.

Q. What doth this teach us?—A. That to neglect our souls, and beautify our bodies in this world, is the certain way to ruin both our soul and body hereafter.

Q. What benefits shall believers when raised receive from Christ?—A. They shall be openly acknowledged and acquitted by Christ, Matt. xxv. 34—40.

Q. When shall the righteous be acknowledged and acquitted by Christ?—A. In the day of judgment.

Q. What is meant by being acknowledged by Christ? —A. Our being owned by him as his brethren and bride.

Q. Whom will Christ thus acknowledge?—A. His friends and children, who were not ashamed uprightly to confess him on earth, Luke xii. 8.

Q. What are we to understand by Christ's acquitting us in the day of judgment?—His declaring the pardon of all our iniquities, and the injustice of all the calumnies and reproaches ever cast upon us, Acts iii. 19.

Q. In what doth Christ's acquittance of our real faults in the day of judgment differ from the pardon we receive in justification?—A. The acquittance in justification changeth our law-state, and is very secret; but the acquittance in the day of judgment makes no change on our state, and is very public and open, before God, angels, and men, at once, Rev. ii. 17, Luke xii. 8.

Q. Why shall believers be *so openly* acknowledged and acquitted?—A. For the glory of God, their own honour and joy, and the shame and confusion of their enemies.

Q. How doth this open acknowledgment and acquittance of believers tend to the glory of God?—A. It publicly shews the greatness of his love, grace, mercy, justice, and truth to his people, 2 Thess. i. 10.

Q. How doth it tend to the honour and joy of believers? —A. Their good name is thus finally vindicated, and Christ's new name publicly called on them, Matt. xxv.

16

Q. How doth it tend to the confusion of their enemies?—
A. As they shall be thus publicly proven fools and enemies
to God, in disregarding and injuring the saints, and liars in
reproaching them, Deut. xxxiii. 29.

Q. On what grounds shall the saints be thus acknowledged and acquitted?—A. On the foundation of Christ's
infinite and everlasting righteousness, Rom. v. 21.

Q. What shall Christ do with the wicked in the day of
judgment, instead of acknowledging and acquitting them?
—A. He will deny all saving relation to them, publish their
sins before the whole world, and openly condemn them to
the punishment of hell, Matt. vii. 23.

Q. What benefits shall believers receive from Christ after
the day of judgment?—A. They shall be made perfectly
blessed in the full enjoyment of God to all eternity, Psalm
xvi. 11, and xvii. 15, Isa. lx. 19, 20.

Q. What is meant by our being *perfectly blessed?*—A.
Our being wholly freed from all misery and want, and fully
possessed of all happiness, Rev. xxi. 4. 7.

Q. In what does our highest happiness consist?—A. In
the full enjoyment of God, Psalm lxxiii. 25.

Q. What of the saints shall be blessed with this happiness?—A. Their whole man, 1 Thess. iv. 16, 17.

Q. How will the bodies of the saints be blessed with it?
—A. Their ears shall be ravished with the sweet melody
of heaven; their lips filled with the high praises of God
and the Lamb; and their eyes captivated with the view of
the glorious bodies of other saints, and especially of Christ's
glorious body, Rev. xix. 1, John xvii. 24.

Q. Will Christ's body be unspeakably more glorious than
the bodies of the saints?—A. Yes; in all things he hath
the pre-eminence; and the glory of his Godhead shines in
and through it, Col. i. 18, Isa. lx. 19, 20.

Q. How will the souls of believers be perfectly blessed
in heaven?—A. Their minds shall be ravished with sweet
sights, and their will with sweet embraces of God.

Q. With the views of what shall our mind be ravished?
—A. With the views of the divine persons and perfections,
of Christ as Mediator, and of all the attributes, truths, and
works of God, as centering in him.

Q. What views of the divine persons shall we have?—
A. We shall see the distinctness of all the three; and that
they are one in essence, and in one another, 1 John iii.

Q. What perfections of God shall we then see?—A. All his known perfections, especially his grace, love, mercy, wisdom, power, holiness, justice, and truth, with the amiable oneness and connection between them.

Q. What views of God's works shall we then have?—A. We shall see the glorious nature, beautiful connections and ends of the works of creation and providence, and especially of redemption, Rev. i. 5, 6.

Q. What views of Christ as Mediator shall we then have?—A. We shall clearly see the glory of his undertaking, of his person as God-man, and of his offices, relations, and works, John xvii. 24.

Q. What views of divine truths shall we then have?—A. We shall see all the truths of the Bible in their glorious matter, beautiful connection, and relation to Christ, and to God in him, Psalm xxxvi. 9.

Q. Will there be any ordinances in heaven to instruct us in the knowledge of these things?—A. No; we shall see them all in a clear and immediate manner.

Q. What is meant by our will's embracing God?—A. It is our spiritual feeling and experience of that goodness which we now believe, and shall then see to be in God.

Q. In what manner shall we enjoy God after the day of judgment?—A. Fully and familiarly, 1 Cor. xiii. 12.

Q. How will our enjoyment of God be *full*?—A. We shall be filled with as much of God's glory and goodness as we can hold, Eph. iii. 19, 1 Cor. xv. 28.

Q. Will there be different degrees of glory in heaven?—A. Yes; though all be full, yet some shall be able to contain more of God than others, Isa. xxii. 24.

Q. Who shall be able to contain most of God's fulness?—A. Those who are possessed most of his grace on earth.

Q. How will our eternal enjoyment of God be *free* and *familiar*?—A. As nothing shall ever stop our access to, or hinder our full enjoyment of him, 1 Thess. iv. 17.

Q. What will be the effect of this full enjoyment of God?—A. Perfect likeness to God, and joy in him.

Q. How doth perfect likeness to God flow from full enjoyment of him?—A. The full views of his glory, and sense of his love, will transform us into a perfect conformity to his image, 1 John iii. 2.

Q. How doth perfect joy flow from it?—A. As present

full enjoyment of God, and certainty of its eternal duration, raiseth joy to the highest, Psalm xvi. 11.

Q. Can ever believers be surfeited with the fulness of God?—A. No; for his fulness, like running water, is eternally fresh and new to their souls, Rev. vii. 17.

Q. What will be the saints' employment in heaven in expressing their joy?—A. They will admire God and the Lamb, and sing hallelujahs for evermore, Isa. li. 4.

Q. How long shall the saints be perfectly blessed in the full enjoyment of God?—A. To all eternity, Isa. lx. 15.

Q. How should we improve the view of believers' eternal happiness?—A. By admiring the riches of God's love, and studying holiness to make us meet for heaven.

Q. What shall become of the wicked through eternity? —A. They shall lie amidst the flames of hell, and *have no rest day nor night, but be tormented with fire and brimstone in the presence of the holy angels, and of the Lamb*, Rev. xiv. 10, 11, Isa. xxxiii. 14.

Q. What shall the wicked do for ever in hell?—A. They shall continually roar, curse, and blaspheme God; weep, wail, gnash their teeth, and gnaw their tongues for pain, Matth. xiii. 50, Rev. xvi. 10, 11.

Q. 39. *What is the duty which God requireth of man?*

A. The duty which God requireth of man is obedience to his revealed will.

Q. What call you obedience to God?—A. Our doing that which he commands from regard to his authority.

Q. Do we not obey God, if we do what he commands, even though we do it not because he commands it?—A. No; regard to God's authority is the very *form* of all true obedience, Deut. xii. 32, and xiii. 18.

Q. Why should we obey God?—A. Because he made, preserves, and redeems us, Psalm c. 2, 3.

Q. In what manner must we obey God?—A. Constantly, humbly, universally, and from love.

Q. Why should we obey God humbly?—A. Because of his greatness, and the meanness of our best service.

Q. Why should we obey God constantly?—A. Because we are his property, and do *always* depend on him.

Q. Why should we obey God universally in every thing? —A. Because *all* his commands are very good.

Q. Why should we obey God from a principle of love?
—A. Because of his infinite love and loveliness, and the
excellency of his commands, 1 John iv. 19, Psalm xix.

Q. Is any other besides God lord of our conscience?—
A. No; God is the *one Lawgiver*, James iv. 12.

Q. Wherein doth the obedience which we owe God, and
that which we owe to men differ?—A. We are to obey God
for his own sake, and men out of regard to God.

Q. What is our duty, if men command what God bids,
or forbid what he commands?—A. We are to obey God
rather than men, Acts iv. 19, and v. 29.

Q. What is the rule of our obedience to God?—A. His
revealed will in his word, Mic. vi. 8, Isa. viii. 20.

Q. What is the secret will of God?—A. His purpose or
decree respecting that which comes to pass, Eph. i. 11.

Q. Is our fulfilling of the secret will of God any obedience?—A. No; for his secret will is unknown to us, it is the
rule of God's conduct, not of ours; it ascertains future
events, but doth not prescribe our duty.

Q. 40. *What did God at first reveal to man for the
rule of his obedience?*
A. The rule which God first revealed to man for
his obedience was the moral law.

Q. When did God first reveal this rule of obedience?—
A. He wrote it on Adam's heart in creating him.

Q. Why is this rule called *a law?*—A. Because it not
only directs, but binds us to our duty.

Q. Why is it called *the moral law?*—A. Because it constantly directs and binds *the manners* of all men.

Q. Were not the ceremonial and judicial law grafted
upon the moral law?—A. Yes; the ceremonial upon the
first table, and the judicial on the second.

Q. Was not the ceremonial law an obscure gospel?—A.
Yes; in as far as its rites and services represented Christ,
and his righteousness and grace, Heb. x. 1.

Q. How may the types of the Old Testament dispensation be distinguished?—A. Into typical persons; typical
classes of persons; occasional typical things; miscellaneous typical institutions; typical places; typical oblations;
typical seasons; and typical purifications.

Q. What *particular persons were* typical?—A. Adam,
Abel, Enoch, Noah, Melchizedeck, Abraham, Isaac, Jacob,
16*

Joseph, Job, Moses, Aaron, Bezaleel, Aholiab, Phineas, Joshua, Gideon, Samson, Boaz, Samuel, David, Solomon, Elijah, Elisha, Jonah, Eliakim, Isaiah, Daniel, Zerubbabel, Joshua the high priest, John Baptist, and perhaps Cyrus, &c.

Q. What did these typify?—**A.** Jesus Christ in his marvellous birth, excellent qualifications, solemn call to his work; saving offices and relations; his work of obedience and suffering for his people; and the glorious reward of it; his usefulness to his people, in promoting their deliverance, instruction, holiness, and comfort.

Q. Which were the *typical classes* of persons?—**A.** The Israelites in general; their first born males; the unmarried brothers of such as left widows childless; the voluntary bound servants; the hanged malefactors; the sojourning strangers; the Nazarites; Nethinims; Levites; priests; high-priests; holy prophets; and the kings of David's family.

Q. What did these typify?—**A.** The high-priests and kinsmen redeemers typified Jesus Christ, in his person, endowments, and work, as our great Redeemer, and High-priest. The strangers represented the Gentiles as objects of God's gracious care, and the others were emblems of the saints, and figure of Christ in his dignity, his service of God, his sufferings for men, and his management of the church and kingdom of God.

Q. What were the *occasional typical things?*—**A.** Noah's ark; Jacob's ladder; Moses' burning bush; the cloudy pillar; the sweetened water of Marah; the manna; the the rocks yielding water; the well of Beer; the cluster of grapes from Eschol; Aaron's budding rod; the brazen serpent; the healing pool of Bethesda; the waters of Shiloah; the deliverance of the Hebrews from Egypt; their passage through the red-sea; their travels in the wilderness, their entrance into Canaan; their wars with their heathen neighbours; and their return from Babylon.

Q. What did these typify?—**A.** Most part of the former pointed out Christ as the Saviour, Mediator, nourishment, comfort, or medicine of his people. The ark and burning bush represented also the church as containing them that are saved, and as much exposed to persecution and trouble. The six last particulars typified the erection and fate of the Christian church; and the conversion and fate of her true members, with respect to their spiritual condition.

Q. Which were the *miscellaneous typical institutions?*
—A. CIRCUMCISION, which was a seal of the covenant;
sanctification of fruit trees; offering no base things to God;
scourging of bond women for whoredom; protection of
fugitive servants; exclusion from the congregation of the
Lord; wearing of proper apparel; blue fringes; not cutting
of flesh for the dead; abstinence from blood, and fat or animals torn, or dying of themselves; leaving of gleanings in
fields or vineyards; avoiding of mixed garments, sowing
of mixed seeds or plowing with oxen and asses together, or
gendering with cattle of different kinds; tenderness to animals; not muzzling the ox while treading out the corn;
covering of excrements in the camp; and temporary freedom from the service of war.

Q. What did all these signify?—A. In general, that being renewed in the spirit of our minds, through our union
to Jesus Christ, as made of God to us wisdom, righteousness and sanctification, and redemption; we should deny
ungodliness and worldly lusts, and live soberly, righteously,
and godly; in simplicity and Godly sincerity; doing justly,
loving mercy, and walking humbly with our God.

Q. Which were the *typical places?*—A. Canaan; the
cities of refuge; Jerusalem; Zion; the tabernacle and
temple.

Q. What did these signify?—A. Canaan, Jerusalem,
and Zion represented a new covenant state; and typified
the state of the gospel church, and of the heavenly glory.
The cities of refuge typified Jesus Christ, and our state of
safety through him, in his covenant, and church. The
tabernacle and temple represented Christ's manhood, the
gospel-church, and heavenly state; and were emblems of
true believers as the residence of God.

Q. Which are the *typical utensils?*—A. The ark of the
covenant; the pot of manna; the table of shew-bread with
its loaves; the golden altar with its incense; the golden
candlestick with its oil; the silver trumpets; the brasen
lavers, and sea; the brasen altar; the altars of earth and
stone; the altar of Ebal.

Q. What did these signify?—A. The pot of manna,
and the table of shew bread, but especially the silver trumpets, typified the ordinances and preaching of the gospel:
the other represented Christ as the fulfiller of the broken
law, advocate with the Father, light of the church, or means
of purification from and atonement for sin. And even the

pot of manna, and table of shew-bread, may denote him as
the provision and supporter of his people.

Q. Which were the *typical oblations?*—A. The burnt-
offerings; the sin-offerings; the trespass-offerings; the
peace-offerings; the meat-offerings; the drink-offerings;
the holy anointing oil; the soul ransom money; the tithes;
the first fruits; and the things voluntarily devoted to God.

Q. What did these signify?—A. The oil signified the
Holy Ghost and his influences; the others signified Jesus
Christ, as devoted to the service of God, and the salvation
of his people : Jesus Christ as satisfying the justice of God,
expiating our sins, and thus become our spiritual peace-
maker, provision, and comfort.

Q. Which were the *typical seasons?*—A. The hours of
the daily sacrifice; the weekly sabbath in its ceremonial
use; the feast of new moons; the passover and feast of unleavened bread; Pentecost; the feast of trumpets; the fast
of general expiation; the feast of tabernacles; the year of
release; and jubilee.

Q. What did these signify?—A. The season of Christ's
appearance in our nature to fulfil all righteousness; and
the seasons of the powerful virtue of his death, and spread
of his gospel, in the New Testament church. The three
last also prefigured the happiness of the heavenly state.

Q. Which were the *typical purifications?*—A. Purifications from defilement contracted by holy things, by touching or eating unclean beasts, by childbirth, by leprosy, by
running issues, and by touching or approaching dead
corpses;—and the trial of suspected adultery, and the expiation of uncertain murder.

Q. What did all the washings, sprinklings and shavings,
used in these purifications, signify?—A. That by the application of Christ's blood and Spirit, for the removal of
the guilt and filth of sin, and the destruction of its power,
we become clean before God.

Q. Are the ceremonial and the judicial law now abro-
gated?—A. Yes; Gal. v. 1. Heb. viii. 13, Col. ii. 14.

Q. Why is the ceremonial law abolished?—A. Because
Christ the substance of its types is already come, Heb. x.

Q. Why is the judicial law *as such* abolished?—A. Because the Jews are now cast off from being a nation peculiarly separated to the Lord, Rom. xi.

Q. Can the moral law be abolished?—A. No; the obligation of the moral law is invariable, and constant from creation through all eternity, Psalm cxix. 144.

Q. Why so?—A. Because it depends on the nature of God, and man's relation to him as his reasonable creature.

Q. Upon whom is the moral law binding?—A. Upon all men, Rom. ii. 14, 15, Psalm cxlvii. 19, 20.

Q. Why hath God given a law to men?—A. For his own honour and their happiness, Psalm cxlvii. 19, 20.

Q. How is the law for the honour of God?—A. As it shews that he is absolute ruler over all, James iv. 12.

Q. How is it for the happiness of men?—A. As in *keeping* God's command *there is a great reward*, Psal. xix. 11.

Q. How many things are often included in a law?—A. Two; its precept or command, and its sanction.

Q. In what does the precept of a law consist?—A. In shewing us our duty, and binding us to it.

Q. What is the sanction of a law?—A. The threatening or promise annexed to the precept, in order to deter us from sin, and excite us to duty, Deut. xxx. 16.

Q. Is a threatening always annexed to God's law?—A. No; it is only annexed when the persons under it are *actually* fallible, Gal. iii. 10, Lev. xxvi.

Q. Is a promise a necessary part of God's law?—A. No; it is never annexed to it, but when the law is either formed into a covenant, or made a rule of life to such as are within the new covenant, Deut. xxxviii.

Q. With what different forms hath God clothed the moral law?—A. With the form of the *law of nature*, of the *covenant of works*, and of a *rule of life*.

Q. What is the *law of nature*?—A. The moral law written on Adam's heart in his creation, binding him to perfect obedience under pain of eternal death, but promising him no reward of his obedience, Rom. ii. 14.

Q. What is the form of the law *as a covenant of works?*—A. The moral law considered as binding to perfect obedience under pain of eternal death, and promising eternal life as the reward of obedience, Gal. iii. 10. 12.

Q. What is the form of the moral law *as a rule of life?*—A. The moral law as binding to perfect obedience under pain of fatherly chastisements, and have the promise of gracious and fatherly rewards annexed to obedience, Psal. lxxxix. 30, 31, 32, 1 Cor. xv. 58.

Q. In what do the law of nature and the law as a covenant differ?—A. Chiefly in the law as a covenant having a promise of eternal life annexed to obedience, which the law of nature hath not, Gal. iii. 12.

Q. Wherein do the law of nature, and the law as a rule of life, differ?—A. Chiefly in that the law of nature was perfectly written on man's heart in creation, was given by an absolute God, and required obedience under pain of eternal death; which is not the case with the law as a rule of life, Ezek. viii. 4, Luke i. 74, 75.

Q. In what do the law as a covenant of works, and the law as a rule of life, differ?—A. Chiefly in their author, subjects, sanction, design, and acceptance of obedience.

Q. How do they differ in their *author?*—A. An absolute God gives the law as a covenant; but Christ as Mediator gives the law as a rule of life, which is therefore called *the law of Christ*, Gen. ii. 16, 1 Cor. ix. 21.

Q. Is the law as a rule, enforced with the authority of God as our Creator and Preserver?—A. Yes; but that authority is sweetened and heightened by his being our God, Redeemer, and Father in Christ, Luke i. 74, 75.

Q. How do the law as a covenant and as a rule, differ in their *subjects?*—A. All men in their natural state are under the law as a covenant; but believers only are under the law as a rule of life, Rom. vii. 4—6.

Q. Are not believers under the law as a covenant?—A. No; they are wholly delivered from, and completely dead to it, Rom. vi. 14, Gal. ii. 19, and iv. 4, 5.

Q. To what of the law as a covenant, are believers dead? —A. To its commands, promise, and curse.

Q. How are they dead to the command of it?—A. As no obedience can be required of them as the condition of their eternal life, Phil. iii. 9, Heb. xii. 28.

Q. How are they dead to the promise of it?—A. Their persons are not in the least justified, nor eternal life procured by their good works, 1 Cor. iv. 4.

Q. How are they delivered from the curse or threatening of it?—A. As they cannot incur God's wrath, or be condemned to hell for their sin, Rom. viii. 1. 33.

Q. By what means are believers delivered from the law as a covenant?—A. By their union to Christ, who fulfilled and magnified it in their name and stead.

Q. Why is Christ called *the end of the law for righteousness?*—A. Because he fulfilled and abolished the types of the ceremonial law, and answered the demands of the moral with his perfect righteousness, Rom. x. 4.

Q. Wherein do the law as a covenant and as a rule differ in their *sanction?*—**A.** The sanction of the law as a covenant, is eternal life or death ; but the sanction of the law as a rule, is fatherly rewards or chastisements.

Q. What is believer's obedience to the law as a rule rewarded with ?—**A.** With much freedom from spiritual plagues, and sweet communion with God here, and additional degrees of glory in heaven, Isa. lxiv. 4, 5.

Q. Why call you these *fatherly* or *gracious rewards ?*—**A.** Because though they are given to obedient believers, yet they are not given for their obedience' sake, but flow from God's fatherly grace and love, Rom. v. 21.

Q. If it is not for the sake of their good works that believers are rewarded, how is it that the more holy they are, the more happiness they receive ?—**A.** Because the receiving of much purchased holiness prepares for receiving the more abundant purchased happiness, Dan. xii. 3.

Q. Is not holiness itself happiness?—**A.** It is the very height of happiness, Psalm xvii. 15.

Q. Are more diligent and holy believers less indebted to Christ for their happiness, than more slothful believers ?—**A.** No ; they are the deeper in the debt of God's free grace, being first indebted for more grace, and then for more glory, Luke xxii. 28—30, 1 Cor. xv. 10.

Q. Doth believers' obedience always go before their privilege, according to the law as a rule ?—**A.** No ; first the privileges of regeneration, justification and adoption are bestowed ; then follow duty and privilege by turns, till they perfectly unite into one in glory.

Q. What mean you by fatherly chastisements ?—**A.** All those troubles which believers meet with in this world after their conversion on account of their sin, Heb. xii.

Q. What are the heaviest of believers' chastisements?—**A.** The terrors of God, and hiding of his face, with the occasional prevalency of sin and Satan ; which are terrible as hell to the saints, Psalm lxxxviii., Rom. vii.

Q. Why are these called *chastisements*, and not punishments ?—**A.** Because they tend not to the hurt, but to the advantage of the saints, Heb. xii. 6. 10, 11.

Q. Would it not more effectually stir up believers to obedience, if it entitled them to eternal life, and their disobedience exposed them to eternal death ?—**A.** No ; that would disparage the righteousness of Christ, hinder our improvement of it as the great motive of obedience, and

fill us with so much of the spirit of bondage, as to disqual-
ify us for gospel-obedience, 2 Cor. v. 14.

Q. How is the righteousness of Christ, as *the alone condition of our eternal life*, the great motive to holy obedience ?
A. Therein we clearly see the constraining love of Christ;
the holiness, goodness, and greatness of God ; the purity,
goodness, and binding force of his law ; and the vileness of
sin ; and have assurance of strength for, and a gracious reward of our obedience.

Q. How long doth the sanction of fatherly rewards and
chastisements continue annexed to the law as a rule of
life ?—A. Only in this world, 1 Cor. xiii. 10.

Q. Why hath the law as a rule of life no such sanction
in heaven ?—A. Because there the saints are by grace infallibly established in holiness, and there work and reward
are become entirely the same, Rev. iii. 12.

Q. How do the law as a covenant and as a rule differ in
their *design* ?—A. The original design of the law as a
covenant was, that man might procure life by it ; but the
design of it as a rule, is to teach men how to improve the
spiritual life which they freely receive from Christ, and testify their thankfulness to God for it, Gal. iii.

Q. How do they differ in *acceptance of obedience* ?—A.
The law as a covenant accepts nothing less than perfect
obedience ; but the law as a rule, though it require perfect,
admits of God's accepting our sincere obedience for Christ's
sake, Rev. viii. 3, 4. 1 Cor. xv. 58.

Q. What mean you by *sincere obedience* ?—A. Our uprightly endeavouring to obey the whole law of God.

Q. Can any man since Adam's fall attain life by his obedience to the law ?—A. No ; *As many as are of the work
of the law are under the curse*, Gal. iii. 10.

Q. Is the moral law then of any use to men ?—A. It is
of very great use to them, Psalm xix. 7—10.

Q. To whom is it of use ?—A. To all men in general,
and to believers and unbelievers in particular.

Q. Of what use is the moral law to all men ?—A. To
show them their duty, and bind them to it ; to discover to
them the holiness of God, their own sinfulness, and inability to keep the law, and their need of Christ and his righteousness, Micah vi. 8, Gal. iii. 11, 12, 21.

Q. Of what use is the moral law to believers ?—A. To
show them what their sins deserve ; how much they are obliged to Christ for fulfilling the law in their stead ; and how

they should express their gratitude to him for his kindness to them, Titus ii. 12, 13, 14, and iii. 8.

Q. How then is it said, *The law was not made for a righteous man?*—A. The meaning is, that it was not made to terrify, curse, and condemn a righteous man.

Q. Of what use is the law to unbelievers?—A. To awaken their conscience, and drive them to Christ, or bind them over to more dreadful wrath if they refuse him.

Q. How is the moral law made known to men?—A. Either by being written on their hearts, or by revelation in the word of God, Rom. ii. 15. 18.

Q. In what different ways is God's law written on men's hearts?—A. Either by nature, or by grace.

Q. In what do the natural and gracious writings of the moral law on men's hearts differ?—A. Since the fall, the *first* merely impresseth some knowledge of the law in our conscience, without influence from the word of God; the *last* consists in the Spirit's powerful application of the word of God to our heart, thereby conveying to us the knowledge of the law, and an inclination and ability to keep it, Rom. ii. 14, 15, Jer. xxxi. 33.

Q. On whose hearts is God's law written in a natural manner?—A. On the hearts of all men, Rom. ii. 15.

Q. On whose heart is it written in a gracious manner?—A. On the hearts of *believers only*, Jer. xxxi. 33.

Q. What are the properties of the moral law of God?—A. It is spiritual and holy, just and good, perfect and exceeding broad, Rom. vii. 12. 14, Psalm xix. 7—10.

Q. How is God's law *spiritual?*—A. It reaches our heart, and requires obedience from spiritual motives, in a spiritual manner, and to spiritual ends, Luke i. 74.

Q. How is the law *holy?*—A. It is the transcript of God's holiness commanding every thing holy, and condemning all impurity, 1 Peter i. 15, 16, Matthew v.

Q. How is God's law *just?*—A. It binds to give every one their due, and requires no more than God originally gave man ability to perform, Psalm cxix.

Q. How is God's law *good?*—A. The keeping of it tends greatly to his glory and our advantage.

Q. How is God's law *perfect?*—A. It is a complete standard of right and wrong, requiring every duty in the highest degree, Matth. v. 48, Psalm cxix. 9.

Q. How is God's law *exceeding broad?*—A. It binds

17

our whole man at all times, and in every situation ; and requires many duties in every case and season.

Q. 41. *Wherein is the moral law summarily comprehended ?*
A. The moral law is summarily comprehended in
the ten commandments.

Q. What do you mean by *summarily* comprehended ?—
A. It means, that all the moral laws of God may be reduced to one of these commands, Matth. xxii. 37. 39.

Q. How many rules are necessary for understanding the
ten commandments ?—A. Six.

Q. What is the first rule ?—A. That every command
requires many duties, and forbids many sins, which are nôt
expressly named in it.

Q. What is the second rule ?—A. That wherever a duty
is required, the contrary sin is forbidden ; and wherever a
sin is forbidden, the contrary duty is required.

Q. What is the third rule ?—A. That wherever a sin is
forbidden, all sins of the same kind, and all occasions,
causes, or appearances of these sins, are forbidden ; and
wherever any duty is commanded, all duties of the same
κind, and all the means of performing them, are commanded.

Q. What is the fourth rule ?—A. That whatever we
ourselves are bound to, we are obliged to do what in us lieth
to cause others to do the same.

Q. What is the fifth rule ?—A. That that which is forbidden may never be done ; but actions required, are only
to be performed when God giveth opportunity.

Q. What is the sixth rule ?—A. That the same sin is
forbidden, and the same duty required, in different respects,
in many commandments.

Q. Where, and to whom, were the ten commands most
solemnly delivered ?—A. To Moses, and the children of
Israel, at Mount Sinai, Exod. xx.

Q. How were the ten commands there delivered ?—A.
God solemnly proclaimed and wrote them.

Q. What solemnity attended God's proclamation of the
law ?—A. Terrible thunders and lightnings, Exod. xix.

Q. What was the design of this ?—A. To shew how
dangerous it is to be under the law as a covenant, or to
break it as a rule of life, Gal. iii. 10, Deut. iv. 24.

Q. Whether was it the covenant of works, or of grace,

which was delivered at Sinai?—A. The law simply, as given with such awful solemnity, was the covenant of works, published to drive Israel to Christ; but the covenant of grace was delivered in the preface and ceremonies.

Q. On what did God write the ten commands?—A. On two tables of stone, Deut. x. 4.

Q. Why did God write his law on tables of stone?—A. To shew the perpetual obligation of the law; and to represent the natural hardness of our hearts in which the Spirit writes it, Jer. xxxi. 33, Ezek. xxxvi. 26, 27.

Q. Why did God write his law on two tables?—A. To distinguish our duty to God from our duty to man.

Q. How many commandments were written in each table?—A. Four in the first, and six in the second.

Q. 42. *What is the sum of the ten commandments?*

A. The sum of the ten commandments is, To love the Lord our God with all our heart, with all our soul, with all our strength, and with all our mind, and our neighbour as ourselves.

Q. What is the fulfilment of the moral law?—A. Love to God, to ourselves, and to our neighbour.

Q. How is love the fulfilment of the law?—A. As it must be the principle, motive and substance of every act of our obedience to the law, 1 Tim. i. 5.

Q. What is the sum of the first table of the law?—A. To love the Lord with all our heart, soul, strength, and mind, Matth. xxii. 37. Luke x. 27.

Q. What do you mean by that?—A. It is to love him in the most ardent and judicious manner, to the utmost of our power, and far above all other things.

Q. What necessarily belongs to this superlative love to God?—A. Our loving him for himself, devoting our whole man to his service, centering our soul in him as its only rest, and contemning all things in comparison of him, Psalm lxxiii. 25, 26.

Q. Why should we thus love God?—A. Because he is infinitely lovely in himself, and good to us, 1 John iv.

Q. By what marks is our superlative love to God manifested?—A. By our hatred of all sin; carefulness to please God; readiness to suffer for him; grief for his dishonour; frequent thoughts of him; love to his people, word, and ordinances; and constantly study to be like him.

Q. What is the sum of the second table of God's law?
—**A.** To love our neighbour as ourselves, James ii. 8.

Q. What do you mean by that?—**A.** To love our neighbours as truly and constantly as ourselves; and to do them all the good we would wish them to do to us in like circumstances, Rom. xii. 9—21. Matth. vii. 12.

Q. If one would wish others to give him an opportunity of sinning, as of drunkenness, &c. should they do so to him?—**A.** No; to promote sin is *hatred* not *love.*

Q. Who is our neighbour, whom we must love as ourselves?—**A.** All men, even our enemies, Matth. v. 44.

Q. Should we love all men alike?—**A.** No.

Q. Whom should we chiefly love?—**A.** The saints.

Q. Why should we love the saints above others?—**A.** They are most like God, and dearest to him.

Q. How is our love to be exercised towards all men?—**A.** In esteeming, pleasing, helping, sympathising with, and praying for all men, Rom. xii. 10—21.

Q. How is our love to be exercised towards the saints?—**A.** In delighting in them as our chief companions.

Q. How is our love to be exercised towards our enemies?—**A.** In forgiving, praying for, and rendering them good for evil, Luke vi. 27, 28, &c.

Q. Why should we love our enemies?—**A.** That we may obey God, and be like him, who shews mercy to sinners, and makes his sun to rise on the evil and unjust.

Q. What things are considerable about the commands?—**A.** Their preface, the commands themselves, and the reasons annexed to several of them.

Q. 43. *What is the preface to the ten commandments?*

A. The preface to the ten commandments is in these words, "I am the Lord thy God, which have brought thee out of the land of Egypt, out of the house of bondage."

Q. 44. *What doth the preface to the ten commandments teach us?*

A. The preface to the ten commandments teacheth us, That because God is the Lord, and our God and Redeemer, therefore we are bound to keep all his commandments.

Q. What doth the preface to the ten commandments contain?—**A.** General reasons for our keeping them all.

Q. Might not God, by mere authority, require us to yield obedience to his law?—A. Yes: Dan. iv. 34.

Q. Why then doth he annex reasons of obedience to it? —A. Because of our aversion to obey his law; and to shew the greatness of our obligation, and the kindness of God in giving as such encouragement to our duty.

Q. Why are these reasons of obedience placed before the commands?—A. To shew that we must first believe in, and receive God as our God and Redeemer, before we can be enabled to obey any of his commands, Gal. v. 6.

Q. Must we then first receive the comforts and blessings of the gospel, before we can, and that we may be able to perform the duties of the law?—A. Yes.

Q. What blessings?—A. Union with Christ, justification through his righteousness, the love of God shed abroad in our hearts, the solid hope of heaven, &c.

Q. What is the first reason of our obedience to God's law contained in the *preface?*—A. That the Lawgiver is *the Lord*, or *Jehovah*, Exod. xx. 2.

Q. What is the force of this reason?—A. That because God is being itself, gave us our being, and will give being to all his promises, we ought to obey him.

Q. What is the second reason of obedience contained in the preface?—A. That the Lawgiver is *our God*.

Q. What is the force of this reason?—A. That God, being our master, head, husband, father, friend, and portion, we ought to love, obey, and submit to him.

Q. In what different respects may God be our God?—A. He is the God of all men by creation and providence; of all church-members by external covenant; and the God of all saints by special covenant in Christ.

Q. Are we not the more obliged to obey God, that he is our God in various respects?—A. Yes.

Q. Under what stronger obligations to obedience are church-members, than Heathens?—A. God hath blessed them with his word and ordinances; and they are more solemnly bound to be his by their baptism, &c.

Q. Under what stronger obligations to obedience are believers, than nominal Christians?—A. God hath favoured them with distinguished blessings, and stands in particular relations to them, 1 John iv. 10.

Q. What is the third reason of obedience contained in the preface?—A. That the Lawgiver is *our Redeemer*.

17*

Q. From what did God redeem Israel of old?—**A.** From the land of Egypt, and house of bondage.

Q. How can these words in the preface respect such as are not Israelites?—**A.** As God has delivered all church-members from what resembles the bondage of Egypt.

Q. From what hath God delivered all church-members?—**A.** From the bondage of Popery or Paganism.

Q. From what other bondage hath God delivered believers?—**A.** From the bondage of the law, sin, Satan, and the world, Isa. xlix. 24, Gal. i. 4, John viii. 36.

Q. How doth this spiritual bondage resemble the bondage of Egypt?—**A.** As in Egypt, Israel's bondage was very cruel, they being required to make brick without straw, and had their male children drowned in the river Nilus; so unconverted persons are required to perform duties, while they have no strength; and have all their apparently good works and resolutions buried in the floods of their corruption, Gal. iii. 10, Rom. vii. 13.

Q. Who are our cruel taskmasters in our spiritual bondage?—**A.** Our conscience and our lusts, Titus iii. 3.

Q. Why doth our conscience harrass us?—**A.** Because we cannot fulfil the task of duty which the law prescribes us.

Q. Why doth our lust harrass and disquiet us?—**A.** Because we cannot fulfil the task of sin which they prescribe, nor fulfil one lust, but at the expense of another.

Q. Do sin and Satan, like Pharaoh, obstinately refuse to let us go from our spiritual bondage?—**A.** Yes; but God redeems us with a *strong hand*, Eph. i. 19.

Q. Is God's redeeming us from our spiritual bondage a very strong reason of our obedience to him?—**A.** Yes; God having redeemed us by *such* price and power, we are wholly and eminently his; and therefore ought to be wholly devoted to his service, Luke i. 74, 75.

Q. Is our serving of God a requital of his redeeming us?—**A.** No; God neither requires, nor can our good works be any proper requital of such amazing favours; for when we have done all *we are* but *unprofitable servants*, Psalm cxvi. 12, Luke xvii. 10.

Q. Why then doth God require obedience, because he has redeemed us?—**A.** That we may thereby acknowledge our obligation to him for his redeeming grace, and sink deeper in its debt, Psalm cxvi. 12, 13.

Q. Wherein do the four commands of the first table of

the moral law differ?—A. The first command respects the *object*, the second the *means*, the third the *manner*, and the fourth the appointed *time* of our worship.

Q. 45. *Which is the first commandment?*
A. The first cammandment is, "Thou shalt have no other gods before me."
Q. 46. *What is required in the fitst commandment?*
A. The first commandment requireth us to know and acknowledge the only true God as our God, and to worship and glorify him accordingly.
Q. 47. *What is forbidden in the first commandment?*
A. The first commandment forbiddeth the denying, or not worshipping and glorifying the true God as God and our God; and the giving of that worship and glory to any other which is due to him alone.
Q. 48. *What are we specially taught by these words,* before me, *in the first commandment?*
A. These words, *before me,* in the first commandment, teach us, That God who seeth all things, taketh notice of, and is much displeased with, the sin of having any other god.

Q. What are the general duties required in this command?—A. To know, acknowledge, worship, and glorify the true God, 1 Chron. xxviii. 9. Matth. iv. 10.
Q. What ought we to know concerning God?—A. That he is, what he is, and what he hath done.
Q. Why must we know *that God is?*—A. Because this is the foundation of all religion and duty, Heb. xi. 6.
Q. Why must we know *what God is?*—A. Because without the knowledge of the divine perfections and persons, we cannot discern him as the only true God.
Q In what respect ought we to know God?—A. As an absolute God, and as he is in Christ.
Q. Why must we know him as an absolute God?—A. That we may see how contrary his nature is to sin, and how unfit an absolute God is to be the enriching portion of sinners, Deut. iv. 24.
Q. Why must we know God as he is in Christ?—A. Because in Christ his glory is most brightly displayed in such a way as is engaging to sinful men, 2 Cor. v. 19.

Q. What different kinds of knowledge of God are there?
—**A.** Notional and saving knowledge.

Q. In what do these differ?—**A.** Notional knowledge is acquired by natural study, changes not our state, but renders us proud; saving knowledge is taught by Christ's Spirit, and humbles and sanctifies us.

Q. Is notional or head-knowledge good in itself?—**A.** Yes; but we can, and often do use it very ill.

Q. Can adult persons have saving knowledge without some measure of head-knowledge?—**A.** No; Isa. xxvii. 11.

Q. Is it enough that we know God *merely as God?*—**A.** No; we must know him *as our God* in Christ.

Q. What is understood by knowing God *as our God?*—**A.** The discerning him as our father, king, shepherd, husband, portion, &c. Isa. xxxiii. 22, and lxiii. 16.

Q. How may we attain to this knowledge of God?—**A.** By searching the scriptures in the fear of God, and by the assistance and illumination of his Spirit, John v. 39.

Q. What is to be understood by *acknowledging God?*—**A.** Our owning and avouching him for God and our God, Deut. xxvi. 17, John xx. 28, Psal. xci. 2, Exod. xv. 2.

Q. In what different ways are we to acknowledge him as God and our God?—**A.** By profession and practice.

Q. How must we acknowledge God *by profession?*—**A.** By professing to hold all his truths which represent him *as God or our God*, from a regard to his authority.

Q. In what manner ought we to acknowledge God by our profession?—**A.** In a plain, constant, humble, bold, and public manner, Matth. x. 32, Heb. x. 23.

Q. Why should our profession be *plain?*—**A.** That no divine truth may be buried amidst doubtful expressions.

Q. Why should it be *constant* or steadfast?—**A.** Because God and his truths are always the same Heb. xiii. 8, 9.

Q. Why should it be *humble?*—**A.** Because of our own, and others daily miscarriages, Rev. xi. 3.

Q. Why must our profession be *bold?*—**A.** To make the opposers of truth and holiness ashamed, and to encourage its friends in their adherence to it, Phil. i. 17. 28.

Q. When should we most boldly avow our profession?
—**A.** When iniquity and error most abound, Mark viii.

Q. Why so?—**A.** That we may restrain, and put to shame the boldest of men in error and wickedness.

Q. Why should our profession be *public?*—**A.** That we may not appear ashamed of Christ, and may excite others to embrace his truths, Luke xxii. 8, Matth. v. 16.

Q. How are we to acknowledge God as God, and our God *in our practice?*—A. By exercising towards him all suitable graces, honouring him with all due worship, and doing all things with an eye to his glory.

Q. What graces are we to exercise towards God ?—A. Faith, hope, love, fear, repentance, zeal, thankfulness, watchfulness, humility, resignation, patience, &c.

Q. Can we exercise one of these graces without exercising them all ?—A. No ; they are inseparably united in their nature and exercise, 2 Peter i. 4—10.

Q. Why is faith necessary ?—A. Because without faith we cannot receive nor worship God as our God, nor acknowledge him to be true, Heb. xi. 6, 1 John v. 10.

Q. Doth this command require faith in Christ as Mediator ?—A. Yes; for without this we could not acknowledge the truth of God in his word ; nor can we receive and worship God as God, and our God, but through Christ, 1 John iii. 23, John xiv. 6, Eph. ii. 18.

Q. How can the moral law require such faith from us, as could not be required of Adam, who had the law written on his heart ?—A. God's law binds us to credit whatever discoveries of himself or his will he makes to us.

Q. Doth this command require us to believe all the truths of the gospel with application to ourselves ?—A. Yes ; and if we do not, we make God a liar, instead of owning him as God and our God, 1 John v. 10.

Q. What is *hope* in God?—A. An expectation of all promised good things from God, Lam. iii. 26.

Q. Why is it required that we hope for *all the good* things which God hath promised ?—A. To acknowledge God as our *infinitely* gracious and liberal God, Psalm cxxx. 7.

Q. Wherein do faith and hope differ ?—A. Faith especially respects the faithfulness of God, and truth of his promise; hope especially respects the goodness of God, and the good things he hath promised : hope respects only future things, but faith respects also what is past or present.

Q. Why is love to God required in this command ?—A. To acknowledge God infinitely excellent in himself, and gracious and kind to us, Psalm cxvi. 1—6.

Q. How should our love to God be exercised ?—A. In

our choosing, esteeming, desiring, delighting in, and remembering him in his perfections and excellency.

Q. How can we sinners love the holiness and justice of
God?—**A.** We must receive Christ, in whom God's holiness and justice will be as amiable and lovely to us, as his
mercy and goodness, Hab. i. 13, 1 John i. 9.

Q. What call you the *fear of God?*—**A.** Not a slavish
terror of God as a destroyer ; but a filial awe of him as a
holy, great, powerful, and just Father, Heb. xii. 28.

Q. Why is this fear necessary?—**A.** To acknowledge
the majesty, power, holiness, &c., of God, Psal. lxxxix. 7.

Q. Why is repentance required from us?—**A.** To acknowledge the goodness and holiness of God ; and to give
up with the service of sin and Satan as our god.

Q. Are faith and repentance precepts of the gospel strictly so called?—**A.** No; they are required by the law ; and
it argues great ignorance to say, that faith, which believes
and receives God as our God, and repentance, which turns
from all other gods to the true God, are duties, not of the
law, but of the gospel, Matth. xxiii. 23.

Q. What is *holy zeal?*—**A.** An active spiritual concern
for the glory and truths of God, and indignation against sin,
John ii. 17, Acts xvii. 16, Psalm cxix. 139.

Q. For what should we be zealous?—**A.** For all the
truths of God, and every thing belonging to him, Jude 3.

Q. Why should we be zealous for the smallest truths?—
A. Because the glory of God is concerned in them ; they
are confirmed with the blood of Christ ; and the contempt
of them makes way for our giving up with greater truths,
Matth. v. 19, Luke iv. 10, Prov. xxiii. 23.

Q. For what truths should we be particularly zealous?—
A. For such as are presently opposed, which are therefore
called *the word* of Christ's *patience*, Rev. iii. 10.

Q. Are we to be equally zealous for all God's truths?—
No ; our zeal is to be proportioned to the natural or circumstantial importance of truth, Matth. xxiii. 23.

Q. Wherein lies the evil of carelessness about divine
truths relative to the discipline and government of the
church?—**A.** It shews great pride, as if we thought Christ
had instituted trifles ; and much selfishness, as if we sought
only our own happiness, not the honour of Christ ; and besides, the neglect of these things introduceth the ruin of
fundamental truths, Jude 3, 2 Tim. iii. 13.

Q. What are the qualities of right zeal?—**A.** It must

be only for what is founded on scripture ; and directed by knowledge ; managed with meekness and prudence; and attended with constancy, humility, and regard to the glory of God, Rom. x. 2, Gal. iv. 18, 1 Tim. vi. 11.

Q. Why is zeal necessary ?—A. To testify our high esteem of God, and his truths and ordinances.

Q. Why is thankfulness necessary ?—A. To acknowledge God as the God and author of all our mercies.

Q. What is *watchfulness?*—A. A disposition to guard against the snares of God's enemies, and to wait on him for his favours and blessings, 1 Pet. v. 8. Isa. viii. 17.

Q. Why is watchfulness necessary ?—A. To testify that our whole dependence is on the true God, and prevent our acknowledging and turning aside to other gods.

Q. What is *humility* towards God ?—A. A deep impression of our meanness and vileness before him, Job xl.

Q. Why is humility towards God necessary ?—A. To acknowledge God's greatness and holiness ; and prevent an idolatrous self-conceit, Isa. vi. 5. Matth. xvi. 24.

Q. What should we think meanly of before God ?—A. Our wisdom, riches, righteousness, beauty, &c.

Q. What is *resignation ?*—A. A willingness to be disposed of in our work and lot as God pleaseth, Acts xxi.

Q. Why is resignation necessary?—A. To acknowledge God's wisdom, and absolute dominion over us.

Q. When is resignation most difficult?—A. When God calls us to difficult duties, or visits us with heavy afflictions, Isa. vi. 8, 9. Lev. x. 3.

Q. What is *patience ?*—A. A bearing of afflictions with calmness of mind, 1 Pet. ii. 23.

Q. Why is patience necessary ?—A. To acknowledge the justice, wisdom, and love of God in afflicting us.

Q. What do you understand by the *worship* of God ?— A. It is a more immediate approach to God, and giving him the glory due to his name, Psalm xcvi. 8, 9.

Q. Wherewith ought we to worship God ?—A. With our soul and our body, 1 Cor. vi. 20.

Q. How are we to worship God with our soul alone ?— A. In meditation, admiration, &c. Psal. cv.

Q. What do you understand by *meditation?*—A. Our thinking of God and spiritual things.

Q. What should be the principal subjects of our meditation ?—A. The divine perfections, persons, and works ; Christ in his person, natures, and offices; the covenants of works and grace ; the law of God ; and beauty of holiness; the vileness and danger of sin, &c.

Q. Why is such meditation necessary ?—A. That we may know and acknowledge God more and more.

Q. What of God should we admire and wonder at ?—A. Every thing he is or doth, especially his love and sovereign grace, Psal. xxxvi. 7. and cxxxix. 17, 18.

Q. Why is admiration of God necessary ?—A. To acknowledge the absolute incomprehensibleness of God.

Q. How are we to worship God with soul and body jointly ?—A. By prayer, praise, receiving the sacraments, &c.

Q. How doth prayer glorify God ?—A. It acknowledgeth his omniscience to see all our sins, and his ability and readiness to supply all our wants, Phil. iv. 19.

Q. How doth praise glorify God ?—A. It is a confession to God himself, or others, of his infinite excellencies.

Q. How doth giving and receiving of the sacraments glorify God ?—A. We therein acknowledge God our *master*, whom we serve ; our *food*, on which we live ; and our *portion*, wherewith we are enriched, Gen. xviii. 7. 10.

Q. How do we acknowledge God as God, and our God, in other acts of life besides immediate worshipping of him ? —A. By making his glory our chief end in them ; and rendering to ourselves and others what is due, on his account, 1 Cor. x. 31. Tit. iii. 11, 12.

Q. Why is worshiping and glorifying God *accordingly* subjoined to our knowing and acknowledging him as God, and our God?—A. To show, that all our behaviour, and especially our worship, must correspond with the perfections of God, and his relations to us, and our knowledge and acknowledgment of them, 1 Cor. xxviii. 9.

Q. How must our worshipping and glorifying of God correspond with his being *a Spirit?*—A. In our seeking chiefly for spiritual blessings, and having a spiritual frame and end in every thing that we do, John iv. 24.

Q. How must they correspond with God's *infinity?*—A. In our making God the proper centre of all our desires, Psal. xxvii. 4, and lxxiii. 25, 26.

Q. How must they correspond with his *eternity ?*—A. In our caring chiefly for our eternal interests.

Q. How must they agree with his *unchangeableness?*— A. In our constant maintaining honourable apprehension of God ; and stedfastness in our duty.

Q. How must our worship and practice correspond with the *wisdom* of God ?—A. In our viewing, admiring, imitating, and relying on it, 2 Pet. ii. 9.

Q. How must they agree with the *power* of God ?—A. In our expecting his accomplishment of the most difficult-like promises: and our attempting the performance of the most difficult duties in his strength.

Q. How must they correspond with the *holiness* of God ? —A. In our earnest endeavours to increase in holiness, and daily blushing before God because of our impurity.

Q. How must they agree with the *justice* of God ?—A. In our standing in awe to sin, rendering every one his due, and boldly asking and expecting from our just God all the blessings which Christ has purchased for us.

Q. How must our worship and practice correspond with the *goodness* of God ?—A. In our esteeming all our enjoyments his free and undeserved mercies, and boldly asking the supply of all our wants from him.

Q. How must they correspond with the *truth* of God ?— A. In our believing his word, particularly his promise; living a life of faith on his Son; and studying to be like God in uprightness and sincerity, 2 Chron. xx. 20.

Q. How must they correspond with his being the *one only* God ?—A. In our renouncing all other lords and lovers; and refusing to give any thing the place of God in our hearts, Hos. xiv. 3. 8, Psalm lxxiii. 25, 26.

Q. How must they correspond with God's being the *living* God ?—A. In our receiving and improving him as our life, and devoting our life wholly to his service.

Q. How must our worship and practice correspond with God's subsistence in *three persons*?—A. In our worshipping the Father, through the Son and by the Spirit: and studying to maintain distinct communion with each of the divine persons, 2 Cor. xiii. 14, Eph. ii. 18.

Q. How must they correspond with God's being *in Christ*?—A. In our daily making use of Christ in his person and offices, as the way to the Father, Col. ii. 6.

Q. How must they correspond with God's relations of Father, husband, master, &c.? A. In our improving these relations to encourage our kindly dependence on, and obedience to him as our God, Exod. xv. 2.

Q. How must our worshipping and glorifying God correspond with our knowledge and acknowledgment of him ?— A. They must flow from a saving knowledge of him; and

18

our delight and diligence therein must increase in proportion to our knowledge and profession.

Q. Is not our whole duty, in some respect, required in this command?—A. Yes; for it is a knowing, acknowledging, worshipping, or glorifying God, 1 Cor. x. 31.

Q. Doth this, or any other command, require any thing but what is really our privilege?—A. No; to enjoy and serve God as our God, is our highest honour and happiness, Deut. xxxiii. 29. Psalm xix. 11.

Q. Is not the neglect of any duty required in this, or any other command, a sin forbidden in it?—A. Yes.

Q. What sins are more generally forbidden in the first command?—A. Atheism, profaneness, and idolatry.

Q. What is Atheism?—A. The denying, or not having a God, Eph. ii. 12, Psalm xiv. 1.

Q. How many sorts of Atheism are there?—A. Three; Atheism in heart, in word, or in practice.

Q. What is heart Atheism?—A. The doubting of God's existence, and desiring that there were no God.

Q. Can any be fully persuaded in their heart that there is no God?—A. No; for the proofs of his existence are so clearly engraven on the works of nature, and impressed on our conscience, that it, however stupified, cannot but bear witness to this truth, Rom. i. and ii.

Q. What is Atheism in word?—A. An affirming that there is no God, Ezek. viii. 12.

Q. How many ways may we be guilty of verbal Atheism?—A. Either by expressly denying that there is a God, or by maintaining errors directly contrary to any of his perfections.

Q. What are some of these errors?—A. Denying the divine equality of Father, Son, and Holy Ghost; denying the providence of God, or divinity of his word; maintaining that sinners can satisfy his justice for their sin; or ascribing any thing mean or sinful to him.

Q. What makes men endeavour to persuade themselves and others, that there is no God?—A. It is that they may indulge themselves, in wickedness, without dread of danger and punishment for it, Ezek. viii. Psalm x.

Q. What is Atheism in practice?—A. Our living as if there were no God, Ezek. viii. 12, Eph. ii. 12.

Q. When do we live as if there were no God?—A. When we live ignorant or forgetful of God; repine at his providence, neglect his worship; allow ourselves in sin, particularly secret sin, and that which is opposite to the graces required, as in unbelief, distrust, despair, hatred of God, bold prying into his secrets, impenitence, indifference about the truth and glory of God, unthankfulness, pride, incorrigibleness, impatience, &c. Jer. ii. and iii. &c.

Q. What is the *profaneness* forbidden in the first command?—A. Our not worshipping and glorifying God as God, and our God in Christ, Mal. i. 6.

Q. What is *idolatry?*—A. The giving of that honour and glory to any other which is due to God alone.

Q. How many kinds of idolatry are there?—A. Two, gross and secret idolatry.

Q. What is gross or open idolatry?—A. The external worshipping of sun, moon, stars, angels, men, images, or any other creature, instead of God, 2 Kings xxi.

Q. Did all the Gentile world, before Christ's incarnation, and a great part of it since, live in such gross idolatry?—A. Yes; Rom. i. 24, 1 Cor. i. 21.

Q. How should we be concerned for these idolaters?—A. In praying earnestly that God would deliver them from this great misery, by sending his word and Spirit among them; and in encouraging all suitable means of spreading the gospel in those places, Psalm xlv. 3, 4, 5.

Q. When are we guilty of secret and refined idolatry?—A. When, while professing the true God alone, we think of, love, or depend on any thing more than him.

Q. What are our most common idols or false gods which we honour with refined idolatry?—A. Imaginary beings, ourselves, other men, the world, the devil, second causes, and the gifts, graces, and ordinances of God, &c.

Q. How do we make imaginary beings an idol?—A. When we boast of false gifts, ascribe events to what men call *fortune, luck* or *chance*, 1 Sam. vi. 9.

Q. What about ourselves do we ordinarily make an idol of?—A. Our wisdom, will, righteousness, strength, beauty, belly, reputation, &c. Isa. xiv. 13, 14.

Q. How do we make an idol of our wisdom?—A. When we boast of it, rely on it, prefer our notions to God's word, and measure his truths by them.

Q. How do we make our will an idol?—A. When we are too much concerned to get it accomplished.

Q. How do we make self-righteousness our idol?—A. By depending on, and preferring it to the *righteousness of God* offered to us in the gospel, Rom. x. 3.

Q. How do we make our strength an idol?—**A.** When we boast of, rely on, or ascribe our works, and especially our religious performances to it, Isa. x. 13, 14.

Q. How do we make our beauty an idol?—**A.** By providing clothes or ornaments above our ability; valuing ourselves on account of our beauty; and being more careful about our external form and dress, than to be clothed with Christ's righteousness, and made all-glorious within, Isa. iii, 1 Pet. iii. 3, 4, 1 Tim. ii. 9, 10.

Q. How do we make our belly our god?—**A.** By being more careful for, and pleased with food to it, than to receive and delight in God as our portion, Isa. xxii. 13.

Q. How do we make our reputation our idol?—**A.** When we are more concerned for our own honour than for the glory of God, 2 Kings x. 16. 31, John v. 44.

Q. How do we make other men, and especially our relations, our idol?—**A.** In obeying them rather than God; or thinking of, loving, desiring, and delighting in them, more than God, 1 Sam. ii. 29, Deut. xxxii. 18.

Q. How do we further make ourselves or others our god?—**A.** By doing any thing more out of a view to their or our advantage, than to the glory of God, Zech. vii. 5.

Q. What of the world do we often make our god?—**A.** Its customs, riches, honours, and pleasures.

Q. How do we make the world our god?—**A.** By thinking habitually on it, and that even when worshipping God; by immoderate and inordinate desire after it; grudging for the want of it; taking satisfaction in it when God is absent; trusting to it; and despising others, particularly the saints, because they have little of it, Psalm iv. 6.

Q. How do we make the devil our God?—**A.** By hearkening to his temptations, embracing his doctrines, obeying his laws, and consulting, or entering into compacts with him, 2 Tim. ii. 26, 2 Cor. iv. 3.

Q. What are the doctrines and laws of the devil?—**A.** Whatever is contrary to the doctrines and laws prescribed in the word of God, 1 Tim. iv. 1, 2, 3, and vi. 3, 4, 5.

Q. In what forms is Satan especially consulted with?—**A.** As a physician and teacher, Isa. viii. 19, Lev. xx. 6.

Q. How do men consult the devil as a physician?—**A.** When they apply to him, or to charmers and wizards, for cures to men or beasts; or apply for a cure that which hath plainly no natural tendency to gain the end.

Q. How do men consult the devil as a teacher?—**A.**

When they observe superstitious omens of good or bad fortune; or consult dumb persons, wizards, star-gazers, &c.; use charms, or cast any kind of lots, to discover their marriage, future lot, or things lost.

Q. What evil is there in pretending to tell men's fortunes by studying the planets or stars?—A. Hereby men arrogate to themselves the knowledge that is proper to God; and make their lot depend on the heavenly bodies, rather than on the will of God, Isa. xlvii. 13, Deut. xxix. 29.

Q. Are there any that enter into compacts with the devil? —A. Yes; the scripture often speaks of such, and says they ought not *to live*, Exod. xxii. 18, Lev. xx. 6.

Q. How do we make second causes of things an idol? —A. By using unlawful means, trusting in lawful means, and ascribing events to them rather than to God, Isa. xxxi.

Q. When do we make an idol of God's ordinances, gifts, or graces?—A. When we love and seek them chiefly for themselves; or rest in, depend on, and boast of them more than God, Jer. vii. 4, Phil. iii. 5, 6.

Q. When is our idol most subtle and indiscernible?— A. When it is a solitary idol; is in our heart; is the lawful object of some fear, love, and delight; or is worshipped in our use of lawful means, Matth. x. 37, 38.

Q. How may we discern our secret idolatrous love to a creature?—A. When it abates our love to God, carries off our heart in his worship, or makes us abridge the performance of it, Luke xiv. 26, 27, Phil. ii.

Q. What are some means of curing our Atheism and idolatry?—A. Earnest prayer for the experience of God's powerful grace, diligent searching of his word, watching against the first motions of sin, shunning the company of the wicked, and frequenting the company of the most serious saints, Psalm cxix. 48, 49.

Q. What is the argument to enforce the first command? —A. That all our Atheism and idolatry is *before God*.

Q. What do these words, *before God*, in the first commandment teach us?—A. That God seeth our most secret Atheism and idolatry, and is much displeased therewith.

Q. How doth it appear, that God is much displeased with those sins?—A. He often forbids them; and hath often severely punished men for them, 1 Kings xi. and xiv.

Q. Why is God so much displeased with these sins?— A. They are an attack on his being, a denial of his perfections, and rob him of his distinguishing honour.

18*

Q. 49. *Which is the second commandment?*

A. The second commandment is, " Thou shalt not make unto thee any graven image, or any likeness *of any thing* that *is* in heaven above, or that *is* in the earth beneath, or that *is* in the water under the earth. Thou shalt not bow down thyself to them, nor serve them; for I the Lord thy God *am* a jealous God, visiting the iniquity of the fathers upon the children, unto the third and fourth *generation* of them that hate me; and showing mercy unto thousands of them that love me, and keep my commandments."

Q. 50. *What is required in the second commandment?*

A. The second commandment requireth the receiving, observing, and keeping pure and entire, all such religious worship and ordinances as God hath appointed in his word.

Q. 51. *What is forbidden in the second commandment?*

A. The second commandment forbiddeth the worshipping of God by images, or any other way not appointed in his word.

Q. 52. *What are the reasons annexed to the second commandment?*

A. The reasons annexed to the second commandment, are, God's sovereignty over us, his property in us, and the zeal he hath to his own worship.

Q. How prove you that this command respects the means of worship?—**A.** Its forbidding the use of images in the worship of God, because not of God's appointment, infers a requiring of the use of the means of worship appointed by God, and these only.

Q. Why should God only appoint the means of his own worship?—**A.** Because he *only* knows sufficiently what means of worship do best suit his own honour, and our advantage; and he *only* can authorize and make means effectual, Deut. xii. 32. and v. 32, James iv. 12.

Q. What is the principal medium of worshipping God aright in our fallen state?—**A.** Christ as a Mediator.

Q. Is not Christ as Mediator the proper object of worship?—**A.** Christ the Mediator *as God* is the proper object of worship; but *as Mediator* he is the way and medium by which alone we come to God, John xiv. 6.

Q. Are we then in our worship first to come to the Mediator, and then come to God?—**A.** No; we are all at once to come to God as in Christ, John xiv. 6. 9.

Q. What are the instituted means of worshipping God? —**A.** His ordinances which he hath appointed in his word, Psalm cxlvii. 19, 20, Prov. viii. 34.

Q. Why are these means of worship called *ordinances?* —**A.** Because they are established by the supreme authority and will of God, Deut. vi. 1, 2. 6. 20. 24, 25.

Q. What are the principal ordinances of God's worship? —**A.** Meditation, self-examination, prayer, reading, preaching, and hearing God's word, administering and receiving the sacraments, singing of psalms, religious fasting, thanksgiving, instruction of families, religious conference, oaths, vows, and lots, with church-government and discipline, Psalm cv. 2, 2 Cor. xiii. 5, &c.

Q. What is self-examination?—**A.** Our serious trial whether we have real grace, and in what case our graces and lusts are, by comparing our heart and life with the marks God has prescribed in his word, Matth. v., vi., vii.

Q. Why is self-examination necessary?—**A.** To acknowledge God as our judge, obtain assurance of his love, prevent spiritual security, discover our sins and wants, beget thankfulness and earnestness in prayer, &c., 2 Cor. xiii. 5, &c. Lam. iii. 42, 1 John 1—5.

Q. How prove you, that singing of psalms is God's ordinance?—**A.** In scripture it is often commanded, and the saints are often employed in it, Col. iii. 16.

Q. In what doth singing of psalms properly consist?—**A.** In praising God with our lips, for what he is, and has done, with cheerfulness of heart, Psalm cx. cxlv.—cl.

Q. May we not use harps, organs, and other musical instruments, in praising God?—**A.** No; for these, though used in the temple-service, were not used in the Jewish synagogues, nor in the New-Testament worship, nor are suited to the spiritual nature of it, John iv. 23, 24.

Q. In what manner should we sing psalms?—**A.** With understanding, love, and affection to God.

Q. What psalms should we sing in praising God?—**A.** Those psalms which we find recorded in scripture.

Q. Must we sing every expression in these psalms as relating to our present case ?—A. No ; we must sing some as expressive of what has been or may be our case.

Q. How are we to sing these psalms in which the psalmist prays for his wrath on his enemies ?—A. With a satisfaction of heart in these bright displays of God's justice in destroying his incorrigible enemies.

Q. What is religious fasting ?—A. The setting apart some time for solemn humiliation, confession of sin, pleading with God for mercies, and devoting ourselves to his service, Joel ii. 12—20, Neh. ix., Ezra ix., Dan. ix.

Q. Why is such voluntary humiliation called *fasting* ?—A. Because on these occasions we are to abstain from all unnecessary food, Dan. x. 3, Jonah iii.

Q. Is this abstinence any part of religion in itself ?—A. No ; but, it is a means of preparing us for humiliation and earnest prayer, Jonah iii. 7, 8.

Q. When are we called to fasting ?—A. When we have fallen into some great sin, when some judgment is inflicted or threatened, or some great mercy to ourselves or others very much needed, Joel ii. Ezra ix. x.

Q. When are we to set apart time for the solemn thanksgiving ?—A. When God hath bestowed some signal favour on us, or our brethren, Exod. xv. 2 Chron. xx.

Q. How many kinds of solemn fasts and thanksgivings are there ?—A. *Secret* in a closet, *private* in a family or society, and *public* in a congregation or country.

Q. Who have power to appoint general fasts and thanksgivings ?—A. Both the civil magistrate and the church, as the needs of the state or the church call for it, 2 Chron. xx. 3, Ezra viii. 21, Jer. xxxvi. 9, Joel i. ii.

Q. May church or state give up their own power, or claim the power of the other in this matter ?—A. No : for both are only stewards of that power ; the state under God as Creator, and the church under Christ as Mediator, Psal. lxxxii. 1, Eph. i. 22.

Q. In what are we religiously to instruct our families ? —A. In all the truths and ways of God, Deut. vi. 7, 20.

Q. Why ought our families to be thus instructed ?—A. To fit them for the more profitable reading and hearing of the word of God, Gen. xviii. 19, Psal. lxxvii. 1—8.

Q. What do you understand by religious conference ?—A. Our speaking with one another of the truths of God, and experiences of his dealings with us, Psal. cxvi.

Q. How should religious conference be managed?—A. With delight, humility, and prudence, Psal. lxvi. 16.

Q. What is a religious vow?—A. A solemn promise by which we *bind ourselves* to avoid or perform something for the honour of God, Numb. xxx. Psalm cxix. 106.

Q. What is necessary to make a vow or promissory oath lawful?—A. That what we engage be good in itself, and in our power to perform, Numb. xxx. Psalm cxvi. 14.

Q. To whom are all religious vows to be made?—A. To God only as our party, Psalm lxxvi. 12.

Q. How many kinds of religious vows are there?—A. Sacramental and occasional.

Q. What is an occasional religious vow?—A. It is when either a particular person, or a number of persons together, solemnly engage to serve the Lord, and cleave to his truths, Judg. xi. 31, Neh. x. Deut. xxix.

Q. How prove you, that secret personal covenanting with God is a duty?—A. From Isa. xliv. 5. *One shall say, I am the Lord's*, &c. Psalm cxix. 106.

Q. How prove you, that public covenanting with God is our duty?—A. The Old Testament church practised it with God's approbation; and it is no ceremonial service, but is promised to take place under the New Testament, Isa. xix. 18, 2 Cor. viii. 5.

Q. What seasons are pointed out in scripture as fit for public covenanting?—A. When a people hath received some great mercy, is threatened with great judgments, or is essaying to reform from, or withstand great apostacy, 2 Chron. xv. 12, and xxxiv. 31, Neh. ix. and x. &c.

Q. In what manner should religious vows be made?—A. Voluntarily from faith in and love to God; with knowledge of what we vow; and sincere resolution, in the strength of Christ to perform it, Jer. iv. 2, Psal. cxix. 106.

Q. What is an oath?—A. It is a solemn calling of God to witness the truth of what we affirm or promise; and requiring him to avenge it, if we deal falsely.

Q. How are oaths distinguished?—A. Into *assertory*, by which we affirm the truth of facts; and *promissory*, whereby we engage to avoid or perform something.

Q. Is swearing lawful under the New Testament?—A. Though swearing rashly, unnecessarily, or by any creature, is expressly forbidden, Matth. v. 34—37, James v. 12; yet necessary and reverential swearing *by God alone* is allowed, 2 Cor. i. 23.

Q. In what sense are all oaths to be taken?—**A.** In the plain sense of the words, without equivocation, or mental reservation, Psalm xxiv. 4, and xv. 2.

Q. What is a lot?—**A.** It is a solemn appeal to God, for arbitration in distributing and deciding some things controverted, Acts i. 24. 26, Prov. xvi. 33.

Q. What is required to make assertory oaths and lots lawful?—**A.** That they be necessary in matters of weight, and will end strife, Josh. vii. 14, Jer. iv. 2.

Q. What call you church government?—**A.** It is that order which Christ hath appointed in his visible church.

Q. For what end is church-government appointed?—**A.** To be a hedge for protecting the doctrine and more immediate worship of God, and making every one in their station active in his service, Eph. iv. 12, Tit. i.

Q. Is the civil magistrate head of this government?—**A.** No; it is wholly distinct from the civil government; for Christ says, *My kingdom is not of this world.*

Q. Has the civil magistrate no concern with the church? —**A.** Yes; as her nursing father, he ought to take care that peace and order be preserved; truth kept pure and entire; blasphemy and heresies suppressed; discipline, and all other ordinances of God, duly settled, administered, and observed: for which end he may call synods, and provide that every thing done in them be according to the word of God, 2 Chron. xix. xxix. and xxx. &c.*

Q. Is the Romish pope head of Christ's visible church? —**A.** No; he is *Antichrist*, the *man of sin*, 2 Thess. ii.

Q. Who then is the *alone* king and head of the church? —**A.** Jesus Christ, and none other, Matth. xxiii. 8—10.

Q. What things are considerable in church-government? —**A.** The officers, courts, and subjects of it.

Q. What different kinds of officers hath Christ appointed in the New Testament church?—**A.** Ordinary and extraordinary, 1 Cor. xii. 28.

Q. Which were the *extraordinary* officers?—**A.** Apostles, evangelists, prophets, and workers of miracles.

Q. Which are the *ordinary* officers in Christ's church? —**A.** Pastors and teachers, ruling elders and deacons.

Q. How prove you the divine institution of pastors?—**A.** The scripture declares, that Christ gave to his church *pas·tors and teachers*, Eph. iv. 12, 13.

---

* See Confess. Chap. xx. 4. xxii. 3, and the scripture quoted.

Q. What names are given to pastors in scripture?—**A.** They are called *teachers, rulers, ministers, shepherds, overseers, bishops, &c.* Heb. xiii. 17, &c.

Q. Doth the scripture require, or allow of any bishop ruling over other pastors?—**A.** No; it forbids all lordly rule in the church; never distinguisheth between bishops and presbyters, but calls the same persons by both names; and ascribes the highest power in the church to presbyters, even the ordination of an evangelist, Luke xxii. 25, 26, Tit. 1. 5. 7, 1 Tim. iv. 14, Phil. i. 1, &c.

Q. What is the office of a pastor?—**A.** To rule in the church, and to administer the word and sacraments, 1 Cor. iv. 1.

Q. How prove you, that ruling elders are appointed by Christ?—**A.** The scripture plainly suggests that there are elders who *rule well*, and yet do not *labour in word and doctrine*, 1 Tim. v. 17, Rom. xii. 8, 1 Cor. xii. 28.

Q. What is their office?—**A.** To concur with pastors in ruling and inspecting the manners of the people.

Q. How prove you the divine institution of deacons?— **A.** Deacons were ordained by the apostles; and their office is frequently approven of in scripture, Acts vi. 3, 1 Tim. iii.

Q. What is a deacon's office?—**A.** To take care of the poor, and serve at the Lord's table, Acts vi.

Q. What courts hath Christ appointed for government in his church?—**A.** Sessions, presbyteries, and synods.

Q. What is a *session?*—**A.** That court in the particular Christian congregation, which consists of a pastor or pastors, elders and deacons.

Q. What divine warrant have we for kirk sessions?—**A.** The light of nature, and law of necessity, the institution of Christ, alluding to such courts in the Jewish synagogues, and the apostolical example, do fully warrant them, Matth. xviii. 15—21, Acts xiv. 23, &c.

Q. What is the business of sessions?—**A.** To admit church-members, rebuke offenders, and suspend them from the sacraments, and manage all the ecclesiastic affairs of a particular congregation, 1 Tim. v. 17.

Q. What is a presbytery?—**A.** A church court consisting of ministers and elders from several congregations.

Q. How prove you the divine warrant of a presbytery? —**A.** From its being expressly approven in scripture; and from the apostolic example of presbyteries at Jerusalem, Ephesus, and Corinth, 1 Tim. iv. 14, Acts xi., &c.

Q. What is the business of a presbytery?—**A.** To rule in affairs too hard for sessions, to ordain pastors, excommunicate offenders, &c., 1 Tim. iv. 14.

Q What is a synod?—**A.** It is the meeting of several presbyteries in one court, Acts xv.

Q. What scripture warrant have we for this court?—**A.** In Acts xv. we find that the rulers from sundry churches met together, disputed and determined a point of controversy in the church.

Q. How prove you this was not a meeting for consultation only?—**A.** From the scriptures calling their determinations a *burden* and *decrees*, Acts xv. 28. and xvi. 4.

Q. What power have synods?—**A.** To rule in ecclesiastic affairs that are too hard for presbyteries.

Q. Have they power to impose any new articles of faith? —**A.** No; but to interpose their authority in favour of what is according to the word of God, 1 Cor. iv. 1.

Q. What are the privileges of the subjects or private members in the church?—**A.** To receive all the ordinances of Christ suited to their case; and if blameless, and of adult age, to choose their own officers.

Q. How prove you that adult Christians have a right to choose their officers and particularly their pastors?—**A.** They are commanded to *try the spirits;* they *chose two,* one of which was to be an apostle; the apostles caused them choose their deacons, and *ordained elders by suffrages* in the churches: and the very light of nature requires Christians liberty to choose their own spiritual physician and guide; and represents it as most absurd, that a temporal possession should entitle a man, however profane, to choose spiritual guides to the church, 1 John iv. Acts i. 23—26. vi. 3, and xiv. 23.

Q. Do church officers derive their authority from the church?—**A.** No; they derive it from Christ, 1 Cor. xii.

Q. Have all church members a right to rule in her?—**A.** No; for if all were rulers, there could be none to be ruled, Heb. xiii. 17, Acts xx. 28, 1 Thess. v. 12.

Q. What are the spiritual terms of communion with the visible church in all her sealing ordinances?—**A.** That men be in appearance saints and faithful, Psalm xxiv. 3, 4, Eph. i. 1, 1 Cor. v. 11, 2 Thess. iii. 6.

Q. Is it not enough if men be real saints?—**A.** No; what God hath joined together, it is at our peril if we put asunder, Matth. v. 19.

Q. To what are church-members to be faithful?—A. To the relation they stand in to God or men, and to the trust which they have received, and the vows they are under, whether personal or national, Phil. iii. 17.

Q. How are we to be faithful to the relations we stand in?—A. By performing the various duties of them.

Q. How ought we to be faithful to the trust reposed in us as church members?—A. By conveying to posterity the truths of God as fully and clearly, and his ordinances as pure and entire as we received them.

Q. How are church members to be faithful to their vows? —A. By still continuing to acknowledge the obligation of their vows, and endeavouring to perform the duties engaged to in them, Neh. x. 26, Psalm cxix. 100.

Q. Doth a church member's selling or giving up any of the truths of Christ which he hath once received, or is by oath bound to, make him scandalous?—A. Yes ; as much as a servant, though a saint, his selling of his master's goods at his own hand, Prov. xxiii. 23, Matth. v. 19.

Q. What is church discipline?—A. The method which Christ hath appointed for correcting and reclaiming scandalous church members, Matth. xviii. 15—18.

Q. What call you *scandal?*—A. An open sin, which grieves the godly, and tempts others to sin.

Q. How many kinds of scandal are there?—A. Two ; *private* scandal, which is known only to a few, and *public* scandal, which is known to many.

Q. What is the first step of discipline with respect to private scandal?—A. He that knows it should secretly tell the offender his fault, and reprove him for it, Lev. xix. 17.

Q. What is to be done if the offender confesseth and promiseth amendment?—A. The reprover is to rest satisfied, and carefully to conceal his brother's fault, Lev. xix. 16.

Q. What must be done if the offender denies or defends his fault?—A. The reprover is to reprove him again before one or two witnesses, Matth. xviii. 16.

Q. If the offender still continues obstinate, what is the next step of discipline?—A. The offended person is to tell that church judicatory to which the offender is most immediately subject, Matth. xviii. 17.

Q. What is the first step of church discipline with respect to public offences?—A. They are to be brought before a church judicatory, Acts xv. 5, 6.

19

Q. What is to be done with an offender, if he continues to disregard church-judicatories?—**A.** He is to be excommunicated, or solemnly cast out from communion with the visible church, Matth. xviii. 17, 18, 1 Cor. v.

Q. What is meant by one's being *delivered to Satan?*—**A.** That his person is cast out from Christ's visible church into the visible kingdom of the devil, 1 Cor. v. 5.

Q. On whom should this sentence be passed?—**A.** On those whose sin is gross and manifest, and who continue obstinate in their wickedness, 1 Cor. v. 1 Tim. i. 20.

Q. For what end are church-censures necessary?—**A.** For reclaiming offenders, deterring others from sin, for vindicating the honour of Christ and the gospel, and preventing God's wrath from falling on the church.

Q. In what manner should offenders be reproved?—**A.** With great prudence, meekness, and plainness.

Q. Why must we rebuke with great prudence?—**A.** Because if we choose not fit time, place, and words, the end of the rebuke may be entirely lost, Prov. xxv. 12.

Q. Why must we reprove with great meekness?—**A.** To prevent the offender's passion, and cause him take the rebuke as designed for his good, Gal. vi. 1.

Q. Why must we reprove with great plainness?—**A.** That offenders may not think their sin less than it is, or be too lightly affected with it, Acts viii. 20—28.

Q. What doth the second command require with respect to all these ordinances of God?—**A.** The receiving, observing, and keeping them pure and entire, Deut. vi.

Q. What is meant by receiving the ordinances of God?—**A.** The knowledge and embracement of them.

Q. What is meant by observing them?—**A.** Our doing what they require, and waiting upon God in them.

Q. What is meant by keeping these ordinances pure?—**A.** Our allowing nothing to be added to them.

Q. What is meant by keeping them entire?—**A.** Our suffering nothing to be taken from them.

Q. What sins are more generally forbidden in the second commandment?—**A.** Profaneness, idolatry, and superstition.

Q. What is the profaneness forbidden in the second commandment?—**A.** Our opposition to, contempt of, or indifference about the ordinances of God; and neglecting to receive, observe, and keep them pure and entire.

Q. What is the idolatry forbidden in the second command?—A. The worshipping of God by images, saints, angels, &c.

Q. How did the Pagans break this command?—A. By using images in the worship of their false gods.

Q. May not we make images of mere creatures?—A. Yes; if they are not to be used for a religious use.

Q. What different kinds of images of God are forbidden in this commandment?—A. Images made by men's hands, and images made by their fancies, Deut. iv. 15.

Q. Is it idolatrous to make an image of any divine person; of the Father as an old man; of the Son as a babe; or man hanging on a cross; or of the Spirit as a dove; or to conceive any such fanciful idea of these persons?—A. Yes.

Q. Is it idolatrous, when we read of God's hands, feet, &c. to fancy him as having such members?—A. Yes.

Q. Is it idolatrous to paint God as light, or the Trinity as a triangle, or body with three heads?—A. Yes.

Q. Why must we make no images of God with our hands or fancy?—A. Because God hath forbidden it; and it misrepresents him as material, finite, &c. and so as no God at all, Deut. iv. 15—19, Isa. xl. 18—20.

Q. May not such images help to instruct the ignorant?—A. No; they are teachers of lies, Hab. ii. 18, Jer. x. 15.

Q. Is an image, or imaginary idea of Christ, as a suffering or glorified man, helpful to our faith?—A. No; it is very hurtful to it; for it divides the natures of Christ in our conception of him, whereas faith must still view them as united in one person, Isa. ix. 6, John i. 14.

Q. What is superstition in the worship of God?—A. Our taking from, or adding to his ordinances.

Q. May not men appoint teaching ceremonies in the worship of God?—A. No; Isa. i. 12, Col. ii. 20—23.

Q. Why so?—A. Because they cannot bless nor render effectual these ceremonies; and so they lead men's minds away from the spirituality of God's worship.

Q. How prove you, that God will not bless nor approve ceremonies of men's appointment used in his worship?—A. He gives men no authority to appoint them; but condemns these appointments as will-worship, Col. ii. 20.

Q. Doth not God command us to do all things *decently and in order?*—A. That command requires us to choose the fittest times and places for worship, and to perform it in a grave manner; but doth not allow men to appoint ceremonies as parts of God's worship, 1 Cor. xiv.

Q. Among what sect of professed Christians is the saddest mixture of idolatry and superstition to be found ?—A. Among the *Papists*, and those of the *Greek church*.

Q. How are the Papists guilty of idolatry ?—A. In their worshipping images of the Trinity; the bread in the sacrament; the cross, angels, and saints, especially the Virgin Mary, and their images or relics; bowing at the name of Jesus, or towards altars, or the east; swearing by creatures, or by touching and kissing the gospels, &c.

Q. How are the Papists guilty of superstitious taking away from God's ordinances ?—A. In denying the use of the cup in the Lord's supper, and of the scripture to the people; and in taking away the second commandment from their catechism, and the public offices of their church.

Q. Why do they deny the people the use of the cup in the Lord's supper ?—A. To exalt their clergy, who claim it as their due.

Q. Why do Papists deny the people the use of the scripture ?—A. That they may not, by reading it, discover their errors in doctrine, and corruptions in worship, &c.

Q. Why do they so conceal the second commandment ? —A. Because it condemns their images and superstition.

Q. How are the Papists guilty of superstitious adding to the ordinances of God?—A. In their adding five bastard sacraments; offering the bread in the Lord's supper as a sacrifice; abstaining from flesh in Lent; using vain fastings, superstitious holy days, vestments, fonts, altars, &c.; adding cream, oil, spittle, and the sign of the cross in baptism; baptising of bells; praying on beads, &c.

Q. Is it not sinful for Protestants to preserve monuments of idolatry and superstition, by keeping images of the Pagan gods, of Christ as man, &c.; or superstitiously observing their holy-days, as New Year's Day, Fasten's-even, Christmas, Pasch, &c. ?—A. Yes; Gal. iv. 10.

Q. Will it excuse us from sin, if we do these things with no bad intention ?—A. No; to think that innocent intentions justify bad actions, is Popish doctrine.

Q. Why are most men so fond of pompous ceremonies in the worship of God ?—A. Because they do not relish the spiritual nature of his ordinances, and think themselves capable of bettering his institutions.

Q. What are the three reasons annexed to the second

commandment?—A. God's sovereignty over us, his property in us, and the zeal which he hath for his own worship.

Q. How is God's *sovereignty* over us a reason for keeping this command?—A. God being Lord of all, it is most suitable to his wisdom and authority that he prescribe all the means of his worship, James iv. 11, 12.

Q. How is God's *property* in us as our God a reason for keeping this command?—A. These whose God he is, have the strongest reason to obey his ordinances, and beware of spiritual whoredom, and showing themselves wise above him, Deut. xii. 32, Exod. xv. 2.

Q. How is God's zeal or jealousy for his own worship, a reason of keeping this command?—A. As it makes it profitable to keep, and dangerous to break it, Deut. iv. 24.

Q. How doth God's zeal for his own worship show itself?—A. In his rewarding the keepers, and punishing the breakers of his commands, Deut. v.—xii. xxviii.

Q. How doth God reward the keepers of his commands? —A. In esteeming them lovers of him, and shewing mercy to thousands of them, Exod. xx. 6.

Q. How doth God punish the breakers of his commands? —A. In counting them haters of him, and punishing their sin to their third and fourth generation, Exod. xx. 5.

Q. How can God justly punish children for their parents' sin?—A. Because children are the property of parents, and so parents are punished in them, 1 Kings xiv. xvi.

Q. Whether doth this threatening respect temporal or eternal punishment?—A. If the children continue to approve their parents' sin, by walking in it, the threatening respects both temporal and eternal punishment; but otherwise, it respects only temporal strokes.

Q. If the children become saints, how is this threatening executed?—A. The temporal strokes are often inflicted, but are made to work for their good, Isa. xxvii. 9.

Q. 53. *Which is the third commandment?*

A. The third commandment is, " Thou shalt not take the name of the Lord thy God in vain; for the Lord will not hold him guiltless that taketh his name in vain."

Q. 54. *What is required in the third commandment?*

A. The third commandment requireth the holy
19*

and reverend use of God's names, titles, attributes, ordinances, words, and works.

Q. 55. *What is forbidden in the third commandment?*

A. The third commandment forbiddeth all profaning or abusing of any thing whereby God maketh himself known.

Q. 56. *What is the reason annexed to the third commandment?*

A. The reason annexed to the third commandment is, That however the breakers of this commandment may escape punishment from men, yet the Lord our God will not suffer them to escape his righteous judgment.

Q. What is to be here understood by the NAME of God? —A. Every thing whereby God maketh himself known.

Q. By what doth God make himself known?—A. By proper names, titles, attributes, ordinances, words, and works, Exod. xxxiv. 6, 7, &c.

Q. What are the *proper names* of God?—A. They are either essential, as *Jehovah, Jah, Lord, God;* or personal, as the *Father, Son, Holy Ghost,* &c.

Q. What are the *titles* of God?—A. Creator and Preserver of men; God and Father of Christ; *Father* of lights, mercies, or spirits; *God* of glory, peace, patience, comfort, and salvation; *God* of Abraham, Isaac, and Jacob; *holy One,* and *Rock* of Israel; *King* of kings, saints and nations; *Lord* of glory; *Hearer* of prayer, &c.

Q. What doth the third command require with respect to God's names, titles, attributes, ordinances, words, and works?—A. The holy and reverend use of them.

Q. What do you mean by the *holy use* of them?—A. Our using them with holy natures, out of regard to God's holy law, and with a view to promote holiness.

Q. What do you mean by a *reverend use* of them?—A. Our using them with a filial fear of God upon our spirit, manifested in our outward conduct, Psalm lxxxix. 7.

Q. Can an unregenerate man use God's names, &c., rightly?—A. No; he always profanes them, Isa. lxvi. 3.

Q. When are God's names, titles, and attributes, used in a holy and reverent manner?—A. When we think, speak, write, or hear of them, with a holy awe of God in our hearts, and to promote a holy fear of him in our lives, Deut. xxviii. 58, Psalm lxxxix. 7, Heb. xii. 28.

Q. When are God's ordinances used in a holy and reverend manner?—A. When we approach them with holy hearts and hands; and wait upon, and seek after the *great God*, and *holy One* of Israel in them, Psalm lxxxix. 7.

Q. When is God's word used in a holy and reverend manner?—A. When we receive it in our heart as the word of the great God, to make us holy, Psalm cxix.

Q. When are God's works used in a holy and reverend manner?—A. When we discern God in them and improve them chiefly to advance his glory, Psalm cxxxvi.

Q. What is forbidden in the third commandment?—A. The profaning or abusing of any thing whereby God makes himself known.

Q. How are God's names and titles profaned?—A. By our thinking, speaking, writing, or hearing of them, rashly, lightly, or maliciously.

Q. Are they not dreadfully profaned by rash invocations in common speech; as, O Jesus! O Christ! O Lord! O God! Goodness! good God! or horrid imprecations of curses, confusion, damnation, &c.?—A. Yes.

Q. Are they not also dreadfully profaned, when they are used in charms to drive away devils, witches, diseases, &c?—A. Yes; Acts xix. 13—17.

Q. How is God's attribute of *spirituality* profaned?—A. By our conceiving of him as any way corporeal; neglecting to worship him in spirit and in truth; and by our contempt and ignorance of spiritual things.

Q. How is God's attribute of *infinity* profaned?—A. By our conceiving of him as more present in heaven than in earth, or in one place than another; and our filling his place in our hearts with other things.

Q. How is God's *eternity* profaned?—A. By our neglecting to think of his eternal purposes and love; and our not preparing for an eternity to come.

Q. How is God's *unchangeablenes* profaned?—A. By our conceiving that prayer can change his purpose, or fearing that sin may alter his love; and by our unstedfastness in our Christian profession or practice.

Q. How is the almighty *power* of God profaned?—A. When it is despised, distrusted, resisted, or when trusted on for assistance in sin, Isa. xxxvi. xxxvii.

Q. How are God's infinite *wisdom* and knowledge profaned?—A. By our curious prying into his secrets, measuring the mysteries of his word by our reason, judging the hearts and intentions of others, despising or distrusting his direction, or charging with folly his words or works.

Q. How is God's *holiness* profaned?—A. By our disliking it, mocking at sin, at saints, or holy things, and neglecting the diligent study of holiness in heart or life.

Q. How is God's *justice* profaned?—A. By our not imitating it, not fearing to live in sin, not embracing Christ's righteousness for satisfying it, and not expecting all blessings from it through his merits.

Q. How is God's *goodness* and mercy profaned?—A. By our not enlarging our hearts to receive it; being discouraged, by our sinfulness, from seeking grace or glory; offering our good works to God as a price of salvation; or sinning because grace doth abound.

Q. How is God's *patience* abused?—A. By our not admiring it; contemning lesser strokes and warning; and not imitating it in our patient waiting on God, and bearing with such as offend us.

Q. How is God's *truth* profaned?—A. By our suspecting his sincerity, discrediting his word, or expecting the accomplishment of promises without using the appointed means, 1 John v. 10.

Q. How is God's being the *living God* profaned?—A. By our neglecting to improve him as our life, and by not living to him, Jer. ii. 13.

Q. How is God's being the *one only* God profaned?—A. By dividing our heart and life between him and idols.

Q. How is the mystery of the *Trinity* profaned?—A. By ridiculing it; by erroneous conceptions and representations of it; and by indifference about distinct communion with the three persons in it, 1 John ii. 22, 23.

Q. How is Christ as Mediator profaned and abused?—A. By our neglecting him as the way to the Father; expecting salvation through him in ignorance and unrighteousness, or partly by our own works and strength; or by using his name to authorise any wickedness, 1 Cor. 23.

Q. How are God's ordinances in general profaned?—A. By our using them in an ignorant, carnal, careless, hypocritical, legal, lifeless, or licentious manner.

Q. When do we use the ordinances of God *ignorantly?* —A. When we use them without knowing their institution, nature, and ends, Acts xvii. 23.

Q. When are the ordinances of God used *carnally?*—A. When we attend upon them only with our bodies, or for some carnal advantage, John vi. 26.

Q. When are they used *carelessly?*—A. When we attend them without earnest concern to find God in them.

Q. When are they used in a *hypocritical* manner?—A. When, in attending on them, we study to appear saints when we are not, or to seem better than we are.

Q. When are God's ordinances used in a *legal* manner? —A. When we attend on them to atone for our sins, or to purchase grace or glory to us, Isa. lviii. 1—7.

Q. When are they used in a *licentious* manner?—A. When they are used as a means of performing or covering some malicious, lascivious, or covetous design.

Q. When are they used in a *lifeless* manner?—A. When we attend on them with sleepy or drowsy bodies, or without the active exercise of spiritual grace.

Q. Is it a very great sin to indulge ourselves in a *sleepy* attendance on God's ordinances?—A. Yes; it is a *mocking of God to his face,* and turning the means of salvation into poison to our soul, Lev. x. 2 Cor. iv. 4.

Q. Is not the more particular abuse of God's ordinances also forbidden in this command?—A. Yes.

Q. How is *meditation* profaned?—A. By our thinking on trifles, or mostly on the circumstantials of religion; or having our mind easily led aside from spiritual objects.

Q. How is *self-examination* profaned?—A. By our trying ourselves by unscriptural marks; or without an impartial and earnest desire to know our real state and case, Rev. iii. 17, Isa. lviii. 2—7, Luke xviii. 11.

Q. How is *prayer* profaned?—A. By our not praying in Christ's name; praying for unlawful things, or for things lawful without due submission to God's will; by rash calling on God to *save, bless, guide, preserve, &c.?* or by calling on Satan to *take* or *hurt* any.

Q. How is prayer further profaned?—A. By superstitious limiting it to particular days, hours, or words; and using indecent gestures or words; or, in social prayer, words not easily understood.

Q. How is *singing of psalms* profaned?—A. By our neglecting to join with others in it; wanting affections suited to the expressions sung; attending more to the melody of the voice than the frame of our heart; and by sudden wearying of the exercise, &c.

Q. How is the *preaching* of God's word profaned?—**A.** By preaching without a regular call, or chiefly for gain or honour; by preaching error, or truth in a wrong manner; or preaching with theatrical gestures, or in words the hearers cannot understand, or which tickle their fancy or passions, rather than touch their conscience, 1 Cor. ii. 1—5.

Q. How is the *reading* and *hearing* of God's word profaned?—**A.** By reading and hearing it out of curiosity, chiefly to inform our judgment, or to pass the time, or sound jests, rather than to make us holy.

Q. How is the *administration* of *baptism* and the *Lord's supper* profaned?—**A.** When these ordinances are administered by such as are not *true gospel-ministers*, or to such as are not *proper members of the visible church;* or are administered in a *private* and superstitious manner, Matth. xxviii. 19, 1 Cor. x. 16, 17, and xi. 23—29.

Q. How is the *receiving* of the sacraments profaned?—**A.** When we attend on them without due preparation, or suitable exercise of grace; and when we rest in them as infallible securities of salvation; or neglect to improve them after receiving them, 1 Cor. xi. Luke iii.

Q. How is *fasting* profaned?—**A.** In our fasting for wicked or doubtful causes; or to further strife, or atone for sin; or without faith's view of a crucified Christ, and sincere resolution to turn from the sins which we confess.

Q. How is *religious instruction* of families profaned?—**A.** When it is not performed in a careful, patient, and impartial manner; nor suited to the capacities of those who who are instructed, Deut. vi. 7.

Q. How is *religious conference* profaned?—**A.** By our studying therein to shew our abilities; or talking mostly on disputable and circumstantial points.

Q. How are *religious vows* profaned?—**A.** By our vowing what is sinful, trifling, doubtful, or impossible; vowing to serve God on condition he will save us; or by vowing in our own strength, or without a serious resolution to perform our vows, Eccl. v. 4.

Q. How is *public covenanting* profaned?—**A.** By forcing men to it; admitting such as are ignorant and profane; or covenanting in such a manner as tends to promote division, contention, and pride.

Q. How is *swearing of oaths* profaned?—**A.** By our swearing what is trifling, false, or doubtful; or without a due call, and fear of God upon our spirit, Jer. iv. 2.

Q. Is it not dreadful wickedness to cry out on slight occasions, *The Lord knows, God knows ;* or to confirm our assertions with *od, troth, faith, conscience, soul, devil, fiend,* and other minced oaths ?—**A.** Yes ; and such profane swearers ought not to be credited.

Q. How are *lots* profaned ?—**A.** By our using them to discover future events, or things lost ; or to determine trifling disputes, or such as human prudence might have easily decided ; or when we reflect on the lot after it is cast.

Q. Is it a great sin to play at cards or dice?—**A.** Yes ; for it irreverently calls God to be arbitrator in a trifle ; is the source of much idleness, strife, and profane swearing ; and a chief delight of profane persons ; and leads in men to heathenish affections, words, and practices, Prov. xvi. 33, 1 Thess. v. 22.

Q. How is *church government* profaned ?—**A.** By setting up false forms of it ; despising and opposing it; or preventing it, to please the humours, and support the carnal interests of men, Micah vi. 16.

Q. How is *church discipline* profaned?—**A.** When it is inflicted in a disorderly, proud, and partial manner, or upon improper objects ; when it is despised, opposed, used as a satisfaction for sin, exchanged for money, or removed without evidence of repentance.

Q. How is God's *word in general* profaned ?—**A.** By our denying, despising, ridiculing, and jesting on it, misapplying, or wresting it to sinful purposes.

Q. How is God's *law* profaned ?—**A.** By our contracted views of its extent ; presenting our vile righteousness as an obedience to it; seeking happiness by it ; or despairing of life because of its rigour.

Q. How is the *gospel* of God profaned ?—**A.** By our discrediting his offers ; turning it into a new law ; or taking encouragement to sin from the grace of it, 1 John v. 10.

Q. How are the *decrees* of God profaned or abused ?—**A.** By our curious prying into, deriding, or misrepresenting them ; or taking encouragement from them to neglect the use of appointed means, Deut. xxix. 29.

Q. How is God's work of *creation* profaned ?—**A.** By our making his creatures occasions or instruments of pride, intemperance, lust, or other wickedness ; and by sporting at their hurting or destroying one another.

Q. How is God's work of *providence* profaned ?—**A.** By our neglecting to study the language of them ; misinterpreting, quarrelling with, and fighting against them; and our ascribing the events thereof to second causes, or what is profanely called *chance*, Jer. v. 3, 4.

Q. How is God's work of *redemption* profaned?—A. By our denying or deriding any part of it, disregarding an interest in it, and not walking worthy of it.

Q. What reason is annexed to this third command to deter us from profanation of God's name?—A. A very dreadful one; namely, that *the Lord will not hold him guiltless that taketh his name in vain.*

Q. What doth the Lord's not holding him guiltless mean? —A. That the Lord will not suffer such as profane his name to escape his righteous judgment.

Q. Should men punish the more gross blasphemies and profanation of God's name?—A. Yes; *he that blasphemeth the name of the Lord shall surely be put to death.*

Q. Why then do such gross profaners of God's name so often escape punishment from men?—A. Because many magistrates and great men are principal profaners of God's name, or want due zeal for his glory, Micah iii. 1, 2.

Q. Can any such as profane God's name by perjury, habitual profane swearing of broad or minced oaths, escape God's wrath?—Yes; he will make their plagues wonderful, except they repent, Deut. xxviii. 58, 59.

Q. Do not such profane persons often escape visible judgments in this life?—A. Yes; but their torments in hell shall be the more dreadful, Rev. xvii. 20.

Q. How shall the plasphemers of God's name be punished in hell?–A. Their cursing and blasphemy shall become their everlasting punishment; their profane tongues shall for ever burn in hell fire, and they shall gnaw them for pain, Luke xvi. 24, Rev. xvi. 10, 11.

Q. Why doth God so punish profane swearing?—A. Because it is so heinous a crime, committed without any provocation from God, or any temptation of profit or pleasure to the sinner.

Q. 57. *Which is the fourth commandment?*

A. The fourth commandment is, "Remember the Sabbath-day to keep it holy. Six days shalt thou labour, and do all thy work. But the seventh day *is* the Sabbath of the Lord thy God; *in it* thou shalt not do any work, thou, nor thy son, nor thy daughter, thy man-servant, nor thy maid-servant, nor thy cattle, nor the stranger that is within thy gates. For *in* six days the Lord made heaven and earth, the sea, and all that in them *is*, and rested the seventh day: wherefore the Lord blessed the Sabbath-day, and hallowed it."

Q. 58. *What is required in the fourth commandment?*

A. The fourth commandment requireth the keeping holy to God, such set times as he hath appointed in his word; expressly one whole day in seven, to be a holy Sabbath to himself.

Q. 59. *Which day of the seven hath God appointed to be the weekly Sabbath?*

A. From the beginning of the world to the resurrection of Christ, God appointed the seventh day of the week to be the weekly Sabbath; and the first day of the week, ever since, to continue to the end of the world, which is the Christian Sabbath.

Q. 60. *How is the Sabbath to be sanctified?*

A. The Sabbath is to be sanctified by a holy resting all that day, even from such worldly employments and recreations as are lawful on other days; and spending the whole time in the public and private exercises of God's worship, except so much as is to be taken up in the works of necessity and mercy.

Q. 61. *What is forbidden in the fourth commandment?*

A. The fourth commandment forbiddeth the omission or careless performance of the duties required, and the profaning the day by idleness, or doing that which is in itself sinful, or by unnecessary thoughts, words, or works, about worldly employments or recreations.

Q. 62. *What are the reasons annexed to the fourth commandment?*

A. The reasons annexed to the fourth commandment are, God's allowing us six days of the week for our own employments, his challenging a special propriety in the seventh, his own example, and his blessing the Sabbath-day.

Q. What is to be here understood by the *Sabbath* day?
—**A.** A day of holy rest, Exod. xxxi. 17, Isa. lviii. 13.

Q. Doth the light of nature require the observance of a Sabbath?—**A.** It requires, that some part of our time be set apart for the public service of God; but shews not *what* particular time, or *how much* time.

Q. What part of time doth the fourth command require for a Sabbath to the Lord?—**A.** One whole day in seven.

Q. Whether is this commandment moral or ceremonial?—**A.** It is *moral*, and binding on all men in all ages.

Q. How prove you that?—**A.** It, with the other commandments, was written by God on tables of stone, and published in the midst of the moral law; it is enforced by moral reasons, and did bind strangers as well as Jews: and the Sabbath was appointed in Paradise, before there were any ceremonies, Exod. xx. 8—11.

Q. Is not the observance of the precise day of the week ceremonial?—**A.** That circumstance is changeable, but not properly ceremonial.

Q. How then was the Sabbath called *a sign* to the Israelites?—**A.** This was only an additional use of the Sabbath, added to the principal and moral end of it.

Q. Ought not men to maintain a holy frame of spirit every day?—**A.** Yes; Gal. v. 25, Rom. viii. 6.

Q. What need then is there of a weekly Sabbath?—**A.** That God may be more solemnly worshipped, the finishing of his principal works remembered, spiritual love encouraged, heaven represented, men's souls more regarded, and the bodies of men and beasts refreshed.

Q. What special marks of honour hath God put upon this fourth commandment?—**A.** It is introduced with a solemn charge to *remember* it; it expresseth both what is required, and what is forbidden; and hath most reasons annexed to it, Exod. xx. 8—11.

Q. Why hath God put such special honour upon the fourth commandment?—**A.** Because sin, Satan, and the world, do so much oppose the right observance of it; there is least light of nature for it; and a conscientious regard to it greatly promotes our keeping of the other commands.

Q. Doth this command require any more time than one whole day in seven for the worship of God?—**A.** It respects the time of worship in general, and so extended to the Jewish holidays; and still implicitly requires days of fasting and thanksgiving, and time every morning and evening for our worshipping God in secret, and in our families.

Q. Doth God fix the precise time for fasts and thanksgiving, and for our secret and private worship, as he did for the Jewish holy days ?—A. No; he appoints the duties, and their general season; but allows men to fix the precise day or hour, according to the general rules of edification, Joel ii. 3, 2 Chron. xx., Ezra ix. x., Jonah iii.

Q. May the church appoint *holy days*, to remember Christ's birth, death, temptation, ascension, &c. ?—A. No; as God hath abolished the Jewish holy days of his own appointment, so he hath given no warrant to the church to appoint any: but hath commanded us to labour six days, except when Providence calls us to humiliation or thanksgiving; and expressly forbids us to observe holy days of men's appointment, Col. ii. 16, Gal. iv. 10, 11.

Q. What is the difference between a fast day and a holy day ?—A. The day of a fast is changeable, and esteemed no better in itself than another day; but a holy day is fixed to a certain time of the week, year, or moon, and reckoned better in itself.

Q. How much of one day in seven is to be kept as a Sabbath to the Lord ?—A. The whole natural day, consisting of twenty-four hours, Deut. v. 14.

Q. When doth the weekly Sabbath begin ?—A. In the morning immediately after midnight.

Q. How prove you that?—A. As Christ rose early in the morning, and the evening after is called the evening of the same day; and Moses said, *To-morrow* (not this night) *is a Sabbath to the Lord,* John xx. i. 19, Exod. xvi. 23.

Q. How then is it said, Lev. xxiii. 32, *From evening to evening shall ye celebrate your Sabbath?*—A. That related to the ceremonial, not to the weekly Sabbath.

Q. When was the weekly Sabbath first instituted ?—A. Immediately after the creation, Gen. ii. 3; and it was observed by the godly patriarchs, as Enoch, &c.

Q. Why then have we no express accounts of the observance of it till Israel came out of Egypt ?—A. Because till then the scripture-history is very brief.

Q. On which day of the week was the Sabbath at first appointed ?—A. On the *seventh ;* for thereon God rested from creation-work, Gen ii. 2, 3.

Q. How long did the weekly Sabbath continue on the

seventh day ?—A. From the beginning of the world to the resurrection of Christ, Heb. iv. 4—10.

Q. On which day of the week is the Sabbath now appointed ?—A. On the *first* day, Acts xx. 7, 1 Cor xvi. 1, 2.

Q. Why was it fixed on that day ?—A. To keep up the remembrance of Christ's resting from his sufferings, and rising from the dead, Matth. xxviii. 1, Heb. iv. 10.

Q. How prove you, that the Sabbath was changed from the *seventh* to the *first* day of the week ?—A. The *first* day of the week, or *eighth day*, was prophecied of as a Sabbath ; and the apostles and primitive Christians did always, after the resurrection of Christ, meet for public worship on it, and called it *the Lord's day*, Ezek. xliii. 27, John xx. 19. 26, Acts xx. 7, 1 Cor. xvi. 1, 2, Rev. i. 10.

Q. How prove you, that the example of the apostles is a sufficient warrant ?—A. Because, by being inspired by the Holy Ghost, they taught and enjoined nothing but the will and command of Christ, 1 Cor. xi. 23.

Q. How prove you the reasonableness of changing the Sabbath from the *seventh* to the *first* day of the week ?—A. Because resting from the purchase of redemption is more glorious than resting from creation work, Rom. i. 4.

Q. Why was this change expedient ?—A. That Christ might shew his divine authority, and set up a standing evidence of his incarnation and resurrection ; and make the time, as well as matter of New Testament ordinances, point to himself, Heb. iv.

Q. Are all Christians then bound to keep this fast day Sabbath till the end of the world ?—A. Yes ; and hence it is called, *the Christian Sabbath.*

Q. Why then does Paul say, *Let no man judge you in respect of Sabbath-days*, Col. ii. 16. ?—A. His meaning is, that, under the New Testament, we should not adhere to the ceremonial and Jewish sabbaths.

Q. Why are the persons required to observe this command so expressly named in it?—A. That none may pretend he is exempted from keeping the Sabbath.

Q. Why is the charge of keeping this command principally directed to parents, masters, and magistrates ?—A. Because they should not only observe it themselves, but also oblige those under them to keep it, Gen. xviii. 19.

Q. If superiors keep the Sabbath themselves, can their inferiors' open breach of it be charged on them ?—A. Yes ; if they could have hindered it, 1 Sam. iii. 13.

Q. Why is it required that labouring beasts rest on the Sabbath?—A. That they may share of the benefit of God's Sabbath (or rest) ; and may not, with their labour, give disturbance to men, Exod. xxiii. 12. and xx. 10.

Q. Who sanctify or hallow the Sabbath day?—A. God doth it, and men ought to do it.

Q. How doth God sanctify the Sabbath?—A: By making it holy by his command and example, Exod. xx. 11.

Q. How do men sanctify it?—A. By keeping it holy.

Q. How are we to keep the Sabbath-day holy?—A. By a *holy* rest and holy employment on that day.

Q. What are we to rest from on the Sabbath-day?—A. From all worldly employments and recreations.

Q. In what manner must our whole man rest from these? —A. In an holy manner, Deut. v. ix.

Q. How must our rest on the Sabbath be *holy*?—A. It must be the rest of *holy* persons, in order to our promoting and delighting in *holy* exercises, Isa. lviii. 13.

Q. In what holy employment should we be exercised on the Sabbath?—A. In the public and private exercises of God's worship, Isa. lxvi. 23. Prov. viii. 34.

Q. How should we prepare for the Sabbath before it come?—A. By self-examination, timeous laying aside of our earthly business, thinking of the solemnity of the Sabbath, and longing for the approach of it, Neh. xiii.

Q. Why should we earnestly long for the Sabbath?—A. Because on it God often giveth his people sweet and sanctifying communion with himself, Isa. lviii. 13, 14.

Q. How are we to be employed in the morning of the Sabbath-day?—A. In rising early to meditate on divine things, especially the work of redemption ; in reading God's truths, praying to, and praising him in secret, and with our families, Psalm xcii.

Q. Should not our awaking on the Sabbath much impress us with the views of our eternal state?—A. Yes.

Q. What are the public exercises of God's worship on the Sabbath day?—A. Prayer, singing of Psalms, reading, preaching, and hearing God's word ; and administration of the sacraments, Luke iv. 16. Acts xx. 7.

Q. In what should we be employed, when going to and from public ordinances?—A. In meditation, ejaculatory prayer, and religious conference, Psalm cv. Mal. iii. 16.

Q. How should we be employed in the evening of the

Sabbath?—A. In meditating on, repeating, and praying over what we have heard; and instructing our families and calling them to give an account of what they have been hearing, Psalm i. 2. Mark iv. 34.

Q. Why ought we to call our families to an account of what they have heard?—A. To cause them hear with more attention, and remember what they hear.

Q. In what manner is the Sabbath to be sanctified?—A. With sincerity, carefulness, delight, and reverence.

Q. In what, besides the exercises of God's worship, may we be employed on the Sabbath?—A. In works of necessity and mercy, Mat. xii. 1—13.

Q. What call you *works of necessity?*—A. Such as could by no means be done before, nor delayed till the Sabbath is over; as quenching the fire of houses, defending ourselves against enemies, &c.

Q. What call you works of mercy?—A. Such as necessary eating and drinking, relieving the poor, visiting the sick, feeding or relieving cattle, &c.

Q. What is in general forbidden in the fourth command?—A. The profanation of the Sabbath.

Q. How many ways is the Sabbath profaned?—A. Five ways; by omission, or careless performance of the duties required; by idleness, or doing that which is in itself sinful; and by unnecessary thoughts, words, or works, about worldly employments or recreations.

Q. Are not days devoted to humiliation and thanksgiving profaned in the same manner?—A. Yes.

Q. Do we profane the Sabbath by reading and praying at home, when we should be attending public ordinances?—A. Yes; it is to set one divine ordinance against another.

Q. Is it very sinful to neglect attendance on public prayers, and singing of psalms, while we punctually attend sermons?—A. Yes; it evidenceth our enmity against the glory of God, and the more spiritual things; for in sermons men can more show their parts, and feed their curiosity, than in prayer, and especially in praise, which so eminently tend to exalt God alone, Psalm xcvi. 1.

Q. How is the Sabbath profaned by *careless performance* of the duties required?—A. By our worshipping God, or being employed in the works of necessity or mercy, without a holy and spiritual frame of heart.

Q. How is the Sabbath profaned by *idleness?*—A. By our lying more in our beds on it than upon other days; or spending the time in sleep or sloth in our houses, gardens, or fields, Isa. lviii. 13. Matth. xx. 6.

Q. How is the Sabbath profaned by doing that which is in itself *sinful?*—A. By lying, stealing, drunkenness, whoredom, &c. committed on that day Ezek. xxii. 28.

Q. How many ways is the Sabbath profaned by carnal or worldly thoughts, words, or works?—A. Three ways; before, on, or after the Sabbath.

Q. How do we profane the Sabbath by them, before it come?—A. By so oppressing our bodies or minds with earthly business and cares, as to unfit us for performing the duties of the Sabbath, Isa. lviii. 13. Mal. i. 13.

Q. How do we profane the Sabbath by what is done after it is over?—A. By plunging our bodies or minds into such a hurry of worldly business soon after the Sabbath, as destroys the impression of Sabbath exercises, and hinders the improvement of them, Amos viii. 5.

Q. How is the Sabbath profaned by *carnal thoughts?*—A. By our thinking on worldly business, or chiefly on the circumstantials of religion, on that day, Isa. lviii. 13.

Q. What carnal thoughts are most sinful on the Sabbath?—A Such as we entertain while engaged in God's worship.

Q. How do we profane the Sabbath by *carnal words?*—A. By talking of worldly affairs, common news, or mostly of the circumstantials of religion, Isa. lviii. 13.

Q. How do we profane the Sabbath by *carnal looks?*—A. By idle or curious gazing on our own or others person, dress, houses, beasts, fields, &c. on that day.

Q. How do we profane the Sabbath by *worldly words?*—A. By our journeying to visit friends in health, or carry on business; by carrying in water, or garden-stuffs; walking in fields for recreation; gathering in crowds in streets or houses for carnal conversation; or applying medicines, without *absolute necessity*, to prevent the hinderance of our earthly labour on another day, Jer. xvii. Neh. xiii.

Q. Is it very sinful to make cheeses or hay, or to sell fish, or bear burdens, reap corn, &c. on the Sabbath, when otherwise we must suffer great loss?—A. Yes; we are unworthy of the Christian name, if we prefer our carnal gain to the glory of God, Neh. xiii. 15—22.

Q. Is Sabbath breaking a very horrible crime?—A. Yes; it is a sin against great love, and the source of many other sins; God commanded a man to be stoned to death for gathering sticks on the Sabbath; and hath threatened and destroyed nations for breach of it, Ezek. xx.

Q. How many reasons are annexed to the fourth command?—A. Four, Exod. xx. 9, 10, 11.

Q. What is the first reason?—A. God's *allowing us six days* of the week for our own employments, while he has taken but one to himself.

Q. What is the force of this reason?—A. That when God hath taken to himself so much less time than he might have claimed, and given so much to us, we should cheerfully give him that which he hath reserved for himself.

Q. What is the second reason annexed to the fourth command?—A. God's *challenging a special propriety* in the seventh day as a holy Sabbath to himself.

Q. What is the force of this reason?—A. That the Sabbath being God's right, it is very sinful to rob him of it, Mal. iii. 9.

Q. Whether is it worse to rob God of his time or honour, or to rob men?—A It is far worse to rob God.

Q. Why then is robbery of God so common among men? —A. Because they are ignorant of God; and do not consider, that robbery of him, and particularly breach of Sabbath, shall be punished with eternal torments in hell.

Q. What is the third reason annexed to the fourth command?—A. God's *own example*, in working six days in creation-work, and resting on the seventh.

Q. Wherein lieth the force of this reason?—A. That it it is the greatest honour to imitate the example of God.

Q. What is the fourth reason annexed to the fourth command?—A. God's *blessing* the Sabbath day.

Q. How doth God bless the Sabbath day?—A. In setting it apart for his worship and imparting blessings to men.

Q. Where lieth the force of this reason?—A. That when God has set apart a day to bless us, we should carefully wait on him to receive his favours.

Q. Can one who allows himself in Sabbath-breaking, prosper in religion through the week?—A. No; for he neglects on Sabbath to wait for, and receive the blessing of God, which alone makes rich in good works.

Q. What connection hath our obedience to the second table of God's law with our obedience to the first?—A. Obedience to the first table is as it were the root, and obedience to the second the fruit; so that none can properly perform the duties of one table, while he neglects those of the other, Matth. xxii. and xxiii.

Q. 63. *Which is the fifth commandment?*

A. The fifth commandment is, "Honour thy father and thy mother; that thy days may be long upon the land which the Lord thy God giveth thee."

Q. 64. *What is required in the fifth commandment?*

A. The fifth commandment requireth the preserving the honour, and performing the duties, belonging to every one in their several places and relations, as superiors, inferiors, or equals.

Q. 65. *What is forbidden in the fifth commandment?*

A. The fifth commandment forbiddeth the neglecting of, or doing any thing against the honour and duty which belongeth to every one in their several places and relations.

Q. 66. *What is the reason annexed to the fifth commandment?*

A. The reason annexed to the fifth commandment is, a promise of long life and prosperity, (as far as it shall serve for God's glory and their own good) to all such as keep this commandment.

Q. Doth very much of practical religion lie in a proper performance of the duties of the second table of the law? —**A.** Yes; the same acts which are done out of obedience to men, are *civil*, when performed out of regard to God's authority, are *religious* obedience, James i. 26.

Q. When do we perform the duties of the second table in a religious manner?—**A.** When we perform them from love and regard to God, chiefly for his glory, depending on his promised strength, and hoping for acceptance only through Christ, Col. iii. 17, 1 Pet. iv. 11.

Q. What doth the second table of the moral law contain?—**A.** Our duty to man, Matth. xxii. 39.

Q. How do the six commands of the second table differ? —**A.** The fifth command respects man's various relations, the sixth his life, the seventh his chastity, the eighth his wealth, the ninth his good name, and the tenth the most inward dispositions of his heart, Deut. v. 16—21.

Q. In what different relations do men stand to one

another ?—A. In the relation of superiors, inferiors, or equals.

Q. Whom do you understand by *superiors?*—A. Such as are above others, as parents above their children.

Q. Why are all superiors called *father and mother* in the command ?—A. Because, like parents, they have authority over, influence upon, and ought dearly to love their inferiors.

Q. Whom call you inferiors?—A. Such as are below others, as children are below their parents.

Q. In respect of what are persons superiors or inferiors to one another ?—A. In respect of age, authority, influence, gifts, or graces.

Q. Whom call you equals ?—A. Such as have much the same authority, age, influence, gifts, or graces.

Q. What are the principal classes of superiors ?—A. Parents, husbands, masters, ministers, and magistrates.

Q. What are the principal classes of inferiors ?—A. Children, wives, servants, people, and subjects.

Q. How may the duties belonging to these relations be performed ?—A. By our exercising the graces respecting men in general, and fulfilling the duties belonging to our particular stations, Matth. vii. 12.

Q. What graces respecting men in every station are necessary?—A. Temperance, meekness, humility, gentleness, goodness, peaceableness, and brotherly kindness.

Q. What is *temperance?*—A. The due abstinence from meat, drink, and fleshly pleasures, 1 Cor. ix. 25.

Q. Why is temperance necessary ?—A. To keep us sensible of our duty, and mindful of heavenly things.

Q. What is *meekness ?*—A. A calmness of spirit under provocations and injuries, 1 Pet. ii. 23.

Q. Why should we study meekness ?—A. It is pleasant, profitable, and honourable, and makes us like Christ.

Q. How may we attain meekness?—A. By daily views of the patience and mercy of God, and of the meekness of Christ ; by maintaining the exercise of reason in our souls, and low thoughts of ourselves, Psalm lxxxvi. 15.

Q. In what doth humility towards man consist ?—A. In meddling only with our own affairs, cheerfully giving every man his own due honour, and esteeming others better than ourselves, Eph. v. 21, and iii. 8.

Q. Why should we study humility towards men ?—A. It tends much to render us happy, by preventing jealousy, discontent, anger, and envy; and it is very honourable, being respected both of God and men.

Q. How may we attain this humility?—A. By considering how vile we are in God's sight; and that all the good things which we have are his free gifts, 1 Cor. iv. 7.

Q. Wherein doth *gentleness* or lenity consist?—A. In our kindness and condescension to others; easiness to be persuaded to good, and dissuaded from evil; and readiness to consider, bear with, and put the best construction on the tempers, words, or actions of others.

Q. Why should we study lenity and gentleness?—A. It makes us like God; renders conversation pleasant; and we need that others exercise lenity towards us.

Q. Wherein doth *goodness* or *benignity* consist?—A. In believing good of, and wishing and doing good to, and rejoicing in the welfare of others, 1 Cor. xiii. 4—7.

Q. How is goodness to be exercised towards such as are in misery and distress?—A. In pitying, supporting, comforting, and relieving them, 1 John iii. 17. Heb. xiii. 16.

Q. How is goodness to be exercised towards our enemies?—A. In praying for their conviction or conversion, and waiting for opportunities to render them good for evil.

Q. Why should we study goodness or benignity?—A. It makes us like God, happy in ourselves, aud eminently useful to others, Matth. v. 43—48.

Q. Wherein doth *peaceableness* consist?—A. In our readiness to part with some degrees of our right for the sake of peace, and to exert ourselves to make or maintain peace between others, Gen. xiii. 8, 9.

Q. How far ought we to pursue peace with men?—A. As far as we can without sin, Heb. xii. 14.

Q. Why should we follow peace?—A. That we may resemble the God and Prince of peace,—adorn our profession, and render ourselves and others easy, Matth. v. 9.

Q. How should we study peace?—A. By praying for the Spirit of peace; study to be humble, to observe the good that is in others, and to avoid envy, tale-bearing, and rash censuring, Phil. ii. 3. Prov. xxvi. 20.

Q. In what doth *brotherly kindness* consist?—A. In our love to, and familiarity with the saints, on account of Christ's image in them, Psalm cxix. 63, and xvi. 3.

Q. Why should we exercise this kindness towards the saints?—A. They are the most *excellent ones of the earth,* most precious in God's sight, and shall be our everlasting companions in glory, Psalm xvi. 3, and cxix. 63.

Q. In what proportion should the saints be loved?—A. According to the degree of Christ's image in them.

Q. Why may we not measure our love to them by the agreement of their sentiments with ours, or the measure of their good offices to us?—A. Because this would be to love them for our own, not for Christ's sake.

Q. What are the advantages of love among saints?—A. It honours Christ, proves their saintship, promotes their communion with God, and with one another, and stirs up others to study religion, John xiii. 35, Matth. v. 16.

Q. How may love to the saints be attained?—A. By receiving the spirit of adoption into our heart, and the exercise of love to Christ, 1 John i.—v.

Q. What is the duty of parents to their children?—A. To love, protect, correct, provide, and pray for them; instruct them in the principles of religion; encourage them to duty; and dispose of them in callings and marriage, as best suits their disposition and advantage.

Q. How are parents to correct their children?—A. With due severity, without passion, with an eye to God's glory, and their children's spiritual good, and looking up to God for his blessing on their corrections.

Q. How should parents instruct their children?—A. By teaching them the truths and duties of religion as early and seriously as possible, Prov. xxii. 6, Deut. vi.

Q. How are children to be encouraged to their duty?—A. By urging them to it early, often, earnestly, and with the most gaining motives; and by commending or rewarding them when they do well, Psal. xxxiv. 11.

Q. How should parents manifest their love to their children?—A. By shewing a tender regard to their bodies, and much more to their souls, Isa. xlix. 15, Gal. iv. 19.

Q. Is it a true parental love, to love the bodies of our children most?—A. No; we have this love in common with beasts; and such parents are guilty of the blood of their children's souls before God, 1 Sam. ii. and iii.

Q. What is the duty of children to their parents?—A. To esteem, honour, love, and obey them, Eph. vi.

Q. How ought children to honour their parents?—A. By speaking honourably of, and humbly to them; and by reverend carriage before them, Mal. i. 6.

Q. How are children to show their love to their parents?

—A. By delighting in their company and instructions, cheerfully bearing with their infirmities and providing for them when old and infirm, Gen. xlvii. 12.

Q. How are children to obey their parents?—A. By cheerfully submitting to their reproofs and corrections, performing their lawful commands, and hearkening to their reasonable advice in their calling and marriage.

Q. What may be the reason why the mother is expressly mentioned in this command?—A. Because she suffers most in the birth and bringing up of children ; and is most ready to be despised by them, Prov. xxiii. 22, and xxx. 17.

Q. What are the duties of husbands to their wives?— A. Faithfulness, love, sympathy, protection, instruction, and prayer with and for them, Eph. v. 25.

Q. What are the duties of wives to their husbands?— A. Faithfulness, love, sympathy, submissive hearkening to their counsels, and endeavoring with meekness to win them to Christ, if they be wicked, 1 Pet. iii. 1—7.

Q. In what are husbands and wives to be faithful to one another?—A. With respect to their soul, body, bed, name, estate, and secrets intrusted to them.

Q. How are they to exercise love towards one another? —A. By a deep concern for one another's eternal salvation, and an earnest care to please, and hide one another's infirmities, James v. 20, 1 Pet. iii. 1—7.

Q. What is the duty of masters to their servants?—A. To use them with gentleness ; give them due food, wages, and instruction ; pray for and with them ; restrain them from sin ; and cause them to attend the worship of God in public, private, and secret, Col. iv. 1, Gen. xviii. 19.

Q. What is the duty of servants to their masters?—A. To honour and obey them ; pray for them, and the success of their work ; be faithful and diligent in their service ; and submit cheerfully to their reproof, advice and instruction, Titus ii. 9, 10, Eph. vi. 5—8.

Q. What is the duty of ministers to their people?—A. To settle among them by a regular call ; take care chiefly for their souls ; pray much for them ; administer all the ordinances of Christ in them faithfully, diligently and affectionately ; and be patterns of a holy conversation among them, 1 Thess. ii. 3—13, Acts xx. 17—32.

Q. What is the duty of people to their ministers?—A. To love, esteem, and pray for them ; provide them subsistence; support their good name; and receive gospel ordinances dispensed by them as from Christ, 1 Thess. v. 12.

Q. What is the duty of magistrates to their subjects?— **A.** To govern and defend them with wisdom and clemency, establish and execute good laws, promote religion, discourage evil-doers, and encourage such as do well.

Q. If the magistrate be an Episcopalian, or otherwise different in religion, or a bad man, doth that any way lessen his power?—**A.** No; it only makes him less capable of using his power aright, as it would do in the case of a natural father; but till he prove a tyrant, his power is never lessened, Rom. xiii. 1—7, Jer. xxvii. 17.

Q. Whom call you a *tyrant?*—**A.** One that either never had a right to govern, or hath lost it by employing his power for the destruction, not the good of his subjects.

Q. What is the duty of subjects to their magistrates?— **A.** To defend, honour, obey, pray for, and pay due tribute to them, 1 Pet. ii. 17, 1 Tim. ii. 1, Titus iii. 1.

Q What is the duty of superiors in age, gifts, or grace, to their inferiors in these things?—**A.** To instruct, advise, and encourage them in that which is good; and to walk as patterns of holiness before them, Titus ii. 2.

Q. What is the duty of inferiors in age, gifts, or grace, to their superiors in these things?—**A.** To love, esteem, and honour them; to imitate their good pattern, and follow their admonition and advice, 1 Pet. v. 5.

Q. What is the duty of equals one to another?—**A.** To prefer one another, desire and delight in one another's good, and be mutual examples in holiness.

Q. How many ways is the fifth command broken?—**A.** Two ways; by neglecting the graces and duties required, and by committing the contrary sins.

Q. What are the sins of parents against their children? —**A.** Cruelty, untenderness, wasting their earthly portions, giving them too much of their will, loving them more than Christ, loving some better than others, without regard to their virtue, training them up in ignorance or wickedness, and opposing their reasonable inclinations in their calling or marriage, Deut. xxviii. 56, 1 Sam. iii. 13 and ii. 29.

Q. What are the sins of children against their parents? —**A.** Irreverent speeches or carriage towards them; refusing to submit to their instruction, reproof, or advice; wasting their substance; grieving their spirit; neglecting to support them when old and infirm ; and contemning their consent in their calling and marriage, Gen. xxvi. 34, 35.

Q. What are the sins of husbands against their wives ?
—A. Unfaithfulness, hatred, bitterness, haughtiness, and ill-grounded jealousies, &c., Col. iii. 19, Mal. ii. 14, 15.

Q. What are the sins of wives against their husbands ?
—A. Unfaithfulness, hatred, imprudent speeches, irreverent and haughty carriage, disobedience, groundless jealousy, prodigal wasting their estate, &c., 1 Pet. iii. 1.

Q. What are the sins of masters against their servants ?
—A. Requiring them to do what is sinful or above their strength ; rigorous upbraiding or correcting them for their faults ; withholding from them due food, wages, or the benefit of family instruction and worship ; casting them off when sick, &c., Chr. iv. 1, Eph. vi. 9, Jer. x. 25.

Q. What are the sins of servants against their masters ?
—A. Despising, defaming, disobeying, or serving them with eye service ; wasting and abusing their master's property ; neglecting to attend on family instruction or worship, &c., Col. iii. 22, 2 Sam. xix. 26, 27.

Q. What are the sins of ministers against their people ?
—A. Forcing themselves on them ; seeking chiefly their own carnal gain ; carelessness in praying, studying, or dispensing gospel ordinances ; preaching error, or truth unfaithfully and unseasonably ; and shewing themselves patterns of a loose and carnal conversation, Isa. lvi. 10—12.

Q. What are the sins of people against their ministers ?
—A. Hatred, contempt, and slandering of them ; neglect of prayer for, and of the ordinances dispensed by them ; grieving them with their unbelief and wickedness ; and withholding due subsistence from them, 2 Chr. xxxvi. 16.

Q. What are the sins of magistrates against their subjects ?—A. Ruling them with cruelty and oppression ; requiring and encouraging that which is evil, and discouraging what is good ; exposing them to enemies ; or chiefly seeking their own carnal advantage, 1 Sam. viii., Mic iii.

Q. What are the sins of subjects against their magistrates ?—A. Restraining prayer for them, reviling of them, disobedience to, and rebellion against them ; and refusing to pay them just tribute, 2 Pet. ii. 10, Jude 8.

Q. What are the sins of superiors in age, gifts, or grace, against their inferiors in these things ?—A. Despising and disregarding them ; or encouraging them to sin by their example or advice, Rom. xiv. and xv,

Q. What are the sins of inferiors in age, gifts, or grace, against their superiors?—**A.** Despising and contemning them, or their good instruction or pattern; and following their bad example or advice, Isa. iii. 5.

Q. What are sins of equals one against another?—**A.** Selfishness, hatred, haughtiness, dishonouring, defaming, and enticing one another to sin, Eph. iv. 31.

Q. What is the only reason annexed to the fifth commandment?—**A.** That the keepers of it shall live long in the land which the Lord God giveth them, Deut. v. 16.

Q. What is meant by this long life?—**A.** The long continuance of life, with the blessing and prosperity of it.

Q. Do all that honour their parents, and are faithful in all relative duties, live long and prosperously?—**A.** They either do so, or have the want of it made up by the full enjoyment of God, Isa. iii. 10, Psal. xix. 11.

Q. With what limitation is this, and all promises of temporal blessings, to be understood?—**A.** *As far as it shall serve for God's glory, and their own good.*

Q. What is the danger of stubborn and rebellious children?—**A.** God hath cursed them, and commanded such to be stoned to death; and they often come to a miserable and disgraceful end, Deut. xxi. xxvii. Prov. xxx. 17.

Q. How is the fifth command, *the first command with promise,* when the second hath a promise annexed to it?—**A.** The fifth is the first of the second table, and is the only command having a promise peculiar to itself.

Q. Why are reasons annexed to the first five commands? —**A.** These five are, as it were, the foundation of the rest, and some of them less enforced by the light of nature.

Q. If we perform the relative duties required in the fifth, can we break the following commands?—**A.** No; if we rightly regard ourselves and neighbours in relative duties, we can neither murder, commit adultery, steal, lie, nor covet, Rom. xiii. 9.

Q. 67. *Which is the sixth commandment?*

A. The sixth commandment is, "Thou shalt not kill."

Q. 68. *What is required in the sixth commandment?*

A. The sixth commandment requireth all lawful endeavours to preserve our own life and the life of others.

Q. 69. *What is forbidden in the sixth commandment?*

A. The sixth commandment forbiddeth the taking away of our own life, or the life of our neighbour unjustly, and whatsoever tendeth thereunto.

Q. What doth the sixth commandment require ?—A. —The preservation of life, Eph. v. 28, 29.

Q. Whose life doth it command us to preserve ?—A. The life of ourselves and others, 1 Kings xviii.

Q. Of what life are we to study the preservation ?—A. Of our spiritual and natural life, Deut. xxx. 15, 16.

Q. What means are we to use for the preservation of our life ?—A. All lawful means, and these only.

Q. Can unlawful means promote or preserve the life of our soul ?—A. No, James i. 15, Ezek. xviii. 4.

Q. May we lie, deny Christ's truth, or otherwise sin, to preserve our own life, or that of others, especially of eminent saints ?—A. No ; to save men's natural life by sin, is to murder our soul, and make an attack on the life and honour of God, Amos ii. 12, 13.

Q. How then is Rahab commended for saving the life of the spies by a lie, Heb. xi. ?—A. She is only commend-mended for their faith in receiving the spies, but not for the lie which she made to save them.

Q. May we not, in some cases, omit the public duties of God's worship, in order to defend our lives ?—A. Yes ; for God declares that he *will have mercy and not sacrifice.*

Q. What are the lawful means of preserving our natural life ?—A. A calm and cheerful temper ; the moderate use of meat, drink, sleep, physic, labour, rest, or recreations ; and defending it with clothes, houses, and armour.

Q. How are we to promote and preserve our spiritual life ?—A. By diligently attending on gospel ordinances, and receiving and improving Christ in them, Is. lv. 1, 2, 3. 6, 7.

Q. What calmness of spirit is necessary to promote our spiritual life ?—A. Our conscience quieted with the blood of Jesus ; our spirit meekened by the love of God ; and comforted with the views of our saving relation to him.

Q. What is the food by which our spiritual life is preserved ?—A. Christ's flesh and blood, John vi. 32—57.

Q. What medicine must heal our spiritual maladies ?—A. God's love, Christ's blood, and his spirit's influence.

21*

Q. With what raiment must our soul be clothed?—A. Christ's imputed righteousness, and imparted grace.

Q. In what labour must our soul be exercised to promote its life?—A. The labour of love to God and man.

Q. What rest is necessary for promoting spiritual life?—A. Our solid satisfaction in God as our *all*, Psal. xvi.

Q. What recreation is necessary to promote spiritual life?—A. Our walking with, and rejoicing in God, through our Lord Jesus Christ, as our king and friend.

Q. Where must our soul dwell for safety and health?—A. In God as in Christ, Psal. xci. 1—9. and xc. 1.

Q.—With what armour must we defend the life of our soul against sin, Satan, and the world?—A. With the shield of faith; the breast-plate of righteousness; the helmet of the hope of salvation; the sword of the Spirit, which is the word of God; and with earnest prayer, Eph. vi.

Q. Can we sinfully *exceed* in using these means of spiritual life?—A. No: we never use them enough.

Q. How are we to preserve the life of other men's bodies?—A. By a ready forgiving of injuries; assisting and defending the innocent; punishing murderers with death; promoting peace between man and man; and by charitable distributions to the necessities of the poor.

Q. How are we to promote the life of other men's souls?—A. By prayer for God's grace to them; restraining them from, and reproving them for sin; instructing and encouraging them in the ways of God; and providing them with the outward means of grace to the utmost of our power.

Q. What is forbidden in the sixth command?—A. All murder, or unjust taking away of man's life.

Q. Is it unlawful in every case to kill?—A. No; it is lawful to kill hurtful beasts, or innocent beasts for food; and to kill men in lawful war, necessary self-defence, or when justly sentenced to death by the magistrate.

Q. For what are magistrates to condemn men to death?—A. For idolatry, blasphemy, witchcraft, murder, adultery, sodomy, bestiality, incest, &c. Lev. xx. and xxiv. &c.

Q. Can we break this command with respect to beasts?—A. Yes; by killing, torturing, and abusing them; or by exciting them to kill and torture one another in sport and cruelty, as at matches of cock-fighting, bear-baiting, and bull-baiting, Exod. xxiii. Numb. xxiii. Prov. xii. 10.

Q. Is accidental manslaughter murder?—A. No; except it spring from culpable negligence in us, John xx.

Q. Are duels or set combats between men lawful?—A. Duels appointed by public authority, which tend to prevent the shedding of more blood, are sometimes lawful; but private duels are always sinful, 1 Sam. xvii.

Q. How prove you private duels are sinful?—A. They spring from pride and revenge, expose men's lives without ground, pour contempt on the authority of God, and of the magistrate, and make men martyrs for sin.

Q. How may the murder of men be distinguished?—A. Into the murder of their body and of their soul.

Q. Which of these is worst?—A. The murder of souls.

Q. In what different ways are men guilty of murder?—A. In heart, gesture, word or deed.

Q. How do we commit murder in our *heart?*—A. By indulging passion, hatred, anger, envy, malice, and devising, desiring, and delighting in the hurt of any.

Q. In what doth lawful and sinful anger differ?—A. Holy anger seeks the glory of God, and the good of the offender, and the destruction of his sin; but sinful passion and anger seek our own honour, and the hurt of the offender, Exod. xxxii. Numb. xx. Eph. iv. 26, 31.

Q. Wherein lieth the evil of sinful passion?—A. It unfits for duty, renders reproof hurtful, magnifies injuries, excites others to sin, and opens our heart to Satan.

Q. How do we commit murder in our *gestures?*—A. By envious, disdainful, and fierce looks; by beholding the distress of others with pleasure or unconcern; enraged gnashing with the teeth, foaming with the mouth, &c., Gen. iv. 5, Luke x. 30—32, Obad. 12, Acts vii. 54.

Q. How do we commit murder in our *words?*—A. By contentious brawling, wrathful imprecation, disdainful and passionate speeches; and by writings tending to grieve, enrage, and hurt men's soul or body, or approve of it.

Q. How do we commit murder in our *deeds?*—A. By such actions as injuriously hurt men's soul or body.

Q. Doth the sixth commandment forbid only the actual taking away of life?—A. No; murder in God's sight includes whatever tends unjustly to take it away.

Q. What things tend to the murder of men's bodies?—A. Sparing of murderers; withholding the necessary means of life; excess in meat, drink, grief, or pleasure; lust; covetousness; ambition; revenge; oppression; smiting; wounding; and grinding the face of the poor, &c.

Q. What are the most ordinary means of murdering men's bodies?—**A.** Unlawful war, drunkenness, gluttony, and uncleanness, Jer ii. 35, Prov. v. 11.

Q. When is war unlawful?—**A.** When it springs from covetousness and ambition, is raised without first trying peaceably to adjust differences, or tends only to maintain trifling claims, 2 Kings xiv. 8.

Q. Wherein doth gluttony consist?—**A.** In eating too often, too much, or too strong or delicate food.

Q. Wherein doth drunkenness consist?—**A.** In an excessive desire of liquor, drinking too often, too long, or too much, Isa. v. 11, 12. 22.

Q. When do we eat or drink too much?—**A.** When we eat or drink more than satisfies and strengthens nature, and especially when we eat or drink till we partly lose the use of our reason, Jer. v. 8.

Q. Wherein lies the evil of gluttony and drunkenness? —**A.** They murder our body, by breaking its constitution, and make us like beasts in stupidity; and drunkenness often makes men like devils in wickedness, Prov. xxiii.

Q. Wherein doth the abominable nature of drunkenness further appear?—**A.** It abuseth God's bounty, our time and money, breaks all God's commands, defaces his image in man, exposes to all wickedness and danger, draws on many heavy curses, and hastens men to hell to drink the cup of God's eternal wrath, Isa. xxviii., Gal. v. 21.

Q. What shall we then think of such as boast of their ability to drink much, or of making others drunk?—**A.** Such glory in their shame and likeness to Satan; are near vengeance, and under the curse of God, Isa. v. 11—22.

Q. At what season is revelling, gluttony, and drunkenness, most criminal?—**A.** When God is threatening or inflicting very heavy judgments on us, or our land; for then they most daringly contemn God's justice and power, hasten his wrath, and are rarely pardoned, Isa. xx. 13.

Q. Wherein doth the great evil of murdering men's bodies appear?—**A.** It destroys man, who is the image of God, and our own brother; it is directly contrary to our natural conscience and affection; and is more frequently pursued with God's visible judgment than most of other sins, Gen. iv. and ix. 6, Rev. xvi., xvii., xviii.

Q. What is the worst kind of bodily murder?—**A.** A man's murdering of himself, Matth. xxvii. 5.

Q. Is it not better to kill ourselves, than live in torment, or be barbarously and disgracefully killed by others?—A. No; self-murder is an evidence of pride, discontent, and despair; God alone is master of our life; torment here is far easier than hell; and after death there is no place for repentance, 1 Sam. xxxi., 2 Sam. xvii.

Q. Can no self-murderer be saved?—A. One may give himself a wound, of which he may die in a lingering manner, and yet repent before death; or a child of God may, in a frenzy of distraction, kill himself; but it seems impossible for such as deliberately kill themselves, by an immediate death, to repent or be saved, 1 John iii. 14.

Q. How then could Samson, who drew down the house upon himself, be saved?—A. His design was not against his own life; and he had God's special allowance to part with it, in order to slay a multitude of the Philistines, Judg. xvi. 28—30.

Q. How are we in general rendered guilty of spiritual murder?—A. By every sin we commit, Ezek. xviii. 4.

Q. How do we murder our own soul?—A. By sinfully defiling it, and drawing God's curse on it; and especially by refusing Christ the Saviour of souls, Hos. xiii.

Q. How do we murder the souls of others?—A. By vexing and grieving them; neglecting to prevent their sin, or reprove them for it; and encouraging them in it, by command, example, or advice, Lev. xix. 17.

Q. Who are principally guilty of murdering other men's souls?—A. Heads of families, ministers, magistrates, and professors, Ezek. xxii. Mich. ii. iii. Zeph. iii.

Q. How do heads of families murder their children and servants?—A. By denying them family instruction and worship in due season, careless performance of these duties with them, indulging and encouraging them in sin.

Q. How do ministers murder other men's souls?—A. By entering into the ministry without God's call, which renders their labour unprofitable; by neglecting due pains for their people's instruction and conversion; by preaching error, or truth in a wrong manner; by administration of the sacraments to the ignorant and profane; and by their loose and carnal example, Jer. xxiii.

Q. How do ministers murder men's souls by a wrong way of preaching truth?—A. By preaching the law as a covenant, as it might and should be obeyed by us to render us welcome to Christ as a Saviour; by insisting chiefly on circumstantial points; by preaching to a multitude as if they were all saints, or in such a manner as makes saints discredit their relation to Christ, or forget the duty of the present times, Ezek. xxxiii. Jer. xxiii.

Q. How do magistrates murder other men's souls?—A. By not providing their subjects with schools, and a pure gospel ministry; and by not punishing, but encouraging error, superstition, and gross immorality, Mich. vi. 16.

Q. How do professors murder other men's souls?—A. In causing others to stumble at religion by their ungodly example; dropping or corrupting God's truths and ordinances; or sinning away his presence from the means of grace, Ezek. xvi. Isa. vi. 9, 10, and lix.

Q. Are we not then all very guilty of murder, and especially spiritual murder, before God?—A. Yes, surely.

Q. How may we be cleansed from our blood guiltiness?—A. By the application of Christ's blood to our conscience for the pardon of all our sin, 1 John i. 7, Zech. xiii. 1.

Q. What are the best means of preserving us from more blood-guiltiness?—A. The consideration of its dreadful nature; avoiding temptations to it; and especially having the love of God in Christ shed abroad in our hearts by the Holy Ghost dwelling in us, Eph. iv. 30, 31, 32.

Q. 70. *Which is the seventh commandment?*

A. The seventh commandment is, " Thou shalt not commit adultery."

Q. 71. *What is required in the seventh commandment?*

A. The seventh commandment requireth the preservation of our own and our neighbour's chastity, in heart, speech, and behaviour.

Q. 72. *What is forbidden in the seventh commandment?*

A. The seventh commandment forbiddeth all unchaste thoughts, words, and actions.

Q. What is required in the seventh commandment?—A. The preservation of chastity, 1 Thess. iv. 3—7.

Q. What do you understand by *chastity?*—A. Cleanness and purity from irregular fleshly pleasure.

Q. Whose chastity ought we to preserve?—A. Our own and our neighbour's, 1 Cor. vii. 2. 35, 36.

Q. Wherein is our own and our neighbour's chastity to be preserved?—A. In heart, speech, and behaviour.

Q. Why should we preserve our own and our neighbour's chastity?—A. Because we are men, not beasts; Christians, not Heathens; and therefore our bodies and souls ought to be pure temples for the Holy Ghost.

Q. By what means are we to preserve our chastity?— A. By watchfulness over our minds and senses; temperance in eating and drinking; seasonable fasting; fervent prayer; the fear and spirit of God dwelling in us; and by faith in Christ, and his promises of sanctification; diligence in our callings; and lawful marriage, Job xxxii. 1.

Q. What is marriage?—A. A lawful joining together of a man and woman in individual fellowship during life.

Q. Who instituted marriage?—A. God instituted it before the fall, to teach us that marriage is very honourable, and the privilege of all men, Gen. ii., Heb. xiii. 44.

Q. What are the ends of marriage?—A. The mutual help of parties, regular increase, and education of mankind, affording the church a holy seed, and preventing of uncleanness, 1 Cor. vii., Gen. ii., Mal. ii.

Q. When is a marriage lawful?—A. When it is contracted, with consent of their parents, between one single man and a woman come to years of discretion, duly distant in affinity and blood, and of the same religion.

Q. May parents force, or without good reason oppose their children's inclinations to marriage?—A. No.

Q. How distant in affinity and blood must those be who marry together?—A. Persons in a direct descent must never marry together, nor any nearer than cousins in the oblique descent; nor must we marry any nearer relations of a late husband or wife than of our own, Lev. xviii.

Q. Why must those who marry together be duly distant in affinity and blood?—A. That friendship may spread in the world, and unnatural lust be discouraged.

Q. Why must they be come to the years of discretion? —A. That they may be capable to choose their yoke-fellow, and manage the affairs of their family, Prov. xxxi.

Q. Why ought they to be of one religion?—A. That they may walk together *as heirs of the grace of life*, and not seduce one another from the fear of God, 2 Cor. vi. 14.

Q. Ought professed Christians to marry *only* with such as appear to fear God?—A. Yes; otherwise they disobey God; pour contempt on religion, in preferring riches, beauty, or parentage to it; hinder their prayers; take into their bosom a means of deadening their soul, disordering their family, and ruining their seed, 2 Cor. vi. 14.

Q. What is forbidden in the seventh commandment?—
A. All unchaste thoughts, words, looks, or actions.

Q. How is unchastity committed in our *thoughts*?—A.
By filthy dreams, devising or desiring opportunities of unchastity, or by delighting in imaginary views of committing it, Jude 8, Job xxxi. 1.

Q. How are we guilty of unchastity in our *words*?—A.
By reading, hearing, speaking, or writing of uncleanness, or temptations to it, with pleasure; and especially if the style be immodest, Eph. v. 4.

Q. Whence doth men's pleasure in reading, hearing, or speaking immodest language, proceed?—A. From the fire of uncleanness burning in their heart, Prov. vii. ix.

Q. How are we guilty of unchastity in our *looks*?—A.
In viewing immodest pictures with pleasure, or beholding other objects with unchaste desires towards them, Ezekiel xxiii., Matth. v. 28, Prov. xxiii. 33.

Q. How are we guilty of unchastity in our *deeds*?—A.
By incest, Sodomy, bestiality, self-defilement, and other unnatural lusts, Lev. xviii. 6—24, and xx. 11—21, Gen. xxxviii. 9, Rom. i. 24—27; lascivious salutations, wanton embraces and dalliances, Prov. vii. 13, and vi. 29; such gestures as shew the levity and filthiness of the mind, or tempt others to unchastity, Isa. iii. 16, Gen. xxxviii. 14. 16, Prov. vii. 10—12; and by fornication, adultery, rape, polygamy, and retaining of concubines, Gen. xxxiv, 2 Sam. xi. and xiii, 1 Kings xi. 3.

Q. What is polygamy?—A. It is to have more wives or husbands than one at the same time, 1 Kings ii. 1. 3.

Q. How prove you that polygamy, and keeping of concubines, are very sinful?—A. As these practices are contrary to God's command, and the first institution of marriage, which makes only twain one flesh; and have bred great disorder in families, Lev. xviii. 18, Gen. ii. and xvi.

Q. How then did Jacob, David, and other saints, indulge themselves in those practices?—A. Custom, and the darkness of the times had blinded their consciences.

Q. What, besides the above kinds of unchastity is forbidden in this command?—A. Whatever tends to encourage any manner of unchastity, Prov. v. vii. and xxiii.

Q. What things encourage and excite to unchastity?—
A. Idleness, gluttony, drunkenness, vain gadding, excess

in carnal mirth, lascivious books and pictures, vows of single life, undue delay of marriage, unjust divorce or desertion, wanton attire, frequenting light and lewd company, Ezek. xvi., Jer. v., Gen. xxxiv., &c.

Q. How do vows of single life lead to unchastity?—A. They expose men to temptations to fornication.

Q. What is unjust divorce?—A. It is when one married person is by law disjoined from the other, for other causes than adultery and obstinate desertions, Matth. xix.

Q. What is desertion in a married state?—A. It is when one married person departs from, and refuseth to dwell with the other, 1 Cor. vii. 15.

Q. What attire may be called wanton?—A. Attire above our station and ability, especially if framed or put on in a light and lewd manner, Prov. vii. 10. 16.

Q. Wherein lieth the evil of vain apparel?—A. It consumes that which should pay our just debts to God and man, wastes much precious time in putting it on, contradicts our Christian character of modest sobriety, draws our heart from God, excites our neighbours to envy or lust, and exposeth our land to ruin, Prov. vii. 10. Zeph. i. 8. 1 Pet. iii. 4. Isa. iii. 16—26.

Q. Is it lawful for one sex to wear attire proper to the other?—A. No; it is *an abomination to the Lord*, Deut. xxii. 5.

Q. How are persons guilty of frequenting light and lewd companions?—A. Either more *secretly*, by often accompanying with one or a few such persons; or more *openly*, by attending stews, stage-plays, balls, promiscuous dancings, common penny-weddings, &c.

Q. How do you prove, that stews or bawdy-houses are abominable?—A. They are condemned in scripture, and are a nursery for incest and adultery, &c. Lev. xix. 29.

Q. How prove you balls, and common penny-weddings, sinful?—A. They are public meetings of light persons, who debauch one another with pride, drunkenness, vain and immodest jests, wanton dalliances, &c. Gal. v. 21.

Q. If these balls or weddings are used to collect charity for the poor, doth that render them lawful?—A. No; if we *do evil that good may come, our damnation is just.*

Q. Wherein lieth the evil of promiscuous and vain dancing?—A. The Scripture represents it as the work of drunken and impudent persons; it inflames lust; indisposeth for religious duties; and is contrary to the modest

22

soberity required in Christians, Exod. xxxii. 19. Matth.
xiv.

Q. Doth not the scripture examples of Miriam, David,
&c. warrant our dancing, Exod. xv. 20. Judges xi. 34.
1 Chron. xv. 29. Eccl. iii. 4. 2 Sam vi. 14. 16. Psalm xxx.
11. cxlix. 3. and cl. 4. Jer. xxxi. 4. 13. Lam. v. 15.?—A.
No: for, besides that the most of these texts respect religious worship; the word rendered *dance* in the two first,
and six last, signifies a *pipe*, or a *company of singers;*
that in Chronicles and Ecclesiastes, *to leap, or rejoice
greatly;* and that in Samuel, *to praise* or *praise by play-
ing on an organ.*

Q. How prove you stage plays sinful?—A. Sin and
especially carnal lust, is therein made the subject of diver-
sion and jest; which convenes light and lewd persons, inflames their lust, and excites their vanity, Eph. v. 4.

Q. Wherein lies the great evil of adultery, fornication,
and other uncleanness?—A. It greatly offends and dishonours God; ruins our soul, body, character, and estate; injures others; and is very rarely repented of.

Q. 73. *Which is the eighth commandment?*

A. The eighth commandment is, " Thou shalt not
steal."

Q. 74. *What is required in the eighth commandment?*

A. The eighth commandment requireth the lawful
procuring and furthering the wealth and outward
estate of ourselves and others.

Q. 75. *What is forbidden in the eighth commandment?*

A. The eighth commandment forbiddeth whatsoever doth, or may unjustly hinder our own or our
neighbour's wealth or outward estate.

Q. What is required in the eighth commandment?—A.
The lawful procuring and furthering of our own and our
neighbour's wealth, Eph. iv. 28, 2 Cor. xii. 14.

Q. Is it lawful for men to have any peculiar property in
the good things of this life?—A. Yes: for if all things were
common, stealing would be impossible, and so there would
be no need for this commandment.

Q. Why then had the primitive Christians in Judea all
things common?—A. It was from their own choice, and
not from any command of God, Acts iv. and v.

Q. Had they any peculiar reason for this course ?—A. Yes ; Christ had forewarned them of the sudden desolation of their land, and loss of their wealth even though they should not dispose of it to their brethren.

Q. What means are we to use for promoting our own and our neighbour's wealth and outward estate ?—A. All lawful means and these only, Eph. iv. 28.

Q. By what lawful means are we to promote our own wealth ?—A. By choosing lawful and suitable callings, diligence in them, and prayer for God's blessing on our labour ; by a prudent and frugal use of outward enjoyments ; by requiring our just dues ; and rendering to every one their due, especially to the Lord.

Q. What is a lawful calling ?—A. One in which we can glorify God, and do good to men, 1 Cor. x. 31.

Q. What is a proper and suitable calling ?—A. One which answers our station, inclination, ability, and the place of our abode.

Q. What do you mean by a frugal use of things ?—A. Our care to answer every purpose in a suitable manner, with as little expense as possible, John vi. 12.

Q. May we sue our neighbour at law to recover what he owes us ?—A. Yes ; if it is of much importance, and if he is capable to pay, and disregards more peaceable methods of obtaining it, Deut. i. 16, 17.

Q. How prove you that ?—A. From God's appointing magistrates, and giving laws for the recovering of civil rights ; and because otherwise the outward estates of the godly would be a prey to the wicked, Deut. xxv.

Q. How then doth Christ say, *If any man sue thee at law, and take away thy coat, let him have thy cloak also?* —A. The meaning is, that we should rather lose a little, than carry on litigious contests at law, Matth. v. 40, 41, 42.

Q. And how doth Paul say, *There is a fault among you, that ye go to law one with another,* 1 Cor. vi ?—A. The meaning is, that it is sinful for Christians to carry their pleas and differences before Heathen magistrates, to the scandal of religion, when they might compose them among themselves, 1 Cor. x. 32, Eph. iv. 32.

Q. How are we to give our wealth to the Lord ?—A. By setting apart sufficient time for his worship on our labouring days ; and giving of our substance to support ministers, teachers, and the poor, 1 Cor. ix. 14.

Q. How is this a mean of promoting our wealth ?—A.

As what is thus given from love to the Lord, is lent to him, and he will repay it with usury, Prov. xix. 17.

Q. How doth the Lord repay what is thus lent to him? —A. By succeeding and directing our endeavours to gain more ; and wonderfully providing for us or our posterity, when reduced to straits, Hag. ii. 19, Psal. xxxvii. 25, 26.

Q. When should we especially give charity or alms ?—A. When our prosperity, or the wants of the poor, are exceeding great ; or when we profess deep humiliation or thanksgiving before God, Neh. v. Isa. lviii. 6, 7.

Q. Who are bound to give alms ?—A. All men, except such as are in *deep poverty*, Eph. iv. 28.

Q. To whom should we give alms ?—A. To all that are in need, especially to poor saints, and poor relations.

Q. Why should we especially give alms to poor saints? —A. Because they are dear in God's sight, can pray down blessings on us ; and Christ will peculiarly reward this charity at the last day, Gal. vi. 10, Matth. xxv. 35.

Q. Why should we give alms ?—A. To testify our obligation to God for our all, and evidence our love to our brethren, Gal. vi. 10, Prov. iii. 9, 10, Luke vi. 35. 38.

Q. In what manner should we give alms ?—A. Cheerfully, from love to God and man ; with proper secrecy ; and in proportion to our ability, and our neighbour's necessity, 2 Cor. viii. 14, and ix. 7.

Q. In what proportion ought we ordinarily to give to the poor, and other pious uses ?—A. It seems most agreeable to scripture, to give, *if possible*, about a *tenth part* of our income at least, Gen. xiv. 20, and xxviii. 22.

Q. How may we be able to spare so much?—A. By labouring diligently in our callings, and retrenching all unnecessary expenses in our diet, clothes, &c.

Q. Wherein lieth the evil of expending on vain apparel, unnecessary food, furniture, &c., what should be set apart for pious uses?—A. Hereby we murder the poor, banish the gospel, starve the ministers of Christ, and souls of men, that our intemperance, pride, and other lusts, may be satisfied, Neh. xiii. 10, 11, Mal. iii. 8, 9.

Q. By what means are we to promote the wealth of others ?—A. By kindness and justice towards them.

Q. How are we to exercise justice towards our neighbours ?—A. By studying sincerity in our words and deeds to them ; faithfulness to our promises, contracts, and trusts ; by buying and selling at just prices ; paying just debts, restoring pledges, and what lost things we have found, and what we have unjustly taken from others.

Q. Why must we restore what we know we have gotten unjustly?—A. Because otherwise we continue in our theft, and cannot expect pardon from God, Lev. vi. 4, 5.

Q. What if by such restitution we should expose our character, and give away all we have?—A. We may make restitution in such a secret manner as not to blemish our character; and if this is impossible, better expose our character, and give away all our substance than expose ourselves to God's wrath, Lev. vi. 4, 5.

Q. To whom are we to make restitution?—A. To the persons from whom the goods were unjustly taken, or their heirs; or if none of these can be found, to the poor.

Q. What is forbidden in the eighth command?—A. Stealing, or injustice towards the wealth of any.

Q. From whom is it possible for men to steal?—A. Either from themselves or their neighbour.

Q. How do men steal from themselves?—A. By idleness, churlishness, imprudent management, prodigality, rash suretiship, and injustice towards others.

Q. What is *idleness?*—A. It is to live without a calling, or to be slothful in business, Prov. xviii. 9.

Q. Wherein lies the evil of idleness?—A. It renders us useless and hurtful to men, dishonours God, and makes us a ready prey for the devil, 1 Tim. v. 13, Matth. xx. 6.

Q. May not believers, whose provision is secured by God's covenant, be idle?—A. No; they must work with their hands, and be *diligent in business,* Rom. xii. 11.

Q. Why then are we commanded to *be careful for nothing?*—A. That forbids only an anxious and sinful care, by which we distrust God's kindness and promise, but not the diligent use of means to promote our wealth.

Q. Doth not such diligence hinder our serving of God?—A. No, it promotes it; nay, is a serving of God, when performed in obedience to his command, Exod. xx. 15.

Q. What is *churlishness?*—A. An aversion to use our wealth in providing things necessary and decent for our place and station, in order to heap up riches. Isa. xxxii. 7.

Q. Wherein lieth the evil of churlishness?—A. It is a distrust of God's providence; an adoring the world as our God; and an injuring of our outward estate, by withholding the expense of means to promote it, Isa. xxxii. 7.

22*

Q. May we not pinch ourselves to give to the Lord ?—
A. Yes ; but not to increase riches, 2 Cor. viii. 2.

Q. What call you *imprudent management ?*—A. Our not
using aright the means and opportunities of procuring and
furthering our wealth, Prov. x. 4, 5.

Q. How prove you imprudent management sinful ?—A.
A good man will guide his affairs with discretion.

Q. What is *prodigality ?*—A. An unnecessary wasting
of our wealth on food, raiment, or other things, above our
ability and station ; or in gluttony, drunkenness, gaming,
whoring, balling, and extravagant charity.

Q. What do you call extravagant charity ? Prov. xxiii.
21.—A. That which is given to such as we know to be in
no need, or who will be encouraged in idleness and wickedness by it ; as charity given to beggars, who are able, but
unwilling to work ; or to monks and friars, to build monas-
teries, and support superstition, 2 Thess. iii. 10.

Q. Wherein lieth the evil of extravagant charity ?—A.
It robs ourselves, and such as are truly needy, and devotes
to sinful purposes what belongs to God.

Q What is *rash suretiship ?*—A. Our engaging for the
payment of such sums of our neighbour's debt, as, if required from us, will much hurt our outward estate.

Q. Wherein lieth the evil of rash suretiship ?—A. It is
directly contrary to God's command, and hath brought
many to outward misery, Prov. xxii. 26, 27, and vi. 1, 2.

Q. How doth injustice towards others injure our wealth ?
—A. It brings the curse of God into our estate, either as a
moth to consume it, or as a plague to slay our own and our
children's souls by it, Deut. xxviii.

Q. How doth the curse of God consume men's wealth ?
—A. It deprives them of prudence to keep it, blasts their
endeavours to increase it, and permits others unjustly to
bereave them of it, Zech. v. 4. Job xx.

Q. How doth the curse of God slay the souls of men by
their wealth ?—A. By permitting them to improve it as an
excitement to, and instrument of spiritual idolatry, carelessness about salvation, pride, uncleanness, &c.

Q. How do men steal from their neighbour ?—A. By
taking or keeping from him any part of his wealth, without
his voluntary consent and leave, Judg. xvii.

Q. How may stealing be distinguished with respect to
the *thing stolen ?*—A. Into stealing of time, office, persons,
or goods.

Q. How are we guilty of stealing time?—A. By spending the time which belongeth to our master, in idleness, or in our own or other men's work; wasting time in unnecessary visits, idle talk, and tempting others to do so, &c.

Q. How are we guilty of stealing offices?—A. By depriving our neighbour of his office and business, and sinfully procuring one to ourselves, 2 Sam. xv.

Q. What is *man-stealing?*—A. It is the stealing of men, women, or children, in order to marry or inslave them; enticing our neighbours' servants from them, &c.

Q. What is stealing of goods?—A. The unjust taking from others corn, cattle, money, grass, &c.

Q. How may stealing be distinguished with respect to its *extent?*—A. Into stealing of the loan of a thing while we design to restore it; and stealing with a design to retain it as our property.

Q. How many ways can stealing be committed?—A. In thought, look, word, or deed.

Q. How is stealing committed in our *thoughts?*—A. By devising, desiring, and delighting in it, or contriving how to hide or excuse it, 1 Kings xxi. 2 Kings v.

Q. How is stealing committed in our *looks?*—A. By viewing what is our neighbour's with an evil eye, and taking pleasure in seeing others stealing, Josh. vii. 21.

Q. How is stealing committed in our *words?*—A. By commanding, encouraging, defending, denying, or excusing theft, or lying for advantage, 2 Kings v.

Q. How is stealing committed in our *deeds?*—A. By our actual bereaving our neighbour of his wealth and outward estate, without his consent, Prov. vi. 30.

Q. How may stealing be distinguished with respect to its *openness?*—A. Into *public stealing*, which is from public communities, or by public authority; and *private stealing*, 1 Kings xxi. Josh. vii.

Q. How may stealing be distinguished in respect of the *quality* of the thing stolen?—A. Into *sacrilege*, which is the stealing of things dedicate to a holy use; and the *stealing of common things*, Acts v. Exod. xxii.

Q. How may stealing be distinguished with respect to the *manner* of transacting it?—A. Into theft, strictly so called, robbery, and oppression.

Q. What is *theft*, strictly so called?—A. The injuring our neighbour's wealth secretly, without violence.

Q. What is *robbery?*—**A.** Our taking by violence and force, what belongs to our neighbour, Job i. 15. 17.

Q. What is *oppression?*—**A.** It is a mixture of theft and robbery, whereby we violently take from our neighbour what is his, under pretence of law and right, Mic. ii.

Q. How are we guilty of common public theft?—**A.** By debasing the coin, steeling out of public treasures, trading in running goods, defrauding magistrates of their due tribute; and magistrates also, by making an improper use of public revenues.

Q. How prove you smuggling sinful?—**A.** It is the occasion of lies and false swearing; steals from our nation and common parent; and often God's curse quickly consumes what is gained by it, Zech. v. 4.

Q. How are we guilty of private theft?—**A.** By using unlawful, or too base callings; direct thieving; resetting thieves; breach of trust; detaining just wages, revenues, or lost things which we have found; and by deceitful borrowing, bargaining, or bankruptcy.

Q. When have we an *unlawful trade* or calling?—**A.** When we have a calling which tends not to the glory of God, and good of mankind, 1 Cor. x. 31.

Q. Who have an unlawful calling?—**A.** Fortune-tellers, gamesters, stage-players, sturdy beggars, &c.

Q. How far is the business of musicians and dancing-masters sinful?—**A.** Not as it moderately refreshes the natural spirits, and teaches a decent behaviour; but only in so far as it promotes balls, lascivious dancing, vanity, and lust, Isa. v. 12, Amos vi. 5.

Q. Whether is an unlawful calling, or a simple act of theft, worst?—**A.** An unlawful calling is by far the worst, as it is a continued and deliberate theft.

Q. What mean you by *direct thieving?*—**A.** The secret taking away our neighbour's property without his consent, removing land-marks, &c. Josh. vii.

Q. How are we guilty of *resetting* thieves?—**A.** By saving thieves from public justice; keeping, concealing, or buying goods which we have reason to believe are stolen, &c.

Q. How are we guilty of theft by *breach of trust?*—**A.** By neglecting any thing that engagement, office, or relation binds us to do, for promoting our neighbour's wealth; and especially by enriching ourselves at the expense of those whose trustees we are, Luke xvi.

Q. Who are ordinarily most tempted to this theft?—A. Advocates, tutors, stewards, servants, &c.

Q. How are we guilty of theft in *detaining wages?*—A. By withholding from servants the whole, or part of their wages, without ground, or for weak reasons; and delaying the payment of them beyond the due time, James v. 4, Deut. xxiv. 15.

Q. How is theft committed in *detaining just revenues?*— A. By our careless or wilful neglect to pay taxes, or rents of land, houses, or money, in due time, Prov. iii.

Q. How is theft committed in *detaining things lost?*—A. By our concealing them, especially when they are sought for; or demanding more for restoring them than the owner is pleased to give, Lev. vi. 3, 4.

Q. How are we guilty of theft in *deceitful borrowing?*— A. By our borrowing without a sincere design, and probable view to pay it at the time set; by careless injuring of the thing borrowed, or in trust; and by refusing or neglecting to return it in due season, Psalm xxxvii. 21.

Q. By whom is theft committed in bargains and merchandise?—A. By both sellers and buyers.

Q. How do the sellers commit theft in bargains?—A. By selling stolen and insufficient goods as lawful and sufficient; by overrating, and too highly commending their goods; by taking an advantage of the buyer's necessity, ignorance, or credulity; and by using unjust weights and measures, 1 Thess. iv. 6, Prov. xi. 1, and xx. 9. 23.

Q. How do the buyers commit theft in merchandise?— A. By sligting and underrating the goods; by unnecessarily buying them on trust to the seller's hurt; by taking advantage of his ignorance, necessity, or trust in them; and by undue delay of payment, &c. Prov. xx. 5. 14.

Q. What rules should we always observe in bargains? —A. To do to others as we would wish they should do to us in the like case; and when we are in doubt concerning the true value of goods, rather to hurt ourselves than our neighbour, Matth. vii. 12, and xx. 15.

Q. How do we commit theft in bankruptcy?—A. In rendering ourselves bankrupts by sloth and prodigality; concealing part of our substance from our creditors; preferring some in payment, whose claims are not better than others; not paying up the abatements which they allow us, if ever we be able, &c. Rom. xii. 11, and xiii. 8.

Q. How are we guilty of public robbery?—A. By ravaging, and levying contributions in our enemies' country, destroying their trade, and taking their ships, in an unlawful war; or doing so in a lawful war, in any other design or degree than to promote a solid peace ; and by forcing communities from their just rights and privileges.

Q. How is private robbery committed?—A. When one, or a few, do, without warrant from the magistrate, take any thing from their neighbour by violence, Job v. 5.

Q. How are men guilty of public oppression?—A. By unjust inclosures, depopulations, forestalling, ingressing, monopolies, unjust taxes, &c. Mic. ii. vi. Isa. v.

Q. What are unjust inclosures?—A. The inclosing of fields common to a city or country, for the interest of one or a few, under a pretence of right, Mic. ii. 2.

Q. What is forestalling?—A. Our buying up goods coming to the market, and hoarding up corn in dearth to enhance the price, Prov. xi. 26.

Q. How are we guilty of sinful ingrossing?—A. By adding house to house, field to field, and trade to trade, when one is sufficient for our family; and by buying up the most part of any sort of goods to raise the price, Isa. v.

Q. What is a sinful monopoly?—A. Our restraining of others by law from selling a particular sort of goods, in order that they may raise their prices *too high*.

Q. When do magistrates oppress with unjust taxes?—A. When they chiefly lay them on the poor and laborious, in order to ease or support naughty and idle persons; or when, without extreme necessity, they make them so heavy, as the subjects can scarce pay them.

Q. What are the branches of private opression?—A. Extortion, rigorous exaction of debts, and vexations, lawsuits, Amos v. 11. Matth. xviii. 28. Prov. iii.

Q. How is oppression committed by private extortions? —A. In servants demanding excessive wages, proprietors burdensome rents, and usurers unreasonable usury; or in masters, tenants, and borrowers, refusing due wages, rents, or usury, matth. vii. 12.

Q. Is it lawful to receive usury or reward for the loan of our money?—A. Yes; if it is not from the poor, but from such as can give it, and in a moderate proportion, Psalm xxxvii. 26. Luke vi. 35, and xix. 23.

Q. How then did God forbid the Israelites to take usury?—A. He forbade them to take it from their brethren and poor strangers; but allowed them to take it from others, Exod. xxii. 25. Deut. xxxi. 20. Lev. xxiii. 35, 36, 37.

Q. How is oppression committed in rigorous exaction of debts?—A. By our exacting what is owing us, to the utter ruin of our neighbour's outward estate; detaining for pledges what is necessary to support their life, and upbraiding such as are willing to pay, with their inability.

Q. How is oppression committed by vexatious law suits? —A. By our making a trade of buying pleas and weak rights; going to law, without first trying all peaceable means to adjust differences; or contending at it on trifling and unjust grounds, Matth. v. 1 Cor. vi.

Q. How is sacred robbery and oppression committed? —A. In our persecuting men for the truth; bereaving them of God's ordinances; tearing away their beloved pastors; forcing on them a false religion, or pastors without a due call, 1 Kings xii. and xiii.

Q. How is secret theft committed?—A. In our denial of sacred dues, and making merchandise of sacred things.

Q. Who are guilty of sacrilege, by withholding sacred dues?—A. All in general, and professors, magistrates, ministers, and heads of families in particular.

Q. How are men in general guilty of this sacrilege?— A. By the want of due holiness in heart, neglect of fervent prayer for, and giving a holy example to others, or of the due support of God's ordinances and ministers, or teachers, and the poor, Neh. xiii. Mal. iii. 8, 9.

Q. How is the want of due holiness in heart and life, and restraint of prayer, a spiritual theft?—A. A holy disposition and pattern, with fervent prayer, is a debt required of us for our neighbour's sake, as well as our own; and without them, we are means of hindering the enriching blessing of God, and bringing his curse on ourselves, our family and country, Gen. xxxix.

Q. How do professors in particular sacrilegiously defraud others?—A. By neglecting to convey to their posterity the truths and ordinances of God, as full, clear and pure, as they received them; and not endeavouring to spread the gospel where it is not, Judges ii. Psalm lxxviii.

Q. How do magistrates sacrilegiously defraud men?— A. By neglecting to support faithful ministers and teachers, or to encourage charity-funds; and by otherwise disposing of the money due to these purposes, 2 Chron. xxix.

Q. How are ministers guilty of sacrilege?—A. In buying, seeking, or accepting presentations; making their benefice their chief motive to their work, and receiving it without a right to it before God; spending their time and talents in idleness and worldly business; neglecting the duty, frequent, and faithful administration of God's ordinances to their people; suiting their doctrine, worship, discipline, government, and private practice, to the sinful humours of men, for the sake of carnal honours, favours, or gain, Isa. lvi. 10, 11, 12. Jer. xxiii.

Q. How do parents and masters sacrilegiously defraud their families?—A. In withholding from them their due privilege of time to worship God, and of family-worship, and of proper instruction in the things of God, Jer. x. 25.

Q. How do we commit Simony, or make merchandise of sacred things?—A. By giving, receiving, contemning, forsaking, or prizing them for carnal gains, Acts viii. 18.

Q. What sacred things do men make merchandise of? —A. God's presence, truths, ordinances, gifts, and revenues; the souls of men; and offices wherein men represent God, Acts viii. 18—20, Rev. xviii. 13.

Q. How do we make merchandise of God's presence? —A. By prosecuting carnal ends at the expense of his absence; and contriving worldly business in time of his worship, &c., Ezek. xxxiii. 31, Zech. vii. 5.

Q. How do we make merchandise of God's truths?—A. By hiding, denying, perverting, opposing, or even professing them for carnal honour, pleasure, or gain.

Q. How do we make merchandise of God's ordinances? —A. By carnal ends in dispensing or attending on them, and by neglecting, corrupting, or administering them to improper persons, for carnal favour, honour or gain.

Q. How do men make merchandise of God's gifts?—A. By pretending to buy, sell, or compliment others with pardon of sin, the gifts of the Holy Ghost, absolution from church censures, &c., Acts viii. 18, 19.

Q. How do we make merchandise of sacred revenues? —A. In complimenting our friends with them; or voluntarily giving them to support sacrilegious traders or church-officers not appointed by Christ, as lordly bishops, cardinals, deans, monks, friars, &c., 1 Sam. ii. 36.

Q. How are men's souls made merchandise of?—A. In men's buying or selling imaginary freedom from purgatory; selling themselves to Satan; giving or receiving hire to judge or swear falsely; plead an evil cause; committing whoredom ; or otherwise sinning, or suffering sin in others for carnal favour, honour, pleasure, or gain.

Q. How do we make merchandise of those offices in which men are God's deputies?—A. By procuring offices in the state, and especially in the church for unworthy persons, from any carnal view, Judges ix., 1 Sam. ii. 36.

Q. How is the bestowing of offices in the church after this manner *especially* sinful?—A. As hereby, for carnal favour, honour, pleasure, or gain, the offices of Christ's house are sold to unworthy persons, and they are set up to receive sacred honours and revenues, murder men's souls, and trade in selling divine things, Titus i.

Q. Why should we carefully avoid stealing?—A. It greatly injures ourselves and others, is contrary to scripture, reason, and the nature of God, and exposes to his wrath, Zech. v. 4, 1 Cor. vi. 10, and v. 11.

Q How can stealing be contrary to the nature of God, when he commanded the Israelites to *borrow* of the Egyptians without paying again, and to take the Canaanites' possession from them?—A. The Egyptians owed the Israelites wages for their labour : and God commanded Israel to ASK, (as the word should be rendered,) not to BORROW from them: and besides, God, who is supreme proprietor of all things, could as justly turn out the rebellious Egyptians and Canaanites, and give their property to Israel, as a master can turn out a rebellious servant, and give his place and privileges to another.

Q. How may we attain to true and genuine honesty ?—A. By a solid trust, and living on God in Christ as our Father and portion ; the application of Christ's death, for crucifying the world to us, and us to it ; and by living in the view of God's omniscience, the shortness of our life, the judgment to come, and the unprofitableness of gaining the whole world, if we lose our own soul.

Q. 76. *Which is the ninth commandment ?*

A. The ninth commandment is, " Thou shalt not bear false witness against thy neighbour."

Q. 77. *What is required in the ninth commandment ?*

A. The ninth commandment requireth the maintaining and promoting of truth between man and man, and of our own and our neighbour's good name, especially in witness-bearing.

23

Q. 78. *What is forbidden in the ninth commandment?*

* **A.** The ninth commandment forbiddeth whatsoever is prejudicial to truth, or injurious to our own or our neighbour's good name.

Q. What is more generally required in the ninth command?—**A.** The maintaining and promoting of truth between man and man, Zech. viii. 16. 19.

Q. What truth is to be maintained and promoted?—**A.** Truth in matters of doctrine and fact, Col. iii. 9.

Q. What do you understand by *maintaining* of truth?—**A.** Our standing to, and abiding constantly by it.

Q. What do you understand by *promoting* of truth?—**A.** Our studying to make it duly known and believed.

Q. How should we thus maintain and promote truth?—**A.** By constant study to be as good as we appear; to speak as we think, and as things really are, and when we should speak of them, 2 Chron. xix. 9.

Q. What is more especially required in the ninth command?—**A.** Our maintaining and promoting our own and our neighbour's good name, Rom. i. 8.

Q. Why ought a good name to be carefully maintained and promoted?—**A.** It *is more precious than great riches;* and renders men very useful for promoting the glory of God, and good of mankind, Prov. xxii. 1.

Q. Whose good name are we to maintain and promote?—**A.** Our own and our neighbour's good name.

Q. How ought we to maintain and promote our own good name?—**A.** By deserving and defending it.

Q. Can we deserve a good name before God?—**A.** No; in his sight *all our righteousness is as filthy rags,* Isaiah lxiv.

Q. How may we deserve a good name from men?—**A.** By living meekly, peaceably, *soberly, righteously, and godly in this present world,* Matth. v. 17, Titus ii. 12.

Q. How are we to defend our own good name?—**A.** By vindicating it against reproaches and false accusations; and by modest commendation of ourselves only when there is need, in such a manner, as all the praise may redound to God's free grace, 2 Cor. x. xi. and xii.

Q. Who ought to maintain and promote their own good name?—**A.** All men, especially ministers, magistrates, and professors, Luke i. 6, Sam. xxiii. 4.

Q. Why ought ministers, magistrates, and professors, es-

pecially to maintain and promote their own good name?—
A. Because the blemishes in their character principally
tend to the blasphemy of God's name, and do harden others
in their sin, 2 Sam. xii. 14.

Q. In respect of whom are we to maintain and promote
our neighbour's good name?—A. In respect of ourselves
and others, Rom. xii. 10, 1 Sam. xxiii. 14.

Q. How are we to maintain and promote our neighbour's good name in respect of ourselves?—A. By considering that which is good in them with esteem, delight, and
thankfulness; by ready receiving good reports concerning
them; by contemning and discouraging bad reports, tale-
bearers, and whisperers; and by grief for reproof of, and
endeavoring to reclaim them from their real faults.

Q. How are we to maintain and promote our neighbour's
good name in respect of others?—A. By commending and
vindicating them behind their back; by concealing their infirmities; and by reproving them before others only when
there is need, and in such a way as doth not darken their
real excellencies, 1 Sam. xxii.

Q. When may we lawfully report our neighbour's faults
to others?—A. When others are in danger of being insna-
red by not knowing them; when private admonition cannot claim them; when public shame is their proper punishment; or when our hiding of their faults would hurt the
temptation of the innocent, Phil. iii. 2.

Q. Wherein is truth, and our own and our neighbour's
good name, to be especially maintained and promoted?—
A. In witness-bearing; for what is said in witness-bearing,
is a most solemn appeal to God, and most firmly establishes,
or more deeply wounds truth, and our own and our neighbour's good name, Prov. xiv. 1 Sam. xxii.

Q. What is more generally forbidden in the ninth commandment?—A. All injuring of truth, Col. iii. 9.

Q. Whereby do we injure truth?—A. By simple falsehood, wilful lying, equivocation, mental reservation, forgery,
and hypocrisy or dissimulation.

Q. What call you *simple falsehood?*—A. Our representing any doctrine or fact according to our conception of it,
but otherwise than it really is, and in terms tending to lead
others into a mistake, Job xxi. 34.

Q. Is all use of terms seemingly representing things
otherwise than they are, sinful?—A. No; it is no sin to
use figures, metaphors, ironies, and hyperboles, if their sig-

nification is so intimate or fixed by custom, as to leave no proper danger or mistake, Eccl. xi. 9.

Q. What figures are used in scripture?—**A.** The whole is put for a part, and a part for the whole, &c.

Q. What is a *metaphor* and allegory?—**A.** The representation of spiritual things by the names of natural; as when Christ is called a *lily, rose, sun,* and *shield,* &c.

Q. What is *irony?*—**A.** The using terms which seem to commend things, with such an air as that they severely reprove them, Eccl. xi. 9, 1 Kings xviii., xxii.

Q. What is a *hyperbole?*—**A.** The expressing things as if much greater or less than they are; as when the cities of Canaan are said to be *walled up to heaven,* which, according to the eastern idiom of language, signified no more than their great height.

Q. What is *wilful lying?*—**A.** Our maintaining as a truth that which we doubt of, or know to be false.

Q. How are we guilty of lying?—**A.** By neglecting to speak the truth when called to it, for reproving sin, or bearing witness to facts; by asserting or denying things more strongly than our information will bear; by making promises without a sincere design, and probable views of performance, or breaking them without weighty reasons; and by relating known falsehoods.

Q. How may lies, in relating known falsehoods, be distinguished?—**A.** Into *jocose lies,* made to raise wonder and sport; *officious lies,* made to gain some carnal advantage, or prevent some hurt; *pernicious lies,* springing from malice, and tending to hurt our neighbour's soul, character, or estate; and *lies of mere compliment,* at meeting of friends, table, &c., to please men, and display our imaginary breeding.

Q. What is *equivocation?*—**A.** Our using expressions of a double signification in a true sense, in order to make others understand them in a false one.

Q. What is a *mental reservation?*—**A.** Our concealing in our minds some things necessary to be added to what we express, to make our speech agree with our thoughts.

Q. Must we always relate the whole history of a fact, if we relate a part of it?—**A.** No; but we ought always to relate as much of it, as renders what we say strict truth, and as much as tends to excuse our neighbour's deeds.

Q. What is *forgery?*—**A.** Our making and passing of money, writs, speeches, &c., under false names,

Q. Wherein doth *hypocrisy* consist?—A. Sometimes in pretending to be worse than we are ; but especially in pretending to be better than we are.

Q. How may this last and common kind of hypocrisy be distinguished ?—A. Into hypocrisy *respecting our state*, and hypocrisy *only respecting our exercise*.

Q. What is hypocrisy *respecting our state?*—A. Our habitual pretension and appearance to be saints, when we are not ; which constitutes us proper hypocrites.

Q. Do hypocrites ever think themselves true saints ?—A. Yes ; perhaps they ordinarily do so, Matth. vii.

Q. What appearances of saintship may hypocrites have ? —A. The gifts of prayer and knowledge, the common convictions and comforts of the Holy Ghost, and an outwardly zealous and tender practice, Isa. lviii. 2, Heb. vi.

Q. What are the marks of a hypocrite?—A. The *habitual* performance of religious duties *to be seen of men ;* greater zeal against sin in others than in ourselves ; with a partial concert to observe only *some,* not *all* the commands of God, Matth. xxiii. 4—33.

Q. What is hypocrisy *respecting our exercise only?*—A. That by which saints, or profane persons, sometimes do good to be seen of men, and esteemed better than they are ; and by which saints are often more careful of the outward than inward part of religious duties.

Q. Why may not saints, and profane persons, be called *hypocrites* from this their hypocritical exercise?—A. Because saints habitually disallow their hypocrisy ; nor doth it represent them in another state than they really are ; and the hypocrisy of the profane is so scanty, that it doth not make them appear saints, Rom. i. 14—24.

Q. Wherein doth the evil of falsehood, lying, and dissimulation, appear?—A. They are the offspring of Satan, an abomination to God, break the bonds of society, and expose men to eternal wrath, John viii. 44, Prov. vi. 19.

Q. What is more especially forbidden in the ninth command ?—A. Whatsover is injurious to our own or our neighbour's good name, Psalm xv.

Q. How do we injure our own and our neighbour's good name ?—A. By defiling and slandering it ; and by flattery.

Q. In what doth flattery consist?—A In unnecessary and false commendation of men to their knowledge.

Q. Wherein lieth the evil of flattery?—A. It is the oc-
23*

casion of lies, and slander of others; it hinders self-examination, and inflames our pride, &c. Prov. xxix. 5.

Q. How do we defile and stain our own good name?—
A. By openly committing any thing imprudent or wicked,
which may be a blot to our reputation, Eccl. x. 1.

Q. How do we defile our neighbour's good name?—A.
By tempting them to commit such imprudent or wicked
things as blot their reputation, 1 Kings xiii.

Q. What is slander or defamation?—A. Our unjust
charging of ourselves or others with that which is bad.

Q. How many ways are men guilty of slander?—A. In
thoughts, and deeds, but most formally in words.

Q. Whom do men slander in thought, word, and deed?
—A. Either themselves or their neighbours.

Q. How do we defame ourselves in our *thoughts?*—A.
By judging ourselves hypocrites when we are saints; or
judging ourselves otherwise guilty of sin than we are.

Q. How do we practically slander ourselves in our *deeds?*
—A. When we acquiesce in the calumnies cast on us;
when saints live in such a dejected manner, as if under
sentence of eternal death; or when we provoke others to
slander us.

Q. How do we provoke others to slander us?—A. By
our going to the utmost bounds of our Christian liberty; and by being slanderers of others, haughty, and proud
boasters of ourselves, or busy bodies in other men's matters.

Q. How do we defame ourselves in our *words?*—A. By
falsly accusing ourselves; imprudently revealing our own
faults, or denying the gifts and graces which God hath bestowed upon us, 2 Sam. i. 10. Exod. iv. 10.

Q. How do we slander our neighbours in our *heart?*—
A. By rash, harsh, and partial judging and disesteeming of
them, or by desiring and delighting in their infamy.

Q. What call you rash judging of others?—A. Our
judging of their conduct without careful examination of its
circumstances; and especially judging their thoughts, designs, and eternal state, Matth. vii. 1—5.

Q. What mean you by *harsh* judging of others?—A.
Our condemning their practice in things indifferent, inter-
preting their words and actions in the worst sense; and
viewing their afflictions as evidences of their distinguished
wickedness, Rom. xiv. Acts xxviii. 4.

Q. What mean you by *partial* judging of others?—A.
Our judging of them on the report of adversaries, or in-

sufficient informers, and under prejudices of our own, at their person, principles, party, or nation; and condemning them for sins less than those in which we allow ourselves.

Q. How do we practically slander our neighbours in our *deeds?*—A. By not duly informing them of evil reports passing on them, that they may vindicate themselves; by groundlessly shifting fellowship with them; seeking out, ready listening to, easy belief, and firm remembrance of evil reports concerning them; encouraging tale-bearers; and by neglect of proper means to refute slanders, and bring slanderers to deserved punishment and shame.

Q. How do we slander our neighbours in our *words?*—A. By charging them with faults of which they are innocent; or charging them with their real faults in an unchristian manner, Psalm l. 20. 2 Sam. xvi. 3. and xix. 26, 27.

Q. How may slander of our neighbour in words be distinguished?—A. Into upbraiding and backbiting him.

Q. What do you understand by *upbraiding* him?—A. Our slandering a man to his face, either in a more serious or scornful manner, 2 Sam. vii. 7, 8. 1 Cor. v. 11.

Q. Wherewith do such slanderers usually upbraid their neighbour?—A. With his religion, qualities, offices, exercises, and sentiments; his natural infirmities of baldness, lameness, &c.; and his real faults, Matth. v. xi, xii.

Q. Is it very sinful to upbraid men with their holiness and religion?—A. Yes; it is a reproach of God himself in and by his image in men, Psal. xxii. 8, 9.

Q. Is it very sinful to upbraid men with their natural defects?—A. Yes; it is a reviling of God as the author of these defects, Lev. xix. 14. 2 Kings ii. 23.

Q. How do we slander men in charging them with their real faults?—A. By twitting them with sins of which they have evidenced their repentance; and charging them with their sins in a light and passionate manner, 2 Sam. xvii.

Q. Why is it very sinful to upbraid men with these sins for which they have evidenced sorrow?—A. Because it is a counteracting the conduct of God in pardoning them.

Q. Why is it very sinful reproachfully to upbraid men with their sins unrepented of?—A. Because it tends to harden them much in their sin.

Q. In what do such upbraiding for sin and Christian reproof, differ?—A. Such upbraiding for sin flows from pride, passion, and hatred at the sinner; is attended with a love to his sin; and is expressed in a way tending to expose and exasperate him ; but Christian reproof flows from love to the glory of God, and the offender's soul, and hatred at his sin ; and is expressed in a meek and calm manner.

Q. What is *backbiting?*—A. Our scornful or serious defamation of our neighbour in his absence, Psalm xv. 3.

Q. Is it very sinful to scoff at our neighbour's religion, natural or sinful infirmities, real or feigned, in his absence ? —A. Yes ; it is like a mad-man's casting firebrands, arrows, and death, in his sport, Isa. xxviii. 22.

Q. How do we more seriously backbite our neighbour ? —A. By raising and spreading false reports of him ; representing his real faults worse than they are ; concealing what tends to excuse and extenuate them ; publishing them, when it no way tends to the glory of God, or his good ; hiding or lessening his real excellencies, or putting a bad construction on them, Jer. xx. 10, and xviii. 18.

Q. How do backbiters and whisperers ordinarily cover their hatred at him they defame ?—A. By pretending their esteem of him, or their discrediting, or sorrow to hear such bad reports ; by requiring the slander to be kept secret, &c.

Q. Doth this conduct lessen the guilt of their slander ? —A. No ; it adds dissimulation to it, Prov. x. 18.

Q. Wherein lieth the great evil of slander?—A. It robs God of his glory arising from men's good name, quenches brotherly affection, gives our neighbour such a wound as can scarce be healed, brings dishonour on ourselves, and exposes to eternal wrath, Prov. xxii. 1.

Q. Whether is theft or slander worst?—A. Slander ; for it takes away our good name, which is better than great riches ; renders us more useless, contemptible, and hated ; and is a more lasting and irrecoverable hurt than the loss of our wealth by theft, Prov. xxii. 1, Eccl. vii. 1.

Q. What then makes almost all men delight so much in slandering our neighbours?—A. Pride, and a malicious inclination to make other men's character as bad as their conscience tells them their own should be, Titus iii. 3.

Q. What kind of falsehood and slander is most criminal?—A. That which is committed in *witness-bearing.*

Q. Who are often guilty of falsehood and slander in public judicature and witness-bearing ?—A. The parties at law, advocates, witnesses, and judges.

Q. How are the parties guilty of such falsehood and slander ?—A. By founding pleas on false and forged claims,

boldly denying truths, asserting untruths, suborning or corrupting witnesses, bribing judges, &c.

Q. How are advocates guilty ?—A. By misrepresenting
the case of their client ; contriving and maintaining falsehoods to support their cause; concealing or faintly supporting of truth, or outfacing it with importunity and eloquence,
Acts xxiv. 1—6.

Q. How are witnesses guilty ?—A. By swearing things
false in themselves, or dubious to them ; or witnessing truths
with malice and envy, Acts vi. 13, 14.

Q. How are the judges guilty ?—A. By suffering themselves to be bribed or seduced ; misrepresenting the law ;
and giving verdict or sentence contrary to their own conscience, or the truth, Exod. xxiii. 8.

Q· What peculiar evil is in slander and falsehood committed in judicatures ?—A. It is committed in the more es-
pecial presence of God, or in his name, or when he is solemnly called on to attest it, Psalm lxxxii. 1.

Q. Is it not horrible wickedness to lie or slander in
preaching and prayer, or to support a religious cause, and
gain proselytes to it ?—A. Yes ; it prostitutes God's ordinances, and is a speaking wickedly for God, Job xiii. 7.

Q. By what means may we avoid falsehood and slander ?
—A. By avoiding to meddle with other men's business ;
speaking little ; careful keeping our hearts ; and by living
in the view of our unworthiness, God's omniscience, and the
account we must give to him at the last day.

Q. 79. *Which is the tenth commandment ?*

A. The tenth commandment is, "Thou shalt not
covet thy neighbour's house, thou shalt not covet thy
neighbour's wife, nor his man-servant, nor his maid-
servant, nor his ox, nor his ass, nor any thing that is
thy neighbour's."

Q. 80. *What is required in the tenth commandment ?*

A. The tenth commandment requireth full contentment with our own condition, with a right and charitable frame of spirit toward our neighbour, and all
that is his.

Q. 81. *What is forbidden in the tenth commandment ?*

A. The tenth commandment forbiddeth all discontentment with our own estate, envying or grieving at the good of our neighbour, and all inordinate motions and affections to any thing that is his.

Q. How prove you that this command respecting covetousness is but ONE of the ten ?—**A.** There are *nine* besides it, as the second is manifestly different from the first : and if this command were to be distinguished from its objects, it would make *six*, or rather a *thousand.*

Q. What is required in the tenth commandment ?—**A.** Contentment with our own lot ; and a charitable disposition towards our neighbour, and all that is his.

Q. Are we to be content to live in an estate or practice of sin ?—**A.** No ; sin is contrary to God's law, 1 John iii. 4.

Q. With what then should we be content ?—**A.** With every thing which God in his providence orders for our lot, whether pleasant or afflicting, Heb. xiii. 5.

Q. What manner of contentment with our lot is required of us ?—**A.** Full contentment, Heb. xiii. 5.

Q. What is *full* contentment ?—**A.** Contentment complete in its parts, and carried to the highest degree.

Q Of how many parts doth full contentment consist ?—**A.** Four ; self-denial, readiness to take up our cross, holy carelessness about this world, and satisfaction with our condition in it, Phil. iv. 6, 7, Matth. xvi. 24.

Q. What is self denial ?—**A.** Our looking on ourselves as unworthy any thing but hell, and incapable to choose or provide what is for our true interest.

Q. What crosses must we take up ?—**A.** Manifold afflictions in this world, and especially suffering for Christ.

Q. What is meant by *taking up* the cross ?—**A.** Submitting to it in obedience to God's will, Acts xxi. 13.

Q. In what manner must we take up our cross ?—**A.** Cheerfully, from love to Christ who bare the curse for us, Matth. xvi. 24.

Q. What is meant by a *holy carelessness* about this world ?—**A.** Our reckoning all worldly enjoyment nothing in comparison of God ; and in the diligent use of means, leaving it wholly to him to carve our lot in it.

Q. What mean you by *satisfaction* with our condition ?—**A.** Our pleasure in it, from a persuasion that it is eminently suited to the glory of God, and our real advantage.

Q. In what cases are we especially called to study contentment?—A. When our relations die, or prove crosses to us; and when we meet with prosperity, bodily afflictions, poverty, reproach, spiritual trouble, disappointment, and loss of all things.

Q. What is more generally necessary to our attaining contentment in these cases?—A. Our union to Christ, the sprinkling of his blood on our conscience, our having God in him as our God, and our heart filled with his love.

Q. How may we attain contentment, when our friends and relations die?—A. By considering, that our God lives; that all men must die; that God has taken them away; that if they were gracious, the loan we had of them was a great mercy, death was their great gain, and we shall shortly meet in heaven never to part, Job xix. 25.

Q. How may we attain contentment when our friends and relations prove crosses to us?—A. By taking their bad conduct to us as a reproof of our neglect of duty to them, and especially to God; and by considering, that all men are imperfect, that God is our chief friend, and will soon free us from the trouble of others, Micah vii. 7—10.

Q. How may we attain contentment in a prosperous state?—A. By living on God as our chief portion; beholding and enjoying him in all that we have, and glorifying him with it; by having our heart weaned from the world; and considering, that discontent is most ungrateful to God, and a ready way to provoke him to deprive us of our present enjoyments, Psalm iv. 6, 7.

Q. How may we attain contentment under bodily afflictions?—A. By considering that they are unstinged; are much lighter than our sins deserve, or Christ suffered; and are useful to put us in mind of death, meeten us for heaven, and sweeten it to us, Lam. iii. 39.

Q. How may we attain contentment under poverty?—A. By considering how poor Christ, and many of his dearest saints, have been; that we have more than we brought into this world, or can carry out of it; and that the less we have, the less we have to account for at the last day, 2 Cor. viii. 9. 1 Tim. vi. 6, 7.

Q. How may we attain contentment under reproach?—A. By a firm faith of our new covenant name; and considering how much Christ and his people have been always reproached, how worthless men's applause is, and how our character shall be vindicated at the last day.

Q. How may we attain contentment under the spiritual

troubles of temptation, desertion, &c.?—A. By application of the many sweet promises respecting spiritual trouble; and considering how Christ, and his dearest saints, have been so troubled; that he has a fellow-feeling of our affliction; that it shall speedily be over, and work for us a far more exceeding and eternal weight of glory, Isa. liv.

Q. How may we attain contentment under manifold losses and disappointments?—A. By a diligent study to supply the want of other things with God himself; by considering, that our God cannot be lost, that our wise and gracious Father is the author of all our losses and disappointments, that they are necessary to convince us of the vanity of this world, prevent us from taking up our rest therein, and to prepare a place for God and his fulness in our hearts, Phil. iv. 19.

Q. Doth full contentment exclude lamentation over our afflictions, and the sinful cause of them, or use of lawful means of deliverance from them?—A. No; it supposes and includes these things, Psalm i. 15, and xci. 15.

Q. What are the great advantages of contentment?—A. It makes God delight in doing us good, sweetens every case, and disposeth us to every duty, Isa. lxiv. 5.

Q. What is a charitable frame of spirit towards our neighbour and all that is his?—A. Our readiness to rejoice in our neighbour's welfare, and mourn for his afflictions, as if it were our own, Rom. xii.

Q. What is necessary to our attaining this charitable frame of spirit?—A. Heart-purity and watchfulness.

Q. From what must our heart be purified?—A. From covetous desires after earthly things.

Q. Why is this purity of heart necessary for us?—A. Because the want of it hinders our communion with God, and proper love to our neighbour, Matth. v. 8.

Q. How may we attain this purity of heart?—A. By faith in Christ as our righteousness and strength, by application of God's pure word to our hearts, and by earnest prayer, 2 Cor. vii 1. Gal. vi. 14.

Q. What of our heart must we watch over?—A. Over the first motions of our heart towards sin, and all temptations thereto, Prov. iv. 23. 1 Pet. v. 8.

Q. Why ought we to watch over our heart?—A. Because it is very deceitful, inconstant, and wicked; sin lies very hid in it; the life of religion lies much in keeping our heart bended towards God; and hereby many wicked thoughts are prevented, Jer. xvii. 9. Prov. iv. 23.

Q. Why is watchfulness over our heart necessary to our having a charitable frame of spirit towards our neighbour? —A. Because without it our heart would wander in covetous desires of what is his, Prov. iv. 23.

Q. What sins are forbidden in the tenth commandment? —A. Discontentment, envy, and covetousness.

Q. What is *discontentment?*—A. Our inward disliking and grudging at any thing in our lot, Job v. 2.

Q. How is our inward discontentment of heart outwardly exercised and evidenced?—A. By sullen shifting to look on our enjoyments, or viewing them in a dissatisfied manner; by disliking to hear our lot well spoken of, and pleasure in hearing it dispraised; fretful complaints and murmuring at it; and by living peevishly in trouble, and unthankfully under the receipt of mercies, Esth. v. 13.

Q. Whence doth our discontentment spring?—A. From worldly mindedness, pride, and distrust of God.

Q. Is it any excuse for our discontentment that it flows from our natural temper?—A. No; that shews discontent to be deeply rooted in our heart, James iv. 1.

Q. Are the length, greatness, and suddenness of our affliction, any excuse for discontent?—A. No; for we also receive many great, unexpected, and lasting mercies; we ought to have expected troubles; and besides, discontentment makes our affliction still more grievous.

Q. Are not very provoking injuries an excuse for our discontentment?—A. No; for we do greater injuries to God every day than can be done to us, Matth. xviii.

Q. Is it any excuse of our discontentment that our troubles unfit us for duty, and that we fear they are the first fruits of eternal wrath?—A. No; for it is chiefly discontent that begets that unfitness for duty, and slavish fear of wrath.

Q. What then should we do in such a disordered case? —A. We should flee speedily to the blood of Christ, and grace of God, for relief from our plagues and fears.

Q. Wherein lieth the great evil of discontentment?—A. It embitters our mercies, quarrels with God, provokes him to add to our trouble, unfits us for duty, increaseth our affliction, and hinders the happy fruits of it.

Q. What happy fruits of affliction doth it hinder?—A. The embittering and purging away of our sin; the excitement, trial, and manifestation of our grace; the weaning

24

of our heart from this world, and setting it on things above, Isa. xxvii. 9, Col. iii. 1.

Q. What is *envy?*—A. Our inwardly grudging and grieving at the good of our neighbour, Gen. iv. 4, 5.

Q. How is the envy of our heart outwardly exercised and evidenced?—A. In our sullen and angry looks on our neighbour's enjoyments, grudging speeches concerning them, and unkind behaviour to him on account of them.

Q. What is the object and ground of our envy?—A. The good of our neighbour in honour, wealth, health, relations, gifts, graces, favour, success, &c.

Q. What is the root of envy?—A. Pride and malice.

Q. Wherein lieth the evil of envy?—A. It dishonours God, embitters our enjoyments, makes us like Satan, is dangerous to our neighbour, and destroyers of ourselves, Prov. xiv. 30, Job v. 2. Jam. iii. 14. 16.

Q. What is *covetousness?*—A. An excessive and inordinate desire of any worldly thing, Hab. ii. 5. 9.

Q. Can we exceed in desiring God as our portion, Christ as our Saviour, and the Holy Ghost as our sanctifier?—A. No; these are intimately valuable, and our possessing them in the highest degree, cannot but tend to God's glory, and our own good, Psalm lxxxi. 10, xvi. 5, 6.

Q. How do we exceed in desiring created enjoyments? —A. In desiring them as our chief good, more than God's law allows, or more of them than is meet for us, Heb. xiii. 5.

Q. How do we commit covetousness in the irregular desire of things?—A. In desiring to have them at the expense of our neighbour's losing them, or in order to fulfil some sinful lust with them, Jam. iv. 2, 3, and v. 34.

Q. How is the covetousness of our heart outwardly exercised and evidenced?—A. By greedy looks on the object of our sinful desire, covetous speeches, excessive toil, labour in too many or base callings, endeavours to draw from our neighbour what is his, &c.

Q. Wherein lieth the evil of covetousness?—A. It is idolatry, making a god of its object; breaks all the commands; tempts to all other sins; begets disquiet of mind; unfits us for duty; draws down God's wrath on us and our heirs in this life; and exposeth to hell.

Q. How may we be delivered from envy and covetousness?—A. By faith in, and love to Christ as our Saviour; believing in the views of God as our portion; prayer for the Spirit of Sanctification; and by serious consideration.

Q. What are we to consider in order to cure us of envy and covetousness ?—A. That these sins make us like Satan, and odious to God; that the worst men have often most of this world; that the more we have in it, the more difficult our duty, and the greater our accounts will be; that death will soon strip us of our earthly enjoyments; and that all our envious and covetous desires shall be publicly exposed at the last day, James iii. iv. Tit. iii. 3.

Q. Why is the object of envy and covetousness so particularly expressed in this command, viz. our neighbour's *house, wife, servant, ox,* or *ass?*—A. Because men are so much inclined to these sins, Ezek. xxxiii. 31.

Q. Is not the coveting of these things forbidden in commands 7th, 8th, &c.?—A. Yes; but these commands strike more directly against actual sins; whereas the tenth strikes more directly against the sin of our nature, and first motions of lust, Rom. vii. 7—13.

Q. Why is it necessary that there should be a particular command against the lust of nature?—A. Because, though it be one of our greatest sins, it is much overlooked by us, Rom. vii. 7. 13.

Q. 82. *Is any man able perfectly to keep the commandments of God?*

A. No mere man, since the fall, is able, in this life, perfectly to keep the commandments of God, but doth daily break them in thought, word, and deed.

Q. Ought every man to keep all the commandments of God perfectly?—A. Yes, Deut. xviii. 13, and xii. 32.

Q. Why ought we to keep them perfectly?—A. God requires, and hath a just title to our perfect obedience; and it tends to the advantage of ourselves and others.

Q. What profit can *even* wicked men's attempts to obey God's law bring to them?—A. Temporal mercies in this life, and the lessening their torments in hell.

Q. Why doth God reward wicked men's obedience, or rather shew of obedience?—A. To shew the regard which he hath to the *very resemblance of holiness,* and that he hath no pleasure in the death of sinners, Jon. iii. 10.

Q. But how can he reward wicked men's obedience, when he says, it is an *abomination* to him?—A. This obedience is better in itself than an absolute neglect of duty, 1 Kings xxii. 29, 2 Kings x. 30.

Q. Can any man perfectly keep the commands of God? —A. No mere man, since the fall, is able to keep them perfectly in this life, 1 Kings viii. 46, 1 John i. 8—10.

Q. Why do you say the commands cannot be kept *perfectly* in this life?—A. Because believers keep them *sincerely, not perfectly*, 2 Cor. ii. 2, Rom. vii.

Q. Why do you say, no *mere man* can keep them perfectly?—A. Because Christ, who is not a mere man, but *God-man,* did keep them perfectly, Matth. iii. 15. 17.

Q. Why do you add these words, *since the fall?*—A. Because before the fall Adam was able, and did keep all the commands of God perfectly, Eccl. vii. 29.

Q. Why do you add these words, *in this life?*—A. Because in heaven the saints shall be able to keep the whole law of God perfectly, Jude 24, Eph. v. 37.

Q. How prove you, that believers cannot keep the commands of God perfectly in this life?—A. The scripture affirms *there is no man that doeth good, and sinneth not;* and that if we say we have no sin the truth is not in us, and shews that the best saints failed in those graces wherein they most excelled; Abraham through distrust lied once and again, Moses sinned by passion, Job by impatience, and Peter by cowardice, 1 Kings viii. 46.

Q. How then are Job, Hezekiah, and other saints, called *perfect* in scripture?—A. Because they were upright and sincere, having all the graces in some measure, diligently studying to have them in full measure, and heartily grieved for their imperfections in holiness; and were far more perfect than others, Job i. 8, Luke i. 6, Phil. iii. 12—14.

Q. How is it said, *He that is born of God sinneth not, and cannot sin?*—A. Because he cannot sin against the law as a covenant; nor can he make a trade of sin, by living in it with pleasure, as others do, Rom. vi., vii.

Q. Of what sins may believers be guilty in this life?— A. Of every unpardonable sin, even the worst, as Atheism, unbelief, idolatry, &c., 1 Kings xi. 1—8.

Q. Into what sins do believers most frequently fall?—A. Into more refined and secret sins, Psalm xix. 21.

Q. Wherein do we break God's commands daily?—A. In thought, word, and deed, Gen. viii. 21.

Q. By what *thoughts* do we break God's commands?— A. By low thoughts of God, and his Son Christ; by atheistical, ignorant, idolatrous, profane, proud, idle, carnal, covetous, unclean, or malicious thoughts, &c.

Q. By what *words* do we break God's commands?—A. By idle, proud, profane, angry, obscene, or lying words, &c. Jam. ii. 6. 8, Matth. v. 22. 34—37.

Q. By what *deeds* do we break God's commands?—A. By carnal labour on the Sabbath ; by killing, stealing, committing adultery, &c. Hos. iv. 2.

Q. Do not we also break all the commands of God daily, by omission of required thoughts, words or deeds?—A. Yes; Isa. xliii. 22, 23, 24.

Q. In what different ways do we daily break all God's commands in thought, word, and deed?—A. In our persons, and by partaking in other men's sins.

Q. How do we involve ourselves in the guilt of other men's sins?—A. By permitting when we could have hindered them ; by exciting, causing, encouraging, rewarding, or defending them ; and by not duly reproving for, and mourning over them, Eph. v. 11.

Q. Do we not constantly and practically re-act our former sins, while we continue impenitent for them?—A. Yes.

Q. Can we then conceive how many sins we commit in a day or hour?—A. No; we commit so many in our own persons, and by partaking with others in sin, that God alone can reckon their number, Psalm xl. 12.

Q. 83. *Are all transgressions of the law equally heinous?*

Some sins in themselves, and by reason of several aggravations, are more heinous in the sight of God than others.

Q. Are all sins equally criminal?—A. No.

Q. How prove you that?—A. The scripture represents some sins as greater than others, some sins are more punished than others, and one sin is unpardonable.

Q. Are not all sins infinitely evil?—A. Yes, as they are committed against an infinitely holy God.

Q. How then can some sins be more henious or worse than others?—A. As therein we more fully exert our enmity against God, and do greater injury to his declarative glory, John xix. 11, and xv. 22.

Q. In what different respects are some sins more heinous than others ?—A. Either in themselves, or by the aggravations that attend them.

Q. How are some sins more heinous *in themselves?*—A. As they directly break more commandments, and contain greater injury to God or men, than others.

Q. Whether are sins directly against the first or second table more heinous ?—A. Sins against the first ; for these are an immediate attack on the being, name, worship, and property of God, which are more precious in themselves than what belongs to men, 1 Sam. ii. 25.

Q. What are the worst sins against the first table ?—A. Atheism, idolatry, profane swearing, unbelief, &c.

Q. Why are these more heinous ?—A. Because they are a direct attempt against the being and essential honour of God, or do blasphemously misrepresent him.

Q. What are some of the worst sins against the second table of the law ?—A. Murder, adultery, slander, &c.

Q. Why are these more heinous ?—A. Because they rob a man of his life, wife, or good name, which are more precious than his wealth, Job ii. 4, Prov. xxii. 1.

Q. What sins against the first table break many commands ?—A. Every sin against it ; but especially those against the first commandment break all the ten.

Q. How do these sins break the commands of the second table ?—A. As they are a direct attack upon the being and honour of God, they lose all binding impressions of duty to our neighbour : and moreover, to rob a man of his God, or means of enjoying him, is a greater injury than to rob him of his life, and every other earthly enjoyment.

Q. How then is it, that sins against the first table of the law are ordinarily so lightly accounted of ?—A. It proceeds from our Atheism, pride, and ignorance of God.

Q. What sins against the second table directly break many commandments ?—A. Every sin against it, particularly drunkenness, theft, covetousness, envy, slander, &c.

Q. How doth drunkenness break the commandments of the first table ?—A. Drunkenness makes a god of our belly ; and liquor unfits us for meditation, prayer, and other ordinances, and justly stops our admission to the seals of the covenant ; it occasions our taking God's name in vain, and perverting his creatures to sinful purposes ; and disqualifieth us for remembering the Sabbath to come, or improving the work of the Sabbath past.

Q. How doth drunkenness break the commandments

of the second table?—A. It disqualifieth us for performing relative duties; by it we devote to the service of Satan that money which should support our family, the magistrates, ministers, and poor; and waste time in encouraging others to sin; it breaks our bodily constitution, occasions quarrels and fighting, starves our families, inflames our fleshly lusts, ruins our estate, and tempts us to steal, procures a bad name, and fills our mouth with slander, and incites an inordinate desire of liquor.

Q. How do theft and covetousness break the commandment of the first table?—A. The covetous thief makes riches his God, worships its image and superscription, profanes God's good creatures, and hath his head and heart full of carnal projects on the Sabbath.

Q. How do theft and covetousness break the commandment of the second table?—A. These sins hinder the performance of our duty to our relations; take from our neighbour the supports of his life, and endanger our own; encourage idleness and prodigality, those incentives of lust, procures a bad name, &c.

Q. Why doth the apostle James say, that *though a man should keep the whole law, and yet offend in one point, he is guilty of all?*—A. Because every sin is against the love that is the fulfilment, and tramples on the authority that is the foundation of the whole law, Jam. ii. 10.

Q. What is the second way some sins are more heinous than others?—A. By the *aggravations* attending them.

Q. What call you an *aggravation* of sin?—A. Any circumstances attending it which increaseth its guilt.

Q. From what circumstances are sins aggravated?—A. From the person offending or offended; from the means against which sin is committed; and the quality, time, place, and manner of the offence. 2 Sam. ii. 25.

Q. How is sin aggravated from the *person offending?*—A. The sins of superiors in gifts, graces, age, or station, as parents, husbands, masters, magistrates, or ministers, are more heinous than the same sins committed by their respective inferiors, Hos. v. 1. Isa. xxxviii. 14.

Q. Why are the sins of superiors more heinous?—A. Because their sins prostitute more of the image or authority of God lodged in them, and do more harden and encourage others in sin, 1 Kings xii. 25—33.

Q. How is sin aggravated from the *person immediately offended by it?*—A. Sins committed immediately against

God, Christ as Mediator, or the Spirit and his grace, are more heinous than like sins committed against men; sins against many, are more heinous than like sins against few; sins against saints, particularly weak ones, more heinous than like sins against others; sins against superiors more heinous than like sins against inferiors; and sins against men's souls, than like sins against their bodies.

Q. How is sin aggravated from the *means against which* it is committed?—**A.** Sins committed against the express lettter of the law, clear revelation, manifold warnings, reproofs, convictions, vows, resolutions, mercies, judgments, &c. are more heinous than the same sins committed in contrary cases, Isa. xxvi. 10. Luke xii. 47.

Q. Why so?—**A.** Because, besides the sin itself, there is added an abuse of those clear revelations, warnings, reproofs, convictions, mercies, judgments, &c.

Q. How is sin aggravated from the *quality of the offence?* —**A.** Sin furnished in word and deed, or which cannot admit of restitution, are more heinous than like sins only conceived in thought, or which admit of restitution.

Q. Why so?—**A.** Because, in the former cases, sin spreads wider, and continues longer than in the latter.

Q. How is sin aggravated from the *time of the offence?*— **A.** Sins committed on the Sabbath, in the time of worship, season of gospel light, or of signal mercies or judgments, are more heinous than the same sins committed in other seasons, Matth. xi. 23. 2 Chron. xxviii. 22.

Q. Why so?—**A.** Because, in these cases, besides the sin itself, holy time is profaned, and eminent duties excluded, Isa. xxii. 12, 13. 2 Chron. xxviii. 22.

Q. How are sins aggravated from the *place of the offence?* —**A.** Sins in a gospel-land and in a public or sacred place, are more heinous than the same sins committed in other places, Isa. xxvi. 10. 2 Chron. xxxiii. 4.

Q. Why so?—**A.** Because such sins do pour more contempt on God, and do more harden and encourage others in sin, 2 Sam. xvi. 22. 1 Kings xiii. 1. 33, 34.

Q. How are sins aggravated from the manner of them? —**A.** Sins done deliberately, wilfully, boastingly, maliciously, frequently, obstinately continued in, or relapsed into after repentance, are more heinous than the same sins committed through ignorance, weakness, or the hurry and violence of temptation, or with blushing, or seldom, and not continued in, Psalm xcv. 10. Jer. xliv.

Q. Doth wilful or slothful ignorance excuse our sin ?—
A. No; it is a damning sin in itself, Isa. xxvii. 11.

Q. Which are the worst of all sins ?—A. Unbelief, and
the sin against the Holy Ghost, Heb. x. 26. 29.

Q. What is unbelief?—A. Our refusing Christ as offered in the gospel; or discrediting the record which God has
therein given of his Son with respect to us in particular.

Q. What is the gospel-record God has given concerning
Christ?—A. That in him there is eternal life for sinners of
mankind, even the chief, 1 John v. 11, 1 Tim. i. 15.

Q. How are we to *appropriate* this divine record ?—A.
By believing that *in Christ, as offered to us, there is eternal
life for us in particular*, 1 Tim. i. 15.

Q. Wherein lieth the peculiar evil of unbelief?—A. It
disparageth all the persons of the adorable Trinity, vilifies
all the divine perfections as highly glorified in the work of
our redemption, and most eminently ruins the souls of
men, John xv. 22—24, Heb. iii.

Q. How doth unbelief disparage the divine persons ?—
A. It contemns the Father as the giver of Christ; tramples
on the blood and mediation of Christ, despising him as the
unspeakable gift of God; and resists the Holy Ghost in
the application of his grace, Isa. liii. 1, &c.

Q. How doth unbelief vilify the divine perfections as
manifested in the work of our redemption?—A. It practically calls God's wisdom *absolute folly*, his power *weakness*, his holiness *impurity*, his justice *iniquity*, his love *hatred*, his truth *deceit* and *falsehood*, 1 Cor. i. 23.

Q. Which divine perfection doth unbelief especially oppose and vilify?—A. Redeeming love, in the freedom and
greatness thereof; which shews it to be a most strange and
aggravated wickedness, John iii. 16—18.

Q. How doth unbelief ruin men ?—A. It gives strength
to their other sins, fixeth their guilt upon them, and binds
them over to distinguished and eternal vengeance.

Q. Is unbelief a single sin ?—A. No; it is a collection
of all the worst sins; Atheism, ignorance, idolatry, murder,
slander, blasphemy, &c., attended with many and great aggravations, John xv. 22—24, Heb. iii.

Q. How doth God destroy unbelief in his elect ?—A. By
shedding abroad his *matchless* love in their heart.

Q. What is the sin against the Holy Ghost ?—A. It is
unbelief aggravated to the highest degree; or it is a
known, wilful, malicious, and avowed blasphemy and re-

jection of Christ, and the whole plan of salvation through him, after conviction of his excellency by the common operation of the Spirit, Heb. 4—6, x. 26.

Q. Why is this sin called *the sin against the Holy Ghost?*—A. Because it is committed in direct opposition to the strivings of the Spirit of God, and the abundant evidence which he gives of the truth of the gospel, Heb x. 26—30.

Q. Can every man commit this sin?—A. No; Pagans, ignorant persons, and believers, cannot commit it.

Q. What may be a sure evidence to a distressed soul, that he has not committed this sin against the Holy Ghost? —A. If he is burthened with fears of its guilt and vileness, and desires salvation through the blood of Christ.

Q. Wherein do the sin against the Holy Ghost, and all other sins differ?—A. It is unpardonable, and they are not.

Q. Why is the sin against the Holy Ghost *unpardonable?*—A. Not for lack of mercy in God, or merit in Christ; but because this sin fully and finally rejects the Spirit's application of this mercy and merit, Heb. x. 26. 29.

Q. For what end hath God set up one sin *as unpardonable?*—A. To affright men from sinning against their light; as every sin against light is a step towards *this sin.*

Q. 84. *What doth every sin deserve?*

A. Every sin deserveth God's wrath and curse, both in this life, and that which is to come.

Q. What doth the very least sin deserve from God?—A. His wrath and curse, Rom. vi. 23. See Quest. 19.

Q. What is meant by sin's *deserving* God's wrath and curse?—A. Its being worthy of it, Rom. i. 32, vi. 23.

Q. Whence is it that every sin deserveth God's wrath and curse?—A. From sin's being the very opposite of the divine nature, and an infinite offence to God, Psalm v.

Q. When shall God's wrath and curse be executed?—A. In this life, and that which is to come.

Q. Do not greater sins deserve greater wrath?—A. Yes; and shall be punished accordingly.

Q. Is there any possibility of escaping this deserved wrath and curse of God?—A. Yes; by Christ alone.

Q. 85. *What doth God require of us, that we may escape his wrath and curse due to us for sin?*

A. To escape the wrath and curse of God due to us for sin, God requireth of us faith in Jesus Christ, repentance unto life, with the diligent use of all the outward means whereby Christ communicateth to us the benefits of redemption.

Q. Why are faith, repentance, &c. required of us?—A. Not to atone for our sin, or be the condition of our eternal happiness; but to be the means of receiving and improving the salvation which Christ hath obtained for us.

Q. How can our salvation be wholly of grace, when these things are required of us in order to our enjoyment of it?—A. Because though the law demand these things as our *duty*, yet Christ hath purchased, and, in the gospel, promiseth and bestows them as *free privileges* upon us.

Q. Why doth God require those things from us, when he knows we cannot perform them?—A. To shew us our duty, convince us of our weakness, and chiefly to excite us to embrace his gracious promise, that we may receive them from Christ as our *free privilege*, Gal. iv. 24.

Q. Why is faith placed *first* of the things required of us?—A. Because till we have faith, we can neither repent, nor rightly attend on Christ's ordinances, Rom. xiv. 23.

Q. How prove you that faith must be before repentance? —A. Christ says, *They shall look on me whom they have pierced, and shall mourn:* and till we by faith see God's love, we can never love him, nor turn from sin in him, Zech. xii. 10, Gal. v. 6, Ezek. xvi. 62, 63.

Q. Is there not a fear of God's wrath, and turning from gross sins, and erroneous notions, that may go before faith in Christ?—A. Yes; which is ordinarily called *legal repentance*, Acts ii. 37, and xvi. 30.

Q. Why is it called *legal repentance?*—A. Because the law as a covenant is the great mean of it, and it is found in many while they are under that law, Rom. vii. 9.

Q. How is faith in Jesus Christ necessary to our escaping God's wrath and curse?—A. It *alone* receives Christ, the *only* Saviour from sin and wrath, and all his salvation.

Q. How is repentance unto life connected with our escaping God's wrath and curse?—A. We therein improve salvation as an excitement to holiness; and Christ saves us *from*, not *in* our sins, Luke i. 74, 75.

Q. Why is the diligent use of Christ's ordinances necessary to our escaping God's wrath and curse?—A. Be-

cause in these ordinances salvation is offered and commu-
nicated to us; and by them faith and repentance are begotten and strengthened, Rom. x. 17, Prov. viii. 34.

Q. In what manner must these ordinances be used?—
A. They are to be used diligently, Acts xvi. 14.

Q. Why should we use Christ's external ordinances *diligently?*—A. Because our eternal salvation is so connected with the right use of them, Isa. lv. 1, 2, 3. 6, 7.

Q. Can we rightly use Christ's outward ordinances before our conversion?—A. By no means, Prov. xv. 8.

Q. Why should we then attend them before conversion?
—A. That we may there wait till Christ, who is often present in them, say to our souls, LIVE, Ezek. xvi. 6. 8.

Q. Hath God promised, that if graceless persons, with
natural seriousness, wait upon his ordinances, he will give
them saving grace?—A. No: however, he ordinarily, if
not always gives grace to such; and we may hope he will
give it to us likewise, Prov. viii. 17. 32, 33, 34.

Q. What is the danger of men's neglecting this diligent
use of God's ordinances?—A. Such study to place themselves without the reach of God's mercy; and though their
salvation is *possible,* yet *not probable,* Prov. viii. 34.

Q. Doth Christ bestow saving grace on diligent attend-
ers of his ordinances for their work's sake?—A. No: but
to put honour upon his own ordinances.

Q. What doth Christ communicate, or make over to sinners, by these ordinances?—A. All the benefits of redemption; such as regeneration, justification, adoption, and sanctification, a happy death, and eternal glory.

Q. 86. *What is faith in Jesus Christ?*
A. Faith in Jesus Christ is a saving grace, whereby we receive and rest upon him alone for salvation,
as he is offered to us in the gospel.

Q. Why is faith called *a grace?*—A. Because it beauti-
fies our soul, and is freely given by God to us.

Q. Why is it called *a saving* grace?—A. Because it interests us in Christ and his salvation.

Q Who is the alone author or worker of faith?—A.
God in Christ by the Holy Ghost, Eph. ii. 8.

Q. What is the general immediate object of faith?—A.
The whole word, especially the *promise* of God.

Q. Who is the peculiar mediate object of faith?—**A.** Christ in his person and offices, held forth in the word.

Q. Is not God also the object of faith?—**A.** Yes; by Christ we believe in God, 1 Pet. i. 21.

Q. What is the subject or seat of saving faith as a habit? —**A.** Our whole soul, mind, and will, Rom. x. 10.

Q. What is the work or exercise of saving faith?—**A.** Receiving and resting on Christ, John i. 12.

Q. Are receiving and resting on Christ two different things?—**A.** No; receiving is the beginning of resting and resting is the continuance of receiving.

Q. Wherein doth faith find and receive Christ?—**A.** In the free promise of the gospel, Rom. x. 6. 8.

Q. How do we by faith receive and rest on Christ as found in the promise?—**A.** By believing the promise to be true and good in itself, suited to our case, and to be accomplished to us in particular, 1 Tim. i. 15.

Q. Can faith, or any other grace, be so described, as to make graceless persons rightly understand what it is?—**A.** Though they may think and talk rationally of it; yet till they experience it, they never properly know it.

Q. Whether doth saving faith lie in assent or consent?— **A.** In both: for *with the* whole *heart man believeth.*

Q. What mean you by the *assent* of faith in Christ?— **A.** Its crediting the promises as true to us in particular.

Q. What mean you by the *consent* of faith in Christ?— **A.** The acquiescence of our heart in the method of salvation through Christ, as every way suited to our undone case, and embracing him as in the promise, to save us according to the riches of his grace, 1 Tim. i. 15.

Q. What are the best descriptions of the exercise of faith in Christ?—**A.** The scripture representation of it.

Q. How is faith in Christ represented in scripture?—**A.** As a persuasion, a looking, coming, running, fleeing, flying, and entering into Christ, a receiving and buying of him, a testing and leaning on him, a believing, trusting, living, dwelling, and walking in him, &c.

Q. Why is faith so variously represented in scripture? —**A.** To shew the extensive improvement which faith, as a habit, makes of Christ in his manifold relations to us.

Q. Why is faith represented as a *persuasion?*—**A.** Because it discerns and credits the absolute certainty and truth of God's word and promise, Heb. xi. 13.

Q. Why is faith called a *looking* to Christ?—**A.** Because it views him as a most glorious object, Isa. xlv. 22.

Q. Why is faith called a *coming* to Christ?—**A.** Because by it we leave our natural state, and come to Christ as our glorious friend and home, Matth. xi. 28.

Q. Why is faith called a *running* to Christ?—**A.** Because by it we come to him quickly, and with all our might, Prov. xviii. 10, Isa. xl. 31.

Q. Why is faith called a *fleeing* to Christ?—**A.** Because by it we, as men pursued, escape for our life to Christ as our saviour and hiding-place, Heb. vi. 19.

Q. From what pursuers do we flee to Christ?—**A.** From God's avenging justice, a broken law, raging lusts, a malicious devil, and an ensnaring world.

Q. Why is faith called a *flying* to Christ?—**A.** Because by it we, through supernatural influence, come swiftly to Christ as a Prince exalted, and rock higher than we, Isa. lx. 8.

Q. Why is faith called an *entering*?—**A.** Because it brings us to salvation through Christ as the door, John x.

Q. Why is faith called a *receiving* of Christ?—**A.** Because it takes hold of him as God's great gift, John i.

Q. Why is faith called a *buying* of Christ?—**A.** Because by it we deliberately receive him as our enriching portion, and glorious ornament, Rev. iii. 18.

Q. With what price does faith buy Christ?—**A.** It buys him without money and without price, Isa. lv. 1.

Q. How doth it this?—**A.** As in receiving Christ, we neither offer, give, nor promise any price for him.

Q. Do not we by faith give up ourselves to Christ *as a price*?—**A.** No: we only give up ourselves to him as monsters of guilt and pollution, to be freely pardoned, purged, and saved by him, 1 Tim. i. 15. Isa. i. 18.

Q. Why is faith called a *putting on* Christ.—**A.** Because by it we apply him as our glorious robe of righteousness, and sanctifying head, Rom. xiii. 14.

Q. Why is faith called a *resting* on Christ?—**A.** Because it lays down our weary soul on Christ as a resting-place; and lays the whole burden of our salvation upon the sure foundation of his person and offices, as exhibited in the firm charter of his promise, Psalm xxxvii. 7.

Q. With what is our soul naturally wearied?—**A.** With the labour of wickedness and vanity, or legal fears of God's wrath, Matth. xi. 28. Ezek. xxiv. 12.

Q. Why is faith called a *leaning* on Christ?—A. Because thereby we, as weak in ourselves, depend on Christ as our staff, stay, and supporting friend, Song viii. 5.

Q. Why is faith called a *believing* IN Christ?—A. Because it not only credits what he says, but receives himself upon his word, Heb. xi. 13. Gal. ii. 16.

Q. Why is faith called a *trusting* in Christ?—A. Because it removes doubts of his ability and willingness to save, and fears of his not performing his promise, Eph. i. 12.

Q. Is there no doubting in faith?—A. There is no doubting in the nature of faith, but great doubting is often mixed with faith in our heart, Matt. xiv. 31.

Q. Why is faith called a *living* in or on Christ?—A. Because it daily improves him as our spiritual food, and living and life-giving head, Gal. ii. 20.

Q. Why is faith called a *dwelling* in God or Christ?—A. Because by it we abide in and with God in Christ as our sure habitation, Psalm xc. 1. and xci. 1.

Q. Why is faith called *walking* in and with Christ?—A. Because it makes use of him as our way, guide, and sweet companion, in bringing us to God and glory, Col. ii. 6.

Q. Why is faith called a *waiting* on Christ?—A. Because it always expects nearer access to, and greater blessings from Christ; than we have yet received, Psalm lxii.

Q. Why is faith called a *yielding* to God, and *submiting* to his righteousness?—A. Because by it we humbly give up ourselves to God, that, through Christ's righteousness, he may give us his promised blessings.

Q. Why is faith called a *hungering* and *thirsting?*—A. Because it begets in our soul a painful desire that nothing but Christ and his righteousness can satisfy.

Q. Why is faith called an *eating* the flesh, and *drinking* the blood of Christ?—A. Because with desire and delight it receives and lives on Christ in his person, natures, office, relations, and righteousness, John vi. 32—37.

Q. How is saving faith distinguished in its degrees?—A. Into a weak and strong faith, Matth. viii. 10.

Q. What are the signs of weak faith?—A. Much carnal fear and care about this world, sinful haste to avoid danger, quitting former confidence, and staggering at God's promise, when we meet with temptation, desertion, or other cross providences, Matth. vi. 30. & xiv. 31.

Q. How may weak believers know they have any faith?
—**A.** If their weakness in faith be their heavy burden.

Q. What are the causes of weakness in faith?—**A.**
Carnal security, neglect to exercise faith, much remaining
ignorance of Christ, quenching of the Spirit, careless improvement of divine ordinances, &c.

Q. What are the evidences of strong faith?—**A.** Much
undervaluing of self-righteousness; crediting God's promise when providence seems to contradict it; refusing to
doubt of his love when he hides his face and smites us;
and earnest study to have the loss of created comforts made
up in God himself, Job xiii. 15, Rom. iv. 19, 20.

Q. What are the advantages of strong faith?—**A.** It
brings much glory to God, and good to our soul.

Q. How doth strong faith give much glory to God?—**A.**
As it refuseth to doubt of his love, wisdom, power, and
faithfulness, even when his providence seems to countenance such doubts, Job xiii. 15, Rom. iv. 19, 20.

Q. How doth strong faith do much good to our soul?—
A. It keeps it quiet and easy under trouble, makes us bold
in approaching to God, fills our heart with spiritual joy, and
strongly disposeth us to duty, Isa. xxviii. 16.

Q. Is faith rightly distinguished into a faith of reliance
and a faith of assurance?—**A.** No; the reliance and assurance of faith are properly one and the same.

Q. What is meant by the *full assurance* of faith?—**A.**
Faith's prevalency over unbelief, by which it either contemns or excludes doubting, Heb. x. 22.

Q. When doth faith contemn the doubts of unbelief?—
A. When Christ's glory is clearly manifested to our soul.

Q. When doth faith perfectly exclude doubting?—**A.**
The moment in which it is swallowed up in vision.

Q. What are the properties of saving faith?—**A.** It is an
humble, precious, and useful grace.

Q. Wherein doth its *humility* appear?—**A.** It brings
nothing to God but guilt and sin to be taken away, and re-
ceiveth Christ for our all in all, Phil. iii. 8, 9.

Q. How is faith *precious*?—**A.** As it believes precious
promises, receives a precious Christ, saves our precious
souls, and makes us precious saints, 2 Pet. i. 1.

Q. How is faith a most *useful* grace?—**A.** It is our
spiritual hand to receive Christ, arms to embrace him,
mouth to feed on him, eyes to behold his beauty, ears to

hear his voice, feet and wings to carry us to him, and neck to unite us with him, &c. Song iv. vii. &c.

Q. How is it that we live by faith?—A. As we by it daily depend on Christ as our resurrection and our life.

Q. How is faith a *shield* to us?—A. It places the power, wisdom, and love of God, and the righteousness of Christ, between us and all danger, Eph. vi. 16.

Q. How is faith our *victory?*—A. It employs the power of Christ to slay all our spiritual enemies, 1 John v. 4.

Q. How doth faith work all its great work in us?—A By doing nothing of itself, but employing God in Christ to do all in and for us, Isa. xxvi. 12, Phil. ii. 13.

Q. What is the ground and foundation of our faith?— A. The boundless power, faithfulness, and love of God, through the infinite merit of Christ, as endorsed and made over to us by his word and oath, Heb. vi. 18.

Q. What are the marks of true faith?—A. Poverty in spirit, purity in heart, love to God and man, and a regard to the whole law of God, Matth. v. 3—10.

Q. Doth faith ever evidence its own reality?—A. Yes; a vigorous act of faith will convince us of its reality and saving nature, as much as any marks of it.

Q. What then is the best way to recover lost evidences of faith?—A. Vigorously to renew our acts of faith on some promises applicable to the chief of sinners.

Q. Why ought the promise believed on to be so extensive?—A. Because otherwise unbelief will deter us from laying hold on it, Luke xxiv. 25.

Q. For what doth saving faith receive and rest on Christ? —A. For salvation, Gal. ii. 16, Isa. xlv. 22.

Q. For what kind of salvation doth faith rest on Christ? —A. A great, sure, well-ordered, and eternal salvation.

Q. How is it a *great* salvation?—A. It springs from God's great love, was bought with a great price, and saves us from the greatest evil to the highest happiness.

Q. From what great evil doth this salvation free us!— A. From the filth, guilt, and power of sin; and from Satan, the world, death, and hell, Ezek. xxxvi.

Q. To what great happiness does salvation bring us?— A. To grace and glory, nay, *to God* himself, Rev. v.

Q. For what salvation doth faith receive Christ as a prophet?—A. For salvation from ignorance and blindness, to spiritual knowledge and light, Isa. lx. 1.

Q. For what salvation doth it receive him as a priest?— 25*

A. For salvation from sin's guilt, and God's abhorrence of us and our works, to perfect righteousness in Christ, and divine acceptance of our persons and duties in him, 2 Cor. v. 21, Eph. i. 6, Rom. iii. 24, 25, Gal. ii. 16.

Q. For what doth faith receive Christ as a King?—**A.** For salvation from bondage, disorder, danger, and death; to life, liberty, order, and safety, Ezek. xxxi. 25.

Q. For what salvation doth faith receive Christ in his natures and relations?—**A.** Not for any other branches of salvation but for sweetening and enhancing the salvation flowing from his offices, Psal. xvi. and xxiii. 1—6.

Q. In what manner doth faith receive and rest on Christ for salvation?—**A.** It receives and rests on him ALONE.

Q. Why on him ALONE?—**A.** Because there is no salvation in any other besides him, Isa. xlv. 22, Acts iv. 12.

Q. Must we then, in receiving Christ, renounce and contemn all we think good in ourselves?—**A.** Yes.

Q. What must we renounce in receiving Christ as our prophet?—**A.** Our own wisdom and knowledge, as ignorance and folly, 1 Cor. iii. 18, Prov. xxx. 2, 3.

Q. What must we renounce in receiving him as our priest?—**A.** Our own righteousness as filthy rags.

Q. What must we renounce in receiving him as our king?—**A.** Our own strength, will and pleasure.

Q. What must we renounce in receiving God in Christ as our portion?—**A.** Our *all*, as loss and dung, to win him.

Q. May we not rest on our good works as a mean of recommending us to Christ as a Saviour?—**A.** No; we must come to Christ as our Redeemer and physician, as every way lost and diseased in ourselves, 1 Tim. i. 15.

Q. Must we turn from sin in order to come to Christ by faith?—**A.** We cannot do so; and to essay it, is a robbing Christ of his *distinguished* honour, 1 John iii. 18.

Q. Why so?—**A.** Because God hath appointed Christ ALONE, not us, to be the Saviour from sin, Matth. i. 21.

Q. Could Christ save us, if we were turned from sin before we came to him?—**A.** No; Christ is sent *only* to save lost and ungodly sinners; nor could persons turned from sin receive the chief branch of his salvation, viz. deliverance from sin, Luke xix. 10, Matth. ix. 13.

Q. Are we then to come to Christ with resolutions to continue in sin?—**A.** No; that is blasphemous and impossible, as Christ is infinitely holy, and saves from sin.

Q. In what form then must we come to Christ?—A. As guilty and vile sinners, to be turned from sin by him.

Q. Can we come to Christ of ourselves?—A. No; the Father must draw us; and *faith is the gift of God*.

Q. What then must we do?—A. Pray for the drawing power and Spirit of God, to work faith in us, and wait for his coming in the ordinances of his grace. See Quest. 31.

Q. 87. *What is repentance unto life?*

A. Repentance unto life is a saving grace, whereby a sinner out of a true sense of his sin, and apprehension of the mercy of God in Christ, doth, with grief and hatred of his sin, turn from it unto God, with full purpose of, and endeavour after new obedience.

Q. Why is this mean of salvation called *repentance unto life?*—A. Because it proceeds from, and is an evidence of spiritual life, and issueth in eternal life.

Q. Is there any repentance unto death?—A. Yes; the sorrow of this world, and legal repentance.

Q. What call you the *sorrow of this world?*—A. Excessive vexation and grief on account of worldly losses and disappointments, Judges xviii. 24.

Q. How doth this work death?—A. It wastes our bodies wounds our souls, and tempts to self-murder.

Q. What is *legal repentance?*—A. That fear, grief, and reformation from sin which an unbeliever may have.

Q. Wherein do legal and gospel repentance differ?—A. In their order, cause, object, and fruits.

Q. How do they differ in their *order?*—A. Legal repentance goeth before faith in Christ, gospel repentance (or repentance unto life) follows after it, Zech. xii. 10.

Q. How do they differ in their *cause?*—A. Legal repentance flows from the view of God's justice and wrath in his threatenings and judgments; but repentance unto life flows from the view of God's holiness and love manifested in the death of Christ, and precept of the law.

Q. How do they differ in their *object?*—A. In legal repentance, we are affected chiefly with the guilt of sin, and with gross sins; but in repentance unto life, we are affected chiefly with the filth of sin, the dishonour done to God by it, and with secret and beloved sins, Gen. iv.

Q. How do they differ in their *fruits?*—A. Legal repentance turneth us only from some acts of sin, and worketh death; but repentance unto life turneth us from the love of every sin, and leads to eternal life, 1 Kings xxi. 27.

Q. How doth legal repentance work death?—**A.** It irritates lust, fills us with wrath against God because of his justice and holiness, and promotes self-murder.

Q. Why is repentance unto life called *a grace*?—**A.** It is God's *free* gift, and our *beautiful* ornament.

Q. Why is gospel-repentance called *a saving grace*?—**A.** Because it is an evidence and part of begun salvation, and makes us meet for perfect salvation.

Q. Why is repentance so often joined with faith in scripture?—**A.** Because it inseparably flows from, and attends faith in Jesus Christ, Zech. ii. 10, 1 Tim. i. 5.

Q. Hath it the same hand with faith in our salvation?—**A.** No; it doth receive salvation as faith doth.

Q. Who are the subjects of gospel-repentance?—**A.** Every sinner ought to repent; but only believing sinners do, or can truly repent, Zech. xii. 10.

Q. Who is the author of saving repentance?—**A.** God in Christ by the Holy Spirit, Acts v. 31.

Q. What is the instrumental cause of repentance?—**A.** God's providence, but *especially his word.*

Q. In how many things doth gospel-repentance consist? —**A.** Five, viz. a sense of sin, an apprehension of God's mercy; grief for, hatred of, and turning from sin.

Q. What call you a *sense* of sin?—**A.** A heart affecting view of it in its nature, number, and aggravations.

Q. Why is this necessary in true repentance?—**A.** To make our soul sick and weary of sin, Jer. xiii. 27.

Q. How is this true sense of sin produced?—**A.** By the convictions of God's Spirit, John xvi. 8.

Q. What do you mean by an *apprehension* of the mercy of God in Christ?—**A.** A sight of him as merciful in pardoning our sins, and saving our souls through Christ.

Q. How is the affecting apprehension of God's mercy produced?—**A.** By the Spirit's enlightening our mind in the knowledge of Christ and his mediation, Gal. i. 16.

Q. Why is it necessary in repentance?—**A.** To melt our heart for sin, and keep us from despair.

Q. What is *grief* for sin?—**A.** Our sorrowing for sin, as it dishonours God, defiles and wounds our own soul, and the souls of others, Psalm li. 4—17.

Q. What doth most powerfully excite true grief for sin? —**A.** A believing view of Christ in his sufferings.

Q. How doth this view excite true grief for sin?—A. As in the death of Christ we clearly see the greatness of that divine love against which sin is committed, and the greatness of God's indignation at our sin.

Q. How doth the view of the greatness of God's love, which appears in Christ's death, excite grief for sin?—A. It fills us with indignation and shame, that we have rendered unto God *hatred* for such *astonishing love*.

Q. How doth the view of God's indignation against sin, which appears in Christ's death, excite grief for sin?—A. It fills us with shame and sorrow, that we have delighted so much in that abominable thing which God so hateth, as to punish it with the death of his Son.

Q. What are the properties of true grief for sin?—A. It is a godly, kindly, universal, proportionate, and superlative grief and sorrow, 2 Cor. vii. 10, 11.

Q. How is it a *godly* sorrow?—A. As sin is sorrowed for *chiefly* as against God, Psalm li. 4.

Q. How is it a *kindly* grief?—A. It flows from our love to God, and the faith of his love to us, 1 John iv. 19.

Q. How is it *universal* grief?—A. As we grieve for all known sins with our whole heart, Psalm xv. 17.

Q. How is it *proportionate* grief?—A. As we grieve most for our greatest sins, as original sin, unbelief, and beloved lusts, Psal. li. 3. 5, Rom. vii. 14—24.

Q. How is it *superlative* grief?—A. As we are more grieved for sin than for afflictions, Rom. vii. 24.

Q. Is true grief for sin always sensibly greater than grief for afflictions?—A. No, but it is more deep and lasting, as it continues while we live, Psalm li. 3.

Q. Must tears always attend true grief for sin?—A. Many have tears for sin without true grief, and some may have true grief for sin without tears.

Q. Why is grief for sin necessary in repentance?—A. To make our soul willing to leave sin, Job xlii. 5, 6.

Q. What is *hatred* of sin?—A. A dislike and abhorrence of it, and loathing ourselves for it.

Q. What chiefly excites us to the true hatred of sin?— A. A view of Christ as crucified *for us*, Zech. xii. 10.

Q. How doth the view of this, as the greatest evidence of God's love, stir up hatred of sin?—A. It makes us hate sin as the murderer of God's *dear Son*, and our best friend, Zech. xii. 10, Acts ii. 36, 37.

Q. How doth the view of Christ's death, as the greatest

evidence of God's indignation at sin, excite hatred of it?—
A. It makes us to hate sin because God hates it; and, as
far as possible, as God hates it, Psalm cxxxix. 22, 23.

Q. What are the properties of true hatred of sin?—A.
It is a *gracious hatred*, flowing from love to God; an *universal* hatred of all sin, at all times; a *proportionate* hatred, chiefly bended against our greatest sins; a *superlative* hatred of sin above any other thing; a *self-loathing* hatred, whereby we loath and abhor ourselves as the rest and lodging of sin, Psalm xcvii. 10, and cxix. 104.

Q. Is it not also a *perfect* hatred?—A. Yes, as therein we desire to hate sin with all our heart, and are grieved that any love to sin should remain in us; and it is hatred which cannot admit of reconciliation with sin.

Q. Why is hatred of sin necessary in true repentance?
—A. To make our soul turn from, and war against it.

Q. What do you understand by *turning* from sin?—A. Our leaving the practice of gross sins, and ceasing from the love of every sin, Psalm cxix. 49, Isa. i. 16.

Q. Can we return to these gross sins of which we have truly repented?—A. We cannot return to a course of such sins, nor live always hardened in them, 1 John iii. 9.

Q. To whom do we turn, in leaving the pleasures and service of sin?—A. To God as our Lord and Portion.

Q. Is turning from the pleasures and service of sin different from our turning to God?—A. No; every step we turn from sin is a step towards God, Hos. xiv. 1.

Q. What is the cause of our turning from sin to God?—
A. God's almighty love drawing our heart, Hos. xi. 4.

Q. Can then any graceless man turn from sin?—A. He may turn from the outward practice of some gross sins, but cannot turn from the love of any sin.

Q. In what manner do true penitents turn from sin to God?—*Humbly*, with a deep sense, and free confession of their sin; *universally*, from all sins with their whole heart; and *heartily*, from love to God, with full purpose of heart, and endeavour after new obedience.

Q. What mean you by turning from sin to God with a full purpose of heart?—A. Our fixed resolution of heart to war against and mortify sin, and obey God more and more, in spite of all opposition, Phil. iii. 14.

Q. Are true penitents often turned out of their designed path?—A. Yes; but never from their fixed purpose against sin, Jer. xxxii. 40, Psalm xlviii. 5, and cxix. 100.

Q. How is our full purpose of heart against sin evidenced?—A. By our endeavour after new obedience to the law of God, Psalm cxix. 5, 2 Cor. vii. 1, Heb. xii. 28.

Q. Why is this obedience called *new*?—A. Because it proceeds from a new *principle*, is influenced by new *motives*, directed by a new *rule*, and managed in a new *manner* to a new *end*, Ezek. xxxvi. 26, 27.

Q. How doth it proceed from a *new principle*?—A. It proceeds from a new heart united to Christ, and not from the old corrupt heart, Matth. vii. 17, Luke viii. 15.

Q. How is this obedience influenced by *new motives*?—A. It is influenced by the authority of God, and his love in Christ shed abroad in our hearts; not by the old motives of the fear or favour of men, or legal fear of God's wrath, or hope of his favour, 1 John iv. 19, and v. 2.

Q. How is it directed by a *new rule*?—A. It is directed by the law as a rule of life; not by the law as a covenant, and our own inclination, 1 Cor. ix. 21.

Q. How is this obedience *new* in its *end*?—A. Its end is the glory of God, not self-interest and applause.

Q. What are the properties (or manner) of this new obedience?—A. It is *sincere*, as therein we study to be in reality what we appear: *spiritual*, as all the powers of our soul are employed in it with holy fear and delight: *constant*, as we walk habitually in the ways of God as long as we live: *humble*, as, after we have done all, we count ourselves *unprofitable servants:* and *universal*, as we study conformity to the whole law of God, in thought, word, and deed.

Q. What are the marks of repentance unto life?—A. A careful desire to avoid, and be rid of sin; a humble, free, and ingenuous confession of it; and a holy revenge on it, in cutting short our lusts of their wonted provision, 2 Cor. vii. 11, Psal. li., Rom. vii. 14—24.

Q. For what reasons should we repent of our sin?—A. God's mercies and judgments call us to it; his command, and our baptismal, and other engagements, bind us to it; and except we repent, we shall surely perish.

Q. When ought we to repent of our sin?—A. Immediately without delay; for the present day may be our last; and every day's continuance in sin is a re-acting of our former sins, hardens our heart, and may provoke God to deny us grace to repent, Psal. cxix. 59, 60.

Q. Is the repentance of the thief on the cross any encouragement to delay repentance till our last moments?—

A. No; for it is but an instance of such late repentance; and that in a man who perhaps never heard of Christ before; and at such a time as the like never was, nor will be; namely, when Christ triumphed over Satan on the cross, Luke xxiii. 40—43.

Q. Can we truly repent of ourselves?—A. No.

Q. What then should we do to obtain repentance?—A. Carfully consider our sins, and the sufferings of Christ, and cry, that, as a Prince exalted to give repentance, he may turn us, and we shall be turned, Isa. lv. 7.

Q. 88. *What are the outward means whereby Christ communicateth to us the benefits of redemption?*

A. The outward and ordinary means, whereby Christ communicateth to us the benefits of redemption, are his ordinances, especially the word, sacraments, and prayer; all which are made effectual to the elect for salvation.

Q. Why are the outward means of salvation called *Christ's ordinances?*—A. Because he appointed them as the King and Prophet of his church, Eph. iv. 11, 12, 13.

Q. What is the general property of all the ordinances of Christ?—A. They are *holy* ordinances, Ezek. xliii. 12.

Q. How are they *holy?*—A. They are pure in themselves, appointed for the service of the holy God, and to make us pure and holy, Eph. iv. 12, 13. Prov. viii. 34.

Q. Why are Christ's ordinances called *outward means of salvation?*—A. To distinguish them from the Spirit and his grace, which are inward means of it, John iii. 5, 6.

Q. Why are they called *ordinary means?*—A. Because God seldom conveys grace to adult persons, without the use of them, Acts ix. &c.

Q. What ordinances of Christ are the principal outward and ordinary means of salvation?—A. The word, sacraments, and prayer, Acts ii. 42.

Q. When doth Christ communicate his benefits by his ordinances?—A. When they are made effectual for our salvation, Acts ii. 46, 47. Rom. i. 16. 1 Thess ii. 13.

Q. What do you mean by the ordinances being made effectual to salvation?—A. Their being made means not only of revealing and offering salvation, but of giving the real possession of it to us, Eph. i. 13, 14.

Q. To whom are Christ's ordinances made effectual for salvation ?—**A.** To the elect *only*, Acts xiii. 48.

Q. Why are they not effectual to others ?—**A.** Because divine power doth not attend them to others.

Q. Why then should persons not elected wait upon any of Christ's ordinances ?—**A.** God commands it ; and they know not but they are elected, Prov. viii. 34.

Q. Do the word sacraments, and prayer, equally respect the graceless and gracious state of elect persons ?—**A.** No : the word and prayer respect both states ; but the sacraments respect *only* their gracious state.

Q. How doth it appear that the word and prayer respect both states ?—**A.** Because they are means of bringing us out of a graceless state, and of confirming us in a gracious state, Acts viii. Eph. i. 13, and vi. 17, 18.

Q. How doth it appear, that the sacraments respect only our gracious state ?—**A.** Because they are seals for confirming God's covenant with us, and suppose our entrance into it, Rom. iv. 11.

Q. By what are God's ordinances made effectual to our salvation ?—**A.** By the blessing of Christ, and the working of his Spirit in us, I Thess. i: 5. 1 Cor. iii.

Q. What do you mean by the *blessing* of Christ on ordinances ?—**A.** His institution of them for our salvation, and his saving power attending them.

Q. What mean you by the *working* of Christ's Spirit ? —**A.** His graciously applying the ordinances to our heart, and making us to see and receive Christ in them, 1 Thess. i. 5.

Q. Do Christ's ordinances become effectual in any degree, from any virtue in themselves ?—**A.** No : for the scripture declares, *the word preached did not profit ;* and that it is to some *savour of death :* and daily experience shews, that the persons may receive all these ordinances, and yet be openly wicked, Heb. iv. 2, Isa. vi. 9, 10.

Q. Can the holiness, learning, or diligence of him that doth administer any of these ordinances make them effectual to salvation ?—**A.** No ; few even of Christ's hearers were converted ; and Paul may plant and Apollos water, but it is God that giveth the increase, 1 Cor. iii. 22.

Q. May we then be careless who preach the word, and administer the sacraments to us ?—**A.** No ; for the administration of them in an irregular manner, and by persons

26

unqualified and unsent, tends to prevent the efficacy of them, Jer. xxiii. 32, Rom. x. 14, 15, Heb. v. 4.

Q. How ought the dispensers of word and sacraments to be personally qualified?—**A.** They ought to be blameless, acquainted with God's truths, zealous for them, and able to defend and declare them to others, Titus i., 1 Tim. iii.

Q. How ought they to be called to their office?—**A.** With inward and outward call of God.

Q. Wherein lieth the *inward call* of God?—**A.** It ordinarily consists in a person's being humbly inclined, from love to the glory of God, and compassion to the souls of men, to bestow his gifts in the ministerial work, if God in his providence give regular access.

Q. What is God's ordinary *outward call* to the ministry? —**A.** The invitation or consent of the Christian people to whom he is to minister; with the trial of his gifts, and ordination by a presbytery, Acts xiv. 23, 1 Tim. iv. 14.

Q. How is the word to be preached by such as are duly qualified and called thereto?—**A.** Soundly, sincerely, plainly, diligently, wisely, faithfully, and zealously.

Q. How is a minister to preach *soundly?*—**A.** By preaching nothing but what is founded on the word of God.

Q. How is he to preach *sincerely?*—**A.** By preaching from faith, not for filthy lucre, but the glory of God, and good of men; and by insisting chiefly on the most important subjects, as Christ's excellency, our need of him, the beauty and necessity of holiness, &c., 1 Cor. ii., iii.

Q. How is he to preach *plainly?*—**A.** By using such words, arguments, and order, as his hearers can best understand, and which tend most to affect their conscience.

Q. How is he to preach *diligently?*—By embracing all opportunities of preaching or preparing for it.

Q. How is he to preach *faithfully?*—**A.** By giving saints and sinners their due portion; preaching against the sins of his hearers, without respect of persons; and preaching law and gospel, in such a manner as tends to honour both, Mat. xxii., xxiv., Ezek. iii., xxxiii., Col. i. 28.

Q. How is he to preach *wisely?*—**A.** By suiting his doctrine to the present cases and capacity of his hearers.

Q. How is he to preach *zealously?*—**A.** By preaching from fervent love to God and the souls of men, manifested in a grave and affectionate address to the hearers.

Q. 89. *How is the word made effectual to salvation?*

A. The Spirit of God maketh the reading, but especially the preaching of the word, an effectual means of convincing and converting sinners, and of building them up in holiness and comfort, through faith, unto salvation.

Q. Who makes the word effectual for our salvation?—A. The holy Spirit of God, 1 Thess. i. 5, and ii. 13.

Q. What of the word doth the Spirit make effectual for our salvation?—A. Both the reading and the preaching of the word, but *especially the preaching of it*, Rom. x. 17.

Q. Why doth God especially make the preaching of the word effectual?—A. To maintain the honour of that ordinance, the attendance upon which is most difficult; and which includes a more open testimony for Christ, in opposition to the visible kingdom of Satan, Rom. x. 15—17.

Q. Of what use is the reading and preaching of the word to elect sinners?—A. It is an effectual means of convincing and converting them, Rom. i. and iii., Heb. iv. 12.

Q. How is the word of God a means of conviction?—A. It shews what is sinful, and what is the nature, aggravations, and wages of sin, Rom. iii.

Q. How is the word a mean of converting sinners?—A. It shews why, from what, and to what we should turn; and by it the Spirit of God conveys his converting grace, or the new nature into our heart. See Quest. 31.

Q. Of what use is the reading and preaching of the word to the elect after conversion?—A. It is an effectual means of *building them up in holiness and comfort.*

Q. What is that holiness in which they are built up?—A. Their sanctification of nature and life.

Q. What is that comfort in which they are built up?—A. Assurance of God's love, peace of conscience, and joy in the Holy Ghost. See Quest 35, 36.

Q. Upon what foundation is this holiness and comfort built?—A. On Christ as our portion, righteousness, and strength; and upon God, in his perfections and promises, as made ours in Christ, Isa. xxviii. 16, 1 Cor. iii. 11.

Q. What is meant by building up saints in holiness and

comfort ?—A. It is to make them increase and abound in holiness and comfort, Prov. iv. 18, 2 Peter iii. 18.

Q. How is the word a mean of building us up in holiness?—A. It shews us what is our duty, with the nature, pattern, and motives of holiness; it condemns all impurity; discovers errors, corruptions, and temptations; and fortifies against them, by the Spirit's conveying his sanctifying influences into our heart, John xvii. 17.

Q. How doth the word build up saints in comfort?—A. It reveals the strongest grounds of comfort, such as promises of pardon and eternal life; and by it the love of God is shed abroad in our heart, Psalm cxix. 49, 50.

Q. To what height are we by the word built up in holiness and comfort?—A. Unto complete salvation.

Q. Through what doth the word of God build us up in holiness and comfort?—A. Through faith.

Q. How is it through faith that the word becomes effectual or four salvation?—A. As by faith we receive the word in its convincing, converting, sanctifying, and comforting influence, into our heart, Acts xv. 9, Heb. iv. 2.

Q. Why is the word of God compared to a hammer, fire, light, rain, and milk?—A. As a *hammer*, it breaks; as a *fire*, it melts and purges; as *light*, it instructs; as *rain*, *dew*, or *water*, it refreshes and fructifies; and as *milk*, it restores and nourisheth our heart, Jer. xxiii. 29.

Q. 90. *How is the word to be read and heard, that it may become effectual to salvation?*

A. That the word may become effectual to salvation, we must attend thereunto with diligence, preparation, and prayer; receive it with faith and love; lay it up in our hearts, and practice it in our lives.

Q. Who ought to read and hear the word of God?—A. All men ought to read and hear it, John v. 39, Isa. lv.

Q. How prove you, that all men should read God's word?—A. God commands us to read it, commends for reading it, and caused it to be written in the language of his church in the time it was revealed, Acts xvii. 11.

Q. What is the fruit of ignorance of the scriptures?—A. Manifold errors, and eternal destruction.

Q. How often should we read the Scriptures?—A. Daily, both in secret, and in our families.

Q. Is it not enough if we read the Scriptures only on

Sabbath?—A. No; this is a dismal token of Satan's still blinding our minds, that we see not the excellency of Christ, and wonders of his law, 2 Cor. iv. 4.

Q. Is it not very scandalous for gospel-hearers to be unacquainted with the Scriptures?—A. Yes; as scandalous in itself as gross immoralities of life, Isa. xxvii. 11.

Q. How are we to read and hear God's word, that it may be effectual for our salvation?—A. In preparing for, receiving, and improving the word, read or heard.

Q. How should we prepare ourselves for reading or hearing the word of God?—A. By meditation, self-examination, and prayer, Psalm cxix. 18. 97, 2 Cor. xiii. 5.

Q. On what should we meditate before reading or hearing the word of God?—A. On the greatness and goodness of God its author; on its own excellency, stability, and fulness; on the excellency of Christ, the matter and confirmer of it; and on our vileness, &c. Psalm xlv. 1.

Q. Why is this necessary?—A. To make us read and hear the word with faith, love, humility, and thankfulness.

Q. Concerning what are we to examine ourselves before reading and hearing the word of God?—A. Concerning our state, and our present condition, Lam. iii. 40.

Q. Why is this necessary?—A. That we may, with knowledge and care, apply whatever suits our case.

Q. For what are we to pray before hearing the word?—A. That God would assist the minister, and by him send a fit message to us, applying it with power to ourselves and fit message to us, applying it with power to ourselves and others, Col. iv. 3, 4, Psalm cxix. 18.

Q. Why is prayer necessary before reading and hearing the word?—A. To enlarge our hearts for, and bring the promised blessings into them, Psalm lxxi. 10.

Q. How ought we to receive the word while reading or hearing it?—A. With great attention, reverence, faith and love, Psalm lxxxix. 7, 1 Thess. i. 5, ii. 13.

Q. How must we read and hear with great attention?—A. By careful listening to, and pondering every sentence as we read or hear it, Acts xvi. 14, Isa. lii. 3.

Q. Why is such attention necessary?—A. Because what we read or hear is the truth of God on which our eternal happiness or misery depends, Heb. ii. 1. 3.

Q. Why must we hear the word with great reverence?—A. Because God himself is present in his word.

Q. How must we read, hear, and receive the word with

26*

faith?—A. By believing every divine truth, as, in one respect or other, spoken by God to us, Heb. xi. 13.

Q. Is faith to be exercised in the very same manner towards all the parts of God's word?—A. No; its exercise is to be varied according to the matter read or heard, whether promises or threatenings, &c.

Q. How is our faith to receive the promises of God?—A. In believing that all the blessings lodged in them are made over to us, and shall be given us in due time.

Q. How is our faith to receive scripture threatenings?—A. By believing, that the wrath contained in them is due to our sin, and shall overtake us if we continue in it.

Q. How is our faith to receive scripture prophecies?—A. By crediting the accomplishment of the events foretold, and preparing us for them, Luke i. 25.

Q. How is our faith to receive scripture-doctrines?—A. In embracing them as true, wonderful, holy, and full of grace and mercy to man, 2 Tim. i. 13. 15, 16.

Q. How is our faith to receive scripture precepts?—A. In discerning their holiness and equity, and believing their obligation upon us, and our mournful defects in obedience, Psal. xix. 7—19, Isa. vi. 5, Rom. vii. 14.

Q. How is our faith to receive scripture histories?—A. In crediting them as true, and discerning them as evidences of the truth and holiness of the promises, threatenings, doctrines, precepts, or prophecies; and as encouragements to improve them, Rom. xv. 4, Heb. xi. 13.

Q. Why is faith necessary in reading and hearing the word of God?—A. Because without faith we constantly make God a *liar*, and render his word a *savour of death* to ourselves, 1 John v. 11, Heb. iv. 2.

Q. With what love must we read and hear the word of God?—A. With an ardent love to it *as the word of God*, and mean of our salvation, Psal. cxix. 97.

Q. How must our love to God's word manifest itself?—A. In our esteeming, desiring, and delighting in it, more than in any worldly good thing, Psal. xix. and cxix.

Q. Why is love to the word of God necessary in reading and hearing it?—A. Because of its author, excellencies, and usefulness; and that it may be kindly received into our heart, Acts xiii. 48, 1 Thess. ii. 13.

Q. How are we to improve the word of God when read or heard?—A. By laying it up in our hearts, and practising it in our lives, Psal. cxix. 11. 34, Col. iii. 16.

Q. What is meant by *laying up* the word of God in *our heart?*—A. The laying it up in our memory by remembering it, in our mind by the knowledge of it, and in our will and affections by the constant love of it, Col. iii. 16.

Q. Why is it necessary to lay up God's word in our heart?—A. That we may practise it in our life.

Q. What is meant by *practising* God's word in our life? —A. The daily improvement of it for direction in, excitement and encouragement to our duty, Psal. cxix.

Q. How are scripture promises to be reduced to practice?—A. In our drawing strength and encouragement to our duty from them, 2 Cor. vii. 1 Heb. xii. 28.

Q. How are scripture-threatenings to be reduced to practice?—A. In our standing in awe to sin because of them: and loving Christ for bearing, in our room, the wrath which they contain, Heb. xii. 25, 2 Cor. v. 14.

Q. How are scripture-prophecies to be reduced to practice?—A. In our looking, waiting, and preparing for the events therein foretold, 2 Pet. iii., Isa. vii., viii.

Q. How are scripture-doctrines to be reduced to practice?—A. In our being directed, excited and encouraged to holiness by them, John xv. 3, and xvii. 17.

Q. How are scripture-precepts to be reduced to practice? —A. In our performing the duties required, and abstaining from sins forbidden in them, Deut. xi. 32.

Q. How are scripture-histories of common and temporal affairs to be reduced to practice?—A. In our improving them as motives to prudence, and diligence in our spiritual concerns, Luke xvi. 8.

Q. How are scripture-histories of holy examples to be reduced to practice?—A. In our study to imitate those patterns of good works, Heb. vi. 12, and xii. 1, 2.

Q. How is the scripture-history of God's mercies to be reduced to practice?—A. In our thence taking encouragement boldly to ask, and firmly to expect mercies and blessings from him, Numb. xiv. 19, Psal. cv., cxlv.

Q. How is the scripture-history of God's judgments to be reduced to practice?—A. In our adoring the righteousness of God in them; and laying our account with the like, if we indulge ourselves in sin, Ezek. xvi., xx.

Q. How is the scripture-history of the failings of good men to be reduced to practice?—A. In our learning to distrust our heart, watch against temptations, pray for, and solely depend on the grace that is in Christ, 1 Cor. x.

Q. 91. *How do the sacraments become effectual means of salvation?*

A. The sacraments become effectual means of salvation, not from any virtue in them, or in him that doth administer them; but only by the blessing of Christ, and the working of his Spirit in them that by faith receive them.

Q. Doth the truth or virtue of sacraments in the least depend on the intention or holiness of the administrator?—A. No; for this would place the power of giving grace into the hands of men, and make us uncertain whether we had received the sacraments or not.

Q. By what then are the sacraments made effectual for salvation?—A. *Only by the blessing of Christ, and the working of his Spirit,* 1 Cor. iii. 6, 7.

Q. What doth this teach us?—A. To cry earnestly for Christ's presence in the sacraments, and to beware of resting in them, Song iv. 16, Psal. ci. 2.

Q. 92. *What is a sacrament?*

A. A sacrament is a holy ordinance instituted by Christ, wherein by sensible signs, Christ, and the benefits of the new covenant, are represented, sealed, and applied to believers.

Q. What did the word *sacrament* originally mean?—A. An oath, whereby soldiers bound themselves to be faithful to their general.

Q. Why then are Christ's sealing ordinances called *sacraments?*—A. Because therein we swear, that we will be faithful followers, subjects and soldiers to Christ; and he engageth to bestow all his blessings upon us.

Q. Why are the sacraments called *holy ordinances?*—A. Their author, matter, objects, and ends, are holy.

Q. How many parts are in every sacrament?—A. Two; the sign, and the thing signified.

Q. What call you the *sign?*—A. That outward thing in the sacrament which may be seen, felt, or tasted.

Q. What is the *thing signified* in all sacraments?—A. Christ, and the benefits of the new covenant.

Q. Wherein doth the sign, and thing signified in sacraments differ?—A. The sign is something *natural* and sensible, but the thing signified is *spiritual.*

Q. What is the form of a sacrament?—A. The word of divine institution, which unites the sign and thing signified, and gives us ground to expect his rendering them effectual, Matth. xxvi. 28.

Q. What relation doth the word of institution constitute between these?—A. It makes the sign to *represent*, seal, and *apply* the thing signified.

Q. What is meant by the sign's representing Christ and his benefits?—A. Its carrying a resemblance of him and his benefits, 1 Pet. iii. 21. 1 Cor. ii. 23—29.

Q. What is meant by the sign's sealing Christ and his benefits?—A. Its confirming our interest in Christ and his blessing, Rom. iv. 11. 1 Pet. iii. 21.

Q. Do the sacraments make our interest in Christ or his promise firmer in itself?—A. No: they only further shew the firmness of it, and tend to strengthen our faith in Christ and his promise.

Q. How do you prove, that the sacraments are seals of God's covenant?—A. Because circumcision (and, by consequence, all other sacraments) is called a *seal of the righteousness of faith*, Rom. iv. 11.

Q. What is meant by the sacramental sign's applying Christ and his benefits?—A. That in and by the sign, Christ and his benefits are really made over to us.

Q. To whom do the signs in the sacraments represent, seal, and apply Christ and his benefits?—A. To believers only, Exod. xii. 48. Ezek. xliv. 9.

Q. How doth that appear?—A. Others have no eyes to see, no hand or mouth of faith to receive Christ; and are not in the new covenant, of which alone the sacraments are seals.

Q. Who have a right to partake of the sacraments?—A. Such as are saints in appearance have a right before men; but only real saints have a right before God?

Q. How is it that hypocrites have a right to the sacraments before men, when they have none before God?—A. They have outward appearance of saints; and the wickedness of their heart is unknown to men, Acts viii. 13.

Q. Is it sinful and dangerous for hypocrites to receive the sacraments?—A. Yes; it is a robbing of God, and wounding of their own souls, Matth. vii. 6.

Q. In what do the word and sacraments agree?—A. God is the author, Christ the matter, and the glory of God, and good of his people, the end in both.

Q. In what do the word and sacraments differ?—A. In their subjects, and in their manner of conveying Christ and his grace to us.

Q. How do they differ in their *subjects*?—A. The word is given to all men in general; but the sacraments belong only to such as are in covenant with God.

Q. How do they differ in their *manner* of manifesting and conveying Christ and his grace to us?—A. By the word we are first united to Christ, and it represents him in a more simple manner; the sacraments do more fully confirm our faith, by giving us a visible token that Christ is ours; the word is a disposition to God as our inheritance; the sacraments are an insertment upon this inheritance.

Q. For what end hath Christ instituted sacraments in his church?—A. To keep up the remembrance of his own death; give his people solemn fellowship with them, and their obligations to him; strengthen their grace; and distinguish them from the rest of the world, 1 Cor. x. xi.

Q. How are Christ's sacraments usually distinguished?—A. Into those of the Old, and the New Testament.

Q. What different kinds of sacraments were under the Old Testament?—A. Ordinary and extraordinary.

Q. What were the *ordinary* sacraments of the Old Testament?—A. Circumcision and the passover.

Q. What was the outward sign in circumcision?—A. The cutting off of the flesh of the foreskin.

Q. What was signified by that?—A. The destruction of original sin, which is conveyed by natural generation; pardon of sin; and dedication of the person to God.

Q. When was the sacrament of circumcision instituted?—A. About 2107 years after the creation, Gen. xvii.

Q. What served the church for sacraments before?—A. The sacrifices, &c. which represented Christ's death, and our living by and on him, Heb. x. 1.

Q. What was the *passover*?—A. The feasting on a sacrificed lamb on the 14th day of the month *Abib*, or March.

Q. What was represented by this lamb?—A. Christ the Lamb of God in his death, 1 Cor. v. 7.

Q. Why was this lamb to be an *unblemished male* of

the first year?—A. To represent the purity, excellency, and vigour of Christ as our suffering Surety, Heb. vii. 26.

Q. Why was the paschal lamb to be *roasted?*—A. To shew the severity of Christ's sufferings, Psalm xxii.

Q. Why was not *a bone* of this Lamb to be *broken?*— A. To shew how exactly the Father would uphold Christ in his sufferings, John xlx. 36, Isa. l. 7. 9.

Q. Why was this lamb to be *eaten with bitter herbs?*— A. To keep in remembrance the bitterness of the Egyptian bondage ; and shew that Christ must be received with bitter repentance for sin, Zech. xii. 10.

Q. Why was *nothing* of the lamb to be *left?*—A. To shew that Christ must be wholly received by faith, John i. 12.

Q. Why was the lamb to be eaten with *unleavened bread?*—A. To keep in remembrance Israel's hasty dismission from Egypt ; and shew that Christ must be received with sincerity of heart, 1 Cor. v. 8.

Q. When was the passover instituted?—A. When Israel came up out of Egypt ; and about 2508 years after the creation, and 1492 before Christ.

Q. For what ends was it instituted?—A. To be a type of Christ, a seal of the covenant of grace, and a memorial of a temporal deliverance, 1 Cor. v. 8.

Q. Why was it called the *passover?*—A. Because it was a memorial of Israel's *passing* out of Egypt, and of the angel's *passing over* their houses when he smote the first-born of the Egyptians, Exod. xii.

Q. What made the angel pass over the houses of the Israelites?—A. The sprinkling of their door-posts and lintels with the blood of the paschal lamb, Exod. xii.

Q. What was signified by the angel's passing over their houses on account of this sprinkling of blood?—A. That the blood of Christ, sprinkled on our conscience, is a sure defence from divine wrath, Rom. viii. 1.

Q. What were the *extraordinary*, and less proper sacraments of the Old Testament?—A. Israel's passage through the Red Sea, the manna, rock, &c., 1 Cor. x. 1—4.

Q. What did Israel's passage through the Red Sea signify?—A. Our salvation from bondage, and separation from the world, through the blood of Christ, Eph. i. 7.

Q. What did the manna, and water-yielding rock, signify?—A. Christ's flesh as *meat indeed*, and his blood as *drink indeed*, John vi. 32—57, Rev. vii. 17.

Q. 93. *What are the sacraments of the New Testament?*

A. The sacraments of the New Testament are, baptism, and the Lord's supper.

Q. How do these differ from the sacraments of the Old Testament?—A. The sacraments of the Old Testament more darkly represented Christ as to come; but those of the New clearly represented him as already come.

Q. Do baptism, and the Lord's supper, succeed in the place of circumcision and the passover?—A. Yes; baptism is come in place of circumcision, and the Lord's supper in place of the passover.

Q. Are there no more sacraments under the New Testament, than baptism and the Lord's supper?—A. No more of divine institution; but the Papists have added five bastard sacraments, viz. marriage, ordination, confirmation, penance, and extreme unction.

Q. What is the Popish confirmation?—A. The pretending to confer the Holy Ghost on such as have been baptized, when they come to years of discretion, by the laying on of the bishop's hands.

Q. What is their penance?—A. Their confession of their sins to the priest, and receiving a pardon from him on condition of suffering from punishment for sin.

Q. What is their extreme unction?—A. The anointing dying persons with oil, to confer the Holy Ghost on them, and make them fit for heaven.

Q. How prove you that marriage and ordination, *though of divine institution for other ends*, are no sacraments?— A. Neither of them are appointed by God for seals of his covenant, nor signify the spiritual benefits of it: marriage is common to all men, and ordination is confined to a small part of professed saints.

Q. How prove you that confirmation, penance, and extreme unction, are no sacraments?—A. None of them, as used by Papists, have any warrant in scripture.

Q. In what do baptism and the Lord's supper agree?— A. God is the author, and Christ the matter of both; equal preparation is necessary for both; both ought to be publicly and solemnly dispensed by gospel ministers only; both are seals of the same covenant, and both contain engagements to the same duties.

Q. Why ought baptism and the Lord's supper to be publicly administered ?—**A.** Because they are public badges of the members of the visible church, and of our communion with Christ, and with one another.

Q. Wherein lieth the evil of the prevailing practice of private baptism ?—**A.** It clandestinely obtrudes members into the visible church, occasions the contempt and irreverent administration of baptism, separates the ordinance of teaching from it, confirms the ignorant in the Popish doctrine of its absolute necessity, robs Christians of solemn opportunity to renew their vows, and deprives the parent and child of the benefit of the joint prayers of the Lord's people, and is a breach of our natural vows.

Q. How is equal preparation necessary for both sacraments, when children in baptism cannot be required to examine themselves ?—**A.** In baptism the parent and child are considered as one ; and though the trial and actual exercise of grace, are not required in the child, they are as necessary to the parent, as in the Lord's supper.

Q. If baptism be so solemn, is it not very sinful in professors to attend carefully on sermons, or the Lord's supper and carelessly go off when baptism is administered, as if it were less solemn ?—**A.** Yes; Mal. ii. 9.

Q. In what do baptism and the Lord's supper differ ?— **A.** Baptism seals an entrance into the church and covenant of grace, is administered but once, and to infants as well as others ; but the Lord's supper is a seal of spiritual nourishment, is to be frequently received, and by such only as can examine themselves.

Q. How long are baptism and the Lord's supper to continue in the church ?—**A.** Till Christ's second coming.

Q. 94. *What is baptism?*

A. Baptism is a sacrament, wherein the washing with water, in the name of the Father, and of the Son, and of the Holy Ghost, doth signify and seal our ingrafting into Christ, and partaking of the benefits of the covenant of grace, and our engagement to be the Lord's.

Q. What does the word *baptism* signify ?—**A.** *Washing, dipping,* or *sprinkling,* Mark vii. 4. Heb. ix. 10.

Q. Did not the Jews of old baptize or wash their prose-

27

lytes when they received them?—A. Yes; but they did not use this as a divine ordinance.

Q. When did baptism become a divine ordinance?—A. When *John the Baptist* began his public ministry.

Q. Was the baptism of *John* the same in substance with that of the apostles?—A. Yes; though it did not *so clearly* point forth the Trinity, nor Christ's *actual* incarnation, Matt. iii. Luke iii.

Q. What divine warrant have we for baptism?—A. Christ's express command and example, and the apostolical practice, Matt. iii. 16. John iv. 2.

Q. What is Christ's express command for baptism?—A. *To teach all nations, baptizing them,* &c.

Q. What is the outward sign of baptism?—A. Water applied to the body, Acts viii. 36.

Q. Is the water in baptism as well applied by sprinkling, (particularly on the face, which represents the whole person), as by plunging our whole body in it?—A. Yes; for what is signified by baptism is called *the sprinkling of the blood of Christ;* the apostles baptized many, where there appears no opportunity of dipping their whole bodies, as Cornelius the jailor, &c.; and in cold climates dipping might endanger the life of infants, 1 Peter i. 2.

Q. How then is it said that in our baptism we are *buried with Christ?*—A. That signifies the burial of sin in our soul by our union to Christ, Rom. vi. 4, 5, 6.

Q. Doth not the scripture tell us, that sundry went *down into,* or came *up out of* the water, at their baptism?—A. These places might as justly be rendered, they went *down to,* or *came from* the water, Matth. iii. Acts viii.

Q. What is signified by the water in baptism?—A. The blood and Spirit of Christ, John iii. 5, 6.

Q. Wherein doth water represent Christ's blood and Spirit?—A. As water refreshes and cleanses our body, so do Christ's blood and Spirit refresh and cleanse our soul.

Q. How doth Christ's blood or righteousness refresh and cleanse our soul?—A. When applied to our soul, it takes away the guilt of sin, quiets our conscience, delivers from the terrors of God's wrath, and from the law as the strength of sin, Heb. x. 22, 1 John i. 7, and ii. 1.

Q. How doth Christ's Spirit refresh and cleanse our soul?—A. He takes away the filth and power of sin, and allays the heat of our indwelling lusts, Titus iii. 5.

Q. In whose name are we baptized?—**A.** In the name of God the Father, Son, and Holy Ghost.

Q. What is signified by our baptism in the name of these three persons?—**A.** Our baptism by the authority, and into the belief and profession of these three persons as one God, and distinctly concerned in the work of our salvation, and made over to us, as our ALL IN ALL; together with our dedication of ourselves to their service, and renouncing their rivals, the devil, the world, and the flesh.

Q. In what manner are the three divine persons made over, and to be received by us in baptism?—**A.** The Father as our Father, the Son as our Saviour, the Holy Ghost as our Sanctifier; and all three in one, as our God and portion, 2 Cor. xiii. 14, John xvi. 14, 15.

Q. What blessings are sealed to us in baptism?—**A.** Our ingrafting into Christ, and partaking of the benefits of the covenant of grace, Gal. iii. 27.

Q. What do you understand by *ingrafting* into Christ?—**A.** Our union to him as a branch to the root.

Q. On what root do we naturally grow?—**A.** On the root of the first Adam as a covenant-breaker, which conveys corruption and death to all its branches.

Q. How are we cut off from this poisonous root?—**A.** By God's changing our nature and state.

Q. What benefits of the covenant of grace are most directly signified and sealed in our baptism?—**A.** Regeneration, justification and adoption, Titus iii. 5, Gal. iii. 27.

Q. Are all these included in our ingrafting into Christ?—**A.** Yes; in our union to him as *our life*, we have regeneration; in our union to him as *the Lord our righteousness*, we have justification; and in our union to him as our *Father*, and *elder Brother*, we have adoption.

Q. What engagements do we come under in baptism?—**A.** We solemnly swear to be *wholly* and *only* the Lord's.

Q. What about us do we in baptism devote to the Lord?—**A.** Our whole man, estate, and time.

Q. How is our soul devoted to the Lord?—**A.** It is devoted to be a temple and throne for him, and to have all its powers employed in his service, Psal. xxxi. 5.

Q. How is our body devoted to the Lord?—**A.** Our eyes are devoted to behold his works, and view his word; our ears to hear his voice; and our mouth to speak for and to him; our feet to run his errands; and our hands to do his will, 1 Cor. vi. 20.

Q. How is our estate devoted to the Lord ?—**A.** All we have is to be laid out for the advancement of his glory, as he calls for it, Prov. iii. 9, Isa. xxiii. 18.

Q. How is our time devoted to the Lord ?—**A.** We are bound to employ it wholly in his fear and service.

Q. Are not then baptized persons great robbers of God, in employing their soul, body, estate, and time so much in the service of Satan ?—**A.** Yes, Mal. iii. 8, 9.

Q. How often is baptism to be administered to the same person ?—**A.** Once only, Tit. iii. 5, 1 Peter, iii. 21.

Q. Why so ?—**A.** Because the benefits most directly signified and sealed in it, are *only once* bestowed.

Q. Why is baptism necessary ?—**A.** God commands it; and it tends much to his glory, and our good.

Q. How doth our baptism tend to the glory of God ?—**A.** Therein he solemnly displays his holiness, justice, and love ; and we acknowledge his sovereignty.

Q. How doth our baptism tend to our advantage ?—**A.** It solemnly declares us members of Christ's church, encourageth us to plead the promises, come boldly to the throne of grace, resist temptations, &c.

Q. Doth baptism bring us into God's covenant?—**A.** No ; it supposeth us within it, and seals it to us.

Q. Is it absolutely necessary to salvation ?—**A.** No.

Q. How prove you that ?—**A.** It is no converting ordinance ; Cornelius was accepted of God before his baptism ; and Christ says, *He that believeth and is baptized, shall be saved: and he that believeth not* (but doth not add, *is not baptized) shall be damned*, Mark xvi. 16.

Q. Is it not gross ignorance and Popish error, to maintain, that all infants, or others dying unbaptized, shall be damned ?—**A.** Yes ; Gal. vi. 15, 1 Peter iii. 21.

Q. 95. *To whom is baptism to be administered?*

A. Baptism is not to be administered to any that are out of the visible church, till they profess their faith in Christ and obedience to him ; but the infants of such as are members of the visible church are to be baptized.

Q. May Heathens, or their children, be baptized ?—**A.** No, till they profess their faith in Christ, and obedience to him, Acts viii. 36, 37.

Q. Have those who, in Christian countries, are as ignorant and as profane as Heathens, or their children, any right to baptism ?—A. No ; their guilt is greater than if they had lived in Pagan countries ; and local situation can never entitle to spiritual privileges, John xviii. 36.

Q. To whom then is baptism to be administered ?—A. To all such as profess their faith in Christ, and obedience to him and their children, Acts ii. 38, 39.

Q. When have children a right to baptism ?—A. The infants who have one or both parents visible saints, have a right to it before men ; and the infants of real believers have a right to it before God, 1 Cor. vii. 14.

Q. How prove you, that the infants of visible saints ought to be baptized ?—A. The scripture represents them as holy, as members of the kingdom of heaven, as interested in God's covenant and promise, and of old required that they should be circumcised, 1 Cor. vii. 14, Mark x. 14, Acts ii. 39, Gen. xvii. 7—12.

Q. How prove you, that the holiness of children mentioned 1 Cor. vii. 14. is not the being begotten in lawful marriage ?—A. Because there it is required that one of the parents be a Christian, which is not necessary to the lawful begetting of children.

Q. How doth the circumcision of infants under the law prove that they should be baptized under the gospel ?—A. The covenant confirmed by circumcision, (of God's being the God of his people and their seed,) is called an *everlasting* covenant ; and Christ cannot be supposed to diminish the privileges of his people by his coming, which would be the case, if circumcision of infants were taken away, and nothing put into its place, Gen. xvii. 10. 17.

Q. How doth the relation of believers' children to the kingdom of God, and interest in his covenant and promise, prove their title to baptism ?—A. As they have a right to these things, they must necessarily have a title to the seal of that right, when capable of it.

Q. How are infants capable of receiving baptism ?—A. Their parents can dedicate them to the Lord ; and he can regenerate, justify, and adopt them, Mark x. 14.

Q. How have parents a right to dedicate their infants to God ?—A. Infants are part of their property.

Q. May parents dedicate their infants to any but God ? —A. No ; for God has the original and principal right to our infants, Ezek. xvi. 20, 21.

Q. If infants may be baptized, why doth Christ require
27*

his apostles to teach, and then baptize persons?—A. That order only related to adult persons.

Q. Why then was not Christ baptized till about thirty years of age?—A. Because baptism was not instituted till he was about that age, Luke iii. 23.

Q. Have we any scripture examples of the baptism of infants?—A. There are probable instances of it; as when Cornelius, Lydia, the jailor, &c., their households were baptized, Acts x. and xvi. 15. 33.

Q. Why is not the warrant for infant baptism more express in scripture?—A. Because before baptism was clothed with the form of a sacrament, it was applied to infants as well as to others; and in the apostles' time no doubt was made of infants right to receive it.

Q. Through whom have infants a right to baptism?—A. Through their IMMEDIATE parents *only*.

Q. How prove you that?—A. The *immediate* seed of wicked parents are accursed of God, Deut. xxviii. 18; and if children derive their right to baptism from *mediate* parents, we ought to baptize all pagans and Mahometans, since they are descended from godly Noah, &c.

Q. Why then are the children of profane idolaters called God's children, Ezek. xvi. 20, 21?—A. Not because he had any visible interest in his new covenant; but because they were his by creation and preservation; or perhaps were the first born of Israel.

Q. May not the infants of profane parents be truly gracious?—A. It is possible they may, but are not to be esteemed as such by men till they evidence their grace.

Q. How are we to judge of the children of visible believers?—A. We are to judge them to be within God's covenant, till by their practice they shew themselves strangers to it, Gen. xvii. Acts ii. 38, 39.

Q. Is it not unjust to make children want baptism on account of their parents' ignorance and profaneness?—A. No; no more than to make the children of Heathens want it; or to let children want an inheritance when their parents had none to leave to them: nay, the baptism of such children would be hurtful both to the parents and children, Matth. vii. 6. Ezek. xliv. 7.

Q. How would it be hurtful to the ignorant and profane parents?—A. It would encourage them to believe themselves *good Christians*, and to continue in their ignorance and profaneness, Ezek. xiii. 22. John viii. 41.

Q. How would it be hurtful to their children ?—**A.** Their receiving baptism without any title to it, tends to bring on them a curse rather than a blessing; and the view of their baptism *as regular*, encourageth and hardens them in their sin, Matth. vii. 6. John viii. 39, 41.

Q. Would not the number of church-members be small if none but visible believers and their children were baptized ?—**A.** Better it were so, than that men, who have no evidence of union to, or communion with Christ, should be obtruded as members of his church, by a solemn profanation of baptism, to the reproach of his name, and discredit of the gospel, Phil. iii. 18, 19.

Q. Do hypocrites profane baptism, by bringing their children to it ?—**A.** Yes, in the sight of God, though not in the sight of men, Psalm lxxviii. 36.

Q. How do hypocrites dedicate their children in baptism ?—**A.** They outwardly surrender them to God, while their heart inwardly refuses them; for no man can sincerely devote his child to any other than his own God, Titus i. 16.

Q. Are the duties relative to baptism very numerous and important ?—**A.** Yes, Psal. cxix. 96. 1 Pet. iii. 21.

Q. What is the duty of parents before the baptism of their children ?—**A.** Secretly to examine themselves; solemnly dedicate their child to God; consider what they are to vow in baptism; and to pray for grace to vow and pray aright, Jer. iv. 2.

Q. What is the duty of parents when offering their children in baptism ?—**A.** To exercise faith in a lively manner on that promise, *I will be thy God, and the God of thy seed*, or the like; and to give up themselves and children to be the Lord's, Gen. xvii. 7. Josh. xxiv. 15.

Q. What is the duty of parents after the baptism of their children ?—**A.** To remember and pay their vows by instructing and correcting them; and seriously putting them in mind of their baptismal engagements, as soon as they come to age, Prov. xxii. 6, 15.

Q. How should spectators improve the administration of baptism ?—**A.** In admiring the love of God towards men; renewing their baptismal vows; remembering, and mourning over the breaches thereof; and pleading for grace to the children baptized, and their parents.

Q. How are we to improve our baptism after we come to age ?—**A.** As a *glass* to discover our sinfulness, a *reason* against yielding to temptations, a *spur* to duties and an *encouragement* to plead the promises of God's covenant.

Q. May one, by an improvement of his baptism, have it afterwards become an effectual seal of God's covenant to him?—**A.** Yes, the efficacy of baptism is not confined to the time of administration; and whenever one believes, his baptism then begins to seal the covenant to him.

Q. Is it so with respect to the Lord's supper?—**A.** No; if we communicate in a graceless state, *that act* can never be a means of sealing God's covenant to us.

Q. 96. *What is the Lord's Supper?*

A. The Lord's Supper is a sacrament, wherein, by giving and receiving bread and wine, according to Christ's appointment, his death is shewed forth; and the worthy receivers are, not after a corporal and carnal manner, but by faith, made partakers of his body and blood, with all his benefits to their spiritual nourishment, and growth in grace.

Q. What divine warrant have we for the Lord's supper? —**A.** Christ's institution, and the apostolic practice, Matth. xxvi. 1 Cor. xi. Acts ii. and xx.

Q. When did Christ institute this sacrament?—**A.** *The same night in which he was betrayed.*

Q. Why did he institute it the night before his death?— **A.** To shew, that it was to come in the room of the passover, which was abolished by his death; to manifest his great love to his people in giving them such a solemn pledge of it when entering on his sufferings; and to stir us up the more affectionately to remember his death therein.

Q. Doth Christ's example, in celebrating this ordinance in the evening of a work-day, and in an upper room, bind us to do the like?—**A.** No, for the eating of the passover just before occasioned these circumstances.

Q. What posture is fittest for receiving the Lord's supper?—**A.** Sitting comes nearest Christ's example, and best suits with the nature of that feast, Matth. xxvi. 20. 26.

Q. What are the outward signs in this sacrament?—**A.** Sacramental elements and actions.

Q. What are the sacramental *elements?*—**A.** Bread and wine, (of any kind; for Christ made use of what was at hand), Matth. xxvi. 26—29.

Q. What is signified by the *bread?*—A. Christ's body, or himself clothed with our nature, 1 Cor. x. 11.

Q. What is signified by the *wine?*—A. Christ's blood, or complete meritorious righteousness, 1 Cor. ix. 25, 26.

Q. Why is Christ's righteousness often called his blood? —A. Because the shedding of his blood was the last and most eminent visible act of his righteousness, John xix.

Q. How do bread and wine represent Christ's body and blood?—A. As bread and wine are excellent food to our body; so Christ, in his person and righteousness, is *meat indeed*, and *drink indeed* to our soul, John vi. 32—57.

Q. Are the sacramental bread and wine transubstantiated, or turned into the real body or blood of Christ?—A. No; for such a change of the elements is contrary to sense, reason, scripture, and the very nature of a sacrament; it would divide or multiply the body of Christ, and subject it to corruption, and the torments of hell.

Q. How is transubstantiation contrary to sense?—A. As we see, feel, taste, and smell the elements to have the same substance after consecration as before.

Q. How is it contrary to reason?—A. As by reason, we know the substance of a thing cannot be changed, while its accidents and qualities remain the same.

Q. May not God, by his power, effect such a change?— A. No; for this would destroy the proof of all divine miracles recorded in scripture, 2 Tim. ii. 13.

Q. Can one who believes transubstantiation, in a consistency with himself, believe any other miracles or points of Christianity?—A. No: for if, in opposition to sense and reason, he believes transubstantiation, it behoves him, in consistency with himself, to believe, that there is no Bible, no Christians; that Christ never appeared, wrought miracles, or rose again, &c.

Q. How is transubstantiation contrary to scripture?—A. As the scripture calls the elements *bread* and *wine* after consecration, as well as before, 1 Cor. xi. 26—28.

Q. How is it contrary to the nature of a sacrament?— A. It makes the Lord's supper not a means of remembering Christ, but of making and barbarously eating him.

Q. How would it divide or multiply Christ's body?—A. As it would make as many bodies, or pieces of Christ's body, as there are receivers of the Lord's supper.

Q. How would transubstantiation subject Christ's body to corruption, or the torments of hell?—A. As the elements unite with the substance of men's bodies which shall be corrupted, and many of them cast into hell.

Q. If the elements are not changed into Christ's real body and blood, why did Christ say of the bread, *This is my body?*—A. His meaning is, that it *represented* his body.

Q. How prove you that?—A. No other view will agree to common sense; and the verb *(is)* is frequently used in scripture for *signifies* or *represents*, Gen. xli. 26, 27.

Q. Ought every communicant to receive both the bread and wine?—A. Yes; for Paul says of all the communicants, *Ye eat this bread, and drink this cup*, 1 Cor. xi. 26.

Q. How may the sacramental actions in the Lord's supper be distinguished?—A. Into the actions of the dispenser, and of the receiver.

Q. What are the sacramental actions of the minister?—A. The taking, blessing, and breaking the bread, and giving it, with the wine, to the communicants.

Q. What may the *taking* and *blessing* the bread and wine lead us to think of?—A. Of God's choosing, calling, and furnishing Christ to be our Mediator, Prov. viii. 25.

Q. For what other end does the blessing of the elements serve?—A. To set them apart from a common use, to represent Christ's body and blood, 1 Cor. x. 16.

Q. What is signified by the *breaking* of the bread?—A. God's breaking and bruising Christ for our sin.

Q. What doth the *giving* of the elements to the communicants represent?—A. God's giving Christ, and Christ's giving himself to worthy receivers, John vi. 32. 57.

Q. What is signified by the communicants *receiving* the elements, and *eating* the bread, and *drinking* the wine?—A. The receiving and feeding on Christ's person and righteousness by faith, Matth. xxvi. 26—29.

Q. How is Christ's flesh and blood to be eaten and drunk?—A. Not in a corporal and carnal manner, but by faith.

Q. What do you mean by *corporal* and *carnal* eating?—A. The pretending to eat Christ's body, and drink his blood, as we do ordinarily meat and drink; or by communicating with carnal ideas of his human body.

Q. What are the general ends of the Lord's Supper?—A. The showing forth of Christ's death, and the spiritual nourishment of his people, 1 Cor. xi. 26.

Q. To whom are we to show forth the death of Christ

in communicating?—A. To God, to our conscience, to Satan, and to the world, Gal. vi. 14, Rev. xxii. 12.

Q. How are we to show forth Christ's death to God?— A. By representing it to him by faith as a sufficient satisfaction to his justice, and the accepted price of all the blessings which we need from him, Heb. x. 19. 22.

Q. How are we to show forth Christ's death to our conscience?—A. By our believing application of it, as an answer to all its legal accusations and demands, and as a means of enlightening, softening, and quickening it to all holy duties, Heb. x. 22, and ix. 14, 1 John i. 7.

Q. How are we to show forth Christ's death to Satan? —A. By our believing improvements of it as an *answer* to all his accusations, a proof of the falsehood of his horrible suggestions, a *reason* against yielding to his temptations, and an *ensign*, for defeating his assaults, Rev. xii. 11.

Q. How are we to show forth Christ's death to the world? —A. By professing it as the *centre* and sum of our principles; the *foundation* of our hope, joy, and boasting; and the *reason* of our holy walk, and disconformity to vain wicked men, Gal. vi. 12. 1 John iv. 9, 10.

Q. What spiritual nourishment do believers receive in the Lord's supper?—A. Their souls are comforted and strengthened by receiving Christ and his benefits.

Q. What benefits do believers receive in the Lord's supper?—A. Peace, pardon, sanctification, consolation, foretastes and pledges of eternal glory, Matth. xxvi. 28.

Q. What is the effect of our being nourished with Christ and his blessings?—A. Our growth in grace, 2 Pet. iii. 8.

Q. What names are ordinarily given to this sacrament? —A. It is called the eucharist, the communion, the feast, and the Lord's supper.

Q. Why is it called the *eucharist* or *thanksgiving?*—A. Because Christ gave thanks when he appointed it; and we are to receive it with thanksgiving.

Q. Why is it called a *communion?*—A. Because therein we have sweet fellowship with Christ, and with one another, 1 Cor. x. 16, 17.

Q. Why is it called a *feast?*—A. Because of the great provision and joy that is to be found in it.

Q. What kind of feast is it?—A. A royal feast, a feast of marriage and memorial, and a feast on a covenant and sacrifice.

Q. How is it a *royal* feast ?—A. As Christ, the king of kings, is the *maker* and *matter* of it, and chief *guest* at it.

Q· How is it a *marriage-feast* ?—A. Therein our spiritual marriage with Christ is sealed ; and we receive pledges of our glorious espousals at the last day.

Q. How is it a *feast on a sacrifice* ?—A. Because Christ, as *sacrificed for us*, is the matter of it, 1 Cor. v. 7.

Q. Why is this sacrament called *the Lord's supper* ?—A. Because the Lord Christ instituted it in the evening of the world, and of the day when the passover supper was eaten ; and to represent its excellency.

Q. What are the properties of the Lord's supper ?—A. It is a confessing, commemorating, communicating, confirming and covenanting ordinance.

Q. How is the Lord's supper a *confessing* ordinance ? —A. We therein declare our love to, esteem of, dependence on, and confidence in Christ crucified.

Q. How is it a feast of memorial, or *commemorating* ordinance ?—A. Christ therein testifies his remembrance of us ; and we remember his death, and our own sin as the deserving cause of it, Isa. liii. 1 Cor. xi. 23—26.

Q. What of Christ's death does this sacrament call to remembrance ?—A. The terrible, voluntary, acceptable, and efficacious nature of it ; and the love of God as the moving cause of it, Isa. lii. 13, and liii. 4—12.

Q. In what manner is the death of Christ to be remembered in the Lord's supper ?—A. In a thankful, affectionate, confident, humble, and sin loathing manner.

Q. How is the Lord's supper a *communicating* ordinance ? —A. As we therein familiarly reveal our case to Christ, transfer our sin for pardon, bring our maladies to him for a cure, and receive his exhibited blessings.

Q. How is the Lord's supper a *confirming* ordinance ? —A. Therein our graces are confirmed and strengthened, and God's covenant is confirmed with us, 1 Cor. x. 16.

Q. How is it a feast or a covenant, or *covenanting* ordinance ?—A. God, with delight and pleasure, engages to be our God and Portion ; and we covenant to be wholly and only devoted to his service, Zech. xiii. 9.

Q. Do not believers herein also communicate in one another's affections and prayers, and engage to seek and promote one another's good ?—A. Yes, 1 Cor. x. 17.

Q. How frequently is the Lord's supper to be received ? —A. As often as we can have opportunity.

Q. How prove you that?—**A.** The Christians in the apostolic and primitive ages received it every Sabbath; Christ's death is worthy of frequent remembrance; and we frequently need this ordinance, Acts ii. 42, and xx. 7.

Q. Would not frequent communicating lessen the solemnity of that ordinance?—**A.** No; no more than frequent prayer, meditation, &c. lessen the solemnity of these ordinances: nay, frequent conscientious communicating tends much to advance the truly divine solemnity of it.

Q. How so?—**A.** The more frequently we have communion with Christ, the more deeply would we be affected with the majesty, holiness, and love of God, which shines in this ordinance, Isa. vi. 5, Psalm lxxxix. 7.

Q. What different kinds of communicating are there? —**A.** Worthy and unworthy communicating.

Q. What is necessary to worthy communicating?—**A.** A worthy state, frame, and end.

Q. What call you a *worthy state* for this duty?—**A.** A state of grace, or spiritual union with Christ.

Q. When have we a *worthy frame* for this duty?—**A.** When, in Christ's strength, we actively exercise the graces of his Spirit on him, 1 Cor. v. 8, Song i. 12.

Q. What *worthy ends* ought we to have in communicating?—**A.** The glorifying of God, the obeying of Christ's dying command, receiving spiritual nourishment to our soul, and mortification of our lusts, 1 Cor x. 31.

Q. What is unworthy communicating?—**A.** Communicating without grace, or without the exercise of it.

Q. Wherein lieth the evil of unworthy communicating? —**A.** It is very sinful and dangerous.

Q. How is it *very sinful?*—**A.** It profanes Christ's body and blood, by intermeddling with it as a common thing, or using it as an encouragement and cloak to sin; it is a crucifying him afresh, and putting him to open shame; and is more sinful than the Jews crucifying him.

Q. How is it worse than the Jews crucifying of him?— **A.** The Jews crucified Christ in his state of humiliation, under the notion of an impostor; but unworthy communicating crucifies him as an exalted Saviour and Friend.

Q. What is the *danger* of unworthy communicating?— **A.** We thereby *eat and drink damnation* or *judgment* to ourselves, *not discerning the Lord's body*, 1 Cor. xi. 29.

Q. Who thereby eat and drink *damnation* to themselves? —**A.** Such as communicate in a graceless state.

28

Q. How do these eat and drink *damnation* by their unworthy communicating?—**A.** This sin binds on them the guilt of their other sins, draws down signal wrath, hardens their conscience, and makes it extremely difficult to bring them to repentance, 1 Cor. xi. 29, 30.

Q. Who eat and drink *judgment* to themselves by their unworthy communicating?—**A.** Such believers as do communicate in a carnal, dead, and lifeless manner.

Q. How do they eat and drink *judgment* to themselves? —**A.** Their unworthy communicating exposeth them to heavy chastisements; such as, hiding of God's face, prevalency of sin, outward troubles, &c. 1 Cor. xi. 30.

Q. Whose duty then is it to receive the Lord's supper? —**A.** All Christians come to the years of discretion are under the obligation of God's law to partake of it; but believers only have a proper right to it; and such believers only as have grace in suitable exercise are fit for it.

Q. Are graceless professors, come to age, guilty of any sin if they neglect to partake of the Lord's supper?—**A.** Yes; they are practically guilty of renouncing their baptism, of condemning the death of Christ as unworthy of remembrance, and of despising sacramental blessings as unworthy of their regard, Luke xxii. 19, 20.

Q. What should such persons do, when both their observance and omission of their duty involve them in sin?—**A.** Their only right course is to flee to Christ, that he may draw them out of the state of nature, and furnish them with his grace, and then to communicate, Isa. lv. 1—7.

Q. What is the duty of believers destitute of the suitable exercise of grace?—**A.** To flee to Christ for the quickening and excitement of their grace, and then to communicate; as their sin of neglecting it is greater than that of graceless professors, Prov. xvi. 1. Psalm cxix. 40.

Q. Who may be admitted to the Lord's table by men? —**A.** Such as are in appearance *saints*, and *faithful;* but such as are ignorant, and openly wicked *cannot, without great sin against Christ, be admitted* thereto.

Q. Why ought ignorant, profane and scandalous persons, to be refused admission?—**A.** Because their admission would tend to the destruction of their souls, and to the dishonour of Christ and his church, 1 Cor. v.

Q. Did not Christ admit Judas to the Lord's supper?— **A.** It doth not appear that he did; but though he did, that only infers that hypocrites may be admitted.

Q. May not ministers give tokens of admission to ignorant and profane persons, if afterwards they doctrinally de-
bar them?—A. No; such conduct is very uncandid; lays
Christ's children's bread in the power of dogs; and is like
giving false keys to known thieves, and then charging them
to be honest, 1 Cor. iv. 2.

Q. Is not such persons seeking admission to the Lord's
table, a true sign of their repentance and reformation?—
A. Not in the least; for many seek after this ordinance as
an atonement for past sin, or merely to be like their neighbours, or to cover some wickedness, &c.

Q. Doth the partaking of ignorant and scandalous persons pollute this sacrament to others?—A. The admission
of them may bring the curse of God upon the dispensation
of the sacrament by those who admit them; but their presence doth not directly pollute it to others.

Q. But may not the godly, by partaking with such, hurt
the souls of those ignorant and scandalous persons?—A.
Yes; for it encourages them to believe themselves *good
Christians*, having right to the seals of God's covenant.

Q. Is not the sacrament greatly abused, by forcing men
to partake of it, or by making the receiving of it a qualifi-
cation for a civil office?—A. Yes; John xviii. 36.

Q. 97. *What is required to the worthy receiving of
the Lord's Supper?*

A. It is required of them that would worthily partake of the Lord's Supper, that they examine themselves of their knowledge to discern the Lord's body,
of their faith to feed upon him, of their repentance,
love, and new obedience; lest, coming unworthily,
they eat and drink judgment to themselves.

Q. What is necessary to a right partaking of the Lord's
supper?—A. Serious preparation for it, lively attendance
on it, and careful improvement of it.

Q. What preparation for this ordinance is necessary?—
A. Habitual and actual preparation, Amos iii. 12.

Q. What do you mean by habitual preparation?—A.
Our having on the wedding garment of Christ's imputed
righteousness, and having the habits of grace implanted in
us, Matth. xxii. 12, Eph. iv. 24.

Q. What actual preparation is necessary?—A. Self-
examination, dedication, meditation, and prayer.

Q. Why is self-examination necessary ?—**A.** To excite our graces, and prevent unworthy communicating.

Q. Why should we examine ourselves every time we communicate ?—**A.** Because our heart is very deceitful, and our frame very variable, Jer. xviii. 9. Prov. xxviii. 26.

Q. Of what are we to examine ourselves before communicating ?—**A.** Of our sin and graces, 2 Cor. xiii. 5.

Q. Of what are we to examine ourselves concerning our sins ?—**A.** What they are, how many, how aggravated, what influence they have on our soul at present, what are our beloved lusts, &c. Lam. iii. 40.

Q. Why is this examination of our sins necessary ?—**A.** That we may approach to the Lord's table with due humility, and sense of our needs, Isa. lxvi. 2.

Q. What concerning our graces are we to examine ?— **A.** Whether we be in a state of grace ; and whether our graces be lively or languishing, 2 Cor. xiii. 5.

Q. What are some general marks of our being in a state of grace ?—**A.** A deep sense of our unworthiness of all grace ; grief for the low state, and scanty measure of our grace ; and an earnest desire to have grace rather than any worldly good, Matth. v. 3, 4, 6. Rom. vii. 24.

Q. Of what particular graces are we to examine ourselves ?—**A.** Of our knowledge, faith, repentance, humility, thankfulness, love, and new obedience.

Q. Why are these graces necessary ?—**A.** To prove our right to the Lord's supper, and dispose us to a proper exercise in partaking of it, 1 Cor. xi. 29.

Q. What are we to examine concerning our knowledge ? —**A.** We are to examine whether it be *sufficient* in its quantity, and *saving* in its quality.

Q. How may we know if our knowledge be sufficient in its quantity ?—**A.** If we have some competent knowledge of the divine persons, perfections, and laws ; of man's creation, fall, and inability to recover himself ; of Christ, in his natures and offices ; and of the covenant of grace, and seals thereof, John xvii. 3. 1 Tim. iii. 16.

Q. How may we know if our knowledge be saving in its quality ?—**A.** If it discover the vileness of our own righteousness, humble and purge our heart, and exalt Christ, Isa. vi. 5 and lxiv. 6. Psalm lxxiii. 25, 26.

Q. How may we know if our faith is true and saving ? —**A.** If it humble and purify our heart, make Christ precious to us, and work by love, Acts xv. 9. 1 Pet. ii. 7, 9.

Q. How may we know if our repentance is true and saving?—**A.** If our sin is imbittered to us, by the views of Christ, and the love of God; if we seriously repent of all known sins, and resolve on every known duty.

Q. How may we know if our humility is true?—**A.** If we reckon ourselves the chief of sinners; are ashamed of both our sins and duties before God; and are grieved for our pride, 1 Tim. i. 15. Ezek. xvi. 63.

Q. How may we know if our thankfulness is true and gracious?—**A.** If we study thankfulness for the least of God's mercies, and chiefly for Christ his greatest mercy; and are afflicted in spirit for our ingratitude, Gen. xxxii. 10.

Q. Of what love are we to examine ourselves?—**A.** Of our love to God, to Christ, and his saints.

Q. How may we know if our love to God be true?—**A.** If we are careful to please him, afraid to offend him, and prize his presence in gospel ordinances.

Q. How may we know if our love to Christ as Mediator be true?—**A.** If we love him in all his offices, relations, ordinances, and people; and love him as a pattern of holiness, as well as a purchaser of happiness.

Q. How may we know if our love to the saints is a gracious love?—**A.** If we love them all, poor or rich; and even though they have injured us, and maintain some notions different from ours; and love them in proportion to the appearance of Christ's image in them, Psalm cxix. 63.

Q. How may we know if our obedience is of a gracious nature?—**A.** If we habitually study obedience to all the commands of God; and depend on Christ as our only righteousness and strength, for assistance in, and acceptance of our obedience, Psalm cxix. Isa. xlv. 24.

Q. What shall one do who cannot discern these graces in himself?—**A.** If he is earnestly desirous to have them, is afraid of disobeying Christ's dying command, and hungers and thirsts after communion with him, he is a true believer, and so ought to communicate, Matth. v.

Q. What are we to examine concerning the case and frame of our graces?—**A.** We are to try whether they be growing, or on the decay, strong or weak, and what resistance sin is making to each of them in our soul.

Q. Why is this examination of our case and frame necessary?—**A.** That in communicating we may ask, and

28*

receive Christ in a suitableness to our present need, and be distinctly thankful for our mercies, 1 Cor. xi. 28.

Q. What is self-dedication ?—A.Our solemn renouncing the devil, the world and the flesh ; and taking God for our all, and giving up our persons and concerns to him to be accepted only through Christ, and disposed of to his glory, Psalm cxvi. 16, Hos. xiv. 2, 3. 8.

Q. On what ought we to meditate before communicating ?—A. Upon our own sinfulness ; the love and greatness of God ; the person, offices, and relations of Christ ; the grace and fulness of the new covenant, &c.

Q. Would not spiritual conference on those subjects also prepare us for communicating ?—A. Yes, Luke xxiv.

Q. For what are we to pray before communicating ?— A. For preparation for it, spiritual assistance and enlargement in it, acceptance of our work, and pardon of our miscarriages therein, 2 Chron. xxx. 18, 19.

Q. Why are self-dedication, meditation, and prayer, necessary before communicating ?—A. To open and enlarge our heart, bring God's presence into our soul, enlarge our expectations of his grace, and excite our graces to a suitable exercise, Isa. lxiv. 5, Psalm xlv. 1.

Q. Why is *so great* preparation necessary to our partaking the Lord's supper ?—A. Because of the great sin and danger of profaning it ; and because God in it hath made all things ready for us, Matth. xxii. 4.

Q. What great things hath God made ready for us in this supper ?—A. His house, table, food, blessing, ministers, angels, &c. ; nay, God himself is ready to feast with us, and his covenant to be subscribed by us.

Q. In what manner ought we to approach the Lord's table ?—A, With great humility, holy jealousy of ourselves, ardent desire, joy, and enlarged expectation of his blessings, Psalm v. 7, and xxvii. 4.

Q. If we approach to the Lord's table with an apprehension that we are *fully* prepared for it, what may we expect at it ?—A. To eat and drink damnation to ourselves, and receive a curse instead of a blessing.

Q. If we approach to the Lord's table with great fear of profaning it, what may we expect at it ?—A. That God will fill us with good things, and lift on us the light of his countenance, Luke i. 53, Isa. lxvi. 2.

Q. What graces are to be exercised by us in communicating ?—A. All saving graces ; as faith, knowledge, love, repentance, humility, thankfulness, &c.

Q. How is our knowledge to be exercised in communicating ?—A. In our *discerning the Lord's body.*

Q. What is meant by our discerning the Lord's body ?—A. Our taking up the bread and wine as representations of the person and righteousness of a God man.

Q. Is such a view of the sufferings of Christ in their painfulness, as excites our natural sympathy with him, and anger at the Jews for so abusing him, a proper discerning of Christ's body ?—A. No ; it is a carnal one, and profiteth nothing, John vi. 63.

Q. How is our *faith* to be exercised in communicating ? —A. In regarding the ordinance as instituted by Christ, and in beholding and feeding on Christ, 1 Cor. x. 16.

Q. What great sights may we by faith behold in the Lord's supper ?—A. The worth of souls ; the exceeding sinfulness of sin ; God's perfections, particularly justice and mercy, harmoniously displayed and magnified ; Christ's love that passeth knowledge, his costly purchase of all blessings, and glorious conquest of all enemies, &c.

Q. What is faith to apply as our food in the Lord's supper ?—A. Christ, and all his promises and blessings.

Q. On what promises should our faith be especially fixed in our receiving the elements in the Lord's supper ?—A. On the sacramental promises, *Take, eat ; this is my body, broken for you.— This cup is the new testament in my blood, shed for remission of sins to many ; drink ye all of it,* Matt. xxvi. 26. 28, 1 Cor. xi. 24, 25.

Q. Why is our faith to be especially fixed on these promises ?—A. That we may not only receive Christ, but take the bread and wine as a solemn confirmation of it.

Q. May we not fix our faith on any other doctrine or promise in connection with those ?—A. Yes.

Q. How is our *repentance* to be exercised in communicating ?—A. In mourning for our sin as the cause of Christ's death, and resolving revenge on our lusts on that account, Zech. xii. 10, Psalm li. 17, Jer. xxxi. 18, 19.

Q. How is our *humility* to be exercised in communicating ?—A. In looking on ourselves as most unworthy, and admiring the wonders of redeeming love, 2 Sam. viii. 18.

Q. What is marvellous in and about redeeming love ?—A. The freedom and riches of it ; the contrivance of redemption ; the person of the redeemer with what he is and does, 1 John iii. 1, 1 Tim. iii. 16, Song v.

Q. How is our *thankfulness* to be exercised in communicating ?—A. In our joyful remembering and praising God for what he is, and has, and will do for us ; and in devising what to render him as an acknowledgment of his kindness, Psalm cxvi. 12, 13, and cxlv.—cl.

Q. How is our *love to God* in Christ to be exercised in communicating?—A. In our holy desiring and delighting in him as our Husband and exceeding joy ; and giving up ourselves wholly to him, Psalm xlii., lxiii.

Q. How is our *love to our neighbour* to be exercised in communicating ?—A. In our rejoicing that others share with us of Christ and his benefits ; our forgiving injuries ; and desiring that multitudes may be added to the church.

Q. How is our *new obedience* to be exercised in communicating ?—A. In communicating chiefly out of regard to Christ's command ; and vowing, in his strength, more perfect observance of his law than formerly.

Q. What particular things are we to vow in communicating ?—A. A life of faith on Christ as our only righteousness and strength ; heavenly-mindedness, watchfulness over our hearts, and against all sins, gross or secret, and particularly against beloved lust ; careful performance of the duties of our station, or which we have formerly much neglected, or which especially tend to prevent sin.

Q. How is our *patience* and *resignation* to be exercised in communicating ?—A. In our kindly compliance with God's will, in whatever method, measure, or season he chooseth for visiting us with his sensible presence, Psal. xlii.

Q. How is our *watchfulness* to be then exercised ?—A. In our waiting for the breathings of God's Spirit, and checking the first motions of lusts and temptations.

Q. What is our general duty after communicating ?—A To examine our carriage in communicating, and whether he had communion with God in it or not.

Q. How may we know if we had fellowship with Christ at his table ?—A. If we be more sensible of our spiritual plagues, more desirous of Christ's presence, and more grieved for his absence than before, Isa. vi. 6, Rom. vii. 23, 24.

Q. In what manner should such as have found Christ at his table come from it ?—A. Admiring and praising God for his love ; with fervent love to God and his people ; with joy in Christ, and sorrow for their own defects; watchfulness against temptations; and prayer for the accomplishment of promises, and strength to fulfil their vows.

Q. How ought they to order their following conversation?—A. By living *soberly, righteously,* and *godly,* charitably, peaceably, and heavenly, *in this present world.*

Q. Why should believers so live after communicating? —A. To testify their gratitude, adorn their profession, preserve their comfort, evidence their communion with Christ, and fulfil their engagements to him, Phil. i. 27.

Q. What is the duty of believers who have not found communion with Christ at his table?—A. To search out the sinful cause of their disappointment, justify God, condemn themselves, renew their repentance, double their preparation, and wait upon God on the first opportunity of the like nature, Song v. 2—9, Mic. vii. 7—9.

Q. What are some of these sinful hindrances of believers' communion with Christ at his table?—A. Carnal thoughts or conference about the time of that ordinance; approaching to it in our own strength; inattention to the divine institution, nature, and end of the ordinance; eyeing our own comfort more than the command and honour of Christ; carnal and imaginary views of Christ's sufferings, &c.

Q. What is our immediate duty, if we find we have communion in a graceless state?—A. Seriously and speedily to consider the exceeding greatness of our sin, pray earnestly for the Spirit of grace, and quickly embrace God's promise of pardon, Isa. i. 18, and lv. 7.

Q. Why should all this be done speedily?—A. Because if such blood-guiltiness lie long on our conscience, it makes our repentance most difficult.

Q. 98. *What is prayer?*

A. Prayer is an offering up of our desires to God, for things agreeable to his will, in the name of Christ, with confession of our sins, and thankful acknowledgment of his mercies.

Q. What scripture warrant have we for prayer?—A. The command of God, the example of Christ and his saints, with the promise of God to hear it, Psalm l. 14.

Q. What are some of the scripture representations of

prayer?—A. It is called *supplications, asking, seeking, knocking, inquiring,* &c. Zech. xii. 10, &c.

Q. Why is it so called?—A. Because in it we ought, with humility and earnestness, to seek after God and his favours, as most precious and necessary, Dan. ix.

Q. Why is prayer called *meditation, lifting up our soul, and pouring out our heart?*—A. Because therein our heart is principally concerned, and must be lifted up above this world to God in a full and familiar manner.

Q. Why is prayer called a *looking up to,* a *talking and wrestling* with God, and *taking hold* of him?—A. Because therein we ought, with quietness and constancy, to plead for God's blessings, for the sake of his own love, mercy, and faithfulness; and that even when he seems to reject our requests, Gen. xxxii. 26, Dan. ix.

Q. Why is prayer represented as a *bowing, falling down, and spreading out our hands?*—A. Because in it, our whole man is to be employed in a reverent, humble, and earnest manner, Psalm xcv. Lam. i. 17.

Q. Why is prayer expressed by *crying, sighing, groaning, and breathing?*—A. Because in it, we, under a sense of burdens and danger, ought to seek relief from God.

Q. Why is prayer represented as *odours* and *incense?*—A. Because, when performed in faith, it is most precious and acceptable to God, Song ii. 14, Rev. v. 8.

Q. Who are bound to pray?—A. All men, good and bad, Matth. vi. and vii. 11, Luke xvii. 1.

Q. When ought all men to pray?—A. While they live in this world, Psalm lxii. 8, lxv. 2, and lxvi. 4.

Q. Why not in the other world?—A. Because there the saints shall have *no need*, and the wicked *no encouragement* to pray, Matth. xxv. 10, 11, 12.

Q. Why ought all men to pray?—A. To give glory to God, and obtain blessings to themselves and others.

Q. Wherein lies the sinfulness of neglecting prayer?—A. It is a practical denial of God, a robbing him of his honour, a contempt of Christ as Mediator, a ruining of ourselves and others, &c. Psal. ix. 17, and x. 4.

Q. How then do such as neglect prayer so often prosper in this world?—A. God, by their prosperity, feeds them like bullocks for the slaughter, Psalm. lxxiii.

Q. What kinds of prayer does God require of us?—A. Ejaculatory, secret, private, social, and public.

Q. What is *ejaculatory* prayer?—A. It is a particular

request offered to God, while we are engaged in other business, Gen. xlix. 18, Zech. ii. 4.

Q. Why is ejaculatory prayer necessary?—A. To maintain habitual communion with God, and keep our heart
always in a praying frame, Psalm cxxxix.

Q. What is *secret* prayer?—A. Prayer by ourselves
alone, Matth. vi. 6, Gen. xxxii. 24.

Q. Why is secret prayer necessary?—A. Because every
man has secret sins to confess, secret wants to be supplied,
and secret mercies to be thankful for.

Q. Is not the neglect of secret prayer a sure sign of a
graceless heart?—A. Yes, Psalm ix. 17, x. 4.

Q. What call you *private* prayer?—A. Prayer with our
families, Zech. xii. Josh. xxiv. 15.

Q. How prove you that family prayer is necessary?—A.
Because every family has its particular sins, wants, and
mercies; and God threatens to pour out his wrath upon
such families as call not on his name, Jer. x. 25.

Q. How often at least is secret and family prayer to be
performed?—A. Every morning and evening.

Q. How prove you that?—A. Because on these occasions there is particular need of prayer and ground of praise;
and this is warranted from the morning and evening sacrifice under the law; David's praying evening, morning, and
at noon, &c. Ezek. xlvi. 13. 15, Psal. lv. 17.

Q. What shall we think of those that perform the worship
of God in private and secret only in the evening, when they
are dull and drowsy?—A. Such prefer the world to God,
and offer to him a corrupt thing, Mal. i. 14.

Q. What is *social* prayer?—A. Prayer performed by
two or more persons occasionally, or at such stated times
as they agree on betwixt themselves.

Q. How prove you that social prayer is a duty?—A.
Reason and scripture do both call for it, Mal. iii. 16.

Q. What is *public* prayer?—A. That which is performed in a public congregation, Zech. ix. 1 Kings viii.

Q. Why is prayer to be so much joined with our work,
and especially that which is religious?—A. Because it
tends to compose our heart, opens it for receiving God, and
draws down his blessing on our labours, Luke xviii. 1.

Q. To whom only are we to pray?—A. To God;
Father, Son, and Holy Ghost, as one God, Psal. lxv. 2.

Q. Why must we pray to God only?—A. He only de-

serves religious honour and worship; and he only can
know or supply all our wants, Matth. iv. 10.

Q. Why may we not pray to angels and saints departed ?
—A. They are creatures, and so unworthy of such honour:
nor can they fully know or supply our wants.

Q. For whom are we to pray ?—A. For all men living,
or that shall live hereafter, except such as are known to
have sinned the unpardonable sin, 1 Tim. ii. 1.

Q. Why must we not pray for the dead ?—A. Because
departed saints have no need of prayers, as they have no
wants ; and the wicked in hell are without the reach of
God's mercy, Matth. xxv. 10, 11. 22.

Q. For whom ought we chiefly to pray ?—A. For saints,
ministers, magistrates, professors, the sick, &c.

Q. Why are we especially to pray for these ?—A. Their
work is most hard and useful ; or their sin most dishonouring to God, and hurtful to men.

Q. What should we plead for to saints ?—A. Protection,
comfort, increase and perseverance in grace, &c.

Q. What should we plead for to the wicked and our enemies ?—A. Conviction of sin, pardon, repentance, peace
with God, and all other blessings, Luke xxiii. 34.

Q. What should we plead for to ministers ?—A. Knowledge, prudence, humility, harmony, zeal, spiritual comfort,
success in their labours, &c. Eph. vi.

Q. What should we plead for to magistrates ?—A. Eminent grace, prudence, courage, safety, &c.

Q. What should we plead for to the poor and afflicted ?
—A. Support under affliction, a blessing on it, and deliverance from it in God's time and way, Psalm xxxv. 13.

Q. In whose name are we to pray ?—A. In the name
of Christ alone, John xvi. 23. 1 John ii. 1.

Q. Why may we not pray in our own name ?—A. Because we, and all our services, are worthless and polluted
before God, Isaiah lxiv. 6. Phil. iii. 8, 9.

Q. Why are we to pray in the name of Christ *alone?*
—A. Because he in his righteousness and intercession, is
our *only* way to the Father, Eph. ii. 18. and iii. 12.

Q. What is it to pray in the name of Christ ?—A. To
pray in his strength ; out of obedience to his command ;
with confidence in his promise ; and dependence on his
merit and intercession, as the *only* ground of God's acceptance and answer of our prayer.

Q. How ought we to prepare for prayer ?—A. By emptying our hearts of carnal thoughts and cares; holy humiliation of soul; careful examination of our sins, wants, and mercies; and looking up for the assistance of the Holy Ghost, Luke xi. 1 Pet. iii. 7.

Q. How may carnal thoughts in prayer, and other religious exercises, be prevented?—A. By watchfulness against the first motions of them; and a deep sense of our wants, and of God's greatness, holiness, omniscience, and love, Mark xiii. 37. Eccl. v. 1, 2.

Q. In what manner are we to pray?—A. With faith of the acceptance of our persons in Christ, and of the goodness of what we ask; hope of obtaining it; and with humility, sincerity, fervour, and constancy.

Q. Can we pray aright of ourselves?—A. No; we neither know what we pray for, nor how to pray; the greatest saints, as Moses, Elias, Job, Jonah, &c. mistook in prayer for what they ought not; and all saints daily mistake in the manner of prayer, Numb. xi. &c.

Q. How doth Christ cure these mistakes in us?—A. By giving his Spirit to assist us in our prayers.

Q. Wherein doth the Spirit of God assist us in prayer? —A. In the matter and manner of it, Rom. viii. 26, 27.

Q. How doth he assist us in the matter of prayer?—A. By leading us out to pray for the things which we most need, and God is most ready to bestow, Rom. viii.

Q. How doth the Spirit assist us in the manner of prayer?—A. By implanting and exciting in our soul all these inherent graces which are necessary in prayer.

Q. What graces are necessary to be exercised in prayer? —A. Knowledge, faith, love, repentance, humility, &c.

Q. Why is *knowledge* necessary in prayer?—A. That we may not pray for unlawful things, or to a wrong object, or in a wrong manner, James iv. 3.

Q. Why is *faith* necessary in prayer?—A. To lay hold on the promises and perfections of God as our encouragement; and to depend on the strength, merit, and intercession of Christ, for enabling us to prayer, and obtaining answer in it, James i. 6.

Q. Why should we pray with *hope* and expectation?— A. Because God hath promised, and Christ hath purchased all that we need, Phil. iv. 19, Heb. ix. 12.

Q. Why should we pray with great *humility*?—A. Because we are so vile and unworthy, Luke xviii.

29

Q. Why should we pray with *fervency* and earnestness?
—**A.** Because of the greatness of our need, Psalm lxx.

Q. Why must we pray with *sincerity*, repentance, and love?—**A.** Because if we indulge hatred, dissimulation, or any iniquity in our heart, the Lord will not hear us.

Q. Why must we pray with *constancy?*—**A.** Because of our frequent need, and God's frequent delay to answer our prayer, Luke xviii. 1, 1 Thess. v. 17.

Q. What is meant by praying *without ceasing?*—**A.** Our keeping our heart always in a praying frame; and being frequent in the exercise of prayer, Eph. vi. 18.

Q. What is meant by praying *in the Spirit?*—**A.** Our praying with the *gifts,* and especially with the *grace* of the Spirit, Jude 20, 1 Cor. xiv. 15, Rom. viii. 26.

Q. Wherein do the gift and grace of prayer differ?—**A.** The gift of prayer lieth in conceiving and uttering suitable expressions in an affecting manner; but the grace of prayer lies in the fervency of our desire after God.

Q. In whom is the gift, or grace of prayer to be found?—**A.** Wicked men may have the gift of prayer; but only believers have both the gift and grace of prayer.

Q. Have all saints the gift of prayer?—**A.** Some saints as well as others have very little of it.

Q. Whence doth that proceed?—**A.** From their negligence in searching the scripture, and their own hearts.

Q. May not such wicked men as have the gift of prayer, pray with great warmth of affection?—**A.** Yes.

Q. Wherein do the raised affections of wicked men in prayer, and of believers, differ?—**A.** The raised affections of the wicked flow from fear of God's wrath, false confidence of his love, or the weight of affliction, and encourage their pride; but those of believers flow from desire to be like and with Christ, and are attended with great humility, Psalm lxxviii.

Q. Of how many parts doth prayer consist?—**A.** Three; petition, confession, and thanksgiving; but most properly prayer consists in petition.

Q. Which of these parts will the saints longest retain the use of?—**A.** Of thanksgiving, Rev. v., Psalm cxlv—cl.

Q. What is petition?—**A.** The offering up of the desires of our hearts unto God, Psalm lxii. 8.

Q. Are not mere verbal requests prayer?—**A.** They are prayer before men, but not in the sight of God.

Q. What things may we desire and plead for in prayer?

—A. Whatever is agreeable to God's will of precept and promise, 1 John v. 14.

Q. What is agreeable to this revealed will of God?—A. The removing or preventing of all evil, and the bestowing of every thing good for our soul and body.

Q. Why must we plead for these mercies?—A. Not to change God's will; but to testify our needy dependence on him, and to prepare our heart to receive these mercies with thankfulness, Ezek. xxxvi. 37.

Q. May we pray for all mercies in the same manner?— A. No; we must pray for some mercies absolutely, and for others conditionally, Psalm xxv., Gen. xviii.

Q. For what may we pray *absolutely*?—A. For a new nature, justification, adoption, sanctification, and every other thing inseparable from our eternal salvation, Psal. li. Dan. ix.

Q. Why may we pray absolutely for these mercies?— A. Because our receiving them cannot but tend to the glory of God, and our real advantage, Psalm cxlii. 4—7.

Q. For what mercies must we pray *conditionally*?—A. The good things of this world, sensible comfort to our soul, freedom from temptation, &c., 2 Cor. xii.

Q. Under what condition or limitation must we pray for these?—A. *If they tend to God's glory and our good.*

Q. Why must we pray for them with this limitation?— A. Because it may be for the glory of God, and our real advantage, that we want them, 2 Cor. xii. 9.

Q. What are we to confess in prayer?—A. All our sins, with the several aggravations of them, Psalm xxxii. li.

Q. Why ought we to confess our sins in prayer?—A. To testify our belief of God's holiness and omniscience; and to affect our heart with a sense of our vileness and unworthiness before him, Dan. ix. 3—19.

Q. In what manner are we to confess our sins?—A. In a humble and affectionate manner, with faith's views of a crucified Christ as the propitiation for them.

Q. For what are we to give God thanks in prayer?—A. For all his mercies, spiritual or temporal, Psal. cv. cvii.

Q. What call you mercies?—A. Whatever springs from God's pity, and tends to the good of our soul or body.

Q. Is there ground of thanksgiving in our afflictions?— A. Yes; it is matter of thanksgiving that they are not more severe, and are sent while they may be useful to us.

Q. Why is thanksgiving necessary in prayer?—A. To

acknowledge the goodness and mercy of God, and stir up our heart to love him, Psalm ciii. cxlv.—cl.

Q. What is our duty after offering up our requests unto God?—A. To expect an answer; wait for it in the diligent use of means, submitting the season, measure, and form of the blessing asked to God's sovereign will.

Q. What mean you by an *answer* of prayer?—A. God's granting the very thing we ask in prayer, or something as good, or better, in its place, Psalm xci. 15.

Q. May not God answer wicked men's prayers, which he never accepts?—A. Yes; as in the case of Nineveh, &c.

Q. Doth God accept and answer all the prayers of believers?—A. No; but only those that are offered up in faith, James i. 6, 7, Dan. ix. 1 Kings viii.

Q. When doth God grant the answer of such prayers? —A. When it is most for his glory and his people's good, but not always when they would have it.

Q. Why doth God often long delay the answering of his people's prayers, which he hath already accepted?—A. To keep them in the exercise of waiting on, and crying to him; and that their mercy may be the greater when it comes, Isa. xxx. 18, Luke xviii. 1—8.

Q. How may we know that God hath heard and accepted our prayer, and will grant an answer, though he long delay it?—A. If we are led out to much resignation to his will, waiting on him for an answer in a holy practice, and deep sense of our unworthiness of the least of his mercies, Psalm v. 2, Isa. viii. 17, Gen. xxxii. 10.

Q. 99. *What rule hath God given for our direction in prayer?*
A. The whole word of God is of use to direct us in prayer; but the special rule of direction, is that form of prayer which Christ taught his disciples, commonly called the " Lord's Prayer."

Q. Hath God given us any rule for our direction in prayer?—A. Yes; he has given his whole word in general, and *the Lord's prayer* in particular.

Q. What in the word of God directs us in power?—A. The prayers, histories, doctrines, threatenings, promises, and precepts therein contained.

Q. How do the prayers contained in scripture direct us?

—A. They shew us to whom, for what and whom, and in what manner we should pray, Dan. ix. 1 Kings viii.

Q. How do the threatenings and histories of God's judgments direct us in prayer?—A. They shew us what sins we ought to confess, and what evils we should pray for the preventing or removal of.

Q. How doth the history of God's merciful providences direct us in prayer?—A. They encourage us to it, and shew us what good things God is ready to bestow.

Q. How do the doctrines of God's word direct us in prayer?—A. They shew us what God is, and is disposed to do; what we are and need; and in what manner we may come to God for the supply of our wants.

Q. How do the precepts of God's word direct us in prayer?—A. They shew us what sins we ought to confess, and seek deliverance from; what graces we should crave; and what duties we need strength to perform.

Q. How do the promises of God direct us in prayer?— A. They shew the various cases we may be in, and what blessings God hath engaged, and is ready to give us.

Q. What doth God by promise engage himself to give us?—A. Mercies suiting every case; outward blessings; suitable relief under trouble; spiritual graces, comforts, and remedies; with encouragement in duty.

Q. What outward blessings hath God promised to us?— A. Health, strength, food, raiment, peace, safety, comfort, and success to us and our children.

Q. What spiritual mercy is promised in connection with these outward blessings?—A. Holy joy, thankfulness and heavenly-mindedness, Isa. lx. Ezek. xxxvi.

Q. What afflicted cases do God's promises respect?— A. The case of temptation, desertion, sickness, poverty, persecution, oppression, calumny, &c.

Q. What doth God promise with respect to afflictions? —A. That he will either preserve from, or support in them; moderate their rigour; shorten their duration; and bring good out of them, Isa. xliii. and xxvii. 9.

Q. What spiritual grace hath God promised to us?—A. Regeneration, knowledge, faith, hope, repentance, love, humility, patience, increase of grace, fear of God, and obedience to his commands, Ezek. xxxvi. xxxvii.

Q. What spiritual comforts has God promised to us?— A. Justification, adoption, assurance of his love, peace of conscience, joy in the Holy Ghost, and eternal glory.

29*

Q. What spiritual plagues has God promised to cure ?—
A. Hardness of heart, ignorance of God, forgetfulness of his truths and providences, unthankfulness for his mercies, pride, envy, lust, desponding fears of death, want of grace, greatness of sin, or future apostacy from God, legality, carnal mindedness, &c.

Q. In what duties doth God promise encouragement ?—
A. In prayer, meditation, public worship, fasting, almsgiving, suffering for Christ, sanctifying the Sabbath, &c.

Q. What encouragement in duty hath God promised ?
—**A.** Preparation for it, assistance in it, and a gracious reward of our work, Psal. x. 17. and xix. 11. Phil. ii. 13.

Q. How are we to improve God's promises in prayer ?
A. By pleading and expecting that for Christ's sake he would do to us and others as he hath promised.

Q. What special rule of direction in prayer hath God given us ?—**A.** That form of prayer which Christ taught his disciples, which is commonly called *the Lord's prayer*, because the Lord Jesus prescribed it.

Q. Did Christ prescribe it as a form, the express words of which we are bound to use ?—**A.** No; but as a pattern of prayer, directing us what we should pray for, and in what order we should offer our requests.

Q. How prove you that Christ did not prescribe it as an *express form* of prayer ?—**A.** Because in Matthew, who relates this form most exactly, Christ *only* says, *After this manner pray ye ;* Matthew and Luke relate it differently ; and Christ, and his prophets and apostles, used different expressions in prayer, Matth. xi. and xxvi. Acts i. and v. Eph. iii. John xvii, &c.

Q. May none use set forms of prayer ?—**A.** Yes ; young children, and such as through weakness are incapable to conceive prayer, may use them.

Q. Why may not others confine themselves to set forms of prayer ?—**A.** Because to do so checks the teaching of God's Spirit, inverts the order of prayer, encourageth to sloth, and is most absurd and unreasonable.

Q. How doth confining ourselves to set forms of prayer check the teaching of the Spirit ?—**A.** As the form teacheth us what to pray for, which is the work ascribed to the Holy Ghost, Rom. viii. 26.

Q. How doth it invert the order of prayer ?—**A.** As by this means, instead of our hearts regulating our words, the words of the form must regulate our heart.

Q. How doth it encourage sloth?—**A.** As it makes us careless of self-examination, and of study of the scriptures for instruction in prayer, and stirring up of our heart to seek after the gift or grace of prayer.

Q. How is it most absurd and unreasonable?—**A.** It is as if a hungry beggar could not ask alms, or a drowning man cry for relief, without an express form.

Q. Is not the Lord's prayer a most excellent pattern?—**A.** Yes; for it is a short, full, and orderly prayer.

Q. How many parts does the Lord's prayer consist of?—**A.** A preface, six petitions, and a conclusion.

Q. 100. *What doth the preface to the Lord's prayer teach us?*

A. The preface to the Lord's prayer (which is, "Our Father which art in Heaven,") teacheih us to draw near to God with all holy reverence and confidence as children to a father, able and ready to help us; and that we should pray with and for others.

Q. What is the preface to the Lord's prayer?—**A.** *Our Father which art in heaven,* Matth. vi. 9.

Q. Whose Father is God?—**A.** He is the Father of all men by creation and preservation, the Father of church-members by external covenant relation, and the Father of true believers, by regeneration and adoption.

Q. May unbelievers call God their Father when they pray to him?—**A.** Yes, if they understand it in a consistency with their state.

Q. What for a Father is God?—**A.** A most honourable, rich, wise, kind, mighty, ancient, and eternal Father.

Q. What child-like dispositions ought God's children to have?—**A.** An awe of his majesty, patience under his rebukes, grief for his frowns, zeal for his honour, thankfulness for his favours, contentment with their provision, obedience to his laws, and an affectionate love to him and his children, Mal. i. 6, Psalm xxxix. 9, lxix. 9, and ciii. cxvi.

Q. What doth the preface to the Lord's prayer teach us in general?—**A.** To begin our prayers with exalted and adoring views of God, Neh. ix. 5, 6.

Q. Why is this necessary?—**A.** That our heart may be suitably impressed in the whole of the duty.

Q. What doth God's being called *Father* in this preface teach us?—**A.** That in prayer we should draw near to God with love, boldness, familiarity, and confident faith of success, Eph. iii. 12, Heb. iv. 16, and x. 22.

Q. What doth his being represented as *in heaven* teach us?—A. To pray with great reverence and humility, and be most intent on heavenly things, Eccl. v. 2. Col. iii.

Q. What doth his being called *our*, not *my* Father, teach us?—A. That we should pray with and for others.

Q. Why should we pray with others?—A. Because united prayer is most effectual and prevalent.

Q. How are we to be exercised when joining with another as our mouth in prayer?—A. In assenting with our heart to the requests contained in his words.

Q. Why should we pray for others?—A. To glorify God, and testify our love to our neighbours.

Q. How doth prayer for others glorify God?—A. We thereby testify that we see in God more fulness and mercy than we can receive or contain.

Q. How doth prayer for others testify our love to them? —A. As we thereby employ God to give them the richest blessings, and do them the greatest good.

Q. On whom do we most advantageously bestow our prayers?—A. On the saints; for they can, and will pray effectually for us, James v. 16, Eph. vi. 18, 19.

Q. What in general do we pray for in the six petitions in the Lord's prayer?—A. In the three first we pray for the advancement of God's honour, and in the three last for our own happiness.

Q. Why are those petitions that immediately concern God's honour placed first in order?—A. To show us that God's honour is preferable to, and the spring of all our happiness, 1 Cor. x. 31, 1 Peter iv. 11.

Q. What do we pray for with respect to God's honour? —A. That his name may be hallowed, his kingdom come, and his will be done, Matth. vi. 9, 10.

Q. What do we pray for with respect to our own happiness?—A. Provision to our body; pardon of sin, and preservation from it, to our soul, Matth. vi. 11, 12, 13.

Q. How many of the petitions are for temporal mercies? —A. Only one; namely, the *fourth*.

Q. Why is there but one petition for temporal mercies? —A. To teach us to be more earnest for spiritual blessings.

Q. Why is the petition for temporal mercies placed before those for pardon of sin, and preservation from it?—A. Because our daily bread is a positive mercy; and we cannot receive pardon of, or preservation from sin, unless we have a natural subsistence in this world.

Q. Why are these three last petitions coupled together by the particle *and?*—A. To shew us, that outward advantages are useless to us without pardon of sin, and pardon insufficient without preservation from it.

Q. Why are we taught to use the terms *our* and *us* in the three last petitions?—A. To teach us to pray for temporal mercies, pardon of sin, and preservation from it, to others as well as ourselves.

Q. 101. *What do we pray for in the first petition?*
A. In the first petition (which is, "Hallowed be thy name"), we pray, That God would enable us and others to glorify him in all that whereby he maketh himself known ; and that he would dispose all things to his own glory.

Q. What do we pray for in this petition?—A. That God would hallow his own name, and direct and enable us and others to hallow it, Psalm lxxxiii.

Q. What is meant by *hallowing* the name of God?—A. Shewing forth the holiness and glory of it.

Q. How doth God hallow his own name?—A. By ordering all things belonging to him so as to shew himself glorious in holiness, Exod. xv. 11, Psalm xc. 16.

Q. What things belonging to God shew him to be great, and glorious in holiness?—A. All his ordinances, words, and works, Psalm lxxv. 2, and cxlv. 17.

Q. Why do we pray that God would hallow his own name?—A. Because none else can sufficiently do it.

Q. How ought we and others to hallow God's name?—A. By acknowledging him as our God, and by a holy and reverent use of all things whereby he makes himself known.

Q. What do we in this petition pray for with respect to ourselves and others hallowing of God's name?—A. That God, by his grace, would direct and enable us to glorify himself in all we do ; and prevent and remove every thing that hinders the hallowing of his name.

Q. What things hinder the hallowing of God's name?—A. Atheism, ignorance, unbelief, idolatry, and every other sin. See more on Command 1, 2, 3, 4.

Q. 102. *What do we pray for in the second petition?*

A. In the second petition (which is, "Thy kingdom come,") we pray, That Satan's kingdom may be destroyed; and that the kingdom of grace may be advanced, ourselves and others brought into it, and kept in it; and that the kingdom of glory may be hastened.

Q. What do we pray for in the second petition?—**A.** The destruction of Satan's kingdom, and the coming of the kingdom of God, Psalm lxxxiii. 17, 18.

Q. What for a king is Satan?—**A.** A most base, wicked, and cruel king, Rev. xx. 2.

Q. How is he a most *wicked* king?—**A.** As he commands nothing but sin, 1 John iii. 8.

Q. How is he a most *cruel* king?—**A.** He continually seeks the destruction of the souls and bodies of all his subjects, 1 Peter v. 8.

Q. What kingdom hath Satan in the world?—**A.** A visible and invisible kingdom, 2 Cor. iv. 4.

Q. What is the visible kingdom of Satan?—**A.** All the world without the visible church.

Q. What are the badges of Satan's visible kingdom?—**A.** The open profession and practice of error, idolatry, profaneness, superstition, &c.

Q. Who are the subjects of Satan's visible kingdom?—**A.** Pagans, Mahometans, modern Jews, and heretical, profane, and grossly ignorant Christians.

Q. What is meant by praying that Satan's visible kingdom may be destroyed?—**A.** Our praying that God would root out all idolatry, superstition, error, delusion, ignorance, and profaneness from the world.

Q. What is Satan's invisible kingdom?—**A.** His power and dominion in men's hearts, 2 Cor. iv. 4.

Q. Who are the subjects of Satan's invisible kingdom?—**A.** All unbelievers, 1 John iii. 10.

Q. What are the great supports of this kingdom?—**A.** The curse of the law lying on our conscience, with our own indwelling lusts, 1 Cor. xv. 56.

Q. What kingdom of God are we to pray for the coming of?—**A.** His kingdom of grace and of glory.

Q. What are the properties of God's kingdom?—**A.** It

is a kingdom of riches, righteousness, peace, high dignity, and eternal duration, Rom. xiv. 17, Isa. ix. 7.

Q. What is the external form of God's kingdom of grace?
—A. Preaching of the word, administration of the sacraments, with church government and discipline.

Q. What is the internal form of it?—A. Regeneration, *righteousness, peace and joy in the Holy Ghost.*

Q. Wherein doth God's kingdom more generally come to men?—A. In the conversation of the Gentiles, overthrow of Popery and Paganism, recovery of the Jews from their infidelity, universal spread of the gospel, &c.

Q. How doth the kingdom of God come to a particular person?—A. In his receiving the means of grace, and in his conversation, sanctification, and glorification.

Q. What influence hath the coming of Christ's kingdom on the kingdom of Satan?—A. It destroys it.

Q. What destroys Satan's visible kingdom?—A. The coming of God's visible kingdom of grace.

Q. What destroys Satan's invisible kingdom?—A. God's setting up his invisible kingdom of grace in our heart, Col. i. 13. See Quest. 26. 31.

Q. By what is Satan's kingdom wholly destroyed?—A. By the coming of God's kingdom of glory.

Q. What do we request in praying for the coming of God's visible kingdom of grace?—A. We request that the gospel may be preached in all nations in plenty, purity, and power, and that all people may flow unto it; that the church may be purged from profane and erroneous persons, and have faithful ministers and magistrates; and that professors may steadfastly maintain, and faithfully convey to posterity the whole of God's truths and ordinances, Psalm cxxxii. and cxxxvii. Dan. ix

Q. What do we request in praying for the coming of God's invisible kingdom of grace?—A. That ourselves and others may be brought into it, and kept in it.

Q. How are persons brought into God's invisible kingdom of grace?—A. By regeneration, justification, and adoption, Col. i. Acts xxvi. See Quest. 31. 33, 34.

Q. How are they kept in it?—A. By sanctification, assurance of God's love, peace of conscience, joy in the Holy Ghost, increase of grace, and perseverance therein to the end. See Quest. 35, 36.

Q. Why need believers pray for the coming of God's invisible kingdom of grace with respect to themselves, when they are already in it?—A. They need to pray that it would come in them more and more, Phil. iii. 9—14.

Q. Wherein doth God's kingdom of glory come?—A. In believers receiving benefits from Christ at death, and at the resurrection. See Quest. 37, 38.

Q. What are we to pray for with respect to God's kingdom of glory?—A. That it may be hastened, Rev. xxii.

Q. What is meant by the kingdom of glory being hastened?—A. Not its coming before God's set time; but his quick ordering of things in the world, and our heart, to make way for its coming in due time.

Q. Are believers to long for death and judgment?—A. Yes, if they do it with submission to God's will, and from an ardent desire to be like and with Christ.

Q. 103. *What do we pray for in the third petition?*

A. In the third petition (which is, "Thy will be done on earth, as *it is* in heaven,") we pray, That God, by his grace, would make us able and willing to know, obey, and submit to his will in all things, as the angels do in heaven.

Q. What will of God is here meant?—A. The will of his precept and providence. See Quest. 11. 39—81.

Q. What do we here pray for with respect to God's will of precept?—A. That God, by his grace, would make us and others to know and obey it. See Quest. 24. 35.

Q. Why must we first know it?—A. Because except we know the commands *as the will of God*, we can never obey them from regard to his authority.

Q. Why should we pray that God would make us to know and obey his will?—A. Because of ourselves we cannot know nor obey God's law, nor can any creature teach or enable us to it. See Quest. 18. 26. 31.

Q. What do we in this petition pray for with respect to God's will of providence?—A. That we and others may understand the language of providence, and submit to the dispensations of it, Micah vi. 9.

Q. In what manner do we pray that God's will may be done on earth?—A. *As it is* done *in heaven*.

Q. By whom is God's will done in heaven?—A. By the holy angels, and glorified saints.

Q. In what manner is God's will done in heaven?—A. Cheerfully, readily, constantly, and universally.

Q. 104. *What do we pray for in the fourth petition?*
A. In the fourth petition (which is, " Give us this day our daily bread," we pray, That of God's free gift we may receive a competent portion of the good things of this life, and enjoy his blessing with them.

Q. What is meant by bread in this petition?—A. All temporal blessings, such as food, raiment, health, strength, agreeable relations, habitation, &c.

Q. Why are these called *bread?*—A. Because, like bread, they are necessary for the welfare of our body.

Q. What measure of these temporal blessings may we pray for?—A. A competent portion, Prov. xxx. 8.

Q. What call you a competent portion of them?—A. Such a portion as enableth us to live without being a burden to others; or as much as tends to God's glory, and our good, Isa. xxxiii. 16, 1 Thess. iv. 11, 12.

Q. What besides this competent portion do we request in this petition?—A. God's blessing with it.

Q. What do you mean by God's blessing on temporal enjoyments?—A. His prospering our endeavours to get them; making us to see his love, bounty and faithfulness in them; giving us contentment with, and comfort in them, and enabling us to thankfulness for them.

Q. Why are we in this petition taught to pray for *bread*, and not for dainty meats or riches?—A. To teach us to be content with little, Heb. xiii. 5.

Q. Why are we taught to pray for *daily*, and not for weekly and monthly bread?—A. To teach us a constant dependence on God for temporal, as well as spiritual good things, Acts xvii. 28.

Q. Why are we taught to say, Give us *this day* our daily bread?—A. To teach us to avoid covetous anxiety, and live every day as if it were our last, Luke xxi. 34.

Q. Why is the bread we are to pray for called *ours?*—A. To teach us that we must have a proper right to the bread we ask from God, or crave his blessing on.

Q. What right ought we to have to our temporal enjoyments?—A. A *civil right* before men, which even unbelievers often have; and a *new covenant right* before God, which only believers can have, Isa. xxxiii. 16.

Q. What bread, and other temporal enjoyments, may

30

we not ask from God, nor crave his blessing on?—A. What is gotten by idleness, deceit, and violence.

Q. Why do we ask our temporal enjoyments from God, when we labour for them with our hands?—A. Because it is God who giveth us opportunity and strength for labour, success in it, and a blessing with it, Deut. viii.

Q. Is it not then a profane and beastly practice, to eat and drink without craving God's blessing on, and returning him thanks for our food?—A. Yes, Exod. xxiii. 25.

Q. Why are we to request our temporal mercies as God's free gift?—A. Because we deserve nothing at his hand, but wrath for our sin, Gen. xxxii. 10.

Q. How are the saints, when often so poor, said to *inherit all things?*—A. All things are theirs by covenant right, and do work for their good; and they enjoy as much as is sufficient for them, 1 Cor. iii. 22, Rom. viii. 28.

Q. Whence then is it, that some saints in straits more readily doubt of their daily bread, than of their eternal salvation?—A. It proceeds from the carnality of their hearts.

Q. 105. *What do we pray for in the fifth petition?*

A. In the fifth petition (which is, "And forgive us our debts, as we forgive our debtors,") we pray that God, for Christ's sake, would freely pardon all our sins; which we are the rather encouraged to ask, because by his grace we are enabled from the heart to forgive others.

Q. What is here meant by debts?—A. Our sins.

Q. Why are our sins called debts?—A. Because they arise from our withholding from God what is his due; and they must be satisfied for by bearing punishment.

Q. How is sin the *worst debt?*—A. An angry God is our creditor, who will exact the utmost farthing of it; we can never be able to pay the least part of it: it makes us daily contract more and more; and exposeth us to everlasting imprisonment in hell, Matth. v. 25, 26.

Q. Wherein do we naturally resemble bad debtors?—A. We hate God our creditor; forget and abhor the day of account at death or judgment; endeavour to deny, shift, or excuse our debt; are averse from acknowledging it, &c.

Q. For whose sake are we to ask from God forgiveness of our sinful debts?—A. Only for Christ's sake; for his righteousness alone satisfied God's justice for sin. See Quest. 25. 33.

Q. Why should believers, whose sins are all pardoned in justification, pray daily for forgiveness of sin ?—A. Because they daily need clearer intimations of their past legal pardon, and present fatherly pardon of their sin against the law as a rule, James iii. 2.

Q. What is the argument annexed to this petition ?—A. Our forgiving our debtors, Luke xi. 4.

Q. How do we forgive our debtors ?—A. By gently demanding money debts, and forgiving other injuries.

Q. In what manner are we to forgive injuries done to us ?—A. Heartily, cheerfully, and for Christ's sake.

Q. How far are we to forgive injuries done to us ?—A. Not as they offend God, but only as they hurt us.

Q. Ought we not to endeavour to bring such as injure us to a sense of their sin against God ?—A. Yes.

Q. Ought we to forgive great injuries ?—A. Yes.

Q. Will not that make men despise and injure us more and more ?—A. No ; it rather tends to make them ashamed of injuring us, 1 Peter iii. 16.

Q. Are we to forgive men before they confess their faults to us ?—A. Yes, in our heart ; though it may not be fit, *at least always*, to intimate forgiveness to them.

Q. Is our forgiveing others the condition of God's forgiving us ?—A. No, by no means, Eph. i. 7.

Q. How then is it an argument of God's forgiving us ?—A. As it imports God's ability and engagement to forgive, as Numb. xiv. 17, 18. Jer. i. 20.

Q. How doth it import God's full ability to forgive us ?—A. In regard that it is as if we should say, *Lord, if we hard-hearted sinners can forgive those that injure us, how much more canst thou, who art full of compassion, forgive us who have offended thee !* Matth. vii. 11.

Q. How doth it import God's engagement to forgive us ?—A. As hearty and Christian forgiveness of injuries is an evidence that we are God's children, whose iniquities he is by covenant engaged to forgive, Heb. vii. 11.

Q. By what are we enabled to forgive others ?—A. By God's grace working in our heart.

Q. Can one be forgiven of God, or in faith ask and expect pardon from him, who is not inclined to forgive men their trespasses against him ?—A. No ; Matt. xviii.

Q. 106. *What do we pray for in the sixth petition?*
A. In the sixth petition (which is, " And lead us not into temptation, but deliver us from evil,") we pray that God would either keep us from being tempted to sin, or support and deliver us *when we are tempted.*

Q. What do you mean by *temptation?*—A. Temptation properly signifies an enticing to sin.

Q. Doth God the *properly* tempt any man ?—No; *God tempteth no man,* but only tries them, James i. 13.

Q. What then is meant by God's leading into temptation ?—A. His laying such occasions before men, as their lusts can improve to sinful purposes; withdrawing his grace; and permitting Satan, the world, and the flesh, to seduce them into sin, Joshua vii. 21, Job i. and ii.

Q. What is meant by evil in this petition ?—A. Chiefly sin, the worst of evils, Hab. i. 13.

Q. Who are our tempters to this evil of sin ?—A. Satan, the world, and the flesh ; but especially Satan, who is expressly called *the tempter,* Matth. iv. 3.

Q. How doth the flesh tempt us to sin ?—A. By inclining and exciting us to sinful deeds, James i. 14.

Q. What with respect to the world tempts men to sin?
—A. The men and things of it, Prov. i. 10. 13.

Q. How do the men of the world tempt us to sin ?—By enticing to, encouraging in, or rewarding for it.

Q. What things of the world tempt men to sin ?—The prosperity and adversity of it, Prov. xxx. 9.

Q. How doth prosperity tempt us to sin ?—A. It is an occasion of pride, presumption, security, covetousness, &c.

Q. How doth adversity tempt us to sin ?—A. It is an occasion of discontent, disquiet, and distrust of God's ability and readiness to help us, 2 Kings vi. 23.

Q. What for a tempter is Satan ?—A. A most crafty, malicious, powerful, and active tempter, Rev. xx.

Q. In what do Satan's craft and subtilty appear ?—A. In his exact observation of our constitution ; seizing the most proper seasons of temptation ; proposing the most deceiving baits as shews of religion and friendship ; and hindering us from such duties as do most oppose his designs, as faith, meditation, self-examination, &c.

Q. In what doth Satan's malice appear ?—A. He tempts,

though filled with torment; and though he knows his temptations shall increase his punishment; and where he is certain he cannot prevail, Rom. xvi. 20.

Q. In what doth Satan's activity appear?—A. In his tempting so constantly, especially when he finds any peculiar opportunity; and in the great variety, and frequent changes of the matter and manner of his temptations.

Q. In what doth Satan's power appear?—A. In the great success of his temptations, and terrible pressure of some, Gen. iii., 2 Cor. xii.

Q. Whom doth Satan especially tempt?—A. Eminent saints, novices in religion, proud, malicious, melancholy, discontented, lustful, and idle persons, Job i.

Q. When is Satan most ready to tempt us to sin?—A. When the objects of temptations are near us; when we are idle, secure, under convictions, or attending God's ordinances, or near death; or have met with signal token of God's love, Josh. vii., 2 Sam. xi., &c.

Q. Doth not our heart so join with Satan in his temptations, that we cannot perfectly distinguish between his, and those that proceed from our heart?—A. Yes; though when temptations are sudden, violent, and terrible to nature, they seem chiefly to proceed from Satan.

Q. What are Satan's principal methods of temptation?—A. His producing or strengthening sinful habits; preventing conviction or the success of it; hindering our closing with Christ; injecting blasphemous thoughts; driving to despair, &c., 2 Tim. ii. 26.

Q. How doth Satan produce or strengthen sinful habits in us?—A. By enticing us to sins suited to our tempers, stations, and circumstances in the world.

Q. By what wiles doth Satan persuade us to sin?—A. By representing sin as virtuous or indifferent, or as a small, secret, and profitable thing, which our fortune or situation obligeth us to commit, and which God will easily pardon.

Q. How doth Satan hinder men's convictions?—A. By opposing the faithful preaching of the gospel, hindering reproof for sin, or causing it to be given in such a manner as tends to render it hurtful or useless.

Q. How doth Satan stop the success of our convictions?—A. By dazzling our eyes with the things of this world; suggesting that we are no wiser than others, and are in a good state; and by causing us make vows, and perform duties in our own strength, Rom. x. 3.

30*

Q. How doth Satan hinder men from closing with Christ?—**A.** By keeping them in gross ignorance, persuading them to trust in the general mercy of God, or causing them embrace a *fancied* instead of the *true* Christ.

Q. How doth Satan inject vile and blasphemous thoughts into our mind?—**A.** By secretly whispering them into our soul, exciting us to think on them, and upbraiding us with them, Acts v. 3.

Q. How doth Satan tempt and drive us to despair?—**A.** By keeping us from thinking on the promises and infinite mercy of God, and merit of Christ; driving us from prayer, and other ordinances; and suggesting that we are matchless sinners, reprobates, or such as have committed the sin against the Holy Ghost, &c.

Q. What are the most deceitful temptations of Satan?—**A.** Those delusions in which, as an angel of light, he apes the work of God's Spirit on the souls of men.

Q. How may we know if we are under the influence of Satan's delusions?—**A.** If the influence we are under dispose us to distrust the worship of God, cherish imaginary views of Christ and spiritual things, or rest on frames instead of Christ in his word; or if it render us proud, despisers of others, haters of such as suspect our saintship, averse from impartial trial, neglecters, contemners, or opposers of any truth or duty of religion plainly expressed in scripture, &c.

Q. Have Satan's temptations always equal success?—**A.** No; his temptations succeed to the destruction of the wicked; but are at last wholly defeated with respect to believers, 1 Pet. v. 8, Rom. xvi. 20.

Q. Why then doth Satan tempt believers to sin?—**A.** Because of his great malice and hatred against God and their souls, 1 Peter v. 8.

Q. Whether doth Satan tempt saints or sinners most violently?—**A.** Ordinarily saints, 2 Cor. xii. 7, Eph. vi.

Q. Why doth God suffer the wicked to be tempted?—**A.** To punish them for their sin, Psalm cix.

Q. Why doth God suffer his own people to be tempted?—**A.** To make them sensible of their weakness and wickedness, and of the strength and subtlety of their spiritual enemies; and to cause them depend on his righteousness, power, and wisdom; long for heaven; and be diligent and watchful in every duty, 2 Cor. xii. 7.

Q. What do we pray for in this sixth petition?—**A.** That

God would either keep us from being tempted to sin, or support and deliver us when we are tempted.

Q. How doth God keep us from temptation?—A. By restraining sin, Satan, and the world, from seducing us.

Q. How doth God support us under temptation?—A. By giving us grace to watch against, and resist it.

Q. How doth God deliver us when we are tempted?—A. By giving us grace to conquer the temptation, or recovering us when fallen into sin, 2 Cor. xii. 9.

Q. How doth God recover us when fallen by temptation?—A. By speedily convincing us of sin, turning us from it, pardoning, and overruling it to our good.

Q. Why do we pray that God would keep and deliver us from temptation?—A. Because we cannot keep nor deliver ourselves from it, Psalm cxxvii. 1.

Q. Why may we not pray absolutely for preservation from temptations?—A. Because it may be for God's glory, and our good, that we be tried by them, James i.

Q. What are some means of preservation from temptation?—A. An humble jealousy of our heart; sense of our weakness and wickedness; daily application of Christ's righteousness and strength; careful and constant watchfulness; and cautious avoiding all occasions and appearances of evil, 1 Pet. v. 8, Eph. vi. Rom. xii.

Q. 107. *What doth the conclusion of the Lord's prayer teach us?*

A. The conclusion of the Lord's prayer, (which is, "For thine is the kingdom, and the power, and the glory, for ever. Amen.") teacheth us to take our encouragement in prayer from God only, and in our prayers to praise him, ascribing kingdom, power, and glory to him. And, in testimony of our desire, and assurance to be heard, we say, Amen.

Q. What things are here ascribed to God?—A. An eternal kingdom, power, and glory.

Q. Why are these things ascribed to God?—A. As an adoration of him, and as arguments for his accepting and answering our prayers, Dan. ix.

Q. What do you mean by ascribing these things to God as an adoration of him?—A. Our acknowledging with fear, love, admiration, joy, and thankfulness, that these things belong to him, Neh. ix. 5, 6.

Q. Why are we in our prayers to praise God ?—**A.** Because praise glorifies him, Psalm l. 23.

Q. What do you mean by improving God's eternal kingdom, power, and glory, as arguments in prayer ?—**A.** Our pleading that God, for the sake of these things, would accept our prayers, and grant our requests.

Q. How is God's *eternal kingdom* a reason why he should grant our requests ?—**A.** Since he is a sovereign and everlasting King, it becomes him to maintain his own honour, advance his kingdom, make his subjects obey his will, provide for, pardon, preserve, and deliver them from all his and their enemies, Psalm lxxxiii.

Q. How is God's *eternal power* a reason why he should grant our requests ?—**A.** As it renders him easily and constantly able to maintain all his own prerogatives, and bestow his blessings on his subjects, Num. xiv. 17, 18, 19.

Q. How is God's *eternal glory* a reason of his granting our requests ?—**A.** As to maintain the honour of his name, advance his kingdom, cause his subjects obey his will, provide for, pardon, and preserve them, will brightly display the glory of all his perfections.

Q. Can our arguments in prayer change the will or purpose of God ?—**A.** No ; *He is of one mind, and who can turn him ?* Job xxiii. 13.

Q. Of what use then are our arguments in prayer ?—**A.** They enlarge our heart to receive God's blessings, and encourage us to expect and wait for them.

Q. From whom is all our encouragement and arguments in prayer to be taken ?—**A.** From God only.

Q. How then do scripture saints plead from the greatness of their sin, distress, and danger ?—**A.** That is only an argument, as it gives opportunity for God's great mercy, power, and wisdom, to vent itself.

Q. What doth *Amen*, which is ordinarily added to prayer, signify ?—**A.** *So let it be ;* or, *so shall it be.*

Q. Why is *Amen* to be added in our prayers ?—**A.** To testify our desire and assurance to be heard.

Q. What is the foundation of our assurance of God's hearing our prayers and granting our requests ?—**A.** His perfections, covenant, and promise ; and the infinite merit, and powerful intercession of Christ.